LAST OF THE OLD-TIME OUTLAWS

George West Musgrave (1877–1947). Courtesy The American Heritage Center, University of Wyoming, copyright restricted.

Last of the
Old-Time Outlaws

THE GEORGE WEST MUSGRAVE STORY

Karen Holliday Tanner
John D. Tanner, Jr.

University of Oklahoma Press : Norman

To Jack and Dorothy Tanner

Also by Karen Holliday Tanner
Doc Holliday: A Family Portrait (Norman, 1998)

Also by John D. Tanner, Jr.
Alaskan Trails, Siberian Dogs (Wheat Ridge, Colo., 1998)

Publication of this book is made possible through the generosity of Edith Kinney Gaylord.

Library of Congress Cataloging-in-Publication Data

Tanner, Karen Holliday, 1940–
   Last of the old-time outlaws : the George West Musgrave story / Karen Holliday Tanner, John D. Tanner, Jr.
      p. cm.
   Includes bibliographical references (p.   ) and index.
   ISBN 0-8061-3424-0 (alk. paper)
   1. Musgrave, George West, 1877–1947. 2. Outlaws—Southwest, New—Biography. 3. Criminals—Southwest, New—Biography.
   4. Frontier and pioneer life—Southwest, New. 5. Southwest, New—Biography. 6. Criminals—Paraguay—Biography. 7. Paraguay—Biography. I. Tanner, John D. (John Douglas), 1943– II. Title.

F786.M975 T36 2002
364.1'092—dc21
[B]

                                                      2002020556

The paper in this book meets the guidelines for permanence and durability of the Committee on Production Guidelines for Book Longevity of the Council on Library Resources, Inc. ∞

1 2 3 4 5 6 7 8 9 10

CONTENTS

LIST OF ILLUSTRATIONS

PHOTOGRAPHS

MAPS

ACKNOWLEDGMENTS

No work such as this could be written without the gracious assistance and prior research of others. Jeff Burton, researcher and scholar extraordinaire, indefatigably responded to our multitude of questions, graciously traveled to London to meet with us, and offered an invaluable critique of the manuscript. Fred Nolan read the final manuscript draft and furnished criticism and support of inestimable worth. Despite the demands of overseeing one of the largest cattle ranches in Paraguay, Robert Eaton found the time to answer our unending questions. Both Daniel Buck and Robert DeArment read an early draft of the manuscript and gave us the benefit of their criticism. Larry Pointer shared with us his insights and indispensable notes on Jano Magor Musgrave. Dr. Jerry W. Cooney graciously consented to read the South American chapters and offered valuable counsel. Our good friend Richard Heald read the manuscript, provided suggestions, and shared our frustrations. Martha Beth Walker has been a continual source of family information.

The authors would also like to acknowledge the following who lent their assistance: Al Regensberg, New Mexico State Archives and Records Center; Jim Bradshaw, the Nita Stewart Haley Memorial Library; Nora Mae Tyler, county and district clerk, La Salle County; and Robert Hart, New Mexico Farm and Ranch Museum.

LAST OF THE OLD-TIME OUTLAWS

INTRODUCTION

Alcibiades, whether with good men or bad, could adapt himself to his company.

PLUTARCH

Like Alcibiades, George Musgrave adapted himself to his company, good or bad. Tall and handsome, he readily attracted women; even men noted his good looks. "Damn," recalled Henry Brock, "he was a fine-lookin' feller and lots of fun." But there was another side to Musgrave. Habitually jovial, he could also be low-down tough. Soft-spoken and well-dressed, "he looked more like a senator than a cattle rustler." Yet he was a cattle rustler; a bank, train, stage, and post office robber; and a killer—"guilty of more crimes than 'Billy the Kid' was ever accused of." Affable, yet hard, attractive, yet dangerous, Musgrave was a typical product of the south Texas *Brasada* that spawned him.[1]

South Texas's *Brasada* or Brush Country, region of the mustang, mesquite, prickly pear, and rattlesnake, sheltered equally untamed, rugged, and deadly men. The Comanches and Kickapoos utilized the brush as their launching point for frequent and devastating raids; bandits and outlaws from east Texas and Mexico regarded the brush as a sanctuary. Notwithstanding the dangers that could

be encountered there, the *Brasada*, and its free-running rivers, offered
to experienced cattleman the promise of becoming one of the West's
great stock-producing regions. Settlement swiftly expanded south
and west of San Antonio during the decade of the 1850s.

Rising on Bennett Musgrave's ranch in central Atascosa County,
Texas, West Metate Creek flowed intermittently past the ranch
house and onto La Parita Creek. From within the house, cries of
joy periodically rang out announcing the birth of a new child. They
did again late Sunday afternoon, May 27, 1877.[2]

George West Musgrave inherited his grandfather Joe Walker's
dimpled chin. Time would demonstrate that he also fell heir to
Walker's stature, boldness, and merry disposition.

Who's Who

HIGH FIVE GANG (A.K.A. BLACK JACK GANG)

Charter members:

Will Christian (a.k.a. Black Jack)
Bob Christian (a.k.a. Tom Anderson)
Bob Hayes (a.k.a. John West)
George Musgrave (known aliases: Burr, Bob Cameron, Jeff
    Davis, Bill Johnson, Jess Johnson, Ed Mason, George
    Mason R. W. "Bob" Mason, Jesse Miller, Bob Murray,
    George W. Murray, Robert Sanders, Bob Steward, John
    Stoner, Jesse Williams)
Code Young (a.k.a. Cole Estes, Bob Harris)

Gang replacements:

Sid Moore (a.k.a. Ef Hillman)
Van Musgrave (a.k.a. Bob Lewis, Theodore James, James
    Taylor, Calvin Musgrave)

Principal gang associates:

Johnny "Dutchy" Behmer (a.k.a. Alamo Hueco Dutch)
Cal Cox

Sherman Crump
Hugh Drake
Dan Johnson (a.k.a. Thomas Daniel Mathes, W. W. Wright)
Volney Campbell "Vollie" Musgrave (a.k.a. Collins, Camel
    Musgrave)
Daniel M. "Red" Pipkin
Dud Pruit
James M. Shaw (a.k.a. J. J. Smith)
William S. "Slim" Traynor

PRINCIPAL LAWMEN:

Andrew C. Alexander, deputy U.S. marshal (Ariz.)
Cipriano Baca, deputy U.S. marshal (N. Mex.)
Charles L. Ballard, Chaves County (N. Mex.) deputy sheriff
    (1896–97), deputy U.S. marshal, and sheriff (1907–12)
Charles F. "Doc" Blackington, Socorro County (N. Mex.)
    sheriff (1899–1902)
William M. Breakenridge, Southern Pacific Railroad special
    officer, deputy U.S. marshal (Ariz.)
Holm O. Bursum, Socorro County (N. Mex.) sheriff
    (1895–98)
Ben R. Clark, Graham County (Ariz.) deputy sheriff
Frederick J. Dodge, Wells, Fargo and Co. agent
Joseph S. Dosh, San Lucas (Calif.) constable
James L. "Les" Dow, Eddy County (N. Mex.) sheriff (1897)
    and deputy U.S. marshal
Alexander Ezekiels, deputy U.S. marshal (Ariz.)
Camillus S. Fly, Cochise County (Ariz.) sheriff (1895–96)
Creighton M. Foraker, marshal of New Mexico (1897–1912)
Fred Fornoff, Albuquerque city marshal and Bernalillo
    County (N. Mex.) deputy sheriff
Charles Fowler, deputy U.S. marshal (N. Mex.)
Patrick F. Garrett, Doña Ana County (N. Mex.) sheriff
George H. Green, marshal for the northern district of Texas

William M. Griffith, marshal of Arizona (1897–1901)

Edward L. Hall, marshal of New Mexico (1893–97)

Dee R. Harkey, Eddy County (N. Mex.) deputy sheriff

Fred Higgins, deputy U.S. marshal (N. Mex.), Chaves
County sheriff (1899–1905)

Thomas S. Hubbell, Bernalillo County (N. Mex.) sheriff

J. Smith Lea, deputy U.S. marshal (N. Mex.)

Robert N. Leatherwood, Pima County (Ariz.) sheriff,
deputy U.S. marshal

Horace W. Loomis, chief deputy U.S. marshal (N. Mex.)

William G. McAfee, Grant County (N. Mex.) sheriff
(1897–98)

Porter McDonald, Arizona Ranger (Cochise County)

Charles D. Mayer, White Oaks (N. Mex.) constable

William K. Meade, marshal of Arizona (1885–90, 1893–97)

Robert C. Ross, Texas Ranger (El Paso)

Cade Selvey, Atlantic and Pacific Railroad special agent

Baylor Shannon, Grant County (N. Mex.) sheriff (1895–96)

John H. Slaughter, former Cochise County (Ariz.) sheriff,
deputy U.S. marshal

M. Cicero Stewart, Eddy County (N. Mex.) sheriff
(1897–1906, 1909–12)

John N. Thacker, Wells, Fargo and Co. special agent

Scott White, Cochise County (Ariz.) sheriff (1897–1900),
deputy U.S. marshal

Daniel R. Williamson, Gila County (Ariz.) sheriff, deputy
U.S. marshal

CHAPTER ONE

LA BRASADA

The early residents of McMullen County were, as a class, moral, law-abiding citizens. Of course most of them carried guns, many of them drank whiskey, and not a few gambled. Six-shooters, whiskey, and poker, however, were within the code: these things had no connection with morals; indulgence in them was neither moral nor immoral, but natural to the times. Some of the most upright, honest, and generous-hearted men that ever lived carried—and on occasion used with deadly effect—six shooters, drank whiskey straight, and staked high sums on spotted cards.

J. FRANK DOBIE

At fifty-eight, Joe Walker, owner of the La Parita Ranch, adjoining the Musgraves' St. Rocky Ranch, stood tall and blue-eyed, though his striking blond hair showed tinges of white. In common with his Scotch-Irish forebears, Walker never went out of his way to avoid trouble; such resoluteness was another familial trait that would become apparent in the character of George West Musgrave.[1]

A participant in east Texas's Shelby County War, Walker, a member of the Moderator faction, killed one man in a duel on the main street of Center. Injured, he rode home, dressed his wound, then took

a fresh horse and fled. Later that night, he killed another man waiting in ambush.[2]

Walker's flight from Shelby County began a eighteen-year odys-
sey. Joined by his wife and his growing family, he migrated through
nine Texas counties before he became, in 1858, an original settler
of Yarbrough Bend in McMullen County. Here he joined with other
frontier families who started herds from the maverick longhorn
cattle and the mustang horses that grazed on the open range
between the Frio River and the Rio Grande.

When the Civil War came to Texas, Walker enlisted in the
McMullen County Confederate Militia. He saw no military action;
during and after the war, he and his two sons defended their home
and their livestock against Comanche and Kickapoo Indians, outlaws, and Yankee carpetbaggers.

Indian depredations in the Brush Country effectively ended in
1872. Violence found a new outlet—the Sutton-Taylor feud. Victor
Rose, author of *The Texas Vendetta: The Sutton-Taylor Feud* and an
acquaintance of many of the participants, explained, "The popu-
lation of Texas was divided into three classes: The Yankees, ex-
confederate, and Taylors." A popular ditty of the day read:

> It was an ancient farmer man
> And he stoppeth one of three:
> "By the Colt's improved and Henry gun
> I pray thee tell to me
> If you belong to the Sutton gang
> Or the Taylor companie?"[3]

Even as the feud raged most fiercely, Walker's oldest son, James
"Bud" Walker, courted and married Sophronia Taylor, widow of
feud victim Martin Luther Taylor. The Walkers stood firmly aligned
with the "Taylor companie." Bud, and his younger brother Tom, a
top hand, gambler, and gunman with frequent brushes with the
law, were inevitably drawn into the feud. A decade of outrages and
dozens of deaths concluded with the December 27, 1875, killing of
Jim Taylor, an act that left the Taylor faction leaderless.[4]

Joseph W. Walker
(1818–88). Courtesy of
the Martha Beth
Walker collection.

Though he was a hardened Texan, there was a whimsical side
to Joe Walker's personality, accompanied, perhaps, by an inclination toward larceny, traits later revealed in the character of his
grandson. Once, during a drought and with the range overgrazed,
Walker moved his herd over to the coast near Corpus Christi. There
he met a sea captain who had docked to take on supplies. Walker
traded the sea captain a horse for a barrel of whiskey. He returned
home with the whiskey to learn what he had doubtless foreseen
even as he made the trade—the horse had cast off its hobbles and
had beaten Walker home.[5]

On November 19, 1863, Joe Walker's daughter, Sarah Prudence
"Prudie" Walker, married Bennett Musgrave in Live Oak County,

Texas, uniting two of the Brush Country's pioneer families.[6] Back in February 1838, when Bennett was six months old, Calvin Musgrave, patriarch of the family, had settled in Gonzales (later Caldwell) County, Texas. In 1855, Calvin and his family moved to the southern portion of Bexar County, where he acquired land in the settlement of Pleasanton. The Musgraves joined the Walkers, Tumlinsons, Doaks, Slaughters, Yarbroughs, Odens, and other pioneer families intent upon taming the *Brasada*. In August 1855, Musgrave enlisted in Captain Levi English's Company of Mounted Men, organized for the protection of the frontier within the western portion of Bexar County.[7]

On September 28, 1859, Juan Nepomuceno Cortina, an influential figure in Cameron County, proclaimed his intent to protect the rights and properties of Mexicans in Texas. To combat this threat, Peter Tumlinson organized another volunteer Ranger force in Atascosa County on November 12, and enlisted Calvin Musgrave as well as Calvin's sons, Bennett and Daniel. In Austin, Major John Salmon "Rip" Ford took command of all Texas Rangers. Ford and the Rangers proceeded south toward Brownsville.[8]

On February 4, 1860, as they moved toward La Bolsa on the Rio Grande, Ford's guard encountered an armed group of Cortina's followers crossing the river and opened fire. A running fight ensued with a detachment of Rangers commanded by Bennett Musgrave in the midst of the melee. A charge by Ford's Rangers forced Cortina and his insurgents into the Burgos Mountains. Colonel Robert E. Lee reached San Antonio on February 19, assumed command of the Eighth Military Department, and advanced with his force into the lower Rio Grande Valley. Peace returned to south Texas.[9]

Cortina's defeat did not end Texas's troubles; now civil war threatened. Ignoring the pleadings of Governor Sam Houston, the Texas Secession Convention on February 1, 1861, voted for the withdrawal of Texas from the Union. Calvin Musgrave shared Houston's pro-Union sentiments. Bennett opposed his father's stance. On January 1, 1863, he rode to Rio Grande Station (previously Fort

Duncan, about a mile north of Eagle Pass), and enlisted as a private in Company D of Duff's Partisan Rangers (Fourteenth Texas Cavalry Battalion).[10]

Although Bennett returned from duty unscathed sometime after July 3, tragedy nonetheless struck the Musgrave household. Bennett's mother, Mariah, died unexpectedly on November 18, just short of her fifty-second birthday. Calvin had recently sold his home in Pleasanton and, according to family tradition, moved to Mexico for the remainder of the conflict.[11]

Calvin returned from Mexico at the war's end and resumed raising stock. In March 1867, the Union rewarded his loyalty with an appointment as postmaster for Pleasanton. Atascosa County citizens also elected Calvin's son Daniel sheriff that year and another son, Thomas, county judge the following year.[12]

Reconstruction, Indian raids, feuds, and the Civil War provided the backdrop against which Bennett and Prudie Musgrave began their family. On September 18, 1864, Prudie gave birth to the Musgraves' first child, Samuel Houston Musgrave, who died two years later. In the meantime, Calvin Van Musgrave, called Van, had been born on February 7, 1866. Next came the twins, Adanna "Addie" and Burrell in 1868.[13]

The late 1860s in south Texas were trying years, with or without children. Most families ran cattle, which also proved to be difficult. Ranchers returning from distant battlefields found that in many instances their herds had substantially increased, yet the stock, worked so little, had turned wild and proved difficult to handle. Musgrave's neighbor, Peter Tumlinson Bell, recalled, "They were wilder than deer and antelope ever hoped to be."[14]

Selling the cattle proved equally difficult, but the arrival of the Kansas Pacific Railroad at Abilene in 1867 opened up the marketplace. Bennett Musgrave's herds had joined those of his neighbors driven north up the Chisholm Trail to Abilene, but later they were transported to Ellsworth on the Kansas Pacific road, and still later to Wichita on the Atchison, Topeka and Santa Fe.[15]

In early 1869, Calvin Musgrave deeded 160 acres of land on Metate Creek to Bennett and Prudie, which the young couple used as the foundation of a successful real estate and livestock career. By 1870, they possessed land and livestock valued at six thousand dollars. The new year also brought the birth of a fourth son, LeRoy Polk Musgrave.[16]

Daughter Julia Elizabeth was born in 1872 at the ranch, while Bennett and neighbor George Washington West trailed a herd north. Following a common practice of the day, Musgrave trained several animals as lead steers, which encouraged the wilder cattle to follow. He and other Texas stockmen trailed approximately 350,000 head of cattle north that year. Down from the record high of 600,000 in 1871, the number remained profitable for the cattlemen, as higher prices, plentiful grass, and favorable weather offset the lower numbers.[17]

The success of his 1872 drive encouraged Musgrave to return north in 1873, checking a mixed herd of 2,132 head through Pleasanton. Sporting the ranch's VE, LPO, PW, and SAM brands, the cattle left late in the season, departing Atascosa County in mid-August. On September 18, while the herd was on the trail, the financial empire of Jay Cooke and Company of New York collapsed, triggering the disastrous Panic of 1873.[18]

The Panic of 1873 marked the commencement of a business downturn lasting several years; many eastern entrepreneurs declared bankruptcy. In the West, panic selling of cattle, coupled with a corn shortage that raised the price of feed, depressed cattle prices. Drivers held their herds outside of Ellsworth and Wichita, fed their stock with expensive corn, and hoped for market improvement. As market prices continued to drop, panic shipping increased. Large herds sold at considerable loss. The 1873 drive proved costly to Musgrave. He, like many others, was forced to borrow money to stay solvent. Musgrave returned to Texas. There is no evidence that he ever drove north on the trail again.[19]

Despite financial setbacks, the Bennett Musgrave family lived comfortably on their St. Rocky Ranch during the later 1870s. Under the watchful eye of Watson Stanfield, Musgrave's foreman, Bennett's stock grazed on some thirty-five hundred acres of land; the family ranked among Atascosa County's more prosperous and respected citizens. George West Musgrave joined the family on May 27, 1877.[20] It was a propitious time to be born.

CHAPTER TWO

An Outlaw's Education

*More weird and lonesome than the journey of an Amazonian
explorer is the ride of one through a Texas pear flat. With dis-
mal monotony and startling variety the uncanny and multi-
form shapes of the cacti lift their twisted trunks, and fat,
bristly hands to encumber the way. To be lost in the pear is to
die almost the death of the thief on the cross, pierced by nails
and with grotesque shapes of all the fiends hovering about.*

O. HENRY

A week before George Musgrave's seventh birthday, his older
brother, Van, married neighbor George West's daughter, Ella. Three
days after the nuptials, deputies arrested the new bridegroom for
betting at Spanish monte. Van pleaded guilty and paid a ten-dollar
fine. His marriage rapidly deteriorated. After Christmas 1884, Ella,
six months pregnant, packed her belongings and returned to her
father's home.[1]

In the spring of 1885, still separated from his wife, but with the
birth of their child imminent, Van graduated to horse rustling. Frio
County authorities caught Van, John May, and William Pelham in
possession of three stolen horses and one stolen mare. The three took
up residence in the county jail at Pearsall.

There may have been several reasons for Van's inclination to lawlessness. Jack Culley, veteran range manager of the vast Bell Ranch in San Miguel County, New Mexico, believed that those cowmen who turned to outlawry were men of action, frequently athletic, self-reliant, possessed of endurance, and, without exception, outstanding rangemen. Van displayed all of these characteristics. On the other hand, faced with growing family responsibilities, perhaps he took to outlawry as a source of escape and excitement.[2] Then again, possibly Van also considered rustling a cowboy's rite of passage. One old rangeman argued "that any cowman of open range days who claimed never to have put his brand on somebody else's animal was either a liar or a poor roper."[3]

Nearly a century later, Bennett's nephew had a simpler explanation: "Bennett was the biggest horse thief in south Texas." Bennett had been charged with cattle theft in 1882, though an Atascosa County jury found him not guilty. Van may have followed his father's lead, or possibly may have acted on his father's behalf. Whatever Van's motivation, he became a rustler.[4]

Frio County's grand jury indicted him on three separate charges of horse theft only eighteen days after the birth of his son, Frank Howard Musgrave. The judge continued the cases during the October 1885 court term. Called before the court on April 23, 1886, Van failed to appear and forfeited bond. Once more, the judge continued the cases. Van did appear for the spring court term in April 1887, at which time the judge again continued the cases, as he did in October and during the spring and fall terms of 1888.[5]

The court finally heard the first of Van's three cases on April 24, 1889; he pleaded not guilty. Following the jury's guilty verdict and the judge's five-year sentence, Van appealed the conviction and remained free on bail. The court continued the other two cases.[6]

Van's ongoing legal problems failed to bring about his reform. With two cases outstanding, and while under sentence for the third, he stole a steer on June 10 from Will Cowley in Atascosa County. Sheriff George Duck arrested Van; Bennett posted another five hundred dollars for bail. A Pleasanton jury convicted Van on

March 1, 1890. Sentenced to two years in the state penitentiary, he appealed the verdict and still remained free on bail.[7]

Coincident with their son's legal difficulties, Bennett and Prudie Musgrave began a series of real estate sales that suggest they anticipated Van's flight from Texas. Several factors influenced their decision to follow.[8]

Drought, the scourge of the cattle industry, struck south Texas in 1887–88. The Frio and Nueces Rivers quit running, leaving only small amounts of water standing in holes. The prickly pear wilted until it was no longer a source either of food or moisture for the stock. Doubtless this further encouraged the Musgraves to look for rangeland less subject to the vagaries of the *Brasada*. Moreover, Bennett's father, Calvin, and Prudie's father, Joe, died in 1888. The loss of these patriarchs removed strong ties to Texas. Finally, Bennett and Prudie's siblings also began to leave the Brush Country to seek their fortunes in other areas of Texas and the Southwest.[9]

On March 8, 1889, six weeks prior to Van's conviction on the first of the rustling charges, Bennett and Prudie sold twenty-one pieces of property, which encompassed 8,487 acres, to San Antonio bankers Daniel and Anton Oppenheimer. By the end of 1889, with Van twice convicted and facing two more trials, his parents had sold all of their remaining holdings in Atascosa County and possessed $9,600 and a note for an additional $1,000. The Musgrave family no longer had any land ties to Texas. Questionable wisdom allowed Van to remain free on bail.[10]

Remarkably, Van returned to Pearsall on April 23, 1890, to stand trial on the second charge. The jury returned a guilty verdict; the judge sentenced him to five additional years in the state penitentiary. Again, Van appealed and—amazingly—remained free on bail. The court continued the final case.[11]

By May 1890, Van had been convicted of two counts in Frio County and one count in Atascosa County. He faced two five-year sentences and one two-year sentence at the Texas State Penitentiary at Huntsville. Moreover, one additional case against him remained pending in Frio County. In the summer of 1890, while still on bail, twenty-four-year-old Van Musgrave fled Texas and twenty-four-year-old Bob Lewis arrived in New Mexico Territory. Posing as Lewis, Van hired on as foreman of James Upton's O Bar O outfit, north of Deming.[12]

The Bennett Musgrave family soon followed, driving their remaining stock along the old Texas Pecos Trail through Del Rio to Sanderson and on to Alpine, near old Fort Davis, in Brewster County. Burrell Quimby Musgrave, Bennett's cousin, lived in Alpine. This fact provides the only explanation for their departure from the main trail. In 1920, George told an associate that he had left Atascosa County in 1888 to become a cowboy in New Mexico. His statement, which suggests that at age eleven he left Atascosa County before his family, is contradicted by other evidence.[13]

Bennett and Prudie left Alpine and no doubt drove their herd via Fort Stockton to Pecos, then followed the river and the Goodnight-Loving Trail to New Mexico and a new start at Cedar Hill, on the Pine Lodge Road, thirty-five miles northwest of Roswell. Unaccountably, as several schools existed near their destination in Chaves County, New Mexico Territory, they left thirteen-year-old George in Alpine to attend school.[14]

When school was not in session, George and Burrell's son, Charley Musgrave, one year older than young George and a town bully, cowboyed for the G4 outfit, south of Alpine, on the Rio Grande. One day, returning from the G4's remuda, Charley took a rope and saddle blanket from twelve-year-old wrangler Stafford Waddell. Outraged, young Waddell grabbed a .44 Winchester and ended overbearing Charley's career with a shot between the eyes. George rejoined his parents in New Mexico soon after his cousin's death.[15]

At the onset of the 1880s, southeastern New Mexico was cattle country. Cattlemen gathered the herds at the only settlements of consequence—Seven Rivers, Lincoln, and White Oaks—for drives to shipping points at Las Vegas, Springer, or Engle on the Santa Fe railway. Between 1887 and 1895, Roswell, previously little more than a post office and a store, slowly emerged as the commercial heart

of the Pecos Valley. Roundups began, starting in April and continuing through November. From Roswell, stockmen drove their cattle and sheep to Amarillo or newly founded Clayton on the
recently completed Denver, Texas and Fort Worth Railroad line.
Bennett Musgrave continued to raise cattle while he regularly
dodged the Chaves County tax assessor. As commonly practiced,
Bennett maintained two counts: what he actually owned and what
he owned "for taxable purposes."[16]

His youngest daughter, Fannie Mariah, had matured into a
beautiful young woman much sought after by the gentlemen of
Roswell. On July 25, 1895, twenty-year-old Fannie disappointed
her other suitors and married Dan Johnson, alias Thomas Daniel
Mathes. Texas-born Dan Johnson, previously the foreman of the
Bar V Ranch, sixty miles north of Roswell, enjoyed a reputation as
one of the best cowmen in the Territory. He was also an outlaw. Fannie refused to marry him unless he reformed and changed his name.
A little earlier, Johnson had been hired by the Milne-Bush Cattle
Co. and that evidently satisfied Fannie about his law-abiding intentions. However, he found his promise difficult to keep.[17]

By the time George Musgrave rejoined his family in Chaves
County, he had grown into a tall, handsome, jovial teenager. Ambi-
tious, he also sought excitement. Four months after his seventeenth
birthday, he followed in Van's footsteps and turned to a criminal
career, joining a rustling operation headed by former Texas Ranger
George T. Parker.[18]

Parker and Ernest Bloom (the son of the co-owner of Circle Diamond Ranch, Frank Bloom) rustled a small stock of horses bearing
Rio Hondo horse rancher C. D. Bonney's T brand, and rebranded
them with Bloom's Bar EB brand (bar over reversed E, B connected). They intended to exchange the burnt T horses for cattle
rustled by Musgrave. On September 15, 1894, Musgrave rustled
one neat cow and three cows bearing the Bar V brand of the Cass
Land and Cattle Company. Before the month was over, he stole two
other cows owned by Casinero Barela. When Musgrave delivered
the cattle to Parker, he received nothing in exchange. C. D. Bonney

had rounded up the horses Parker had stolen and had driven them back to their home range at Border Hill on the Rio Hondo.[19]

Parker cautioned Musgrave that "he better get up and get outa the country, they're gonna give him some trouble over these horses." Having made a fugitive out of Musgrave, Parker later testified before the grand jury that Musgrave and Dan Johnson had rustled twelve head of Bonney-owned horses. Without the slightest remorse, Parker then rode to the Musgrave ranch and falsely claimed to Bennett and Prudie that their son owed him money. Parker left Cedar Hill with a number of head of the senior Musgrave's cattle.[20] Musgrave later and rather artfully elaborated:

> My trouble with Parker started over a trade, in which I sold him cattle for horses, he to pay me the difference due me in cash. I was then [seventeen] years old. After the trade it developed that the horses he traded me were stolen property, and he advised me to leave the country, telling me he would look after my property while I was gone and until it was safe for me to come back. Trouble was brewing over the stolen horses and Parker scared me into leaving because I was in possession of the stolen property.
> Taking Parker's advice, I left the country. I [later] learned that Parker had taken practically all of my mother's cattle, even the calves, claiming that I had sold them to him for $500. I had made no such sale to him. Parker had jobbed me in the trade and robbed mother of her stock.[21]

On March 5, 1895, a grand jury indicted Musgrave on two counts of cattle rustling. Eight months later, he and Dan Johnson were indicted on one count each for horse rustling. Seventeen-year-old George Musgrave did not appear in court to answer any of the charges. He had departed Chaves County in the fall of 1894, accompanied by his close friend and fellow Texan, twenty-five-year-old Code Young (who had been using the name Bob Harris). The two friends left Roswell together, then followed separate paths, but later reunited in Grant County.[22]

From Chaves County, George Musgrave fled west past Hot Springs, in Sierra County. One evening about sundown, "a damned fine-lookin' man" rode into the Double S Ranch west of town, astride a large white horse and leading a black horse carrying a pack. Approaching "Salty John" Cox, the camp cook, Musgrave introduced himself as Bill Johnson, the first of his many aliases. Cox, who was not above a little rustling himself, found Musgrave a likable fellow and "always in good humor." George stayed around the Double S for the next month to six weeks while his sore-backed horses recovered. Cox occasionally loaned him a horse, and George would ride south to the Adobe and the Ladder outfits seeking work. Apparently, he did not find any. He then briefly returned to Chaves County only to learn that the search for him remained active.[23]

Musgrave rode west again, first to Hachita, then up north of Deming, where he cowboyed briefly for Jim Upton's O Bar O Ranch and adopted the alias Jeff Davis. The obvious attraction of Upton's ranch was brother Van, still employed as the ranch's foreman. His friend Code Young, using the alias Cole Estes, rejoined Musgrave at the O Bar O.[24]

Young moved on to the Head and Hearst outfit, which adjoined the Diamond A range. He was "just the finest little fellow [but] a business fellow, keen and grey-eyed, he was business all the time." Young was "a sparsely built man, about five feet six inches in height, weigh[ed] about 145 pounds and [was no] more than 25 years of age," recalled Henry Brock who ramrodded the upper division of the Diamond A Ranch at Apache Tejo, near old Fort McLane on the Santa Rita–Janos Trail. When George left the O Bar O, Brock hired on the "splendid-lookin boy" at the Diamond A.[25]

Another friend of Musgrave's in the area was Bob Hayes, thought to be a fugitive from Texas. He had cowboyed for the Bloom-owned Diamond A Ranch near Roswell under the alias John West and now worked for the neighboring Everhart-owned Hatchet outfit in the Playas Valley. Diamond A cowboy Johnny Longbotham depicted him as an awful tough hombre "who didn't care for nothin'." Brock, in his discursive manner, described Hayes as "a ordinary looking, kind of loose-built sort of fellow, not very large, probably five foot nine inches tall. To talk to he was a jolly, jumping sort of fellow. You just had lots of fun with him." During roundup Estes and Hayes stayed with the Diamond A wagon, representing their respective outfits. Musgrave was the only one of the three actually working for Brock. The Diamond A made no distinction between outlaw and lawman. Brock reflected, "We treated the outlaws as guests, and when the posses came for them a day or so later, we gave them the same consideration."[26]

One day Musgrave and Hayes rode north from the lower division of the Diamond A up to Cow Springs, about twenty miles south of Silver City. Seeking out Brock, they asked if they could shoe their horses. Not realizing that they planned to leave, Brock let them help themselves. As Musgrave and Hayes prepared to ride out that afternoon, they asked Brock if they could pick out an old pony to use as a saddle horse. Brock consented, asked the two where they were going, and they answered, "Well, we just took a notion that we'd worked long enough." The next Brock heard, "They had been down in Mexico and stolen a bunch of cattle and brought 'em up to right near Deming and they found out they was bein' trailed by officers and government men and quit 'em. They left these cattle." Discretion demanded that the fugitives seek new surroundings.[27]

During the spring of 1896, George Musgrave adopted the alias Jesse Williams and, in all probability accompanied by Cole Estes and Bob Hayes, drifted to Cochise County, Arizona, then suffering a new outbreak of Indian raids. On March 28, a small band of Apaches had clubbed Alfred Hands to death as he herded goats at his Cave Creek ranch, near San Simon Valley. The *Sulphur Valley News* credited the killing to bronco Apaches from Mexico's Sierra Madre led by Massai.[28]

In Cochise County, Musgrave hired on as a cowboy for Edward J. Roberts, owner of the OH Ranch, taking in most of the range from the Huachucas on the west to the San Pedro on the east, and north from the Sonoro line to the Babocomari grant. Roberts ran about five thousand head of mixed cattle and usually hired a couple of cowboys for the spring, summer, and fall months. Cowman Ed Lemmon, representing the Sheidley Cattle Company's Flying V Ranch in South Dakota, arrived in Arizona about the same time intent upon purchasing five thousand head of cattle from a pool of Cochise County ranchers, including Roberts. It is probable that Musgrave helped round up cattle for delivery at Huachuca for the Flying V. Lemmon later allowed that Roberts's cowboys were a tough crowd. "I found that all but two, Ed Roberts and his stepson [*sic*], Ben Sneed, had killed their man or men."[29]

Reaching Cochise County, Cole Estes, using the identity of Code Young, secured a job in Sulphur Spring Valley working at the 7D. Leonard Alverson managed the outfit for butcher Charles L. Cummings and blacksmith Ed J. Jacklin, both of Tombstone. Alverson later related that Young "was an excellent hand, good cowboy, would shoe horses, sweep, wash dishes or do anything there was to do."[30]

At about the same time Musgrave, Young, and Hayes reached southeastern Arizona, two Indian Territory renegades, Will and Bob Christian, also appeared in Cochise County. The paths of these five young Texas-born outlaws soon crossed.

CHAPTER THREE

The Christian Brothers

"I have been friendly with a number of outlaws. It is a wise thing to be that way. Besides that—don't be shocked—outlaws are more interesting than inlaws. And they are better housemates."

EUGENE MANLOVE RHODES

Like the *Brasada*, the northwest Texas frontier bred some hard characters, and the tough sons of William Mark Christian were no exception. In the 1860s, Kentucky-born Christian had settled on a site in the southeast corner of Baylor County. Comanche raiding parties still harassed the county in 1868 when Sarah "Sallie" Christian (née Duff) gave birth to their first child, a son, Bob. Three years later, brother Will arrived. In 1874, at the advent of the region's buffalo hunting heyday, their small settlement on the Brazos River took the name Round Timber. The Christian boys witnessed the opening of the Western Cattle Trail in 1876, which launched the area's cattle drive epoch.[1]

The boys' father was a "tall, lank, dark-complexioned Indian-like man, and a very hard looking customer—such a one as one would not like to meet alone on the prairie or in the brush." Texas and Oklahoma neighbor Bill Deister recalled that he "always rode a race horse and always had that Winchester in his hand." As he got off his horse, he would always pass that Winchester with his right hand over to his left. In contrast to their father, Bob and Will's mother, Sallie Christian, born about 1854 in Texas, was slim, blue-eyed, with blond hair. Deister continued, "Pa liked the old man, and Mother liked the old lady. The boys were the nicest fellows you ever saw." According to neighbor J. A. Newsom, "Two persons [William and Sallie Christian] could scarcely be found who were more refined in their life and lived more Godly and righteously than they."[2]

The family left Round Timber about 1883 and moved northwest into the Texas Panhandle. Their next move was into the Indian Territory in the late 1880s, certainly by 1889, when William Mark Christian's name first graces the pages of the U.S. District Court records.[3]

On October 27, 1889, Flave Carver ran a booth at the Muskogee Fair, where his patrons bought, sold, and consumed whiskey. U.S. Deputy Marshal John Childers, Jr., later arrested William Christian and his brother Daniel, two of Carver's customers, on the charge of introducing liquor into the Indian country, a violation of the Trade and Intercourse Act of July 9, 1832. The brothers were "regular peddling" whiskey in the Nations and were "very sharp, selling all the time now but very sly," according to Childers. By the time the case reached the U.S. commissioner in 1891, Carver's memory had deserted him; he just could not recall from whom he had acquired the illicit beverage. Because he was a better witness for the defense than for the prosecution, his testimony assured William Christian's discharge.[4]

The family's prairie home was just above the forks of a creek, within the borders of the Creek (Muskogee) Nation, six miles southeast of Wewoka, near the boundaries of the Seminole and Choctaw Nations. Briefly in mid-1895, the Christians shifted their residence to a nearby rental home, a short distance from William H. "Bill" Carr's store-saloon and cotton gin at Violet Springs. Carr, one of the oldest and bravest U.S. deputy marshals, had been attached to the federal courts at Fort Smith, Arkansas; Wichita, Kansas; and

Paris, Texas. He was also a dangerous and totally unscrupulous gunman. Outlaws and lawmen alike shared his favors. At Violet Springs, he illicitly supplied untaxed and forbidden liquor to the surrounding Indian nations.[5]

Young Bob Christian, who earned a reputation for being bold and reckless by boxing, jumping, and breaking fractious horses, began his outlaw career bootlegging Bill Carr's whiskey in the Seminole and Creek Nations. Newsom recalled that soon the Seminole, Creek, Choctaw, and Chickasaw Nations issued warrants for Bob, though there are no records of any liquor charges being brought against Bob Christian at Fort Smith at this time. Newsom asserted that, fearing conviction, he (Christian) went into hiding in the forest along Little River.[6]

Will, portrayed as "the bravest of the brothers, did the head work." Within the Christian family, Bill Deister revealed how their boldness, recklessness, bravery, and cunning led to crime. "Robbery was a Christian family tradition. They would run clear out of groceries, but the next morning, there would be all kinds of stuff—coffee and ham and bacon and flour. They had been robbing."[7]

Bill Dalton, the last of the Dalton gang to be enjoying both life and liberty, had quit Bill Doolin's gang late in March 1894 and hid out, probably at the Christian compound, notwithstanding "Old Man" Christian's later denial. On April 1, Dalton entered Bill Carr's saloon with a companion, probably George "Red Buck" Weightman or Jim Wallace (alias George Bennett). Initial reports differed as to the identity of Dalton's partner, mentioning variously George Thorne and the Slaughter Kid. George "Red Buck" Weightman had used the alias George Thorne and had also recently left the Doolin gang. He and Dalton could still have been traveling together and both could have been at Carr's. The Slaughter Kid, a sobriquet of George "Bitter Creek" Newcomb (Alfred George D. Newcomb), was also associated with James Castleberry. Newcomb, already dead, is not a candidate, nor is Castleberry. Conceivably, journalists heard the man identified as "George" and drew their own conclusions. In that event, one more candidate looms likely. At the time,

Dalton numbered George Bennett (real name Jim Wallace) among his closest associates.[8]

Carr and Dalton reportedly argued, possibly concerning an illicit activity that involved the two. If Weightman accompanied Dalton, possibly he engineered the confrontation with Carr, determined to avenge an earlier arrest. In either case, an argument ensued, and the lawman reached for his gun. Dalton's companion responded in kind. When the shooting ceased, Carr had suffered wounds in the wrist and abdomen; both outlaws, also injured, had been put to flight. Their ability to travel a considerable distance suggests that their wounds were slight.[9]

Later that month, three horses turned up missing near Wewoka, in the Creek Nation: two belonged to Mr. Elliott and one to Tobe Alexander, a Creek Indian. Suspicion immediately focused on the Christians and the many heavily armed men hanging out at their place. On May 22, J. L. Mackey of Guthrie also lost a mare and a horse to rustlers.[10]

The day following Mackey's loss, Bill Dalton, Jim Wallace, and the two Knight brothers, Jim and Jourd, rode into Longview, Texas, to rob the First National Bank. Before the smoke cleared, two townsmen and one outlaw, Wallace, had been killed and two local citizens had been wounded. The three surviving bandits escaped unharmed.[11] A posse followed the outlaws north across the Red River and into the Choctaw Nation, before being thrown off the trail by the tracks of a band of horse thieves. The posse followed the trail of the rustlers who, the authorities later suspected, had supplied the Longview fugitives with fresh horses.[12]

Rumors persisted among the neighbors that Old Man Christian harbored Bill Dalton. Isaac Trett, a young employee of Christian's, sat for hours on the ranch house roof with Christian's daughter and some other women, as if watching the countryside for approaching posses. After Dalton's death on June 8 at Elk (near Ardmore), Oklahoma, deputy marshals from Paris, Texas, continued to keep the Christian home under surveillance. They observed that no one ever went to work in the fields. Indeed, no cultivated fields existed within three-quarters of a mile of the house. The deputies did count fifteen to twenty horses regularly corralled at the house and noticed that men, heavily armed with Winchesters and revolvers, came and went in the night, bringing in new horses and leaving with others.[13]

Following three weeks of observation, officers arrested Old Man Christian, Jim Castleberry, and Trett on charges of horse theft and brought them to Paris, Texas, seat of the Eastern Texas District Court. When they arrived on June 25, the lawmen received a reception "almost in the nature of an ovation. Hundreds pressed them by the hand, and expressed gratification at seeing them alive again. The officers are confident that some of the men captured were implicated in the Longview robbery."[14]

On June 28, the grand jury of the Eastern District of Texas received the case. That same day, arresting deputy Jeff D. Mynett, who had traveled from Paris to Fort Smith, Arkansas, secured a writ for the men's arrest on the same charge from the court of the Western District at Fort Smith. Five days later, officers rearrested the three men and took them to Fort Smith. Nearly eight months later, the Fort Smith grand jury examined the evidence and declined to indict them.[15]

On December 26, Bob Christian and his associates, including West Love and John Champion, robbed Lewis Rockett's general store and post office at Wilburton in the Choctaw Nation of $21.50, a gold watch, and some pocketknives. Two weeks later, Christian, Love, and Champion, joined by Joe Criner and a fifth man (unidentified), appeared in Wilburton at the GR Bar Ranch of George W. Riddle, a prominent Choctaw.[16]

Robert H. Hall, a man with a dubious background who was Riddle's son-in-law, ramrodded Riddle's four-thousand-acre ranch, about a mile south of town. John E. Lewis, one of the GR cowboys, later reflected, "Now Bob was a tricky fellow and he was connected with the famous Christian gang of outlaws."[17]

Riddle had two to three thousand dollars in cash secreted within the house, money recently withdrawn from a bank at Fort Smith.

On the afternoon of January 9, 1895, Hall set off with the money, ostensibly to purchase cattle. He returned that evening, money in hand, claiming to have abandoned his journey because he feared being waylaid by bandits. In reality, his concern may have been that he had failed to be robbed by his accomplices, the Christians. Possibly, he also realized that suspicion would fall heavily upon him if he was robbed while on the road alone. Whatever his reasoning, Hall helped the Riddles hide the cash and then left for his home. Half of the money now reposed in a trunk, and the rest was tucked away in a mattress.

A few hours later Bob Christian, Love, Champion, Criner, and the unnamed fifth man, masked and heavily armed, presented themselves at the Riddle residence demanding the money upon threat of life. Riddle's wife, Elvarine, reluctantly opened the trunk and unstuffed the mattress, revealing the cash. The enriched outlaws then selected three of Riddle's best saddle horses and fled into the darkness.[18]

Suspicion focused on Christian, Love, and Champion. The court ordered their arrest on January 19. Deputy Marshal Jim Brazell arrested Bob Christian at South McAlester on March 25 and jailed him at Fort Smith. Discharged because no witness would identify him, Christian headed back to the Violet Springs and Corner vicinity of Oklahoma.[19]

Bob Hall's plot to fleece his in-laws eventually became evident. He was arrested and indicted for robbery and receiving stolen property. In January 1896, Joe Criner testified that Hall got most of the money taken from "old Judge Riddell" [sic]. However, as Hall was a Choctaw citizen through marriage, the United States had no jurisdiction in the case, and the court dismissed the charges. Hall was subsequently tried in a Choctaw tribal court at Red Oak for conspiracy to rob other members of the tribe, specifically George Riddle. Found guilty, he was sentenced to one hundred lashes. "But here's where the politics came in," said John Lewis. "Green McCurtain [the governor of the Choctaw Nation] was an uncle of

Bob's wife. I saw the whipping and Bob was laughing all the time. They didn't hurt him."[20]

The Riddle robbery did accomplish one thing. Heretofore a loose association involving Bob Christian and various members of the Nation's criminal constituency, the band now metamorphosed into an organized gang under his leadership. Fresh from the two robberies, the Christian gang prepared for their next offense.

The author Lorenzo Walters maintained "on good authority" that in the spring the Christian brothers appeared in the Choctaw Nation and rustled a herd of cattle belonging to the deputy marshal, Jim McAlester. On July 31, 1895, Deputy U.S. Marshal Charles Baird arrested Ed Childers, Frank Young, and Bob Christian for stealing fifteen head of cattle from Jim McAlester the previous November. Considering the similarities, perhaps this is the offense that Walters referred to "on good authority."[21]

Early Saturday morning, April 20, Pottawatomie Deputy Sheriff William C. Turner encountered the brothers, along with "Buttermilk John" Mackey and Foster Holbrook, near Burnett, a dozen miles southwest of Tecumseh, close to the Christian home. When Turner tried to arrest Bob Christian on an outstanding grand larceny warrant, Bob pulled his revolver, responding, "You can go to hell and eat your warrant also." Turner also drew his gun and fired, the bullet glancing off Christian's head, near his left eye. Then all four men returned the deputy's fire. Turner fell from his horse, killed by a bullet from Bob Christian's revolver. Lawmen captured Holbrook that evening and arrested Mackey the following day. Meanwhile, the Christian brothers fled southwest, crossing the Canadian River back into the Choctaw Nation.[22]

Will Christian later related a self-serving account of Turner's killing. In it, Christian claimed to have been a deputy marshal in the Indian Territory, which, had it been true (it was not), would have made his action plausible. While a "deputy," Will learned that in slack times the marshals would plant a bottle of whiskey, then make an arrest, charging the individual with possession of alcohol on the reservation. He virtuously asserted that he resigned because he disapproved of this activity. Later, following his arrest upon leaving a grocery store, Christian maintained that the two deputies promptly produced a bottle of whiskey from his wagon, causing a scuffle in which one of them was killed. Although there is no factual basis for Christian's tale, there are plenty of other documented instances of this long-practiced form of shakedown in Indian Territory.[23]

On May 1, 1895, the gang, now including Bob and Will Christian, John Fessenden, and John Reeves, stole two horses from Caesar Payne, a resident of Sasakwa in the Seminole Nation. Soon thereafter, Bill Carr sought the brothers out and persuaded them to stand trial for the killing of Turner, perhaps suggesting to them that odds favored an acquittal on a plea of self-defense. The Christians surrendered to Carr and Deputy Hank Watts and joined Holbrook and Mackey in the Tecumseh jail. Following a five-day trial in Judge Henry W. Scott's Third Judicial District Court, and a five-hour closing address by the prosecutor, Colonel W. M. Melton, the brothers were convicted of first-degree manslaughter. Will received a five-year sentence, Bob a ten. The court transferred the Christians to the Oklahoma City county jail pending a decision on their motion for a new trial. Mackey, found guilty of second-degree manslaughter, received a two-year sentence. The *Daily Oklahoman* reported that Holbrook was not charged because of his youth and testimony that he had taken no active part in the shooting. Certainly it was for the latter reason. At age nineteen, Holbrook was subject, minimally, to an accessory charge.[24]

Later the next month, Bill Carr, John Fessenden, J. C. Dowd, Will Christian, Sr., John Reeves, and a Mr. Newsom gathered at Frank Rensberger's home near Violet Springs. Under Carr's leadership, the group agreed to send Reeves and Fessenden to Oklahoma City to smuggle guns to the jailed brothers. That same day, fifteen-year-old Tullis "Tulsa" Welch, a Christian family friend, also passed a revolver to Jessie Findley, Bob Christian's girl friend, with instructions that she should pass the gun on to young Louis "Lonie" Miller. Miller would then smuggle it into the jail for Bob Christian. When she could not locate Miller, Findley ended up delivering the revolver herself. Another gun was slipped in, possibly by Miss Emma Johnson.[25]

Shortly after six o'clock on the evening of June 30, the Oklahoma City jailer, John H. Garver, left the door open between his office and the jail while locking up the cells for the night. As he opened the door into the inner corridor, the Christians jumped him. Another prisoner, Jim Casey, awaiting trial for murder, dashed past the struggling men. Garver screamed for his wife to lock the connecting door. As she did, Casey reappeared with a gun and forced her to unlock it. The Christians and Casey bolted out of the door, leaving the stunned jailer and his wife locked inside.[26]

The three men fled south through an alley to Grand Avenue. They spotted Gus White driving his buggy along the street. Will Christian jumped into the front of the buggy while Casey sprang into the rear; a fight ensued over control of the reins. White managed to bring the horses to a halt near the corner of Broadway and Grand Avenue. Chief of Police Milt Jones spotted the escapees. Pistol in hand, he ran toward the buggy. Casey turned and fired at the police chief. Jones fell dead. Policemen Stafford and Jackson opened fire on the buggy, hitting Casey in the neck and head. He died within a matter of seconds.

During the mclee, Bob Christian untied and mounted Jones's horse, tethered in front of the police court, and galloped south. Brother Will, struck in the neck by a bullet, jumped from the buggy and fled afoot down Grand Avenue, dodging more gunfire. He came upon Frank Berg, riding in a cart near the Santa Fe freight station. Seizing the cart, he headed southeast. About a mile east of town, Will abandoned the cart, stole another horse and wagon, and continued on his way to the North Canadian River. Initial reports stated that Will found a log on which he floated down the river and escaped. In fact, he found a log and lay behind it through the night, hiding.[27] According to the *Daily Oklahoman*, "officers Jackson and Stafford were within a very few feet of him at one time—so close that he could of [*sic*] reached out and touched them. [Will Christian] tells of what he heard them say, and how he had his gun cocked with a determination to kill the first man who laid eyes on him, and take his chances with the rest of the pursuers."[28]

The following morning Will walked a few miles to a friend's house and got a horse. Oklahoma County Sheriff C. H. DeFord and his posse found the wagon abandoned three miles southeast of the city.[29]

The Christian brothers regrouped at their father's house, then headed to the home of a friend who fenced their stolen goods "and was kind of a go-between for the outlaws." Neighbor Bill Deister was confused when he mistook one brother for the other and recalled that Bob had been shot through the neck and Leonie (Deister's sister-in-law) had bandaged him. It was close to a week before Will was able to ride again and the brothers left.[30]

Some reports labeled Will's wound serious, though later accounts, and Will's rapid return to the saddle and outlawry, indicate otherwise. By early July, both brothers were again active and, joined by Fessenden, Reeves, Doc Williams, and Ben Brown, on the prowl in the Little River country. On July 7, they stole four horses near Violet Springs and were then spotted east of Paoli in the Chickasaw Nation. Newspapers began to compare them with the desperate Dalton gang.[31]

On Thursday evening, July 11, Deputy Marshal Bud Logue arrested Doc Williams near Purcell on the charge of harboring outlaws and obstruction of federal officers. Taken to Purcell, Williams was placed aboard a train for Oklahoma City. Five days later, deputies arrested Tullis Welch without incident at his father's place, twelve miles east of Oklahoma City.[32]

Jessie Findley's arrest came on July 12, sixty miles east of Norman. The following day, deputy sheriffs W. H. Springfield and William C. "Bill" Wade of Pottawatomie County took her to Oklahoma City. A tall, slender, twenty-two-year-old girl of "backwoods raising and lack of education," Jessie was described by the press as the "solid girl" of Bob Christian and a daughter figure of the senior Will Christian. Jessie's story interested the prosecution. As she talked, Sheriff DeFord continued the hunt, increasingly and cor-rectly convinced that numerous active and former U.S. deputy marshals, sworn to uphold the law, were aiding and abetting the Christians.[33]

On July 20, Sheriff DeFord arrested Hank Watts, one of the deputies suspected of involvement in the plot to free the Chris-tians. DeFord had additional warrants for Deputy Bill Carr and Old Man Christian. The next day, Deputy Sheriff B. F. Owens arrested Carr, who promised to make no attempt at escape. He arrived in Oklahoma City without benefit of shackles. That same day Deputy Marshal Rufus Cannon arrested the senior Christian, ordering, "Throw up your hands, you old duffer, or I'll blow the hell out of you." Cannon manacled Christian and took him to join the others at the Oklahoma City jail.[34]

The court met on July 29 for the preliminary hearing of Old Man Christian. Jessie Findley appeared as the chief witness. On Friday, June 21, she revealed that the Christian family supporters had arranged for guns to be smuggled into the jail and that she had smuggled in one of the revolvers. She could not say whether Old Man Christian knew of her delivery, though he had told her that he had given three more revolvers and four Winchesters to Fes-senden and Reeves to smuggle into jail for his boys.[35]

During the two months following their escape, the Christians and their gang, reportedly a dozen men strong, rode and stole at will. On July 8, they robbed J. C. "Jack" Simmons's store at Violet Springs, taking $380 in cash and an equal amount in merchandise. Sheriff DeFord led a force of perhaps fifty officers in pursuit of the outlaws; Territorial Governor Cary Renfrow offered a reward of $6,000 for the two Christians. Witnesses spotted the two brothers, in the company of a third party, near South McAlester on July 23. Three days later, the Christians and a partner held up John F. Brown's Wewoka Trading Company store at the Seminole capital in the Indian Territory. They took $37, two Winchester rifles, three cartridge belts, cartridges, and clothing. Fortunately for Brown, they failed to grab anyone who could open the safe.[36]

The Christian brothers and several other men, all heavily armed, were sighted at Wilburton on the evening of July 28. Observers anticipated a holdup of the Missouri, Kansas and Texas Railroad "at a point near the South Canadian River."[37]

The following week, on August 1, the gang, now consisting of the Christian brothers, Fessenden, Holbrook, Reeves, and three other men, robbed a store at Lumkee. The gang crossed the South Canadian River into the Choctaw Nation and, on August 6, robbed a store in Calvin, a few miles south of Lumkee. They continued southeast and made preparations to holdup the Choctaw, Oklahoma and Gulf Railway. Their plans were foiled when they encountered a posse on August 9.[38]

Led by two U.S. deputy marshals, W. H. Springfield and F. C. "Carter" Stockton, the posse, including Sam Eaton and the unsavory Bob Hall, approached the gang's encampment on a mountainside five miles south of Wilburton. According to John Lewis, hatred for Stockton prompted Hall to volunteer to guide the posse to the hideout. He hoped the gang would kill Stockton. Hall's effort failed. The posse found four of the outlaws, the two Christians, Fessenden, and Reeves "completely unawares, lying about the camp stretched out upon the ground." The officers fired one volley into the camp and killed Jack Fessenden. Both groups then fled the scene in opposite directions. The *Hartshorne Sun* reported that for the next several days "the woods [were] full of officers on their trail, but the fugitives were no novices in the scouting business and managed successfully to elude their pursuers." A week later, the officers' efforts began to pay dividends. Deputy Marshal Charles Baird arrested Foster Holbrook on August 17 and incarcerated him in the McAlester jail. On August 21, U.S. marshals arrested Irene Champion, said to be another of Bob Christian's sweethearts, along with W. H. Mickle, E. Mickle, and George and Lee Noland, all on charges of harboring outlaws.[39]

While lawmen arrested many of their confederates, the Christians and John Reeves arrived in the vicinity of Paoli about August 12 and added Claude Nuckells and Ted Edwards as reinforcements. On

August 16, four members of the gang robbed J. N. Townsley's ranch near Atoka. While two outlaws held Townsley and two of his cowboys at bay, the other bandits ransacked the house and seized several guns, a gold watch, and $17.80. They left behind several large, but unsigned, postal money orders.[40]

Five days following the robbery, a U.S. deputy marshal arrested John Reeves at the home of Emma Johnson's father. Reeves joined the others in jail.[41]

On August 23, while riding through a large pasture about seven miles west of Purcell, a posse spotted the two Christians, Nuckells, and Edwards, hiding in a brush-lined ravine that meandered through the pasture. The ten deputies surrounded a house where they thought the gang would come for supplies. As anticipated, Bob Christian rode up a gulch toward the house, and one of the posse fired, killing Christian's horse. As the outlaw turned to flee, Deputy W. E. "Jake" Hocker rode to intercept him. A shot from behind struck Hocker.[42]

Who shot Deputy Hocker? The *Daily Oklahoman* initially reported that it was Will Christian. Taking issue, Deputy Marshal Selden T. Lindsey argued that it would have been a physical impossibility for either of the Christians to have shot Hocker in the back. He opined that a member of the posse, loyal to the Christians, attempted to assassinate Hocker. The *Weekly Oklahoman* resolved the issue. The posse had encountered four men, not two: the Christians, Claude Nuckells, and Ted Edwards. As the Christian brothers fled, deduction argues that the bullet hitting Hocker from behind came from the gun of either Nuckells or Edwards. After he fell, both brothers returned and one of them asked, "Are you badly hurt, old man?" "Yes," replied Hocker. "Well, we're sorry, but we let you down as easily as we could." They unbuckled his gun belt and took his rifle, pistol, and horse. The Christians then rode west on Hocker's horse. The remaining nine members of the posse, cut off by the lay of the land, made no effort to stop them.[43]

Little was heard of the Christian gang during September, but on October 6, a train robbery occurred at Caston Switch, just fifteen miles west of the Arkansas line in the Choctaw Nation. Six robbers, thought to be the Christian brothers' gang, failed to open the safe. The total take was reported to be eighty-five cents. However, circumstances suggest that the Christians, joined by Flave Carver, possibly Tom Harless, and several others, robbed the train of one package of registered mail and heisted an undisclosed sum of money from the express car. Although the take likely did not amount to much, certainly it proved more than the reported eighty-five cents.[44]

In late November, after disappearing from view for a while, the Christians robbed Kennedy's store at Savanna in the Choctaw Nation. Then, on the evening of December 5, a gang of three men robbed the Co-operative Store at Coalgate, twenty miles to the west of Stringtown, making off with four to five hundred dollars in cash and sundries. Witnesses identified both Will and Bob, but could not identify the third man. On the same day, the Christians were also identified, incorrectly, as having robbed a store at the Sac and Fox agency, sixty miles north of Coalgate.[45]

On January 18, 1896, two men attempted, but failed, to rob E. A. Robinson's store at Kiowa, in the Choctaw Nation. The two perpetrators, described as "a tall man [Will Christian] and a low heavy set man [Bob Christian] were thought to be the same as those who were successful at Savanna and Coalgate."[46]

To avoid what must have seemed the increasing likelihood of capture, the Christian brothers now left Oklahoma. Following one of the myriad thief runs, it is likely they fled south toward Wichita Falls or Cooke County, Texas. Certainly going to Jack County, along the old stage route, would be reasonable; from Jacksboro, the route led to Shackelford County, via Throckmorton County. From Shackelford County, they probably continued on the old road to New Mexico.[47]

During the winter of 1895–1896, they appeared at Herb Brogden's in the Seven Rivers region of Eddy County, New Mexico. The two brothers had known the Brogden family in Texas and now one of them herded sheep for Brogden while the other went to work as a herder for neighboring sheep rancher Poole. Interestingly, Brogden later related that the two brothers had stayed with him during the months of July to September 1895. If this was true, they would have had to leave the Indian Territory in June, prior to their escape from the Oklahoma City jail. One can only assume that Brogden's inaccuracy was a ruse to protect himself from any charge as an accomplice after the fact. Dee Harkey, a sometime Eddy County deputy sheriff and inspector for the New Mexico Cattle Raisers' Association, later maintained that he had located the two brothers at Jack and Herb Brogden's. They fled into a cane patch, and he was unable to chase them out. "By God! They left there afoot. They's afraid to go horse-back and they left there afoot and went out into that Arizona Country."[48]

In the meantime, Old Man Christian and the remaining family moved away from the Violet Springs area back into an old Indian house on the Seminole County line. Bill Deister recalled, "The next time I went over to their place there was nobody there. Nobody knows when the Christians left there. I never heard from them after that." Mother Sallie Christian later moved to Wichita Falls, Texas. Old Man Christian's later whereabouts remain unknown; presumably he joined her in Wichita Falls.[49]

Oklahoma Territory had seen the last of the infamous Christian brothers. By the spring of 1896, Bob and Will had arrived in Arizona.[50]

CHAPTER FOUR

THE HIGH FIVES

NOTICE OF REWARD
POST OFFICE DEPARTMENT
OFFICE OF THE POSTMASTER GENERAL
WASHINGTON, D.C., JULY 1, 1896
Order No. 416
For the arrest and conviction of any person, in any United States Court, on the charge of robbing a post office FIFTY DOL-LARS in each case wherein the amount stolen is $50 or less.

W. L. WILSON,
Postmaster General

When the Christian brothers reached Cochise County it was spring roundup time. Bob adopted the alias Tom Anderson and found work at the Boquillas Land and Cattle Company's Wagon Rod Ranch, adjoining Ed Robert's OH range. Will took the name Williams and probably first worked for Fred Ruch's Triangle outfit in the San Simon Valley, eight miles northeast of Willcox. Described as a "jovial, powerful, handsome, broad-browed, dark complected six footer" who weighed 202 pounds, he picked up the nickname Black Jack. When Edward Wilson met Will, the latter worked for the F Ranch of the Tombstone Land and Cattle Company's 4 Bars

Sam J. Hayhurst. Courtesy
Arizona Historical Society/
Tucson, AHS #17497.

outfit in Sulphur Spring Valley. Will next went to work nearby,
breaking mules for James E. McNair, manager of the Erie Cattle
Company's Mud Springs ranch in the Sulphur Spring Valley. Before
long, he had hired on to break broncos at the IX Ranch of the Duval
Cattle Company.[1]

On July 9, 1896, Sam J. Hayhurst, a young Texas cowboy seeking
work, appeared at Si Bryant's 7UP Ranch in Leslie Canyon, between
the Swisshelm and the Chiricahua mountain ranges. The next day,
Will Christian rode to the ranch; Hayhurst approached him about
a job. Christian, then under contract to "break some broncs" at Pete
Johnson's ranch near Naco, saw Hayhurst's request as an opportunity to end his own working contract with Johnson. Christian, Hayhurst, and Johnson's foreman, Emmet Hanson, met on a site near
present-day Don Luis and struck a bargain. Hayhurst agreed to
break the horses, and Christian was free to be on his way.[2]

Nineteen-year-old George Musgrave cowboyed on the ranch
adjacent to the one that employed Bob Christian. Already part-

nered with Young and Hayes, Musgrave appears to have been the magnet that attracted all five men into the self-styled High Five gang. The band had no true leader, and they frequently split up for some of their escapades. However, journalists soon focused on the handle Black Jack. From that time forward, there existed an unwarranted presumption that Will Christian led the "Black Jack gang." Nevertheless, old-time acquaintances of the boys invariably called them the High Five gang.[3]

The five fledgling outlaws rode east past the Chiricahua Mountains, across the San Simon Valley, to the Peloncillo Mountains. Wary of encountering any of the Apache raiding parties then known to be active in the Peloncillos, they would have exercised caution as they passed through the mountains and into New Mexico's Animas Valley, where they turned north. About eight o'clock on Monday evening, July 20, the High Fives rode into Separ, New Mexico, site of a cattle-loading station on the Southern Pacific Railroad line. With Hayes and Anderson probably standing lookout nearby, Musgrave, Will Christian, and Young donned masks and held up the store of John D. Weems.[4]

Threatened by the robbers' six-shooters, the store's few patrons lay their heads on the counter. While one bandit covered them, the other two rummaged through the premises. They next turned to the post office, located within Weems's store, and took $20.94 in cash from postmaster Robert C. Milliken. The losses from the store and post office totaled approximately $280: $180 in cash; a large red, orange, and white-striped Navajo blanket; six gray wool blankets; a three-blade penknife with buck-horn handle; three boxes of cigars; French harps; a demijohn of whiskey; a pair of oil-tanned gloves; a new bridle; socks; and miscellaneous provisions. A couple of months later, the Navajo blanket was located at a residence in the foothills of the Chiricahua Mountains. Code Young had given it away.[5]

The gang fled twenty miles south toward Hachita. Disappointed with the haul, they gave away the small change and a pair of new boots to Johnny "Dutchy" Behmer, a cowboy at the nearby Howell ranch. The outlaws then rode west toward Lordsburg. The next morning, Deputy Sheriff Hardin of Lordsburg and R. J. Dunagan started on the robbers' trail and followed it south until their horses gave out.[6]

News of the robbery was telegraphed to Silver City, county seat of Grant County, forty miles north of Separ. Sheriff Baylor Shannon sent out two deputies. The *Western Liberal* cynically editorialized that during the previous year a man had been murdered near Separ and Shannon had sent out no deputies. "It must not be thought that Sheriff Shannon considers robbery a more important crime than murder. The difference is that he considers this a more important year than the last one. There will be an election this year."[7]

Two days after the robbery, Deputies William G. McAfee and Perfecto Rodriguez rode south from Separ to Hachita, and encountered Dutchy. "Was Black Jack's gang here?" McAfee asked him. "Yeah," said Dutchy, "They eat [*sic*] breakfast here." "What did you feed them for?" demanded McAfee. "Because I was afraid to do otherwise," responded the cowboy. "There's a law to protect you," explained the deputy. "Damn little good the law will do me after they shot me in two," fired back the cowboy, his pockets bulging with nickels.[8]

McAfee and Rodriguez pursued the trail southwest into the Sulphur Spring Valley of the Arizona Territory and "traced the robbers to their haunt, thirty miles north of Bisbee."[9] Astonishingly, McAfee and Rodriguez took no action, on the grounds that McAfee "thought it best to be certain as to the identity of the men before arresting them." The *Western Liberal* pointed up McAfee's ineptitude by reporting that when the deputy asked Black Jack if that was his name, Will Christian candidly replied that he was often called by that name. The rattled McAfee then fumbled for some papers inside his coat, only to find himself staring at the outlaw's gun. Christian took McAfee outside and confiscated the deputy's rifle before sending him on his way.[10]

When the deputies arrived back in Lordsburg a week after the robbery, Rodriguez returned to Silver City. McAfee telegraphed

Robert Milliken and asked him to help in the identification of the robbers. Three days later, McAfee, Hardin, and Milliken finally reached the outlaws' camp. Of course, it was deserted.[11]

New Mexico and Arizona lawmen pursued numerous, albeit spurious, leads in their effort to locate the gang. The elusive bandits availed themselves of the security of Arizona's San Pedro Valley, hiding on the Babocomari grant, north of Fort Huachuca, while they planned a new caper—a bank heist at Nogales.[12]

Musgrave's employer, Ed Roberts, planned to import a large herd of cattle from Mexico, due to cross through the port of entry at Nogales, county seat of Santa Cruz County. To pay the unpopular tariff, he arranged for ten thousand dollars in specie and federal bills to be available at the International Bank of Nogales on August 6, 1896. By noon that Thursday, the bank president, John Dessart, had Roberts's money stacked on the counter of the bank awaiting pick-up at one o'clock.[13]

That same day, Musgrave, Hayes, Young, and the two Christian brothers rode down from the Babocomari, along Sonoita Creek, past old Fort Crittenden, across Denton Sanford's ranch, through Calabasas, and along the Benson-Nogales branch of the Southern Pacific railroad. About noon they turned south and followed those tracks to Morley Avenue in Nogales. Most of the townspeople were at lunch; the streets were deserted.[14]

Little more than one hundred yards north of the international border, the five heavily armed men dismounted in front of a newly constructed two-story brick building on the east side of Morley Avenue. Three businesses operated behind the building's ironclad facade: a grocery store, George B. Marsh's hardware store, and the International Bank of Nogales. The High Fives had not come for groceries or hardware. Code Young and Bob Christian held the horses while George Musgrave, Bob Hayes, and Will "Black Jack" Christian entered the bank.[15]

Inside, Major Fred Herrera, the bank's cashier, sat in his chair behind the counter railing. Dessart stood at the desk just in front of the south end of the counter calculating some balances. Hayes trained a brace of pistols on Herrera while Black Jack leveled his Winchester at Dessart.[16]

As Musgrave moved behind the counter, the other outlaws demanded money, and the bank's officers complied. Herrera handed cash over the counter to Dessart, who stuffed it into a sack. Musgrave walked toward the rear of the bank, glanced sideways through a double doorway into the bank's parlor in the rear, and discovered four men discussing the organization of a water company: Morgan R. Wise of Washington, D.C.; Captain W. L. Campbell of Calabasas; Robert EKey (sic), upper Santa Cruz County rancher; and Judge Eb Williams, EKey's attorney in Nogales. Musgrave trained his two revolvers on the entrepreneurs and brought the meeting to order.[17]

Major A. O. Brummel entered the bank, intending to join the meeting in the rear. Alerted, Musgrave ushered Brummel toward the parlor while Black Jack's Winchester remained aimed at Dessart, and Hayes kept his revolvers leveled on Herrera. For a moment, three robbers attempted to cover four parties: the cashier, the president, the group of four, and now the major. President Dessart, sensing an opportunity, or possibly spurred by panic, bolted toward the door and received a glancing blow from Will Christian's rifle as he fled with Black Jack in pursuit. Running past Marsh's hardware store next door, Dessart called out to Harry Lewis to telephone that the bank was being robbed. Bleeding from a scalp wound, Dessart continued his flight across the street and railroad tracks and north past the Arizona Commercial Company. Black Jack shifted his attention, threw down on Lewis, and warned him upon pain of premature death not to make the telephone call.[18]

Inside the bank, Dessert's flight had distracted Musgrave and Hayes. The bank's parlor's inhabitants seized the opportunity and made their bid for freedom through the rear exit. Chaos ensued. Cashier Herrera grabbed his pistol from under the counter and fired at Hayes, who in panic fled through the front door and ran headlong into Black Jack, doubtless drawn back by the sound of gunfire. Still inside, Herrera turned and directed his fire toward Musgrave as the outlaw fled out the bank's back door. Musgrave fell, struggled back up rubbing his knee, and limped away. After passing through Marsh's hardware store, Musgrave joined the others in front of the bank.[19]

On Morley Avenue, sleepy Nogales sprang to life. Frank King, a deputy customs collector, was returning to the customs house from lunch. As he strolled along the railroad tracks across the street from the bank, he spotted armed men. Assuming a bank robbery was in progress, he opened fire and wounded Musgrave's and Black Jack's horses. Four outlaws mounted their horses; one of them helped the injured Musgrave climb up behind him. They raced up Morley Avenue with Musgrave's riderless horse following.[20]

The High Fives spurred their horses north past the Montezuma Hotel where Ben E. Hambleton, a special inspector for the U.S. Treasury Department, grabbed a Winchester and a horse to give chase. As the outlaws passed the Nogales Electric, Light, Ice and Water Company, they came under fire from Nace Burgoea and Harvey Walker. They finally made it over the little hill in front of the railway section house, with John Mapes and Charley Mehan following on foot with guns blazing. When the firing ceased, bullet marks scarred much of downtown Nogales, but there had been only two fatalities—a horse shot by the Winchester-toting Black Jack, and a mule, the victim of Major Herrera's fusillade.[21]

Diego Ramirez of Nogales stated that the robbers got away with forty thousand dollars. On the other hand, Johnny Clarke, who claimed that his father had joined the pursuing posse, reported, "It was never known if they got away with the money or not." Surely, the gang did not secure all of the money that had brought them to Nogales, and certainly not the forty thousand suggested by Diego Ramirez. Indeed, almost four months later, George Musgrave instructed Joe Temple at Huachuca Siding to send word to banker Dessart that the gang planned to pay Nogales another visit, during which they hoped to be more successful. Both Nogales newspapers reported that not a cent was lost. It seems certain that the fleeing Bob Hayes left most of the money on the counter. It appears equally beyond dispute that Musgrave, while behind the counter, pocketed enough cash to forestall the need for another robbery for the next two months.[22]

After passing the railroad section house on Morley Avenue, the fleeing robbers turned east and rode up Beck Cañon. The collector of customs, Samuel F. Webb, formed a posse consisting of Frank King, Chinese inspector Charles J. Mehan, Joseph Carbon, and customs line rider Roman Enriquez. George Christ and Ponciano Sanchez, the chief of police of Nogales, Sonora, with several of his men, also joined the posse. They trailed the robbers about fifteen miles before they caught sight of the gang about eight hundred yards distant in a shallow canyon. The bandits, in turn, spotted their pursuers and raced out of the canyon and into Mexico, near the San Antonio Pass in the Patagonia Mountains. Webb's posse continued on the zigzag trail, back and forth across the international line, and passed on its way three of the gang's horses, including the two that had been badly wounded at the onset of the flight. The outlaws had helped themselves to fresh mounts. That night the posse rode to Lochiel, an Arizona border town made prosperous by smugglers.[23]

The following morning, former customs agent C. B. Kelton and inspectors Albert P. Behan and H. W. Brady, all of Lochiel, joined the posse while Frank King returned to Nogales to notify officials in Bisbee of the bandits' probable trail. From Lochiel, the tracks of the High Five gang led back to the American side of the boundary and directly east toward Ed Roberts's ranch on the upper San Pedro River.[24]

One writer (Jeff Burton, in *Bureaucracy, Blood Money and Black Jack's Gang*) postulated that Ed Roberts promoted, or at least had prior knowledge of, the robbery. The ranchers of the border region felt general disgust with the tariff policies of the federal government. Roberts's association with Musgrave, combined with his wife's later statement that she had met Black Jack at the ranch, adds credibility to the proposition. Coincidence could never explain the timeliness of the bandits' appearance in Nogales. Moreover, five months following the robbery, Roberts's brother-in-law, the copper

Col. William Cornell
Greene (1853–1911).
Courtesy Nita Stewart
Haley Memorial
Library, Midland Texas.

mining magnate Will Greene, reported the gang's whereabouts to
Deputy Marshal Scott White, but instructed the deputy not to mention their conversation to anyone in the Roberts family. Furthermore, as events later revealed, the gang headed back to Roberts's
ranch following the robbery. Burton's thesis remains tenable.[25]

The posse followed the trail to the Roberts ranch, near Hereford,
where it turned up the river toward Mexico. At the international
border, the posse speculated that the gang would go to Bull Springs,
in the Ajo Mountains of Sonora, Mexico, and then head into the
Guadalupe Mountains near the four-corners region of Arizona,
New Mexico, Sonora, and Chihuahua. Mexican officials occasionally cooperated with American legal representatives. The posse
would not have hesitated to pursue the fleeing bandits deep into
Mexico. However, unable to secure fresh horses, the officers were
forced to call off the chase some fifteen miles south of the border.

On August 8, the same day that Webb's posse quit the chase,
Cochise County Sheriff Camillus S. Fly and several of his deputies
arrived in Bisbee and headed for Miles Gibbon's saloon. There they

arrested an unfortunate cowboy, Bob Forrest, as an alleged member of the gang. Forrest was temporarily jailed at Tombstone. He claimed that on August 8, two days following the robbery, he went to Ed Roberts's ranch to get a pair of boots for Musgrave, and that he had no further connection with either the gang or the Nogales robbery. Within forty-eight hours the press reported that Forrest was not believed to be one of the Nogales robbers but could be an important witness.[26]

Meanwhile, unknown to their pursuers, the robbers had wisely split up into two groups. Only three of the bandits—Anderson, Hayes, and Young—headed into Mexico. Musgrave and Black Jack remained north of the line.

While Forrest languished in Tombstone's jail, Pima County Sheriff Robert N. Leatherwood formed another posse in Bisbee comprised of Deputies Broderick and Doyle, Deputy U.S. Marshal Al Ezekiels, and customs inspectors Webb and Miller. Deputy Ezekiels, with a portion of the Leatherwood posse, followed the trail of the three bandits who had turned south. With the aid of Mexican General Juan Fenochio and the *Gendarmería*, they located the outlaws at La Cuerva, but the three fugitives successfully slipped back north of the border.[27]

At Bisbee, Sheriff Fly and his deputies, Billy Hildreth, Burt Alvord, and Will Johnson, as well as customs inspector Frank P. Robson, joined the rest of Leatherwood's posse on August 11. They followed a trail that led toward the San Simon Valley and the forbidding Skeleton Canyon.[28]

Ezekiels' posse, unsuccessful in its pursuit of Anderson, Young, and Hayes, had crossed back into the U. S. by August 11, and set out to rejoin the Fly-Leatherwood posse. Veteran lawman Jeff Milton, a Wells, Fargo agent out of Nogales and a member of Ezekiels' posse, sighted the three desperadoes near the San Simon Valley's Mulberry Wash. Ezekiels declined to pursue. A dismayed Milton protested, "We saw these fellows and we saw them coming out of the mulberry pasture. I says Damned if they ain't them, and the fellow in charge [Ezekiels] of them others they couldn't go. He says

'We'll run them out of the country.' And I says 'that is what we want to do.' But he just quit. That was on the south end of the Chiricahuas." Abandoning the chase, Ezekiels' posse camped that night near old Fort Rucker on Si Bryant's ranch in Leslie Canyon.[29]

The next morning, Milton, Billy Stiles, Felix Mayhew, and a fellow named Randolph left the main posse, rode north through Dos Cabezas Canyon and boarded the train to Tucson to obtain fresh horses. Milton later mused, "I never run on to Black Jack and I'm glad I didn't. I might have got hurt."[30]

Hard-pressed, Anderson, Young, and Hayes discarded much of their equipment, including a packmule, as they headed east across the San Simon Valley. They rode toward Skeleton Canyon, a pass that led through the Peloncillo Mountains into New Mexico's Animas Valley, a site renowned for violence.

About noon on August 12, the Leatherwood-Fly posse, consisting of the two sheriffs, with deputies Doyle, Burt Alvord, John Johnston, Bill Hildreth, and Inspector Robson caught sight of one of the robbers in the foothills of the Peloncillo Mountains. The lone bandit spurred his horse and disappeared into the hills. Determined to cut off the fugitive's flight, Doyle rode up a rock-strewn hill only to be bucked off his horse. Nursing a bruised knee and coping with a broken weapon, not to mention wounded pride, Doyle left the party to ride to Deming. The rest of the posse pressed on toward the foothills.[31]

At four o'clock that afternoon, the posse neared the entrance to Skeleton Canyon, Leatherwood and Robson riding in front. Suddenly shots exploded from the underbrush seventy-five feet in front of the advancing lawmen. As Leatherwood and the deputies leaped from their horses, Robson fell dead; one bullet had lodged in his forehead, a second had penetrated his temple. The posse's return volley killed one of the bandits' horses. Leatherwood retreated on foot as his horse bolted in the direction of the robbers, followed by Alvord's and Robson's horses. The outlaws seized Leatherwood's horse, but it too fell amid the heavy fire.[32]

The three desperadoes now turned their fire toward Bill Hildreth. A bullet grazed Hildreth's neck; his horse fell, fatally wounded.[33] Jeff Milton related the story as he later heard it:

> Bill Hildreth got in behind a tree and they were shooting and the bullets would knock the bark off on one side and then the other. And old Bob [Leatherwood] told me himself, said, "Milton, did I run? I had one of these old long barrel rifles and I used it for a jumping stick," when they got to shooting at him.
>
> Old Bill was the only one left then and was smoking them. Do you know, I can't understand how a man can shoot at a fellow six or seven times and don't kill him. I don't understand. When old Bill got a chance to run—they were shooting both sides of the tree—he got out. He remembered this fellow [Robson] and went back and got him.[34]

Gang confidante Walter C. Hovey (alias Walter Hoffman) later revealed that Hildreth had attempted to ingratiate himself with the High Fives. As a result, Hildreth's participation in the posse made him a primary target of the outlaws' bullets. The *Bisbee Orb* both confirmed and expanded upon Hovey's explanation. "Hildreth was acting as guide for the officers having been driving cattle in that country for years and knows all the water holes and places in the vicinity. The robbers knowing this and being acquainted with Hildreth desired to get rid of him."[35]

As the canyon grew dark, the three outlaws relieved Robson's body of his rifle, revolver, and watch, and then retreated. They rode east through the canyon until they reached the Animas Valley of New Mexico, where they stole supplies from the Gray ranch at Victoria.[36]

The five surviving posse members also withdrew. The next day, Sheriffs Fly and Leatherwood telegraphed Tombstone: "They got two of our horses, we two of theirs. Think we wounded two, not certain, as they were concealed." The sheriffs were too optimistic;

there is no evidence that they wounded any of the three hunted men. Two days following the ambush, Burt Alvord returned to Tombstone and reported that the robbers, concealed in thick undergrowth, could not be seen during the fight. He also related that, lacking a wagon to haul the body, the posse buried Robson where he fell. Former Cochise County sheriff John Slaughter, Bert Cogswell, line rider William King, and two Mexicans joined the posse. That day the posse rested its horses at the Mulberry Ranch on the west side of the San Simon Valley.[37]

The night following the Skeleton Canyon shooting, Young, Hayes, and Bob Christian secreted themselves in the mountains near the Gray ranch, likely awaiting word of the movements of Black Jack and Musgrave. Nevertheless, they were spotted by the Indian scout Tom Horn.[38]

In mid-July, General Nelson Miles had introduced a plan to unite Seventh Cavalry forces and sweep the Peloncillo Mountains from Steins Pass to the border in an effort to drive Apache hostiles toward the waiting *Gendarmería Fiscal* of Colonel Emilio Kosterlitsky. The last week in August, on his return to Fort Grant following the two-week sweep, Horn, attached to Lieutenant Selah R. H. "Tommy" Tompkins's B troop of soldiers and scouts, spied the three outlaws in the hills south of the Diamond A Ranch. As Horn continued on, he passed the butchered remains of a cow that they had killed. Seeking Apaches, not bank robbers, Horn did nothing except report his sightings upon his return to Fort Grant on August 28. Meanwhile, the three High Fives started north up the Animas Valley.[39]

Though the High Fives had fled the area, federal officialdom tightened the noose on the Skeleton Canyon region. On August 15, Edward L. Hall, U.S. marshal for the Territory of New Mexico, sent his chief deputy and brother-in-law, Horace Will Loomis, to the Peloncillo Mountain region to aid in the gang's capture. On August 24, Loomis telegraphed Hall that the "robbers were encamped behind breast-works of a formidable nature and had stood off the deputies so successfully that a considerable force of men would be necessary to dislodge them." Hall, in turn, wired the Justice Department and requested assistance from Fort Bayard (located ten miles east of Silver City) in the form of a troop of cavalry, claiming his deputy could not "procure citizens to aid in the arrest on account of thinly settled country and ranchers being in sympathy with robbers." That night, Hall set off for Fort Bayard, via Lordsburg, to join in the search for the gang.[40]

Two days later, Hall, Loomis, and Troop D of Fort Bayard's Seventh Cavalry rode from the fort, bound for Skeleton Canyon. The next day, Silver City residents read, incorrectly, that the gang was surrounded in Skeleton Canyon and that an attack would be made upon them that night. Deputy Sheriff Simmons formed a posse of Silver City citizens, eager to join with the posses from Deming and Lordsburg. Alas, they found no outlaws, prompting the *Silver City Enterprise* to proclaim that the bandits "became tired of the protracted postponements of the official visit of the U.S. Marshal, [and] took their departure for pastures more prolific of adventure."[41]

On August 28, Young, Anderson, and Hayes passed the night with a ranchman on the outskirts of Deming. Post Office inspector George H. Waterbury reported that in Deming, "Geo. Musgrave has an uncle-brother and sister, who are shielding and feeding them." Information that Waterbury discovered concerning a brother necessarily referred to Van Musgrave; Fannie Johnson was the only sister who could have been in the Deming area at that time. In March 1895, Burrell Quimby Musgrave, whom Waterbury may have believed to be George's uncle, but actually was his father's cousin, moved from Alpine, Texas, and entered the Deming hotel business. He remained in business throughout 1896 before moving to Las Cruces in April 1897. Subsequent events would continue to cast suspicion in his direction.[42]

The next evening, the three outlaws slipped into town, picked up mail at the post office, and purchased ammunition and supplies. Once more identification came only after they had left. The *Western Liberal* caustically noted that New Mexico's Marshal Edward Hall "was guarding the Depot hotel" but sent a posse after the outlaws. The trail of the desperadoes led toward Cookes Peak, eighteen miles north of town. Soon, heavy rain obliterated their tracks, making pursuit impossible.[43]

While the Deming posse vainly sought the three men, most of the town's citizen's confidently anticipated that the outlaws intended to return and hold up the bank. Preparations began: "Cashier Brown made his peace with his Maker and was prepared to die before he would give up a dollar. A number of fighting men laid in ambush in the vault. There was a loaded shot gun or winchester behind every store door in town and no business man went out after a drink without packing a piece of artillery with them."[44]

On the afternoon of the Skeleton Canyon fight, Musgrave and Will Christian hid elsewhere in the San Simon Valley. That night they approached the San Simon Cattle Company's horse ranch, robbed the hands, and helped themselves to dinner and fresh horses. On Tuesday, August 18, Christian and Musgrave dined at the Mulberry Ranch, recently vacated by the posse. Later, the two outlaws came upon Frank Robson's brothers-in-law, Robert Hill and Will Pomeroy, who were bringing Robson's body back from his temporary grave for burial in Mesa. At considerable risk from posses still riding about the area, they informed Hill and Pomeroy of their innocence in the killing of the line rider. They professed a liking for Robson, expressed sympathy for the widow, and promised her financial assistance if it became necessary.[45]

Musgrave and Black Jack left the valley and headed south toward the Mexican customs house at La Morita. Again, a posse learned of their whereabouts and trailed them into Mexico where the lawmen located and destroyed an abandoned camp. Again, the tracks led the posse back into Arizona with the lawmen having little to show for their efforts save the capture of eight horses and a pair of field glasses.[46]

The two outlaws later reached the Mud Springs region of the Sulphur Spring Valley. On August 28, as Deputy Alvord gathered horses left behind by the posse at Mud Springs, he glanced up a nearby hillside, saw the two outlaws, and realized that he was well within rifle shot. The men challenged the deputy by defiantly waving their weapons. Alvord wisely ignored their impertinence.[47]

A month had passed since the Nogales robbery when early Sunday morning, August 30, Camillus Fly's posse rode on another fruitless quest. Heavy rains frequently obliterated the outlaws' trail, and local cowboys and ranchers often assisted the fugitives. The *Prospector* reported Fly's bitterness about the robbers' "cowardly manner of ambushing" and noted Black Jack's anger that Sheriff Fly was riding the outlaw's favorite horse, secured at the Skeleton Canyon shootout. The *Prospector* failed to explain how Fly came to be riding a horse it had previously reported killed, especially since Black Jack had not participated in the Skeleton Canyon fight, casting doubt that his horse played a role in the melee.[48]

At the beginning of September, three unarmed members of yet another posse left camp to round up their horses and were approached by Musgrave and another man, almost certainly Black Jack. The outlaws talked to the marshal for about fifteen minutes, but the officers, being without weapons, were unable to capture them. Gila County Sheriff Dan Williamson later maintained that the gang captured Ezekiels in the foothills of the Chiricahuas and relieved him of his horse, saddle, and guns. "Hayes insisted on killing him but B. J. overruled it." These accounts may, or may not, refer to the same incident, depending upon the accuracy of Williamson's recollection. Both accounts support the *Globe-Democrat*'s assertion that "the outlaws apparently take the greatest pride in openly defying the pursuers and boldly walking into their presence."[49]

On September 12, two weeks after being spotted at Mud Springs, Musgrave and Will Christian brazenly rode into Bowie Station, north of the San Simon 7H Ranch. One of the two walked into Solomon and Wickersham's mercantile store to buy a pair of boots. Pulling on a pair that fit, the desperado whipped out a ten-dollar bill. The crafty Wickersham, anxious to convince the outlaw that there was little money in the store, asserted that he could not change the bill because he had sent his cash to El Paso for deposit aboard the last train. The affable outlaw strolled across the street seeking change as the other entered Wickersham's. He, too, selected a pair of boots and extended a twenty-dollar bill. He, too, heard the shop-keeper's story. Just then the first outlaw hollered to the other that he had made change. The second boot shopper left through Wick-ersham's front door. Musgrave and Christian jumped on their horses and rode off with their new boots safely fitted into their stirrups. Wickersham lost two pairs of boots, but not the $1,349.25 he had hidden deep in a sack of coffee.[50]

The *Prospector* next reported that Musgrave and Will Christian had been seen in Tombstone on September 16, though the editor allowed that, "as they did not show up at our office we cannot ver-ify the report." That same week, Anna Schaefer and two of her Dos Cabezas neighbors rode up to a windmill, where they discovered the two outlaws "armed to the teeth," slaughtering a steer. The men identified themselves, insisted that they would not be taken alive, and offered payment for the butchered steer. From the security of the Dos Cabezas Mountains, the two fugitives then made their way toward New Mexico and a reunion with Young, Bob Christian, and Hayes.[51]

On September 4, four heavily armed strangers emerged from the Mimbres Mountains near Hudson Hot Springs (later Faywood Hot Springs), twenty-two miles northwest of Deming. They split into pairs. One pair continued north toward the mountains near Santa Rita; the other two rode to Hudson, where they entered the McDermott, Fay, and Lockwood store. They called for a drink; the clerk told them to help themselves to the water in the bucket. Pro-fanely rejecting the water, they demanded whiskey. There was none. They paid for some cans of sardines. Demanding another item the store could not supply, they angrily threw the sardines on the counter and rode away to rejoin their companions. Although lawmen doubted their membership in the High Five gang, local cowboys disagreed. Subsequent events suggest the cowboys' opin-ion was probably the more accurate. Hayes, Young, and Anderson were in the area, headed toward the O Bar O Ranch north of

Deming. They sought refuge with Musgrave's brother Van (alias Bob Lewis), the ranch foreman.[52]

The August 6 bank robbery at Nogales resulted in no territorial indictments. However, on September 17, the United States District Court, Third Judicial District of the Territory of New Mexico, held a grand jury session at Silver City. In case no. 1174, the grand jury indicted Jesse Miller, alias Jesse Williams, alias Jeff Davis [George Musgrave]; Cole [sic] Young, alias Cole Estes; Robert Hoy [sic], alias Robert Hayes; Thomas Anderson, and "Black Jack," for the July 20, 1896, robbery of the Separ post office of fifteen dollars in "divers money belonging to the United States." Federal warrants were issued, requiring the posting of a $2,500 bond by each man. The High Fives, having stolen less money to date than the bond required for each gang member, became federal fugitives.[53]

CHAPTER FIVE

DEATH AT RIO PUERCO

TERRITORY OF NEW MEXICO—STATUTES OF 1887
   Chapter 9, page 44
   Sec. 1. If any person or persons shall willfully and mali-
ciously make any assault upon any train, railroad cars or rail-
road locomotive within this territory for the purpose and with
the intent to commit murder, robbery or any felony upon or
against any passenger on said train or cars, or upon or against
any engineer, conductor, fireman, brakeman or any other offi-
cer or employee connected with said locomotive, train or cars;
or upon or against any express messenger, or mail agent on
said train, or in any of the cars thereof, on conviction thereof
shall be deemed guilty of a felony and shall suffer the punish-
ment of death.

When the High Fives reassembled on the O Bar O Ranch, they camped out in the hills. In the morning Van Musgrave sent ranch hand Johnny Longbotham into Deming to buy ammunition for the boys. A crowd of cowboys gathered at the ranch the following evening; the five did not ride in to join them. After Van rode out with food and the ammunition, the gang disappeared into the rain and darkness on what Longbotham later described as the wettest night he ever saw.[1]

As they made their way through the mountain ranges of western New Mexico, the High Fives may have crossed paths with Tom Ketchum. According to Deputy Ben R. Clark of Graham County, Arizona, Ketchum ran into the gang in the mountains north of Deming. Ketchum's "stay in Jack's camp was abruptly terminated by Black Jack's threatening attitude towards him over his refusal to become a member of his gang." Necessarily, the authenticity of this anecdote relies upon the credibility of both Clark and Ketchum, neither a model of veracity. Any chance encounter with the gang north of Deming would have had to take place in September or during a narrow window of opportunity in late October 1896. Considering the convivial nature of the High Fives, and given Ketchum's acknowledged saturnine disposition and outbursts of uncontrolled rage, more likely the gang rejected his application for membership on the grounds of incompatibility.[2]

In late September, they reached Magdalena, a small mining town west of Socorro, then rode north toward a railroad watering station on the Atlantic and Pacific line near the crossing of the Rio Puerco riverbed, thirty-four miles southwest of Albuquerque. On Friday, October 2, the High Fives reached Rio Puerco, and concealing themselves by the water tank, they awaited the arrival of the eastbound train.[3]

Train no. 802 steamed into Rio Puerco at 7:30 that evening. An overheated crank pin on the engine necessitated a brief layover. Conductor Sam Heady stepped off the train and walked forward to the engine to speak with engineer Charles Ross. Five minutes later, the train slowly pulled out of Rio Puerco to begin to its way up a small hill.[4]

As the train started forward, three of the High Fives sprang up the steps onto the tank of Engine 72 and, drawing down on engineer Ross and fireman Abe Reed, ordered Ross to halt the train; he complied. The unscheduled stop brought brakeman L. G. Stevens and conductor Heady forward. Stevens carried a lantern. A bandit fired at the unwelcome light, hitting the bell of the lantern. A second shot shattered the lantern's handle. Stevens, nursing injured fingers, joined Heady in flight to the security of one of the coaches.[5]

One of the outlaws ordered the engineer and fireman off the train. Code Young, standing on the ground, demanded that the fireman climb back on the engine. Young then checked each car to establish whether it was a mail car, an express car, or a baggage car. He singled out the second express car and ordered the engineer back to unhitch it. Young shoved his gun in Ross's back and herded the frightened man back to the car.[6]

Inside the express car, messenger T. G. Hutchinson heard a rapping at his door. He opened the door about a foot; Young fired in the air in front of his face. Hastily slamming and locking the door, Hutchinson went to his desk, grabbed a revolver, filled his pockets with cartridges, turned off his desk lamp, lit a cigar, and sat down to await developments. Outside, Young stepped back as Ross started to uncouple Hutchinson's car. Shots rang out. During the distraction, the engineer bolted for freedom and hid under one of the coaches.[7]

The three robbers still on the engine now commanded fireman Reed to pull out. The train moved forward, crossing the bridge spanning the Rio Puerco. About a quarter of a mile down the track, they ordered Reed to stop the engine and unhitch the first express car. Reed protested that he was not a brakeman and union rules forbade him to do the brakeman's work. His argument fell on deaf ears. Three bandits hustled him to the rear of the first express car while a cohort remained with the engine.[8]

Inside that express car, messenger L. J. Kohler had heard a shot, then three more in rapid succession before the train pulled forward. Convinced that a robbery was in progress, he doused the lights and locked the door. After the rail cars stopped, Kohler listened for fifteen to twenty minutes while Reed struggled to uncouple the car; the chained drawbars thwarted his efforts. Finally, one of the bandits called out, "Wonder if he will open up if we ask him." "No," came the reply. "To Hell with him, we will fix him yet, we'll blow him out." Kohler next heard them decide to go after the dynamite. The three bandits, with Reed in tow, wandered off, calling out for Young while seeking the explosives. They found neither. Young lay wounded, bleeding to death. Conductor Heady heard him cry out, "I am shot, I can't come, I'm done for." But his weak response went unheard by his sidekicks.[9]

A couple more minutes passed before Kohler heard the voices of Cade Selvey and L. J. Bay talking outside his express car. Kohler opened the door and told Selvey that the bandits had gone seeking dynamite. Kohler, Selvey, and Bay left the car to get help from Hutchinson. They located the messenger still barricaded in his express car and convinced him that it was safe to unlock the door. Soon they heard the lone bandit still with the engine call out, "Boys, we had better play it off, we have been here too long."[10]

The four bandits marched fireman Reed about three hundred yards into the brush and there, shaking hands all around, borrowed his tobacco. They called out once more for Young, then rode off into the night.[11]

With the unscheduled stop, many passengers surmised that the train was being robbed. Only one traveler made a move. Deputy Marshal Will Loomis, on his return from serving subpoenas in Gallup, was sitting with his shotgun beside him on the car seat. He had been chasing the gang since mid-August. He had followed their trail from Santa Fe via Deming to Skeleton Canyon and Mexico. Now, improbably, the High Fives had come to him.[12] The *Santa Fe Daily New Mexican* later described Loomis's situation:

> When the second shot came echoing back from the cañon and adjacent foothills he was on his feet, gun in hand. His cartridge belt and valise were at the other end of the coach where the 'butcher boy' keeps his wares. 'Just hand me that cartridge belt,' said Loomis, quietly to the frightened and blanch-faced punter. The fellow went after it on tip-toe. Receiving the belt, Mr. Loomis slipped out of the coach, quietly dropped silently down off the platform.[13]

Loomis, in a letter to Marshal Hall, recalled lying still as his eyes adjusted to the darkness. He gradually focused upon Code Young and engineer Ross, about three cars forward. When Young stepped away from the engineer, Loomis saw his chance and a blast of his shotgun felled the train robber. Young got back on his feet, and fired his six-shooter twice in Loomis's direction. Loomis pulled the trigger a second time, the outlaw staggered a few yards and fell down the bank into the brush. Loomis returned to the coach to get more shotgun shells as the mortally wounded Young tried to make his way toward the others. His accomplices, unaware of his condition, had ordered the fireman to pull the train forward and away from Young. Loomis jumped off as the train slowed. He landed on the first trestle of the bridge across the Rio Puerco and fell about four feet into soft dirt, slightly spraining his ankle. He hesitated to fire again, fearing that he might injure one of the trainmen.[14]

Loomis, too, heard the four bandits call to Young several times before they rode off to the south. The deputy remained concealed by the darkness and listened to voices in the distance, but the men never returned. Concluding that it would be futile to try to track the gang in the darkness, he returned to the train. By now some of the passengers had stumbled upon the dead body of Code Young. Loomis remained with Young's body at Rio Puerco when the train continued east to Isleta Junction.

Before daybreak, a special train carrying Sheriff Thomas S. Hubbell of Bernalillo County, Albuquerque city marshal Fred Fornoff, and deputies Cornelius Murphy, Juan Gonzales, and their horses arrived at Rio Puerco from Albuquerque.[15] At dawn, Hubbell, Fornoff, Murphy, and Gonzales followed the outlaws' trail toward the Datil Mountains while Loomis, aboard the special train, accompanied Code Young's body back to Albuquerque, arriving at 11:30 A.M. An hour later, Loomis and Cade Selvey boarded another train bound for Socorro, in an effort to head off the bandits.[16] From Socorro, Loomis telegraphed Marshal Hall:

Was on the train held-up last night at Puerco bridge. Killed Code Young with my shot gun. The rest of the party left southward. A special train brought four men and horses from Albuquerque under Sheriff Hubbell while I waited there. I will go to Magdalena and start a posse to intercept hold-ups.[17]

The High Five gang headed south with a six-hour lead. Hubbell's posse followed the trail for five miles along the Rio Puerco, then headed southwest toward the Ladrone Mountains. They rode through a gap in the mountains, which led into a box canyon and the remains of a camp. The trail from the camp turned southeast; the posse followed it for some miles until forced to turn east to the Rio Grande to obtain water for the horses. The pursuers reached the river below Sabinal, then followed the road fifteen miles north to Belen, where they spent Saturday night before returning to Albuquerque aboard a freight. Marshal Hall later argued that the inability to capture the bandits could be attributed to Sheriff Hubbell's posse having abandoned the pursuit. Though it is doubtful that his men would have captured the High Fives had they scoured the country as thoroughly as Fornoff later claimed, they should have determined the correct direction of the gang's route, making unnecessary the wild goose chase which ensued elsewhere.[18]

As the Hubbell posse headed toward the Ladrone Mountains, Loomis organized a posse at Magdalena and set off following the trail of four horses headed across the Plains of San Agustin toward the Mogollon Mountains to the southwest. On October 4, as the High Fives headed east, two men passed near Loomis's camp in the darkness, heading south into the Black Range. Daylight revealed their tracks. Believing them to be those of the bandits but deeming it too late to give chase, Loomis and his posse returned to Socorro. He wired Marshal Hall his intention to lead a posse north from Lake Valley, eighteen miles south of Hillsboro, to intercept the bandits. He discharged the Magdalena riders to save the expense of transporting them by train to Deming and Lake Valley, then headed south to raise a new posse. He reached Lake Valley on October 7, organized a posse, and turned northwest toward the Black Range. But all the hunters found were several worn-out horses.[19]

Marshal Hall also sent out two posses, totaling eighteen men from Hillsboro and Deming, to watch the passes and canyons through which the outlaws might travel. Holm Bursum, sheriff of Socorro County, led yet another posse out of Socorro in an effort to intercept the gang. The lawmen were convinced the High Fives would escape to the southwest; the four outlaws avoided capture by heading east.[20]

While the posses hunted the gang, the body of Code Young arrived at the undertaking rooms of O. W. Strong in Albuquerque. Among the large number of people who viewed the remains were A. H. Jones and A. G. Stocket of the Atlantic and Pacific machine shop. They identified Young's body, claiming to have known Young when he lived in Trinidad, Colorado. Albert V. Read, a cowboy from Deming, identified the body as Cole Estes from west Texas, a co-worker at several cattle companies in southern New Mexico. At five o'clock on Monday afternoon, October 5, Young was buried in the public ground at Albuquerque's Fairview Cemetery.[21]

While the posses searched to the southwest, 130 miles east of their hunt the four remaining High Fives prepared to hold up the San Antonio-to-White Oaks stage line. The sixteen-year-old stage line had never experienced a robbery.[22]

At four o'clock on the afternoon of October 7, the High Five gang ended that crime-free record when they held up the stage en route to White Oaks between Mountain Station Ranch and Wash Hale, near the summit of the Oscura Mountains. The stage carried neither passengers nor strongbox. After confessing to driver John Wickwire that they had held up the Atlantic and Pacific at Rio Puerco, the robbers rifled the four mail sacks looking for registered mail. Fortune smiled on the gang. The First National Bank of Las Vegas, New Mexico, had shipped a package to the Exchange Bank at White Oaks. After tearing the package open, they found it contained five hundred dollars in currency. They left the rest of the mail undisturbed. Turning their own horses

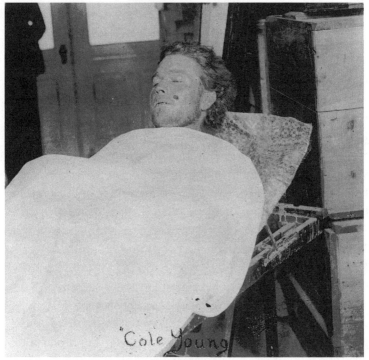

Code Young in death. Courtesy of Wells Fargo.

loose, the bandits seized those attached to the coach. Wickwire, forced to give up his hat and boots, was left to walk barefoot eight miles back to Mountain Station. The gang headed east to Taylor's Well Stage Station, thirty-one miles west of White Oaks. At the Taylor Ranch, they ordered supper. After eating, they robbed station overseer John Mack of $6.50 and again exchanged some horses.[23]

A telegram from San Antonio postmaster Gus Hilton (father of future hotel magnate Conrad Hilton) to officers in Albuquerque carried the news of the holdup and expressed concern that the westbound coach might have also been robbed that night. That fear proved to be well founded. Six hours after the first holdup, the gang stopped the westbound coach about two miles east of Taylor's Well Station. Encouraged by their earlier success, the High Fives again tore open the mail sacks. The bags contained seven pieces of registered mail, but yielded a meager $32.60. The gang could not have been pleased. They next relieved driver Ben Carpenter of his tobacco and knife. Passenger David Tinnen of Albuquerque, returning to Albuquerque to testify as a federal witness in a mail robbery case, hid his pocketbook. The gang helped themselves to Tinnen's hat, gloves, and pipe. Tinnen pleaded that he was a working man; his sad tale struck a responsive chord. They handed him $7.10 as compensation for the new hat before departing. Tinnen recovered his pocketbook, added up his resources, and discovered that he had turned a profit of three dollars. The robbers rode to Manchester, three miles west of White Oaks, where they headed southeast into the Capitan Mountains.[24]

Stage and train robberies in the United States decreased 33 percent during the fiscal year 1896–97, a decline that the postmaster-general attributed to vigorous pursuit, as well as lucrative rewards. He also recognized that highway robbers were desperate criminals, and pursuit necessitated great personal bravery and skill. In spite of the dangers, both real and imagined, a posse had been formed at Mountain Station Ranch three hours following the first robbery. The lawmen rode to White Oaks, where Deputy Sheriff P. S. Tate and additional men joined them. The indefatigable Loomis also set off from Albuquerque, bound for San Antonio, to take up the chase.[25]

Wiley Sidwell, a former cowpuncher for the El Capitan Cattle Company, told a story that a "couple of fellas" with the Black Jack gang hid out in two small log cabins in Copeland Canyon in the Capitan Mountains, pretending to be trappers. The two would have been Will and Bob Christian because Musgrave and Hayes are known to have ridden southeast toward Lincoln to gather information about roundups in the area. Learning of a roundup on the mesa above Picacho, Musgrave and Hayes turned their horses toward Bennett Musgrave's home at Cedar Hill northwest of Roswell, where they reportedly hid for a short time in a cave.

William Kidder Meade, Marshal of Arizona, 1885–89, 1893–97, and his dog, Bob, December 10, 1897. Courtesy Arizona Historical Society/Tucson, AHS #2022.

Meanwhile, the two Christians had headed southeast from Copeland Canyon and stayed briefly with Herb Brogden in the Seven Rivers region. Brogden afterward identified Will Christian as the nefarious outlaw, though lawmen had yet to discover Black Jack's identity. He could only have learned it from Will.[26]

The activities of the High Five gang baffled law enforcement in Arizona and New Mexico. The chases resulting from four months of depredations had netted one outlaw—Code Young. New Mexico's Marshal Edward L. Hall announced rewards of five hundred dollars for the arrest and conviction of any of the robbers, but complained that the well-mounted outlaws constantly replaced their mounts, had their trail obliterated by recurring rains, and had many friends on the ranches. "The men I have been employing are brave men, who would take them, if they could find them; but they are not used to riding and the horses they get will not stand the riding." Hall expressed the need for seven saddle-experienced cowboys, appropriately mounted and familiar with the country, who could bear the hardships and who would pursue the gang day and night. He estimated this would cost one hundred dollars per month per man, plus mounts and expenses, packhorses and two Indian trackers. Marshal William Kidder Meade of Arizona concurred with Hall's assessment and sought authorization to employ fifteen men for thirty days at a rate of five dollars per diem for their services. Fortunately for the gang, the Department of Justice was unwilling to make the investment.[27]

CHAPTER SIX

Revenge

Crime is honest for a good cause.

PUBLILIUS SYRUS

About nine thirty o'clock Monday morning, October 19, 1896, George Musgrave and Bob Hayes (known locally as John West) rode toward a roundup camp on the Rio Felix, about thirty-seven miles southwest of Roswell. Unknown to the cowboys, Musgrave was stalking George Parker.[1]

Near the camp, Musgrave approached cowboys Austin Reeves and Oscar Anderson and asked Reeves if he was with the Diamond A wagon. "No, I happen to be with the CA wagon," Reeves replied. Surprised, Musgrave asked, "Isn't the Circle Diamond wagon here?" "Yes, they're together. The two outfits are working together," Reeves explained. The Circle Diamond was a subsidiary of the Diamond A; Musgrave used the names interchangeably. When asked if he knew George Parker, Reeves replied, "Yes sir, he led the drive this morning." Musgrave inquired which way Parker had gone. "They went out from camp south and were gonna come back up here to the bluff that you see right up there. The two wagons are camped there at this big bluff and the roundup will be throwed together there," replied the cowboy. "Do you know what part of the drive George Parker will be on?" was Musgrave's final question. "Well, it's customary for the man, the boss, to lead the drive and [he] should come in down the Feliz to this roundup ground." Musgrave thanked Reeves and rode on with Hayes toward the roundup camp about one-half mile away.[2]

At the roundup camp, Harry Aguayo and Dan Welch noticed the two riders approaching, their clothes ragged and torn. As the men rode closer, Aguayo and Welch recognized George Musgrave, who called out, "Hello Harry! Are you still here, you must be a good hand." "No, I am still here tho," Aguayo responded. "Who is the cook?" Musgrave asked him. "Sam Butler. The same as when you were with us," answered Aguayo. "Do you think he will give us something to eat? We laid out last night and haven't had anything to eat," Musgrave explained. Aguayo assured the outlaws that Butler would feed them.[3]

Musgrave and Hayes left the CA wagon for the Circle Diamond chuck wagon, got some cold bread and meat to eat, and made themselves at home. Butler, the camp cook, watched them uneasily. The fact that the two men lacked extra horses suggested they were not stray riders looking for work, and the quality of their outfits indicated that they were not "chuck-line" riders. As Butler pondered their intentions, it struck him that one of the men was George Musgrave. Everyone knew bad blood existed between Musgrave and George Parker. The two newcomers finished eating, then took out their Bull Durham tobacco, rolled cigarettes, sat down on bedrolls near the water barrel, and began talking with the hands who had started drifting in from the range. As each hand rode into camp, they would ask Butler to identify him. Before long, George Parker arrived with Les Harmon of the Block Ranch and Billy Phillips of the VV Ranch. As the cowboys looked on, "Parker dismounted and walked toward the water barrel, nodding to Musgraves [sic], apparently not recognizing him. Musgraves stood up quickly and held out his hand as if to shake hands, but instead he pulled out his pistol and shot Parker four times. Parker fell, face down, and died instantly." The *Roswell Record* reported that "the first shot struck

Texas Rangers. L/r seated: George Parker, Robert McNamar; standing: Walter Durbin, Jim King. Courtesy of the Martha Bell Walker collection.

Parker in the left breast and was so close that it set his clothes on fire; the second was in the right shoulder and as Parker fell, he shot him in the top of the head, and after he was on the ground he shot him in the back."[4]

As Parker slumped to the ground, Bob Hayes drew his pistol, trained it upon the cowboys, and threatened, "The first man that flashes a gun I'll kill." Musgrave stood looking down at Parker and vowed, "There are three or four more I'll get before I leave." He told Curg Johnson and Butler, "C. D. Bonney is next on my list." Then, according to Harry Aguayo, Musgrave turned to the cowboys gathered about and warned, "Keep still boys, I will kill the first man that moves. Boys I don't want to hurt any of you but I came a long way to kill this [son of a bitch]! He has caused me a lot of trouble. He reported me to the Law for the things he did himself, forcing me to hide out the last few years. In other words, for branding mavericks when we were partners a few years ago."[5]

Aguayo's recollection was that Musgrave's statement concerning the trek to kill Parker came as Musgrave and Hayes were about to leave, not when he first faced Parker. Whatever Musgrave's words may have been, and whenever he may have uttered them, Aguayo, Reeves, and others all heard him say something that unquestionably established premeditation. However, Musgrave's self-justification is also clear. If these details are essentially true, as surviving evidence suggests, then, according to the code of the era, "Musgrave killed Parker because Parker needed killing." Of course, not everyone viewed the killing as justified. The *Record*, for example, labeled it as "one of the blackest and most damnable murders that has been committed in the territory of New Mexico in years." However, the *Record* lacked most of the details that led up to the shooting.[6]

After the killing, Musgrave and Hayes ransacked Parker's bed seeking arms. George then turned to the outfit's wrangler, Juan Perea, and asked, "How are the horses, and where is my horse, Old Bay Johnny?" Without waiting for an answer, Musgrave ordered Perea, Curg Johnson, and Will Tucker to round up the Diamond A remuda. When they returned with the horses, George roped Old Grant and saddled the gray horse with Parker's new Gallup saddle for himself. He roped Parker's bay cutting horse, Swallow Fork, for Hayes. Musgrave turned to Curg Johnson and said, "Get down, I want that saddle, you won't ever lose nothin by it." When Johnson objected, Musgrave asked him, "How much did it cost you?" "Sixty dollars," replied Johnson. Musgrave put his hand in his pocket as though seeking money, then appeared to change his mind and said, "I'll tell you what I'll do, what is your name? The first time I get to a town where I can send you the money I will send it to you." As Aguayo recalled, he never did.[7]

With new saddles on both horses and their old worn-out saddles left on the ground, Musgrave and Hayes waved their hands to the cowboys and rode off. Only then did the cowboys notice a wisp of smoke coming from the burning clothes on Parker's dead body. Frank Parks and Hamp Collett sent three men into Roswell to notify

Sheriff Charles W. Haynes of Parker's death. Meanwhile, Musgrave and Hayes continued their quest for vengeance.[8]

Musgrave had "announced that there were four men who had been doomed to death and who would surely die at an early day." Although he neglected to identify all of the men on the hit list, Musgrave and Hayes's subsequent actions, as well as the circumstances surrounding the initial horse-rustling charge filed against Musgrave, make it easy to establish who they were.[9]

The two outlaws rode north to the Rio Hondo and the Diamond A headquarters, doubtless intending to even affairs with Ernest Bloom and ranch manager James Sutherland. Pearl Sutherland greeted them; neither her husband nor Bloom was present. The two fugitives asked for food and a change of horses, which she provided, and then continued on their mission.[10]

Musgrave and Hayes spurred their horses west, up the Rio Hondo, to the T Ranch of C. D. Bonney, southeast of Picacho. Bonney was also on the list. When the heavily armed men rode up to the Bonney adobe and asked to see him, Bonney's wife, Sarah, told them that he had left early that morning to round up stray horses. C. D.'s son, Cecil, later wrote that he believed Musgrave wanted to kill his father for his part in the failed arrangement.[11]

More than a few shared knowledge that Parker had plotted with Ernest Bloom, son of Circle Diamond Ranch co-owner Frank Bloom, to swap T-branded horses rustled from Bonney for Musgrave-rustled cattle. Certainly, Jim Sutherland, in his capacity as manager, was aware of the character and machinations of the owner's son. Likely, to spare young Bloom from charges, Parker became dispensable, and an arrangement was made with Dan Johnson to testify against Parker in return for charges being dropped against himself and young Musgrave, an arrangement to which Bonney agreed. It could well be that, needing an additional scapegoat, Sutherland and Bonney reneged on the portion of the agreement covering Musgrave. Johnson, an "old-timer here, being known to all old cowboys as the V bar foreman, until recently in the employ of the Milne-Bush Cattle Co., [and] one of the best cowmen in the territory," probably was not scapegoat material. Musgrave, by virtue of both his youth and absence, was.[12]

That such an arrangement might have existed is further implied by John Cox's account of Musgrave's actions following his flight from Chaves County. "About sundown George rides up [to the horse camp of the Double S Ranch, west of Hot Springs, on the Cuchillo]. And he stayed there, I guess, about a month or six weeks with us. And then he goes back to Roswell and they got after him again over there.[13]

While the terms of the arrangement must remain subject to some conjecture, it seems certain that one existed, just as it seems certain that Musgrave returned to Chaves County believing that he had been exonerated. He had not. Whatever the original terms of the arrangement, apparently they had been betrayed. Accordingly, Musgrave felt morally justified in killing Parker, Bloom, Sutherland, and Bonney.

Leaving the T Ranch, the outlaws first rode north to the Cedar Hill home of Musgrave's father, then fled Chaves County. Although he had not successfully crossed all of the names from his hit list, Musgrave doubtless rode away from Chaves County well satisfied. George Parker, the principal cause of his troubles, and the focus of his hatred, was dead.

CHAPTER SEVEN

Pursued

There has been a gang of outlaws camped within twenty miles of here for two weeks robbed three post offices and terrorizing people, officer say no funds to put posse in field. Cant you stir them up and assure them of compensation?

GEORGE L. BUGBEE
to President Grover Cleveland

Within hours of Parker's death, Deputy Sheriff Charlie Ballard arrived on the scene, accompanied by Mack Minter, Frank Parks, and Mart McClenden. Judge Frank H. Lea rode along to conduct the inquest at the site—forever afterwards known as Parker's Bluff.[1]

At the next morning's inquest, Hamp Collett testified that he had seen the shooting; that Parker had made a move for his gun but Musgrave beat him to the draw. Eve Ball, who later interviewed several of the witnesses, implied that no others admitted to having observed the actual shooting. However, neither the *Roswell Record* nor the *Roswell Register* lacked for witnesses, nor apparently, did Judge Lea, who ruled that Musgrave had "deliberately and with premeditation affected the death of George T. Parker, delivering three mortal wounds, each of a depth of nine inches and of a width one inch."[2]

Charles Littlepage Bal-
lard (1866–1950), taken
in 1898 during the
Spanish-American War.
Courtesy Historical
Center for Southeast
New Mexico, Roswell,
photo no. 1512.

At the conclusion of the inquest, Ballard and his posse drew
fresh horses from the Circle Diamond's remuda and started their
pursuit. That same day, Deputy Sheriff Fred Higgins, accompanied
by Jesse Smith Lea, John Smith, and Les Smith, headed for the Musgrave ranch at Cedar Hill. Later that afternoon, Deputy Sheriff
Legg, Dan Thomas, and Lee Fountain also started for Cedar Hill
from Roswell.[3]

Still more posses assembled. Sheriff Bursum deputized one
group at Socorro while Sheriff Pat Garrett of Doña Ana County
organized another at Las Cruces. Constable Charles D. Mayer of
White Oaks, in Roswell at the time, returned from Roswell to White

Oaks and recruited still another posse. In two days Mayer and his men reached Fairview (now Winston). Before them rose the Black Range and the Mogollon Mountains, dangerous terrain for outlaw hunting. They returned to White Oaks by way of Magdalena, Socorro, and San Antonio. The Bursum and Garrett posses ran across no trail to follow and also gave up the chase.[4]

Meanwhile, Fred Higgins and his party had joined up with Ballard's posse. They trailed Musgrave and Hayes through the Arroyo Seco Cañon and out the head of the Cienega del Macho, north of the Capitan Mountains, and to the Jicarilla Mountains north of White Oaks where snow obliterated the trail. A hundred miles of hard traveling in the bitter cold chilled the posse's ardor. All turned back, save for Ballard and Higgins. The two dogged lawmen secured fresh horses from the Block Ranch, and after killing a calf, cooked enough veal to sustain them for several days, and left the fire blazing through the night to keep from freezing. Though the weather remained miserable, they continued the pursuit through the Jicarillas, down Coyote Cañon to Red Lakes, and along the eastern edge of the Malpais toward the Rio Grande.[5]

More astute lawmen might have anticipated that Musgrave and Hayes would not pass up the opportunity for another strike on the stage line before fleeing the area. In the Oscura Mountains near Cavanaugh's Lake, about twenty-three miles west of White Oaks, the outlaws met Ben F. Carpenter, who was driving the stage to San Antonio at half past eight o'clock, Wednesday night, October 21. Ordered to stop the team, Carpenter, a victim of one of the previous holdups, wisely complied. The robbers liberated the registered mail pouch and suggested facetiously that if San Antonio's postmaster used baskets in the future, it would be unnecessary to slice open government pouches. In the bag, they discovered two letters and one package. One letter contained a check that they discarded; the other held $5 in cash, which they took. They tore open the package and found $152 in gold dust. They chose not to bother with a box holding $2,100 in silver bullion. Although the *Santa Fe Daily New Mexican* reported that "the driver when asked by one of the robbers as to what was in the box, gave it a kick and said it contained a clock," it strains credulity to believe that after finding gold dust in one package, that they would ignore another based only on the driver's word. More believably, as the *Albuquerque Morning Democrat* argued, the silver was too heavy (175 pounds troy weight) for the two fugitives to carry. They boasted of the $785 they had secured from the first two holdups (the official Post Office Department figure was $532.60).[6]

Musgrave directed Carpenter to drive off the road and wait in a secluded spot. Two hours passed before they heard the noise of the approaching White Oaks–bound stage. "Just wait a few minutes," said Musgrave as he tightened his belt and examined his revolver. "Keep quiet while we fix this stage."[7]

Joseph J. Carpenter, driver of the eastbound coach, had just told co-driver Will L. Butler, "Here is where they held us up a week ago," when Musgrave cried out, "And here's where I hold you up again." The second stage met the fate of the first.[8]

The robbers looted the mail sacks, but found only one registered package that contained worthless merchandise. The *Rocky Mountain News* reported that Musgrave, undoubtedly disappointed, then said, apologetically, "I am sorry for you, but I guess you will have to walk." The report continued, "The freebooters then cut the [four] horses loose from the conveyances and disappeared in the hills."[9]

On the morning of October 22, the drivers described one outlaw (Musgrave), as about twenty-three years old, weighing about 170 pounds, five feet eleven inches tall, with dark brown hair, gray eyes, and a sandy complexion. He was called "Rube" by his companion. The other (Hayes) answered to the nickname "Hand," and was described as five feet nine inches tall, about 150 pounds, and about thirty years old.[10]

White Oaks crackled with excitement, but in the absence of both telephone and telegraph, news of the holdups remained confined to the isolated settlement. Early that afternoon, Deputy U.S. Marshal Charles Fowler gathered a nine-man posse, rode out of White Oaks, and followed the bandit's southbound trail along the west side of the Oscura Mountains. Another day passed before Post-master Hilton telegraphed Marshal Hall that no mail had been received from White Oaks for two days and correctly speculated that once again the mail had been held up. Hilton's fears were further heightened by reports that armed men had been seen hiding at the apex of the Oscura Mountains. Young Albert Hallenbeck had spotted a large gray horse with a new saddle at a water hole four miles east of Mountain Station. He had seen a man lying in the grass holding a Winchester, and later Hallenbeck saw two mounted riders carrying Winchesters. Wisely, Hilton held back the next San Antonio stage until the missing White Oaks stage arrived at Mountain Station.[11]

As San Antonio awaited news, the two bandits rode west and crossed to the west slope of the Oscura and San Andres Mountains. They continued on to Rincon, where they crossed the Rio Grande. Musgrave abandoned the large roan horse taken at the time of Parker's killing, later found by Fowler's posse at Hermosa, on the south fork of the Palomas River. From the Rio Grande, the two hunted men rode west to Cow Springs, about thirty miles north of Deming, where they released the four horses taken from the stage-coaches and rustled fresh mounts.[12]

On October 24, Marshal Hall sought Justice Department authorization for a four-man posse, and, not waiting for a reply, boarded the train for Deming. Meanwhile, Sheriff Pat Garrett and Deputy Banner led still another posse northeast toward Tularosa, and Deputy Loomis raced to El Paso and provided Mexican authorities at Juárez with descriptions of the outlaws, believed headed their way. Yet, that same day, riders observed two members of the gang south-west of Silver City at White Signal, no doubt Musgrave and Hayes. They had traveled over two hundred miles in less than three days.[13]

While the posses headed in various directions, Ballard and Higgins reached the Rio Grande and swam across. "That sure was a cold swim. We built a fire on the other side and dried out," Ballard recalled without difficulty. Across the river, cattle had blotted out the trail and the local ranchmen proved none too cooperative in providing information. Ballard wrongly attributed this to fear. The two frustrated lawmen abandoned the chase and headed for Deming, where Ballard asked Marshal Hall to send for Deputy James Leslie Dow, whom he considered "one of the bravest and best officers I ever knew. I was greatly relieved when Les stepped off the train at Deming." Sheriff-elect Dow of Eddy County did not share Ballard's opinion of the local ranchers. The reason, he later informed the *El Paso Daily Times*, was that the High Fives "[had] more friends out there than the officers." Moreover, they had Musgrave's large, extended family ready to lend assistance.[14]

A day or so after the White Signal sighting, cowboys with Ruch's Triangle outfit were rounding up stock when they spotted a couple of the High Fives in the Chiricahua Mountains. The two must have been the Christians rather than Musgrave and Hayes, and it is evident that the four bandits remained split into at least two groups. Indeed, for a short period Musgrave appears to have traveled alone. According to an O Bar O cowboy, Marvin Powe, one day Musgrave rode alone into Upton's ranch north of Deming, and the two reminisced. Musgrave pulled out his six-shooter and picked up Powe's, which rested on the table in its holster. Cocking it several times, Musgrave said, "Marvin, I've got to trade six-shooters with you," and Powe replied, "No you're not. A fella made me a present of the six-shooter and I don't want to give it up." "Well," Musgrave continued, "I hate to do it, but you can get around where you can have a six-shooter fixed. I'm gonna leave you mine. The mainspring is broke in it and the pistols are just alike." On that note, Musgrave collected Powe's pistol, leaving his behind.[15]

On Tuesday, about half past six o'clock on the evening of October 27, Musgrave and Hayes again rode to Separ. Unmasked, they boldly entered the station of the Southern Pacific Railroad Company and robbed express agent Ellis and the pumpman of twenty dollars and the Wells, Fargo Company's Express of an additional fifty-six dollars. Mischievously, they costumed Ellis as an outlaw, masking his face and outfitting him with a cowboy hat. Then they marched the agent and pumpman to the Separ boardinghouse, where they relieved the landlord and his boarders of their funds and forced them to join the growing procession. From the boarding house, the group paraded to John Weems's store, where the armed cowboy patrons were quickly stripped of weapons and money. Musgrave turned his rifle on Postmaster Milliken, and ordered, "Throw up your hand, Milliken; we are after you again." Musgrave shared a bottle of Weems's whiskey with the hostages, while Hayes demanded that Milliken open the safe. When he resisted, Hayes struck Milliken over the head with his gun, inflicting an ugly scalp wound. As the *Silver City Enterprise* later observed, "The Colonel exhibited considerable pluck but his judgment was hidden in the background." Hayes emptied the safe of about thirty-five dollars, then forced open the desk drawer and added one hundred two-cent stamps and three dollars and fifty cents to the growing cache.[16]

As Hayes bullied the postmaster, Musgrave stocked up on whiskey, tobacco, cigars, and other merchandise. With loot in hand, the robbers ordered Milliken and the cowboys to join in the procession with the lodging housekeeper, his boarders, the pump man, and Ellis. The bandits marched the parade, consisting of everyone who had the misfortune of being in Separ that day, about two miles out of town to the stockyards, where they had secreted their horses. After hosting the crowd to a farewell drink, they asked if anyone believed that a Winchester bullet could go through the bodies of thirteen men. With that not-so-subtle warning, Musgrave and Hayes bid the citizens adieu and rode off. The newspapers later reported, "When the passenger train, going west, pulled into the station, the crowd was just returning from the forced march into the country."[17]

Notified of the holdup, the Grant County sheriff, Baylor Shannon, and Frank Galloway of Silver City rode to Separ, where Frank McGlinchey and Steve Birchfield of Deming joined them. Ballard, Higgins, and the newly arrived Dow also started for Separ to take up the trail of the robbers. Meanwhile, Marshal Hall again petitioned the Justice Department for funds, seeking permission to

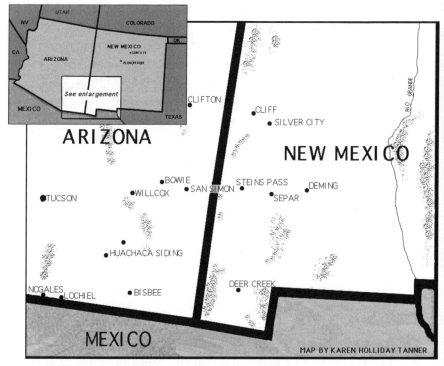

Southern Arizona and New Mexico

employ a posse of seven "good, reliable cattlemen" and Indian trackers. This time the attorney general listened. Five days later Hall
received authorization to expend up to $1,500 to bring in the High
Fives.[18]

On the day that Musgrave and Hayes hurrahed Separ, the Christian brothers robbed Solomon and Wickersham's store and post
office at Bowie. David Wickersham, doubtless recalling the previous loss of two pairs of boots, proved less than accommodating.
He took a shot at Black Jack, narrowly missing the outlaw's head.
With only a paltry fifteen dollars in small change, some boots, and
overalls to show for their efforts, the Christians fled four miles
south to the old Rich Well, where their path crossed that of Dud
Pruit, who was watering Wickersham's Bar Z Bar stock. Pruit, Wick-

ersham's foreman, was related to Musgrave, and locals believed that the boys stopped there occasionally because it was only a short distance from Dun Springs, one of their favorite hiding places in the Chiricahua Mountains. Safely out of sight, the gang issued a well-publicized warning to Wickersham that they would kill him on sight. On Friday, November 6, Wickersham came to Solomonville and, evidently assuming that Black Jack enjoyed being a target, maintained that he had no idea why the gang had it in for him.[19]

The High Fives seemed to be everywhere. On October 29, robbers struck Arturo Elias's store and post office at Solomonville, Arizona, which was then the seat of Graham County. Because their methods were typical of the Black Jack gang, the public, the press, and local officials hastily attributed the robbery to them, but subsequent events established that the culprits were, in fact, a gang of Mexicans led by Ramon Escabosa.[20]

On the evening of October 31, the crew aboard the westbound train out of Deming believed they had spotted High Five gang members hanging around the platform near the mail car. The suspects proved to be tramps. As the same train pulled into Lordsburg, reports circulated that members of the gang were riding on top of the mail car. Investigation revealed the stowaways to be children.[21]

As rumors ran rampant, the gang probably spent most of these days in the San Simon Valley. One day Oscar Cochrane (later the foreman of the San Simon Ranch) and Ben Lucey were at the San Simon horse camp, twenty miles south of the headquarters, when the gang rode in. Cochrane recalled:

> Ben said, "We don't have any beef." "What do you say we bring in one?" they [the gang members] said. Next morn. drove in [a] big San Simon cow and fat calf and killed it. We couldn't say anything, as they'd come in two at a time and ride our horses when [they] wanted to. We had a little corral at north Skeleton Canyon. They'd throw our horses in, catch fresh ones, turn [loose] those [they] was riding, and leave on

ours. Came and went. San Simon never tried to do anything about it. They never did bother us—just robbed our horses.[22]

On October 31, Shannon, McGlinchey, Galloway, and Birchfield tracked part of the gang into the San Simon Valley and set up camp that evening near Squaw Mountain on the west side of the valley. About three o'clock the next morning during Galloway's watch, a noise awakened Birchfield. He grabbed his rifle and roused McGlinchey and Shannon. They saw a person about fifty feet away approaching their camp. Fearful, they hollered into the darkness. The call brought forth no response. Shannon ordered McGlinchey and Birchfield to fire. Their friendly fire killed Galloway. One bullet, later attributed to Birchfield, passed through his right cheek and out the rear of his head. The elusive High Fives were some miles away, preparing for another heist.[23]

On Monday evening, November 2, the four reunited members of the High Five gang robbed the town of San Simon, Arizona. The railroad station agent and Wells, Fargo expressman, Adolph Langlotz, had often boasted he would kill any outlaw who presented himself. "He had sent out to Sears Roebuck and got some kind of fancy coat. The robbers told Langlotz, 'Pull out that coat.' [He] said, 'I just bought it.' 'We don't give a damn; you've been making a lot of talk. We want it.'" Faced with reality, the agent parted with his brand new coat. Adding further insult, the gang relieved Langlotz and his pumpman of their loose change. The outlaws, in what was fast becoming a tradition, fitted the victims with masks. Then they marched them to Thomas R. Brandt's store and post office, where they seized blankets, overalls, and provisions, as well as the cash in the till and $25.75 in postal funds.[24]

The gang forced the agent, pumpman, shopkeeper, and several others who had innocently wandered in to carry the stolen goods to the next store. One of the captives obeyed a command to go inside for four bottles of whiskey. While the storeowner filled the order, the rest of the procession filed in. One outlaw shouted for the shopkeeper to set up drinks for the entire crowd. After all had

a drink, the outlaw insisted, "Now *you* set them up, I have." "But you
have not paid for them yet," protested the beleaguered merchant
turned reluctant bartender. "Well that don't matter, it's your turn to
set them up," came the outlaw's response. The storeowner complied.

As the black comedy unfolded, one of the bandits took down a
jar of candy from the shelf and began to pour it out onto the counter.
"Don't do that," the first outlaw advised, "this is a pretty good old
Boy." Turning to the shopkeeper, he asked the amount of the bill,
then laid down a ten-dollar bill. Not waiting for change, he ordered
everyone back out onto the street. As in Separ, the residents of San
Simon were marched single file about a mile out of town to where
the gang had tied their horses and pack animals. After treating the
folks to another drink before their return hike, the High Fives mer-
rily rode off with between one hundred and two hundred dollars
and a good supply of provisions.[25]

The fugitives again retreated to Ruch's ranch, northwest of San
Simon. There they could climb atop his windmill and, with the aid
of field glasses, spot any threat as it approached. None did.[26]

Following the robbery of San Simon, a frustrated Marshal Meade
wrote to Attorney General Harmon vainly requesting funding.[27]
Meanwhile, in yet another questionable attribution, the *Albuquerque
Daily Citizen* reported that Bob Christian and Bob Hayes had robbed
the post office at Central, New Mexico, near Silver City, taking
$149.08 in money and stamps. However, the *Silver City Enterprise*
did not name the thieves and reported the crime as a burglary:[28]

On election night [November 3], when most of the residents
of Central were interested in watching the votes counted,
some miscreant broke open the post office building and stole
postage stamps and other property, belonging to Dr. R. C.
Anderson, post master, to a value of one hundred dollars.
The thieves also broke into Julius Welgehausen store and
stole a gold watch and chain, album, and other property.
They also robbed the house of a chinaman [*sic*] but the extent
of his loss could not be learned.[29]

This burglary does not conform to the modus operandi of the High Fives. The question of their involvement remains, at best, improbable.

Some citizens of Arizona, increasingly disgusted with the ineptitude of law enforcement and the parsimony of the Justice Department, filed complaints with the federal government. The day of the Central burglary, George Lewis Bugbee, the railroad agent and Wells, Fargo expressman at Bowie, telegraphed his concerns directly to President Grover Cleveland. The White House forwarded Bugbee's complaint to the Interior Department, which, in turn, shuffled it off to the postmaster general. Unable to locate Bowie on the list of post offices, he passed Bugbee's complaint on to the Justice Department.[30]

A post office inspector, George H. Waterbury of Denver, was soon on his way to Cochise County. At Bowie, Waterbury detailed what he perceived to be the difficulty in capturing the bandits. "[They] are thoroughly familiar with the country from White Oaks to Arizona, and will ride 100 miles in twenty-four hours with ease, stealing fresh horses whenever they need them. Thus you will see that these bandits are as bad as Apaches." Marshal Meade believed he had a solution. He telegraphed the self-styled man hunter Tom Horn, then foreman of Burt Dunlap's ranch at Aravaipa, to assist in bringing in the High Fives.[31]

Will Christian and Musgrave rode southwest from Ruch's ranch to Huachuca Siding on November 6. Probably Christian was sporting a spangle-covered sombrero, once the proud possession of a local cowpuncher who had been coerced to hand it over to the covetous outlaw in exchange for twelve dollars. At nine o'clock the next night they reached the Wells, Fargo office at the New Mexico and Arizona Railroad depot, expecting to hit the pay train. When it failed to appear, the station agent and Wells, Fargo expressman, Horace Jewell "Joe" Temple, and an employee in the Huachuca freight office became the targets. Nobly, Christian explained that they did not want to rob any individual person, only the railroad and express companies. Moreover, they did not want to kill anyone, but it would not trouble them if it proved necessary. Temple took him seriously. Christian ordered the agent to open the safe under penalty of death and hovered over the agent to see that it was done—and done quickly.[32] While Christian concentrated on the safe, Musgrave searched the other employee for weapons and came upon the man's money purse. The elderly employee pleaded that it was all the money he had. "The heart of the robber was softened," reported the *Tombstone Porspector*. Musgrave returned the purse.[33]

Christian withdrew the money drawer from the safe and ordered the express agent to dump the safe's remaining contents on the table. When Temple reacted too slowly, Christian again flourished his Colt. As the agent separated cash from the checks, Christian pocketed the cash. Christian and Musgrave passed "jocular remarks about things and persons in general, [and] concluded that they had gotten everything of value." Christian glanced once more into the safe and spotted some small packages, which Temple had failed to produce. He tucked these inside his shirt and the two marched the railroad employees outside.[34]

Musgrave, with Temple in tow, announced that he had an "elegant thirst," and asked if Tom Smith's saloon might still be open. Temple replied that the saloon had closed unusually early that night. Musgrave remembered having seen some wine in the freight house, and with his Colt in one hand and a lantern in the other, ordered Temple to accompany him back inside. Seizing a bottle, Musgrave had Temple sample it before ordering two more bottles uncorked. They took the bottles out to the patient Christian, calmly searching through the packages taken from the safe. Temple pleaded that the contents, which proved to be jewelry, belonged to private individuals who had entrusted their treasures to him for safekeeping. After examining the jewelry by the light of the fire, Christian and Musgrave returned the baubles.

Drinking wine and growing bombastic, the two bandits discussed their holdups at Separ and San Simon and boasted that a few deputies would be killed if the posses continued their pursuit. Musgrave then passed a bottle to the two railroad employees for a farewell drink before he and Christian rode away, richer by $130. They had been at the station from thirty to forty minutes, each with a gun in hand the entire time. They fled in the direction of South Pass. The pursuing posse of Al Ezekiels and William Long lost the trail in the vicinity of Fairbank, about seven miles west of Tombstone. The *Silver City Enterprise* concluded, "Truly these fellows seem ubiquitous."[35]

The day of the Huachuca robbery, Tom Horn responded to Marshal Meade's plea for aid. Due to the roundup and his employer's presence at court in Solomonville, Horn could not comply, but argued that no posse could capture the outlaws because of the inherent handicaps under which posses labored. "I can stand a better show to get them by going alone and will go and get some of them at least and drive the rest out of the country *if there is anything in it for me*. If I undertake the job *no cure no pay* is my mottoe. So if I don't get them it costs no one a cent." Horn further advised Meade, "If you take a Posse down there you will only find *fresh sign*."[36]

About November 9, Black Jack allegedly was spotted in Tombstone. The next day, the High Five gang returned to the Willcox area, broke into Nolt E. Guild's Whitewater Ranch house, and helped themselves to a pair of field glasses. Unfortunately, Guild failed to notify Meade promptly of the bandits' presence in the region. Meade did learn that later in the evening Black Jack and at least one other member of the gang were seen at Pearce, where they brazenly walked into Del Washington's store and post office and made some purchases. They also bought supplies at the Norton and Morgan Company store. The residents were not prepared to confront them, and the boys departed unmolested.[37]

At Bowie, a frustrated Inspector Waterbury complained that "all of [them] are cowboys, who have rode this and the New Mexico ranges for years past, terrorising the people along the route into silence for fear of their lives and stock."[38]

The High Fives were back in the Willcox area near midnight, Friday the 13th. Earlier that day, Sherman Crump, a gang confederate, had come to Willcox to buy a box of ammunition at Soto

Brothers and Chattman's store. Later, about one or two o'clock Saturday morning, he awakened the store's clerk and said he wanted the ammunition he had left there. The clerk let him in and Crump insisted on buying a good deal more. He purchased .38-56-caliber, .44-caliber, and another kind the clerk recalled as .50-82-caliber. Crump said he was going directly home, but he was seen back in Willcox later in the day, as was Cal Cox, foreman for a cattleman down the valley and another suspected gang confederate, who bought still more ammunition—six dollars' worth. Both Crump and Cox paid for their purchases in small change. Residents later learned that the rearmed gang had intended to rob the paymaster's box bound for Fort Huachuca but found it too well guarded by soldiers. Black Jack bragged that they got close enough to hear the guards snoring in their sleep. The High Fives then rode southeast, down the Sulphur Spring Valley.[39]

At midday, Saturday, November 14, two of the outlaws reached Bill Stark's ranch and received a dinner invitation. Rather than hide their identities, the outlaws became "quite loquacious, recounting all of their deeds and various holdups, which would furnish an interesting topic for a blood and thunder novel. Forgetting all precautionary dangers and usual grave demeanor and watchfulness, [they] turned the hour into one of veritable mirth, seemingly enjoying it to the utmost." Meanwhile, Black Jack and another gang member were about two miles away at Brannick Riggs's C Bar Ranch, below Bonita Canyon at the base of the Chiricahua Mountains. Black Jack and his colleague rejected Riggs's similar offer for dinner, remarking that they had recently eaten breakfast and that they were not used to that many meals in a day. They did indicate their need for fresh horses. At the remuda, they roped four of Riggs's horses, explaining, "Mr. Riggs, we want good horses. We are not stealing from you. When we ride them and make a change we will drop you a card so you can come and get them." After repeating that it was not their intention to harm any individual, the fugitives insisted that they would not be taken alive and rode on.[40]

At or near Riggs's ranch, the four outlaws reunited and traveled to Major Edward Downey's nearby ranch in the Pinery Valley for supplies. They spent that night secreted in the Chiricahua Mountains and the next morning rode northwest toward Apache Pass. At the west entrance to the pass, two of them reached Joe Schaefer's Bar ZZ Ranch near Dos Cabezas in time for Sunday morning breakfast. Afterwards, they pulled out two one-pound Bull Durham sacks filled with change from the recent forays and gave them to Mrs. Schaefer. She objected, "You don't owe anybody here for breakfast. We feed anyone and don't charge." An outlaw replied, "Yes, [but] we don't want to carry that, it is too heavy to carry." As they left, the gang told her, "You need not worry about us bothering any of your stock or killing your beef or taking any of your horses. We just work on the big outfits that can afford it." While the two outlaws charmed Mrs. Schaefer, their two confederates descended upon another Dos Cabezas ranch and politely informed the rancher of their plans to leave two horses previously rustled and to take two fresh ones. Before making their way toward Bowie, Black Jack confessed that they had been in Willcox to rob the army payroll.[41]

From Dos Cabezas, the High Fives continued through Apache Pass, crossed the San Simon Valley, and headed for Steins Pass, New Mexico. Perhaps they wanted another chance at an army payroll. Perchance the small railroad settlement was simply along their way. They arrived at Steins Pass on Monday evening, November 16, 1896. There is an unfortunate paucity of information concerning this caper. The *Arizona Daily Star* reported, "They went to Steins Pass to hold up the station but found a woman in charge, and said that they would not molest a woman, but held up the section boss and robbed him." The *Santa Fe Daily New Mexican* merely noted that they robbed "the station and store at Steins station." The *Silver City Enterprise* wrote, "It was reported in this city Tuesday that the station at Stein's Pass on the S.P.R.R. was held up by the Black Jack gang Monday evening." Considering their normal pattern of operations, the gang doubtless planned to rob the Southern Pacific

railroad station and the store/post office. The postmaster general
had appointed Emma Rodgers postmaster on June 23, 1893; she
would maintain the position until January 16, 1899. With a woman
in charge of the post office, with the High Fives' assurance that
they would never rob a woman, and with no postal losses claimed,
it is probable that Mrs. Rodgers was the beneficiary of the gang's
gallantry. It is equally probable that they did hold up the station
office, operated by agent Charles St. John, and also the section boss.
With little to show for their efforts, the High Fives then rode southeast through New Mexico's Animas Valley toward the Continen-
tal Divide and the Playas Valley beyond.[42]

CHAPTER EIGHT

Deer Creek

*There [are] so many people in this country who [want] to be
elected sheriff, and who want to be appointed a deputy sheriff, and who want to be appointed a deputy marshal. There
are enough of these would be officers in the country to take
all the bad men and half of Mexico.*

WESTERN LIBERAL

Musgrave, Hayes, and the two Christian brothers rode all night,
entered the Playas Valley of New Mexico, and at dawn made breakfast at Bud Howell's ranch, two miles south of the old mining town
of Hachita. Then they then headed south down the Old Smugglers
Trail, unaware that a posse was already closing in on them.[1]

On November 7, U.S. Attorney General Judson Harmon approved
New Mexico Marshal Hall's request for $1,500 to fund a manhunt
for the High Fives. In turn, Hall convinced railroad officials to provide free transportation for his men and their horses, and John
Thacker, a Wells, Fargo special agent, offered the express company's
assistance. Marshal Meade had put Deputy Al Ezekiels' posse on
their trail in an effort to prevent the outlaws from turning west, and
a nine-man posse stood by at Separ, ready to move south to cut off
what they assumed would be the gang's flight to Mexico. When

information reached Meade that the High Fives had left Joe Schaefer's ranch and headed east, the strategy designed to effect their elimination became operative.[2]

At two o'clock on Monday afternoon, November 16, even before the High Fives arrived at Steins Pass, the posse, comprised of Charles Ballard, Fred Higgins, Les Dow, Steve Birchfield, Frank McGlinchey, Baylor Shannon, Perfecto Rodriguez, Frank Preiser, and Frank "Pink" Peters, started down the trail leading south through the Playas Valley and toward the Mexican border. The *Western Liberal* took sardonic pleasure in informing its readers that Marshals Hall and Meade, along with agent Thacker, remained at Deming's Depot hotel, "prepared to defend the pretty waiter girls at the expense of their lives, if necessary."[3]

The posse also rode through the night and arrived at Hachita on Tuesday morning. The riders soon discovered the campsite where the gang had breakfasted. Having been tipped off that they intended to head for the Diamond A horse camp at Deer Creek, some seventy miles southeast of Steins Pass, and believing the bandits to be low on provisions, the posse continued south. The lawmen reached Las Cienegas, the Diamond A headquarters ranch, one hour behind the outlaws. After commandeering fresh horses, they rode another twenty-five miles through the darkness, taking a cut-off south of Las Cienegas through Smuggler's Canyon to save some five miles in their effort to beat the High Fives to the Diamond A horse camp.[4]

The lawmen reached the camp at three o'clock on Wednesday morning, November 18. The camp consisted of a corral, a windmill, a newly constructed but empty livestock tank with four foot-high earthen walls partly surrounded by cedar pickets, and a small adobe hut with one window facing away from the corral and tank. The officers explained the situation to Walter Birchfield, the Diamond A superintendent and cousin of posse member Steve Birchfield. Walter not only offered his help, but kept all hands in camp to prevent any warning from reaching Musgrave, who had friends there. Baylor Shannon later claimed that he arrested the

L/r: Stever Birchfield (#1), Baylor Shannon (#2), Charles Ballard (#6), J. Les Dow (#3), Fred Higgins (#4), and C. S. Fly (#5). Courtesy Western History Collections, University of Oklahoma.

cowboys and locked them in the house until the fight was over. The cowboys disputed this, as well as most of Shannon's other contentions.[5]

The officers mixed their tired horses in with the Diamond A herd so as not to be noticed. Ballard, Higgins, Dow, McGlinchey, and Preiser took positions within the tank, next to the windmill and at a right angle to the corral. Shannon, Peters, Rodriguez, and Steve Birchfield hid inside the adobe hut with some of the Diamond A crew. Another eight to ten Diamond A hands, including Henry Brock, waited in the corral.

The posse spotted Musgrave, the Christians, and Hayes just before daylight. Black Jack and Hayes rode up the trail toward the corral and tank hiding the officers, while his brother and Musgrave waited back some two to three hundred yards. Between the two outlaw parties, the scene was bare, without trees or other obstructions. Then, one of the Diamond A boys in the corral stuck his hat through the fence and began to wave off the outlaws. Taking it as a welcoming signal, Black Jack and Hayes continued to ride toward the hidden posse. Henry Brock later recounted, "Well, now I was standing there watching them with a bunch of other fellas and things were pretty tense as they were coming up. We knew what was gonna come off, you know, just waiting for it to open up."

When Black Jack and Hayes were within thirty yards of the officers secreted in the livestock tank, Les Dow yelled to them to surrender. The outlaws jerked their horses' heads up to shield themselves from the posse and began shooting. The posse returned the fire. Bullets struck Hayes in the foot and leg, and he toppled from his horse. Walter Birchfield, who apparently viewed the event from the corral, remembered that "Les Dow shot at Black Jack five times, and it looked like every shot hit him." Appearances proved deceiving. The lawmens' second volley struck Black Jack's horse Barney, a large chestnut sorrel; the wounded stallion started to pitch toward the corral. As the horse lurched, Black Jack's pistol slipped out of its holster. The outlaw leaned across the side of his mount and slapped the dying horse on the side of its head with his hat in an effort to turn him away from the open gate of the corral. The horse fell onto his right side on top of Black Jack's Winchester. Black Jack landed on his feet.[6]

Ignoring the officers' fire, the outlaw grabbed the saddle horn and, with an adrenaline rush, lifted the dying horse sufficiently to jerk the saddle around and recover his rifle. Hayes, unable to rise, continued to fire from a prone position. "He was aclippin' at every head that came up," Brock recalled, covering Black Jack's movements and filling Ballard's and Dow's eyes with splinters off the cedar posts that concealed them. A fatal bullet struck and killed Hayes after he had cocked his revolver on the last round. He could not pull the trigger one more time. "He was jest done in."[7]

While the officers fruitlessly exchanged fire with Musgrave and Bob Christian from afar, Black Jack, keeping the trigger of his Winchester depressed and recycling the action, fanned rounds at the officers as he moved toward an arroyo, just a few feet from his dying horse. "He fired that rifle so fast you would have thought it was a machine gun, and you should have seen the splinters fly from the picket fence around the ground tank," according to Brock.

Black Jack scrambled down the arroyo some two hundred yards or more, losing himself in the scrub oaks and sycamore trees. From there he worked his way up a ridge about sixty yards from the creek bed and headed south, hiding in the soapweed while several of the officers passed by him during their search. He stayed there, safely concealed until late in the evening. "I didn't know [there was] a posse in camp. When all the shooting started, I thought the Diamond A cowboys were trying to get me," he said later. The soapweed seemed an inadequate refuge. "When I realized how far my behind was sticking out from behind that bush it felt as big as a mountain."

New Mexico cowboy John Cox recalled Will Christian claiming, "Them sonsabitches pretended to be follerin' and they passed in forty yards of me. I know damned well they saw me but I couldn't afford to open the fight, five of them on me [sic] one." In recounting this story he heard over fifty years earlier, Cox opined, "By God they just didn't want him, that was all." Henry Brock agreed. Black

Steve Birchfield (l) holding Bob Hayes's six-shooter, and Pink Peters (r) examining Hayes's Winchester. George Parker's saddle (l) and Curg Johnson's saddle (r) in the foreground, November 1897. Courtesy Western History Collections, University of Oklahoma.

Jack had told him that "he was just waiting and the first man that saw, and showed evidence that he'd seen him, was a dead man." Black Jack escaped into the darkness, and no one pursued him. When asked why later, the lawmen unconvincingly maintained that their horses were played out, and, given the outlaw's head start, they knew they would be unable to overtake him.[8]

When the dust settled, cowboys removed the saddles from the slain horses and discovered that Black Jack had been riding George Parker's saddle, while Hayes had been astride that of Curg Johnson. The saddles were returned to Roswell. Walter Birchfield put

Hayes's body in a wagon and had a cowboy nicknamed "Sammy Behind the Gun" drive it into Separ, where the dead outlaw was identified and buried. A memorandum book found on Hayes's body contained notes that indicated that the outlaws "had Loomis spotted."[9]

A number of the lawmen rode into Separ that evening just as the westbound train arrived with Marshal Hall riding in the express car with the guards. When the men rode toward the train, Hall and the guards did not recognize them and thought that they had finally been presented with an opportunity to exterminate the High Five gang. "They jumped out of the opposite side of the car, ran to the ends, climbed onto the platform and prepared for a flanking fire on the outlaws." Fortunately, the guards recognized the members of the posse just before they opened fire and a repeat of the Galloway tragedy was averted.[10]

Newspaper accounts of the events surrounding the shootout at Deer Creek disseminated much misinformation, and lawmen argued with newspapers over who deserved the credit for what actually happened. Even before the arrival of Hayes's body, Frank McGlinchey wired dispatches from Separ to several newspapers claiming that a posse led by U.S. Marshal McGlinchey had killed Hayes and wounded George Musgrave. To compound the many errors, he added a mythical fifth member to the gang. The list of activities attributed to the outlaws, described as "the most desperate gang that ever infested Arizona and New Mexico," also wrongly credited four deaths to the High Fives, including those of an unnamed rancher and an unnamed cowboy in the Animas Valley. The *Santa Fe Daily New Mexican* asserted that George Musgrave was "supposed to be the man who, with Grant Wheeler, blew up the express and mail car near Willcox," while the *Albuquerque Morning Democrat* identified George Musgrave as Black Jack. The version that Grant County Sheriff Baylor Shannon gave to the *Silver City Enterprise* was dismissed by the *Western Liberal* as "evidently inspired by Sheriff Shannon's literary bureau." Les Dow provided the *El Paso Daily International Times* with a generally accurate account of the fight and stated: "No, Sheriff Shannon was not in the fight." The *Western Liberal,* in turn, had little use for Dow's version: "Please do not brag on the fighting ability of men who lay in a dirt tank and only succeeded in shooting the tops of the pickets of the fence that surrounded the tank." The *Eddy Current* rushed to the defense of Dow, Ballard, and Higgins, who "deserve the credit of running the gang down and the cowards who hid deserve no credit."[11] Amid the charges and countercharges, the "irrepressible" George Waterbury announced that, in fact, it had been he who was responsible for sending out the posse that killed Hayes, prompting the *Western Liberal* to note sarcastically: "By the time he gets to Denver he will be telling that he killed Hayes after a terrific hand to hand struggle. The only one of Waterbury's scraps of which there is an actual record made by an interested party, occurred in Albuquerque, when an up country postmaster, after being honorably discharged by the court, blackened Waterbury's eyes for securing his indictment on perjured evidence."[12]

In Deming, Van Musgrave heard talk of the incident and leapt to his brother's defense. He nearly started a riot, but the crowd was restrained by some peace-loving townsfolk.[13]

The day following the Deer Creek shootout, Dutchy Behmer, the High Fives' contact at the Howell ranch, was arrested and charged with being an accessory. At the time of his arrest, he had a horse packed with supplies supposedly for the gang. Three days after Behmer's arrest, Marshal Meade, having received the authorization of the Justice Department, put a posse of ten deputies into the field under the command of White and Ezekiels and instructed them to remain in constant pursuit for the next fifteen days. On Sunday morning, November 22, eight posse members arrived in Tombstone, where they enlisted the services of a guide and took to the field. Deputies Loomis and Ezekiels joined the posse in Bisbee, as did Cochise County Sheriff Fly.[14]

Meade authorized White to call on the services of the commanding officer of the military camp at John Slaughter's San Bernardino Ranch, should he find the civilian force inadequate. By November

27, the White-Ezekiels posse arrived in the vicinity of the San Bernardino Ranch. Ballard and Higgins went into Arizona, where they joined with White at Bisbee. Les Dow returned to Carlsbad.[15]

Meanwhile, what of the outlaws themselves? The morning following the shootout, having traveled over twenty miles on foot through the San Luis Pass, Will Christian reached the Animas Valley headquarters of the Diamond A at Cloverdale. He carefully surveyed the surroundings. When a youngster appeared, Christian questioned him and learned that only Joe Whitmire was at the ranch. Then Christian threatened to double a rope and wear it out on the kid if he lied. Assured of the truth, Christian went to the house and told Whitmire that he needed a good horse; Whitmire invited him to take his pick. After breakfast, Christian rode off on a Diamond A horse and saddle. A day later, he appeared at the Wamel ranch, about forty miles away. Later that afternoon he reached Bud Howell's ranch near Hachita, but, spying a number of guns leaning up against the house, decided to pass it by. That evening, still riding the Diamond A horse, Black Jack reached Ed and Gus Holmigs's ranch, sixty miles from Deer Creek. Before he left, the Holmigs supplied him with a fresh horse, a saddle, and a hat. Farther on, he met James McCabe leading a bunch of horses. "In his usual persuasive way [he] induced Mr. McCabe to give him his pick of the horses. Mrs. Ed Roberts, for whom Musgrave had previously worked, reported that Black Jack arrived at the Roberts's OH Ranch on the San Pedro River one or two days following the Deer Creek shooting. Other reports placed him at different ranches as he made his way to the Mexico line.[16]

In the aftermath of the shootout, Musgrave and Bob Christian hid at various places on both sides of the border. Word circulated in the San Simon Valley that the two went north about ten days after the Deer Creek fight and crossed the Southern Pacific tracks between San Simon and Steins Pass.[17]

By mid-December, some officials believed the three surviving members of the High Five gang had regrouped and were hiding in the vicinity of Globe, Arizona. A week later, reports placed them

Scott White, Cochise County
Sheriff, 1893–94, 1897–1900.
Courtesy Arizona Historical
Society/Tucson, AHS #9156.

at or near J. N. Potter's ranch at Ash Flat in the vicinity of old Fort
Thomas. Yet Deputy White received information that placed Black
Jack in the Chiricahua Mountains on December 13. The *Albuquerque Morning Democrat* concurred that by early December they had
returned to the Chiricahua Mountains and had robbed a Mexican
traveler. Deputy Will Loomis disagreed with these reports and concluded during the first week in December that the High Five gang
had left southeastern Arizona altogether. Apparently, Meade had
reached the same conclusion. On December 19 he wrote the sheriff-
elect of Cochise County, Scott White, "I have decided to make no further efforts for the present looking to the capture of Thos Anderson
[Bob Christian] et al." Having experienced equal lack of success,
Deputies Higgins and Ballard also temporarily abandoned the chase
and returned to Roswell.[18]

At the end of December, Deputy White learned from Colonel
William Greene that Musgrave and Bob Christian had been camped
in the Huachuca Mountains for two weeks and that Black Jack was
in the Swisshelms or Chiricahuas near Sherman Crump's camp.

Greene also believed that they would "go down into Mexico at the H.C. ranch to get fresh horses when they decide to make a move of any kind, that they are laying very quiet now only waiting for a favorable opportunity."[19]

As Marshal Meade decided to abandon the hunt, Marshal Hall increased efforts to capture the gang by announcing the Post Office Department's aggregate reward of six thousand dollars "for the arrest and conviction or for causing the arrest and conviction" of the three bandits, and distributing their descriptions throughout the Southwest.[20]

A number of factors explain the inability of all these law-enforcement agencies to end the crime spree. As Marshals Meade and Hall repeatedly pointed out, sparsely populated southeastern Arizona and southwestern New Mexico, and the proximity of the Mexican border, offered a haven beyond the reach of American lawmen. However, the most significant factors appear to have been the high esteem in which the gang members were held by the residents and a widespread animosity toward governmental officials and policies, particularly the tariff. Leonard Alverson later insisted that many viewed the outlaws as gentlemen who minded their manners and aided in doing the chores. "But the bar room rounders who usually formed parts of the posse would stomp in with their spurs and hats on and spit tobacco juice all over the floor. Start out with lots of whiskey and when it plays out their courage went with it."[21] Well-liked, the High Five gang would help with roundups and assist the ranchers. Many of the ranchers liked to have them around. Alverson continued:

> Once Black Jack stayed all night at Jake Shearers [Double Rod Ranch] and the next evening a posse came along and wanted to know if Jake had seen anything of him. No, Jake had not seen him for ages. Just then little George Shearer pipes up, "Why yes Papa, Black Jack was here last night. Don't you remember he helped mamma with the dishes and put on my shoes and gave me two bits for being a good boy." Jake's

memory still failed him so he said nothing. The posse looked at one another then rode off. There was scarcely a ranch in the country where the Black Jack Christian gang could not get a horse if they wanted or even provisions.[22]

John Cox related a similar story concerning Montague Stevens of the SU Ranch near Reserve, New Mexico:

Montague Stevens had a fella who got into a slight argument and killed this fellow on the chuckwagon and he was a good hand and Montague Stevens is a very honest man, you know, but he said when the officers came he told them exactly where this fella had gone and where he was headed for but they never found him because he was really going in the opposite direction. (Laughs[.]) So all the cattlemen I believe were the same, they protected their cowboys.[23]

Mrs. Anna Zona Ligget told Louis Blachly how the outlaws were warned:

Well, these ranchers, I don't know whether it was a necessity, they never persecuted these outlaws. They'd have been at the outlaws mercy if they did. I know I've heard my brother tell about gettin' up on the windmill and hangin', washin' his clothes and hangin' 'em up on the windmill when the officers were in the house so if there was any outlaws around they wouldn't come to the house.[24]

In the final analysis, the greatest advantage the outlaws had was the fact that they were, in the opinion of San Simon cowboy Oscar Cochrane, "as fine [a] bunch of fellows to meet as you ever saw— jolly, good natured—most agreeable fellows you ever met."[25]

By the end of 1896, the residents of southeastern Arizona believed that the gang had disbanded and had sought safety elsewhere. During the prior six months, the High Five gang had held up one bank, one train, and four stagecoaches. They had robbed a total of eight stores, as well as express depots, railroad depots, and post offices. Two posse members, Frank Robson and Frank Galloway, along with two gang members, Code Young and Bob Hayes, had lost their lives. George Musgrave had killed George Parker. The federal government had expended a considerable amount of money. The rewards offered by the U.S. Post Office and Wells, Fargo exceeded two thousand dollars per outlaw, with an additional one thousand dollars offered for Musgrave's capture. Yet the three members of the gang, Musgrave and the Christians, remained safely outside the reach of the law.[26]

CHAPTER NINE

MAYHEM AND MURDER

The El Paso officers thought they had killed Black Jack, the bandit, but it turned out to be nothing but a peaceable miner. Just so with our competitors—when they think they have captured the plum and a pull for the trade, it turns out to be something else, and our I. W. Harper liquors and Hoffman House segars hold the persimmon.

YRS. RESPY, THE LEGAL TENDER

One evening during the first week in January, a stranger showed up at the express office in Bisbee and asked if there were packages for Jesse Williams (George Musgrave) or Bob Hayes. The newly hired agent unthinkingly replied, "Yes but are these boys not members of the Black Jack Gang?" The stranger answered, "No, they were different men altogether," and walked out without waiting for any packages. A search later revealed a pair of boots and a package awaiting Williams and Hayes. The High Fives had temporarily returned to Cochise County.[1]

Sheriff White had information, evidently accurate, that placed at least a portion of the gang in the neighborhood of Hagin's ranch in Sonora, Mexico. Other reports placed them near Globe. Doubtless a sighting of any group of five or so unknown cowboys would immediately prompt the conjecture—Black Jack gang. Subsequent events, however, suggest that the sightings east of Globe were probably of Van Musgrave and his recently organized gang of horse rustlers.[2]

By mid-January, White and Charlie Ballard, who had again taken up the hunt, decided the outlaws were at Colonel William Greene's Cananea Ranch in Sonora. Securing the aid of a Mexican guide, White, Ballard, and Higgins rode all night in an attempt to surprise their prey but came up empty-handed. A fresh tip placed Black Jack at Billy Plasters's ranch.[3]

Plasters, a native of Grimes County, Texas, ran a few head of cattle on his small ranch at Ochoaville, at the southern end of the San Pedro Valley, almost astride the international line. White learned that Black Jack was hiding at Plasters's place and "playing poker every night with a bunch of Cochise County cowboys and generally having a good time." White, Ballard, and Higgins raided the ranch only to find that the forewarned bandit had fled.[4]

As the gang continued to evade arrest, Meade responded to questions about the size and nature of the various rewards being offered. In addition to the standing Wells, Fargo reward of three hundred dollars, post office rewards approached two thousand dollars for each of the three surviving gang members. Moreover, the citizens of Roswell had posted an additional one-thousand-dollar prize for Musgrave. Though the prospect of money intrigued a number of would-be posse members, collecting required the arrest and conviction of the bandits. They felt it was not worth risking their lives to confront the outlaws directly and wanted a "dead or alive" clause to allow the opportunity to bushwhack them, a substantially safer option.[5]

While Arizona officials tried to establish the High Fives' whereabouts, attention centered in New Mexico on Van Musgrave, who had quit Jim Upton's O Bar O Ranch, formed a gang, and started rustling horses throughout Grant County. Numbered among Van's horse thieves were Hugh Drake, a shirttail relative of the Musgrave boys; Sid Moore, formerly a Pecos cowboy named Ef Hillman;

Hugh Drake, one of Van Musgrave's rustlers and a distant relative. Courtesy of the New Mexico State Records Center and Archives, New Mexico Department of Corrections Glass Negative Collection, Inmate #1516.

William S. "Slim" Traynor, a gunman and former bodyguard; cowboy Hank Weathered; notorious Mexican horse thief Onesimo Rios; and a young Texas boy using the name O'Brien.[6]

Drake, a thirty-year-old native of Gatesville, Texas, grew up in McMullen County, then moved with his family to Ozona, in Crockett County, before heading to New Mexico and a brief career as a horse rustler.[7] Intent upon more than just rustling horses, Moore had served as foreman of Joe Hampson's Double Circle Cattle Company in Graham County, northwest of Clifton, Arizona. About thirty-one years of age, Moore stood five feet ten inches tall, with light blue eyes and light hair, slightly balding on top. "A moody morose disposition when he is seated he usually hangs his head and is apparently brooding over some wrongs. His forehead is deeply wrinkled form a continued practice of frowning."[8]

Old-time cowboy Joe McCauley believed Traynor had been a member of the Dalton gang before he drifted into the Arizona Territory and cowboyed in the Sulphur Spring Valley. He had been linked to the January 30, 1895, robbery of the Southern Pacific at Willcox, along with Grant Wheeler, Joe George, and Jeff Yates. Traynor went to Mexico, drifted to the mines around Nacozari, and hired on with

Dan Hughes as a payroll guard. He quit his job in early 1897, rode north, and fell in with Van Musgrave's horse rustlers. Nothing more is known of the earlier careers of Weathered, Rios, and O'Brien.[9]

By late January, the High Fives began to relocate to the Eagle Creek region of Graham County, an area certainly familiar to Van Musgrave's gang member, Sid Moore. The two bands of outlaws must have been in contact with George Musgrave as intermediary. On Saturday evening, January 30, the J. C. Williams storehouse at Chloride, New Mexico, some one hundred miles east of Eagle Creek, was robbed of a large piece of pork and a new pair of boots. Subsequent events confirmed the involvement of Black Jack.[10]

About the same time, Black Jack was suspected of robbing the Jones Brothers store in nearby Upper Frisco Plaza (now Reserve). Hearing a knock on the door one evening, the bookkeeper opened the door to a man demanding some "baccer." Once inside, the masked intruder promptly drew down on the bookkeeper and ordered him into the back room where the safe was kept. Walter Jones, one of the store's owners, was seated there, and the outlaw demanded that he open the safe. The robber grabbed the contents: $180, along with a watch belonging to Cap Mansul, a six-shooter owned by Dan Higgins, and a Winchester lever-action 10-gauge shotgun. Helping himself to a can or two of meat, some crackers, and a box of shotgun shells, he dipped up a large scoop of peanuts and bid the men farewell. The next morning a party of six or seven men trailed the lone bandit by following peanut shells tossed along the path to Spur Lake, near Luna, where the posse lost the trail. The bandit had eaten all of the peanuts.[11]

Throughout the month of February, as the press continued to speculate as to their whereabouts, the gang lay low. On February 6, a Silver City newspaper noted that Marshal Hall had been informed of Black Jack's capture in El Paso. Will Butler of San Marcial identified the prisoner as John "Jack" McDonald. The next day, Hall and Loomis reached El Paso. As neither had ever seen Will Christian up close, they were unable to identify McDonald as the outlaw and returned empty-handed to New Mexico. When officials established McDonald's true identity, they resumed the search for the real Black Jack.[12]

Two days after McDonald's capture, two men held up the Atlantic and Pacific train number 1, eleven miles west of the Peach Springs depot in Mohave County, Arizona, at the extreme southern end of the Hualpai reservation. One man was killed. According to Hall, the hijackers fit the descriptions of Black Jack, George Musgrave, and Tom Anderson. In Denver, the chief post office inspector, William McMechan, expressed his belief that the dead outlaw was Musgrave. The surviving robber proved to be one James Parker, and the man killed in the robbery effort was Jack Williams of Cedar, Utah. Meanwhile, on February 11, at Silver City, New Mexico, a federal grand jury indicted George Musgrave and the deceased Robert Hayes for the October 27, 1896, robbery of the post office at Separ, New Mexico.[13]

While Black Jack allegedly was being captured in El Paso and chased in northwestern Arizona, Will Christian headed south for the American-owned Bull Springs Ranch in Sonora, Mexico. Cattle-buyer Jim Herron had taken some hands down into Mexico and acquired a herd. The cowboys pushed the cattle north toward the Bull Springs Ranch. Herron rode ahead and found cowboys gathered at the corrals. He spotted a well-groomed man at the kitchen door, eating a sandwich. The stranger wore two six-shooters and a full belt of cartridges; Herron thought he might be an officer looking for Black Jack. The man approached Herron, called out in a Texas accent, "Hello, Jim," and stuck out his hand, remarking, "I know you, don't you know me?" Herron apologized for his failure to recognize the man and accepted the stranger's suggestion that he ride back to the herd with him.[14]

Borrowing a horse owned by Sam Hayhurst, Black Jack joined Herron, explaining as they rode along that his family was from Herron's own region of north Texas, Round Timber on the Brazos River, and that he knew Herron's brother Frank quite well. Herron volunteered the information that Frank ranched on the Mogollon Rim, north of Payson, Arizona. Will Christian eventually identified himself to Herron, explaining that he was in hiding. Growing loquacious, he related that his family had settled at Wichita Falls, that they knew nothing of him or his brother except that they were working for a cow outfit in Arizona, and that at the moment he did not know the whereabouts of his brother, Musgrave, or the rest of the gang.[15]

Christian went on to say that he was tired of the outlaw life, and, though the gang had "made some successful holdups, they had not saved any money. He hoped to go straight, get a ranch, and settle down." Seeking a place to lie low, Christian added that he would ride north to Frank Herron's. "I'll dodge through the country and get up there. If I can quiet down, maybe I can outlive it all."[16]

He rode with Herron and his outfit until the herd reached the border, where Herron sent one of his men into Bisbee to buy some clothes for Christian. Dressed in new clothes, Black Jack rode to Shearer's Double Rod Ranch, where Charley Cook, the foreman, let him swap Hayhurst's horse for another.[17]

Christian's trip to Mexico was short; he apparently returned to Arizona during the third week in February. The *Silver City Enterprise* learned that Christian and six companions had crossed the international boundary line from Sonora, where four others soon joined them. The *Enterprise* presumed the six companions were outlaws. In all probability, they were Herron and his outfit. Just as likely, the four riders who joined Christian north of the line were outlaws George Musgrave, Bill Christian (Tom Anderson), with newcomers Van Musgrave (who now adopted the new alias of Theodore James), and Sid Moore.[18]

The authorities in southern New Mexico had closed in on Van and his men, causing the gang to fold. The newly christened Theodore James and Sid Moore now joined forces with the three surviving High Fives. Pinkerton detectives eventually identified the gang members as Black Jack, George Musgrave, Bob Hayes, Cole [*sic*] Young, Bob Lewis, and Sid Moore. Although they overlooked Tom Anderson (Bob Christian), the Pinkertons apparently possessed information that Lewis and James were one and the same, but failed to link either alias to Van Musgrave. Soon after the reconstitution of the High Fives, authorities found a stolen horse in Willis and Walterwax's Corral in Anthony, New Mexico, that had been sold to the hostlers by Van Musgrave. El Paso lawmen also captured Weathered, Rios, and O'Brien, and recovered at least two dozen more stolen horses, destroying the last vestiges of Van's gang.[19]

Speculation about the Black Jack gang's composition was rife. In addition to the reconstituted gang of five, others had drifted around its fringes. Fifteen-year-old Vollie Musgrave, the youngest of the brothers, served his outlaw apprenticeship with the gang, probably as little more than a messenger boy. Daniel M. "Red" Pipkin was another confederate of the gang. Pipkin later rode with Bronco Bill Walters when they attempted to rob the westbound Santa Fe at Grants on March 29, 1898, and was present again at the robbery of the southbound Santa Fe at Belen, New Mexico. Drake, Traynor, and Jim Shaw complete the list of known associates.[20]

The High Fives headed for Hampson's Double Circle Ranch. They did not stay long. A report in early March placed them in the vicinity of a Dog Springs ranch, near the Mexican border. The news prompted the Santa Fe Railroad to increase the number of guards on its trains running from Lamy Junction and San Marcial. They were next sighted at La Joya, a station on the Atlantic and Pacific line on the east side of the Rio Grande, twenty miles north of Socorro. By March 12, presumably after following the Rio Puerco northward to the Rio Puerco station and then paralleling the Atlantic and Pacific tracks, the gang rode north to Valencia County. That afternoon five "tough-looking characters," on stolen horses bearing the CC brand of Louis Hunning of Los Lunas, stopped briefly at Sol Block's mercantile store in Grants before riding south into the Malpais, where they had camped the previous night. That evening their campfire was clearly visible from the town. Block warned the Grants Atlantic and Pacific station agent, who, in turn, advised stations up and down the line to prepare for a holdup attempt. Citizens also wired Sheriff Tom Hubbell at Albuquerque, who ordered his deputy at Gallup to leave with a posse of eight men. Loomis also led a posse out of Silver City.[21]

A Graham County deputy, Ben R. Clark, later claimed that Jim Shaw told him that Shaw, Black Jack, Red Anderson (alias Red Sanders), and one other man attempted to hold up a train. After successfully stopping the train, they found themselves confronted by a large number of armed men, abandoned their plan, and fled the scene. In the aftermath of this debacle, according to Clark, an angry Will Christian shot and killed Anderson, believing this fringe member of the gang to be an informant. There are numerous anomalies in Clark's account. He confused Tom Anderson with Red Anderson, suggesting that Black Jack killed his own brother. Had there been any such attempt, particularly one occasioning a gun battle, there would be surviving press reports, not to mention particulars in the official correspondence of Marshals Meade and Hall. However, New Mexico's former assistant attorney general, Carl Livingston, picked up and popularized the story; it continues to persist without evidence of veracity.[22]

After reaching the Datil Mountains of Socorro (now Catron) County by March 15, the outlaws passed through Fort Tularosa (now Aragon) and stole four horses. Three days later they rode into San Francisco Plaza (Frisco) about midnight and swapped the four fatigued horses for fresh mounts. Probably intending to rob it, they tried unsuccessfully to persuade Bernabel Chavez to open his store.[23]

Meanwhile, on March 12, in the Tucson courtroom of the United States District Court, First Judicial District, County of Pima, Territory of Arizona, a federal grand jury handed down indictments against Black Jack, George Musgrave, and Tom Anderson for the crime of robbery of personal property belonging to the United States, committed during the San Simon post office robbery. The court immediately issued bench warrants for the three outlaws.[24]

Nine days following the indictment, the High Five gang, leaving behind three horses, stole three more horses and killed an unmanageable horse belonging to the WS Ranch about ten miles west of Alma. When three riders from Lincoln County who had been trailing the stolen horses for over a week reached the WS Ranch, they told the ranch manager, William French, that Black Jack was the object of their pursuit and they believed that the rustlers were traveling toward Clifton.[25]

French reluctantly agreed to guide the men to Clifton. The High Fives, believing that the posse would track them into the hills south of the horse camp, waited there in ambush. However, the posse took a direct route for the Mormon settlement of Pleasanton thirteen miles below Alma, assuming the gang would stop there. With pursuit apparently abandoned, the gang rode south to Gila, in Grant County.[26]

The French-guided posse wandered about and reached Clifton late in the afternoon on the next day. French claimed that, on the advice of Deputy Sheriff Cipriano Baca, he took two of the posse and rode up the Blue River toward the Hugh McKee Ranch, near Double Circle country, for possible word of the gang. They arrived at the ranch next morning to learn that three men, driving a number of horses, had crossed the river before daylight, heading toward the Fort Apache Indian Reservation. French and his followers started an arduous ride toward the outlaws' presumed location. They reached Rausensock Creek at dusk and saw an old cabin, about one hundred yards from the trail. After concealing their horses, the men watched and waited. When a man appeared, one of the Lincoln County posse threw down on him. The man reportedly told them that Black Jack had gone into Clifton, about twenty-five miles south, to see his lady friend. The posse spent the night at the cabin awaiting Black Jack's return. According to French, when he failed to appear the following day, they arrested the cabin's unidentified occupant, took the rustled horses, and rode back to the WS, arriving late that night. They had recovered all of the horses stolen from Lincoln, Socorro, and Grant Counties, with the exception of one belonging to Montague Stevens's SU Ranch and four from the WS.[27]

While French was conducting his futile chase, at least four of the High Fives rode from Gila to nearby Cliff, New Mexico, twenty-five miles northwest of Silver City on the stage road to Mogollon.

They arrived about eight o'clock in the evening of March 22. Unmasked, two of the gang, probably Will Christian and George Musgrave, sauntered into William Heather's store and post office. They nonchalantly approached Heather and his clerk, Layton, drew their guns, and asked where the money and valuables were kept. Heather, who was reading a novel, "thought of his hard-earned cash and then of his happy, tranquil life and concluded to sacrifice the former." While one of the bandits kept the two men covered, the other ransacked the post office department, taking $126.70 in money and stamps and an additional $75 from the store's money drawer. In addition to Heather's gold watch, they helped themselves to assorted jewelry, including two gold rings, an opal scarf pin, and a gold nugget scarf pin. They also grabbed two suits of clothes, two hats, two pair of boots, six suits of underclothes, two overshirts, one and a half dozen handkerchiefs, neckties, an ulster overcoat, tobacco, seven pocketknives, and a six-shooter.[28]

Dressed up in their new suits, Musgrave and Christian cordially invited Heather and his clerk to step up to the bar and have a drink. Heather congenially opened his case of Havanas, inviting the men to partake of a cigar. They rejected his offer, preferring to roll their own cigarettes. Checking Heather's gold watch, they decided that they had tarried long enough. Requesting Heather and his clerk to accompany them, the four men walked to the stable, where Musgrave and Christian selected two of the best stage horses, trading the two from the WS Ranch. Heather, finding the weather chilly, suggested another drink, and the bandits produced one of Heather's bottles. After drinking another round, the outlaws took their prisoners a short distance down the river road, bid them good night, and rode south into the darkness. Heather returned to his store and rang up Sheriff McAfee in Silver City, who organized a posse. Deputies Conant and Myers reached Cliff the following morning.[29]

The deputies followed the tracks south along the Gila River for a quarter of a mile, where the outlaws had turned northwest, doubling back on their route. The gang had cut a pasture fence, passed through the hills behind the store, and fled north to the main road near John Fleming's Warm Spring Ranch. From there, they followed the road northeast up Duck Creek, past the White House, and toward the junction of Five-mile Canyon, where they turned west to Mule Creek, twelve miles distant. Conant and Myers kept on the trail, which led through the Cole Creek country and to Eagle Creek in Arizona, where it disappeared, obliterated by cattle herds. The chase was abandoned. The gang had eluded their pursuers, and a frustrated *Silver City Enterprise* questioned, "Where is [George] Waterbury and all the deputy U.S. Marshals that they cannot stop these fellows from robbing U.S. post offices? It looks as if they were all built with a Waterbury movement which takes a long time to wind up and get started."[30]

Meanwhile, the High Fives transferred their headquarters from Hampson's ranch to Charlie Williams's goat ranch on Cole Creek, eighteen miles east of Clifton. It is a fair conclusion that Moore arranged the relocation with Williams, who shared a two-room adobe house with Bill Jones and his wife. About a quarter of a mile to the east of the house, beyond a canyon entrance, was a large cave that served as the gang's hideout.[31]

A week following the robbery of Heather's store at Cliff, Charles M. Paxton of Clifton approached Marshal Hall in Solomonville. Paxton asserted that his friend James Shaw was also Will Christian's friend. Shaw, a resident of Mule Creek and a postal carrier for the gang, had tired of the association, but feared they would kill him if he failed to do their bidding. Paxton told Hall that Shaw would volunteer to lead the marshal and a posse to the outlaws' camp, the condition being that the gang must all be there. Should any escape, Shaw knew he would be killed.[32]

Several contradictory accounts purporting to explain why Shaw sold out the High Fives have surfaced. A contemporary, Jennie Parks Ringgold, related that for some time Shaw, whom she described as a slender good-looking fellow, about five feet eight inches tall, dark-complected, and very witty, had engaged in a love affair with Mrs. Bill Jones. When Jones discovered his wife's liaison and threatened to kill the paramour, Black Jack graciously volunteered to do the job. Shaw feared for his life.[33]

Still another version, that of Graham County Deputy Ben Clark, claims that Black Jack suspected Shaw of having informed on the gang and intended to kill Shaw for his treachery. Clark's story prompts the question: when and to whom did Shaw betray the gang? It is evident that the High Fives had left Hampson's Double Circle Ranch in early March with the intent of holding up a train. They returned to Graham County in late March, having accomplished little more than the robbery of Heather's store and post office. Possibly, they learned of Shaw's treachery during their sojourn. Subsequent events suggest that they also learned the identity of the individual to whom Shaw betrayed them.[34]

Whichever version or supposition is correct, Shaw feared for his life, panicked, and betrayed the gang to Hall. Shaw's motivation was of no concern to Hall, who, though he possessed warrants only for George Musgrave, Black Jack, and Tom Anderson, agreed to give Paxton and Shaw five hundred dollars to lead a posse to the outlaws' camp. Hall then returned to Santa Fe. Meanwhile, when Deputies Ballard and Higgins left Roswell on March 28, the *Roswell Register* reported "their destination not being exactly known, but, the object being to either capture Black Jack or the fellow who is doing so much robbing on his credit." They went to Santa Fe to confer with Hall, who continued on to Clifton to meet with Shaw and Paxton.[35]

While Paxton and Shaw rendezvoused with Hall, the gang temporarily separated. Word reached Deputy White in Tombstone that, after being seen at or near Ruch's ranch in the Chiricahuas following the Cliff robbery, George Musgrave and another of the gang (either Bob Christian or Van), had fled south into Mexico to hide out with Bennett Musgrave. The senior Musgrave, assisted by his son Vollie, supplied beef under contract to the Rio Grande, Sierra Madre, and Pacific Railroad, which was under construction from El Paso toward Chihuahua.[36]

On April 20, Deputy White passed information, together with considerably more misinformation, to Marshal Meade. There were two men named Christian in the gang, he wrote Meade, and they had left for Indian Territory but were expected back at the end of the month to rejoin their cohorts. Interestingly, White had gleaned the correct names of two of the gang members, but did not associate them with either Black Jack or Tom Anderson; he further informed Meade that he had identified Black Jack as Henry Jackson Hinton. Will and Bob Christian's whereabouts in March and April are now generally known; they were not in Indian Territory. It is possible that White's informant indicated that the Christians hailed from Indian Territory and that the deputy assumed that they had briefly returned there.[37]

As the gang began to regroup in April, rumors about their whereabouts abounded. The *Bisbee Orb* maintained that the outlaws encountered Josh Jones three miles west of the port of entry at La Morita. They took Jones's tobacco and told him that they were on the way to Nogales, where they could get all of the money they wanted. Authorities promptly began to prepare for another raid on the Nogales bank. A few days later, reports were received that members of the Black Jack gang were loitering about Deming. The newspapers complained about the ineptitude of the civil authorities and called upon post offices and citizens of country towns to be on guard. "The citizens of the berg [sic] [Deming] have besmeared themselves with war paint and are holding themselves in readiness to give Jack and his followers a warm reception should they attempt to take the town."[38]

From Tombstone, Sheriff White wrote Marshal Meade that Charles Good (alias Joe Cole) had been sent to entice the Black Jack gang to Texas to rob the Galveston, Harrisburg and San Antonio Railroad east of El Paso, where officers would wait to entrap them. Good reported that George Musgrave had told him Willcox train robbery suspect Grant Wheeler was still at a Mexican hot springs recovering his health and would soon join the High Fives. But

Wheeler reportedly had committed suicide two years earlier, on April 25, 1895. A railroad detective, William M. Breakenridge, tracked him to a ranch down the San Juan River near Mancos, Colorado. With capture certain, Wheeler took his own life. It is difficult to believe that two years after the fact, neither the sheriff of Cochise County nor the United States marshal of Arizona Territory disputed Good's absurd story.[39]

Amid the rumors, two gang members revealed their whereabouts on the night of Saturday, April 3. Black Jack and Sid Moore rode up to the well-known rancher George Smith at his Z Bar P Ranch on Alamocito Creek, about ten miles from Magdalena. Smith recognized them and called out, "I thought I left you fellers over in Arizona the other day." One of the men answered that they had ridden over looking for work, and Smith invited them to step down and share supper. After eating, Black Jack strolled into Smith's room and shot him five times. Moore, sitting on a bench in the kitchen, fired at the cook, Frank Melville. Badly wounded, Melville survived.[40]

One observer saw the outlaws riding south after the shootings. His description comfortably fitted Christian and Moore.[41]

Neighbor and court-appointed receiver Montague Stevens offered an explanation for the killing of George Smith. Smith was a former partner of a neighboring rancher, D. C. Kyle. One day, when Kyle was firing at sheep that wandered onto his range, his bullet struck and killed a Mexican herder. Aware that if he were tried in Socorro County, he would face a jury composed predominantly of Mexican jurors, Kyle faked his own murder by shooting his horse and rubbing blood on the saddle. Leaving his wife to sell their cattle, Kyle fled to Montana. Kyle's Mexican neighbors secured an injunction against any cattle sale; Mrs. Kyle appealed to Smith for aid. He assisted in getting the injunction lifted by posting bond in the amount of the cattle's value. The cattle had just been sold when Smith learned that Kyle had faked his death. The bond would surely be forfeited. At that propitious moment, Black Jack stopped at the Kyle ranch and heard Mrs. Kyle's fears that Smith's reaction would cause her husband to be extradited. Black Jack volunteered to kill Smith.[42]

A degraded sense of chivalry on the part of the younger Christian brother seems insufficient cause to warrant his killing of Smith. If, as Ben Clark claimed, Shaw had betrayed the gang, perhaps it was to Smith that Shaw had revealed the gang's purpose, and Smith, in turn, who had informed authorities. If Black Jack and Moore learned of this on their return from Arizona, possibly Smith's death was punishment for his role in the treachery.

On April 7, a deputy sheriff of Socorro County, A. B. Baca, accompanied by County Assessor Cipriano Baca, traveled from Socorro to Magdalena for the inquest on Smith. They continued on to Baldwin's ranch at Datil, where the recuperating Melville provided them with a description of the gunmen and indicated that Smith had known his killers.[43]

The next day, the two Bacas rode to Smith's ranch to examine the scene, then rode west in quest of the gunmen. The morning of April 12, they rode to Clifton, where they provided Graham County Deputy Sheriff Ben Clark with the killers' descriptions. Clark at once identified one of the killers as Sid Moore but committed a critical blunder when he identified the other as one of the Ketchum boys.[44]

In the morning, the Bacas rode to Morenci, enlisted the aid of Graham County Deputy William T. "Crookneck" Johnson, then returned to Clifton that night. On the morning of April 14, the lawmen took a train to Lordsburg, where they learned that the killers had passed through on the evening of April 8, and had stolen two horses twenty-one miles east of town. The Bacas boarded the train to Willcox, hoping to head off the killers before they could make a dash to the Mexican border. When this proved unsuccessful, the officers returned to Socorro on April 18, concluding a long but fruitless search.[45]

By the third week of April, Deputy White's contacts believed that Black Jack and most of the High Fives were near Fort Thomas, and they expected Musgrave to return to the San Simon Valley about the first of May. Almost four months of 1897 had now passed, and the High Fives, once again at full strength, were still pursuing their lawless activities with impunity as efforts to capture or kill them continued to be ineffective.

CHAPTER TEN

BLACK JACK CASHES IN

But, if it's all the same to you, just give to me instead,
The bouquets while I'm living and the knocking when I'm
dead.

LOUIS EDWIN THAYER

Black Jack went into hiding at the remote cave on Williams's goat
ranch near Cole Creek. With him were Van Musgrave and Sid Moore;
equally cautious, George Musgrave and Bob Christian camped
about one-half mile away from the lair, within earshot, and doubtless with a commanding view of the canyon. Black Jack had sent
one of the fellows from the ranch to W. F. Hagan's store in Clifton to
buy two hundred rounds of ammunition of a very unusual caliber.
Christian did not seem to realize that the purchase would attract
attention, but in fact his rifle was known to be the only one in the
area that used such a cartridge. Indeed, so unusual was the round
to be purchased that no two later accounts agreed on the caliber.[1]

   On the morning of April 27, Graham County Deputy Ben Clark
claimed that he had learned of the purchase of some .35-70-caliber
rounds, and he presumed they were for Black Jack because of the
odd caliber. The *Western Liberal* stated that the cartridges were .45-
90. The *Graham County Bulletin* reported that the unique chamber-

ing was .50-95 Winchester Express, identifying the only cartridge among those named that was both extant and uncommon.[2]

"The officers of the county have been wide awake and gathering in all the information possible so that they might know just when they [the gang] did come," reported Clark to Meade. About nine o'clock on the evening of April 27, Deputy Marshal Higgins learned from the traitorous Jim Shaw that Black Jack and two companions had been seen at the goat ranch. This information, along with the news of the cartridge purchase, convinced Higgins to recruit Clark, William T. "Crookneck" Johnson, and William Hart as a posse to accompany him. Missing from the group was Deputy Charlie Ballard, who had returned to Roswell on April 15.[3]

Guided by Shaw and Paxton, the posse left Clifton at midnight and made its way toward Cole Creek. Doubtless, Higgins neglected to inform Shaw that he only had federal warrants for George Musgrave and the two Christian brothers. He was not empowered to take Sid Moore or Van Musgrave. The posse reached the goat ranch about three-thirty o'clock on the morning of April 28. The men left their horses in the brush.[4]

According to Ben Clark's 1930 recollection, Shaw pointed across the canyon down to the cave and admonished Clark, "If you get into a fight, be sure and do business with the big black fellow [Will Christian] or my life won't be worth the price of a sack of Bull Durham tobacco." Then Shaw fled in the opposite direction. Clark's initial report to Meade makes no mention of Shaw's presence that morning. However, Marshal Hall's report to the Justice Department cites Shaw as an active participant in the ensuing action.[5]

The lawmen hiked in the darkness down the northwest bank of Cole Creek Canyon, opposite the caves; the descent, through loose volcanic rock and prickly pear cactus, proved treacherous. They climbed down to a position about a hundred and fifty yards above Williams's ranch house, located at the southwest mouth of the box canyon. Then they watched for the outlaws to put in an appearance. In his report to Meade, Clark said they waited from about two-thirty o'clock in the morning until sunup. The *Graham County Bulletin*

reported that their wait began about 3:30 A.M. In 1930, again con-
tradicting his 1897 report, Clark wrote that the wait was only a few
minutes, a position he probably adopted to avoid having to admit
that the posse was getting ready to return to Clifton empty-handed.
The *Western Liberal*, always ready to deflate official pomposity, did
it for him, reporting that the posse remained in place until "about
seven o'clock in the morning [when] the supply of liquid courage
the posse carried with them ran out."[6]

As the sun rose over the Big Lue Mountains, the weary lawmen
heard voices coming from the ranch house. Moving west some
seventy yards, they spotted three men emerging from the willows
near a spring, close to the posse's original position two hundred
yards below the mouth of the cave.[7]

"Jack was in the lead & presented his gun, when Marshal Higgins fired & they turned to run when the Posse fired 8 or 10 shots,"
according to Clark's report. Thirty years later, Clark had become
more judgmental: "One of the members of the waiting posse [Hig-
gins], being of an extremely nervous temperament, and probably
over-anxious about his personal safety, opened fire on the outlaws
without warning." Awakened by the gunfire, Bill Jones ran out of
the cabin and saw two of the gang fleeing east, up the canyon, as
the five officers ran in the opposite direction. The *Graham County
Bulletin* reported that, following the initial volley and the clearing
of smoke, "The posse did not know whether their fire had been
effective or not and as the outlaws disappeared in the thick brush
and rocks it was not prudent to follow them." At that moment, no
one realized that Black Jack had been shot.[8]

Dee Harkey heard an account of the shooting from one of the
participants and discussed his conclusion during a 1947 interview
with J. Evetts Haley:

> They got into a shooting scrape and they were running and
> shot back—Now, of course, I wouldn't want to tell this to no
> [one]. You know, those fellars are dead. But [unintelligible]
> boy told me, and I believe he told me the truth. That they shot

back over their shoulder—and by God! They killed this boy
Christian and they didn't know it. And didn't know it until
this boy told them the next day by God! After they found
this outfit, they dispersed . . . and left. So they went back over
when things cleared up you see . . . and by God! they'd killed
him. [Interviewer: Who? Christian?] Yea, they didn't know it
themselves. But then they did. [Interviewer's comment: Killed
him in spite of themselves.] Yea, by God![9]

The Parks family provided what is probably the accurate account
of the discovery of the fatally injured Black Jack. About noon, Bert
Farmer was hauling lumber from Ira Harper's nearby sawmill to
Clifton. He stopped to water his team and came upon a dying man
near a water pool. "Some fellows shot me this morning," said
Christian. Farmer gave Christian a drink and Christian muttered,
"There's nothing more you can do now. I can't live much longer."
Farmer responded, "Hell no, that ain't all I can do for you, I can take
you down to that house." Then he dragged Christian to the Williams
adobe, where Christian soon died. Farmer continued on to Clifton
and reported the incident to a member of the posse. "Did you fellows
know that you killed a man this morning?" "Christ no," responded
the posse member. After discussing the matter among themselves,
the posse members offered Farmer seventy-five dollars if he would
return to Cole Creek Canyon and bring the body back to Clifton.
Farmer accepted the task.[10]

In his report to Meade, Deputy Clark glossed over the posse's
hasty retreat. He wrote that Christian had been mortally wounded
during the gunfire and lived about thirty minutes. In his 1930
account, he reduced this to "a few moments." In reality, Clark had
no way of determining the time of Christian's demise because he
and the rest of the posse had already fled from the scene.[11]

The failure of the posse to remain at the ranch and recover the
body explains the telegram sent that day by Higgins to New
Mexico's Marshal Hall. "Clifton, A. T. April 28, 1897—Had a fight
this morning with Black Jack's gang. Killed Sid Moore 18 miles

east of Clifton. Will bring him in and burry [*sic*] him tomorrow. Fred Higgins."[12]

But what had become of Moore and Van Musgrave? Following the brief fireworks, they remained hidden in the canyon, unaware of the posse's retreat. Leonard Alverson later related that Jesse Williams (George Musgrave) and Tom Anderson (Bob Christian) heard the shooting and got away. Evidently they did not go far, since George Musgrave claimed that he stayed in the area another night. Certainly able to see the posse's flight, Musgrave and Christian after a safe interval would have ventured down to the cave, if for no other reason than to determine their brothers' fates. One of the four then left the cave and rode east.[13]

Shortly thereafter, the Rev. G. H. Adams and Clifton merchant Adam Smith passed an unidentified rider racing east on a well-lathered horse as they rode west from Harper's sawmill toward Clifton. The mystery rider, probably Van Musgrave, told them that he was in a hurry to reach Sacaton, twenty-five miles away.[14]

Adams and Smith approached Williams's goat ranch about eleven o'clock in the morning. The three remaining outlaws, still in hiding, spotted the two men and believed them to be returning deputies. As one raised his gun to fire, Moore recognized Smith and called out, "Don't shoot. That man in the gray suit is Adam Smith of Clifton, a friend of mine." Only later did Smith learn from Sid Moore of his close encounter with death. At the goat ranch, an excited Bill Jones informed the visitors, "A man was killed here this morning." Black Jack's body still lay outside the cabin under canvas.[15]

The next morning, after watching Farmer load Will Christian's body onto a wagon, and convinced that the posse would not return, Moore, George Musgrave, and Bob Christian fled the canyon. There are no reliable reports of which routes were taken by the fleeing outlaws. However, the press, with fair accuracy, did determine the identity of the four fugitives, again adding a nonexistent fifth "tough." "Anderson, George Musgrave, the latter's brother Van, alias Bob Lewis, a Grant County cattle thief; Sid Moore; and his partner, an unknown tough, now comprise the party at large."[16]

J. Smith Lea reported that three days after the killing, George
Musgrave, Bob Christian, and Moore were seen at the San Simon
roundup. Although any roving band of riders might have been
identified as the gang, Lea's report bears the stamp of authenticity—they were headed in the right direction. Moreover, Bob Christian and George Musgrave were known to the San Simon hands.[17]
Lea continued: "[The San Simon boys] were well satisfied that the
three men they saw were Musgrave, Tom Anderson [Bob Christ-
ian] and another Pal, though they did not get to talk to them as they
had done at times before when they used to come into their camps
and eat and tell the boys of their raids. This last time they saw them,
they were on the West side of the San Simon range and going into
the Chiricahua mountains."[18]

When Farmer brought his exanimate cargo into Clifton, the lawmen refused to pay for his services. He, in turn, threatened to bury
the body where they could not find it. Mindful that the reward
would go unpaid without the body, the posse members paid up.[19]

With the arrival of Black Jack's corpse, Fred Higgins needed to
correct his embarrassing mistake. "Clifton, A.T. April 29, 1897—A
little hasty in message yesterday morning. Instead of Sid Moore
we killed Black Jack. Have his body in town. Six responsible men
have identified him. What shall I do with the body. Answer at once.
Fred Higgins."[20]

A new controversy arose. Who killed Black Jack? The *Western
Liberal* succinctly explained the situation: "When the officers found
that there was a dead man they were very jubilant and told all
about it, but could not decide who had done the killing. Deputy
Higgins modestly took the honor, and each of the others, with
equal modesty, also took the honor."[21]

Adopting a somewhat pious attitude, Deputy Ben Clark made
his bid in an offhanded fashion: "It will never be known, and it is
not important that it should be known, who the posseman was that
fired the shot which brought to an end the career of this notorious
outlaw. One other member of the posse and myself owned and
used rifles of the same make and calibre. With one of these Black

Jack was killed. The other member being of the disposition that found pleasure in notoriety and public mention, and I being of a temperament that repels such distinction, I naturally and without hesitation, conceded to the other man the credit, if it can be so considered, for the slaying of Black Jack."[22]

Clark's self-righteousness did not fool W. E. Beck of Morenci; Beck supported Deputy Higgins. "To [Higgins] belongs, and rightfully, the credit for killing Black Jack. This is the opinion of all *fair* minded men here, notwithstanding rumours industriously circulated by certain individuals to the contrary. If the posse had followed Higgins' suggestions the entire three would have been killed or captured with Black Jack."[23]

Amid all the claims and counterclaims, three facts appear certain. First, Deputy Fred Higgins fired the first shot. Second, Higgins probably fired the bullet that struck Christian a mortal wound in the right side, just above the hip, and exited the other side of his body, about two inches higher. Third, due to the posse's precipitant flight, none of them knew that any outlaw had been killed, least of all the notorious Black Jack Will Christian. As the *Western Liberal* fairly judged, "The credit in this case really should be given to chance. It was an accidental shot that killed 'Black Jack.'"[24]

At the inquest held at Clifton the afternoon after the shooting, six people positively identified the dead man as Black Jack. Robert Milliken's confirmation that the body was his established beyond doubt that this was one of the Separ robbers. Deputy Fred Higgins identified the body as "the party who was with Hays [sic] and who escaped" from the Deer Creek shootout. Although the man killed at Cole Creek was indisputably the man who had ridden with the gang that had been pillaging Arizona and New Mexico for the previous ten months, to many, a mystery remained. Who was Black Jack?[25]

The difficulty in securing immediately a correct identification and the subsequent confusion concerning that identification can be traced directly to Deputy Sheriff Ben Clark's bias in numbering the Ketchum brothers as part of the High Five gang. At the inquest,

James Speck, a Morenci resident and one of the six called to identify the body, misidentified it as that of Tom Ketchum. Probably
Clark influenced him. Fred Higgins then telegraphed Hall:
"Identified as Tom Ketchum without doubt." Of course, the dead
man was not Tom Ketchum, who was at that very time in Texas
preparing for the May 14 robbery of the Southern Pacific's train
no. 20 at Lozier. In his self-serving article of 1930, Clark noted
that one of the first individuals to view the body, "a gambler
about town who claimed to be a brother-in-law to William Christian," positively identified Christian. Clark knew full well that
the alleged gambler and self-proclaimed brother-in-law, Speck,
was, in fact, the only witness to attach Ketchum's name to the
body. Clark later claimed that when he traveled to Santa Fe to
question the incarcerated Tom Ketchum, he concluded that there
was no reason to mistake the two. He conveniently omitted the
fact that his wrongful assertion to the Bacas that Sid Moore rode
with the Ketchum boys was what provided the foundation for
all the confusion.[26]

Many southern Arizona cowboys knew that Will Christian was
the man killed at Cole Creek Canyon. Edward Wilson, who had cowboyed with Tom Ketchum before he met Christian, said he was in
Clifton and could have identified Christian's body, but knowing
Black Jack had been bushwhacked, "I kept still. I did not want to
see any one receive a reward for a man killed as he had been."
Leonard Alverson, an old-time acquaintance of Christian's, also
learned that it was Christian who was killed, that he was shot in
the stomach, and that the posse "sneaked back into town." Most
significantly, Scott White reported that Jesse Williams (George
Musgrave) had stated that it was Black Jack who was killed. Musgrave also confirmed to Joseph Mack Axford that Black Jack Will
Christian was the man killed near Clifton.[27]

Will Christian was buried at half past three in the afternoon following the inquest with four hundred witnesses attending. Marshal
Hall subsequently requested $66.25 from the Justice Department
for costs of hauling, dressing, and burying the body. Perhaps the

expenses could have been reduced had officers not stolen Christian's possessions. William French remembered that Cipriano Baca later rode to the WS wearing and displaying Black Jack's boots. Baca had taken the boots from the corpse and afterward gave them to Robert Hanna of Silver City, who placed them on exhibition at the Club House. The boots bore the name "Williams" on the side, doubtless the same ones stolen on January 30 from Chloride shopkeeper J. C. Williams.[28]

Curiously, the posse and coroner's jury's description of the dead man agreed with the description on Black Jack's wanted poster—about 190 pounds, six feet high, and about thirty-eight years of age. Yet, in respect of Black Jack's age, the wanted poster erred by twelve years. Almost certainly, the prospect of reward money influenced the findings. Black Jack had been twice indicted for post office robbery. Arrest and conviction would have in each case resulted in a fifty dollar reward. The postmaster general had posted an additional five-hundred-dollar reward "'for the arrest and conviction or for causing the arrest and conviction' of the persons who on October 7 and October 22 last on four occasions held up and robbed the White Oaks–San Antonio mail coach." Since he had been involved in two of the holdups, the reward for Christian was one thousand dollars. Yet another five hundred dollar reward had been posted for the arrest and conviction of George Smith's murderer. Finally, Wells, Fargo offered its usual three hundred dollars. But all these rewards were payable only upon arrest and conviction. The killing of Christian, like the killing of Young and Hayes, resulted in no rewards for anyone.[29]

Arizona's Marshal Meade, in whose jurisdiction Christian had been killed, remained less than convinced that Black Jack's life had ended. Meade knew Black Jack had not been about thirty-eight years old, but between twenty-five and twenty-seven. He also knew that former deputy Bill Hildreth could, from a photograph, recognize whether the dead man was Tom Ketchum. He wrote to Hall, "As soon as you can get a picture let us see it. From all I can learn Black Jack could not be a man 40 years old."[30]

Chief Deputy Loomis telegraphed Higgins to have the dead body carefully examined, measurements made, and photographs of the face taken. Higgins complied, responding that he had taken two good photographs, measurements, and noted any marks on the body. Nonetheless, a month later Hall advised Meade, "I had a very poor photo of the body, but some one got it, but the photo as far as it is, confirms that fact that the man was Black Jack." Meade must have been both dismayed and suspicious when he learned that no photograph would be forthcoming.[31]

Meade continued his efforts. Now he learned that one of Black Jack's fingers on the right hand, possibly the third finger, previously had been caught in a rope and was damaged. Several days later he learned that a bullet, not a rope, had mutilated Black Jack's little finger. Undeterred, Meade next wrote to Brannick Riggs, very familiar with the members of the High Five gang, and sought Riggs's recollection of Black Jack's "age, height, hair, beard, eyes, complexion, teeth and character of special marks." Riggs, who knew Christian well, offered no help and (perhaps intentionally) confused the issue further by describing Black Jack as "a man well met of easy conversation, frequently smiling. He is probably 35 years old, about 5 feet 6 in height, black hair, beard small and dark, teeth good, sound and even, about 180 lbs, overall well built and of good manners. Talked when he left here of going to South Africa."[32]

The original High Five gang had been reduced to two. George Musgrave and Bob Christian remained at large and under federal indictment. Though no federal warrants had been issued for the gang's two new members, Sid Moore and Van Musgrave, officers were out hunting all four outlaws. A week after the killing of Black Jack, Sheriff White reported that George Musgrave, Tom Anderson (Bob Christian), and a man named Blake (likely Sid Moore) were in the Chiricahua Mountains near Galeyville. White believed that two more of the gang were in the Mulberry country. J. Smith Lea's informants had seen three of the outlaws going into the Chiricahuas about May 1. White's source spotted the three in the Chiricahuas about May 4. That same day The *El Paso Daily International*

Times opined, "George Musgrave, aged 23 [actually he was nineteen], and notable for his dash and daring, even when a beardless cowboy in the Pecos River region of Texas, will doubtless assume Black Jack's place as leader." Though the *Times* expressed the opinion of many, there is no reason to assume that the gang's pattern of decision-making by consensus changed with the death of Will Christian.[33]

The two Musgraves and Moore then headed for the security of Bennett Musgrave's camp in Mexico, while Bob Christian evidently remained in the Chiricahua Mountains.[34]

CHAPTER ELEVEN

THE GREAT GRANTS CAPER

Ha, ha, ha, you and me,
Little brown jug, don't I love thee!
Ha, ha, ha, you and me,
Little brown jug, don't I love thee!

George Musgrave's sojourn in Mexico evidently lasted most of May and June. Bennett Musgrave probably entertained Van and Sid Moore as well. Bob Christian's whereabouts at this time are unrecorded; he may have left the Chiricahua Mountains for a hideaway in the upper San Simon Valley at the southeastern foot of the Pinaleno Mountains.[1]

The gang's two-month absence went largely unnoticed by the lawmen and newspapers of the Southwest. Posses regularly pursued false leads and reported their efforts to journalists who, in turn, arrayed the tabloids with spurious rumors. Misinformation placed the gang, inflated to eighteen in number, at Ruch's Triangle Ranch north of Bowie, "ready for all the deviltry that can be cut out for them." The same account accurately revealed "that Black Jack did not masquerade under that [Tom Ketchum] name." However, it implied that Black Jack was still alive.[2]

Gambler Lon Bass, a former officer from Eddy and more recently of Willcox, agreed to keep his ears open and report to Sheriff Scott White anything significant. An unreliable informant, he volunteered, "If that was the Musgrave gang that robbed the train near San Antonio, Texas, a few days ago [May 14] they will likely be back in this country or around Old man Musgrave before long." Secluded in Mexico, Musgrave and his cohorts had not been responsible for the heist of the Galveston, Harrisburg, and San Antonio Railroad. Credit for the Lozier holdup, their pioneering effort, belonged to the supposedly deceased Tom Ketchum, along with Dave Atkins and Will Carver.[3]

Inaccurate reporting continued into July when an error-ridden Santa Fe dispatch reported: "United States Marshal Hall today [July 2] received information from the New Mexico–Arizona line to the effect that the Black Jack band of desperadoes had disbanded and quit the country. Black Jack Ketchum, their leader, who was shot down in April, was the third member of the band to be killed. George Musgrave and Sid Moore have gone to South America, and Red Anderson, the Panhandle tough, is said to have gone to South Africa."[4]

On July 5, Sheriff Scott White provided William M. Griffith, the newly appointed U.S. marshal for the Arizona Territory, with the first reliable information in over two months. The gang had returned from Mexico and set up camp in the Chiricahua Mountains, drifting between Wood Canyon on the eastern slope and upper Turkey Creek on the western. Tracing their movements from the disappearance of horses and food at ranches where they had worked, White concluded by July 27 that the fugitives had left the Chiricahuas, passed through the Swisshelm Mountains, moved across the San Pedro River, and returned to Mexico. He suspected that they would soon return.[5]

On the night of August 13, someone dynamited the Mule Creek home of Owen C. Wilson, in which Wilson, James Shaw, A. Piper, and Carl Ludy resided. The explosion stunned, but did not seriously injure, the occupants. The next day there was a shooting attempt on

William M. Griffith, Marshal
of Arizona, 1897–1901. Courtesy Arizona Historical Soci-
ety/Tucson, AHS #70935.

Shaw's life as he rode between Pine Ciénega and Clifton. Shaw survived; his horse did not. Initially thought to be an act of revenge
against Shaw by the High Five survivors, the bombing and assassination attempt proved to be part of an ongoing range war between
the small ranchers in the Pine Ciénega vicinity, led by John Wilson
(father of bombing victim Owen Wilson) and the large cattle companies of the Gila and Frisco Rivers and Duck Creek Valley, particularly Thomas Lyons's LC Ranch. The *Silver City Enterprise* soon
identified the would-be assassins as Hugh Martin, "Mart" Childers
(father of Lem Childers, foreman of the LC) and J. W. Davis, alias
John "Red" Tully, who had apparently mistaken Shaw for rustler
Shorty Miller.[6]

On August 19, Creighton Foraker, newly appointed U.S. marshal
for New Mexico Territory, forwarded to the Justice Department the
request of Sheriff Holm Bursum for funds for a two-man posse to
track the Black Jack gang, suspected of being the perpetrators of the

Wilson home bombing. The department replied that Foraker could not use federally paid deputies to aid the sheriff but authorized expenses for one deputy if necessary for a federal process.[7]

That same day, Childers and Tully waylaid Shorty Miller near Mule Creek. Miller suffered two leg wounds before he drove the ambushers away. The next day, Deputy Sheriff Baxter Bishop, Edward Moss, Elgin Holt, James Martin, and both Wilsons followed Miller's attackers to Meader Station, close to where Big Dry Creek joined Little Dry Creek. The pursued turned on the pursuers, firing upon the posse as it approached the stream bank. A fatal bullet, fired from behind a clump of trees, passed through the heart of young Moss. The frightened posse fled the scene on foot, neither bothering to take their horses nor to ascertain Moss's fate. Incensed, nearby rancher Agnes Meader Snider chided the lawmen, "Any man or men that would do that, there's no principle to them," and threatened to go to the site, accompanied only by her young son Bert, to see if she could be of assistance to Moss. The shamed posse returned for the body.[8]

In an attempt to divert suspicion from the large ranchers, LC owner Tom Lyons continued to point the finger at the gang: "It is beyond doubt that the Black Jack gang have been harbored in the vicinity of Mule Springs and the saw mill for some time past and not by the LC outfit either. It seems pretty well known that many of the things taken from Mr. Heather's store did not get much beyond the saw mill. It now appears that the officers are watching the situation and are often found in the houses of those people. This makes the Black Jack people very suspicious and jealous."[9]

Bursum again telegraphed Foraker, informing him of the shootings of Miller and Moss, and mistakenly attributing both to the Black Jack gang. The Justice Department then authorized funding for the second posse member. Foraker dispatched Chief Deputy Will Loomis to Socorro to enlist the services of the ever-willing James Shaw and Cipriano Baca. Deputized, Baca and Shaw rode to the Mogollon Mountains via Patterson and Joseph (now Aragon), then into the Mule Springs country before following a trail to Arizona. In late August, Foraker wrote to Baca at Deer Creek (near Cooney) that the Department of Justice would not cover expenses incurred in Arizona. He cautioned, "Keep out of Arizona unless it is absolutely necessary to go there." Disregarding Foraker's instructions, Baca and Shaw followed the trail to near Whittum, Arizona, where it turned southwest to San Simon and then back toward New Mexico's Animas Valley and Mexico. Meanwhile, the confused *Santa Fe Daily New Mexican* exonerated the Black Jack gang from the killing of Moss but erroneously attributed the shootings to a new outfit: Tom Ketchum, Dave Atkins, Tom Anderson, and Bud Upston.[10]

Another posse, made up of Hinton Moss (Ed Moss's brother), Ben Crawford (Moss's uncle), Loosely Harrington, Will Witt, Edward Head, Melvin Taylor, and the apparently recuperated Shorty Miller, tracked Mart Childers and Red Tully. They cornered and killed Childers near his son Lem's house. When they examined the dead man's rifle, they found it was not loaded. Lawmen later captured Red Tully, who, unlike Childers, survived and served time in the New Mexico Territorial Penitentiary.[11]

Meanwhile, as the *Deming Searchlight* had correctly ascertained, George Musgrave and Tom Anderson (Bob Christian) were in the Animas country. On August 23, two supposed gang members rode into Bowie and tried to cash checks and determine the schedule for the train's arrival. According to Sheriff White, "These men however are not any of the original gang but simply recruits." Accompanied by a third, who had not gone into town, the men camped near Bowie that night and rode off the following morning. A day later, the gang was reported to be back in the Chiricahua Mountains. If they were the High Fives, they eluded detection and left the Chiricahuas for Mexico.[12]

By early October, Baca and Shaw had returned to New Mexico from their fruitless hunt for the gang. Baca reported that friends of his near Springerville, Arizona, advised "that it was of no use to follow the gang or hope to get them or any of them, other than by the merest scratch, being that they were harbored fed and kept informed on his (and every other officers) movements by the ranchers and

cattlemen, these parties do this in self defense." Baca believed that
the only way to capture the gang was to "send in a troop of rangers
and scour the country." Shaw, however, vowed that as a sworn
enemy of the gang he would continue the search alone.[13]

Mid-October brought a report that Jim Shaw had been killed at
his home at Mule Creek, five miles east of the site of Black Jack's
death. In response, the *Sierra County Advocate* speculated, "Jim
Shaw is probably alive and will soon turn up with a Black Jack scalp
dangling from his belt. The supposed evidence of his death is now
believed to be a ruse."[14]

The *Silver City Enterprise* supplied the details:

> On Wednesday of last week [October 13] Deputy Sheriff
> Baxter Bishop found a hat and vest, both of which he iden-
> tified as belonging to Jim Shaw, upon the trail between Har-
> per's old and new sawmills. The hat had been perforated by
> a pistol bullet, which went through the brim on one side
> thence through the crown about the middle of the height of
> the hat and cut the brim where it went out the other side.
> The hat was powder burned showing the pistol had been
> held close to it. The vest showed two bullet holes which
> would have indicated mortal wounds to any human being
> wearing the garment. But there was not a drop of blood
> about either article of apparel. The gun had been held close
> enough to the vest to set fire to a box of matches in one of
> the pockets and burned a large hole in the vest. In one of the
> pockets was found a receipt in favor of Jim Shaw. It is a com-
> mon occurrence for bad men to take their boots off before
> dying, but this is the first case on record where one has taken
> off his vest after death. There is decidedly too much of this
> gallery play around this section of the country and it only
> serves to keep up the tension of recent unpleasant excite-
> ments. Wiley Rainbolt who was arrested near the place where
> Shaw's clothing was found, said that he saw a man who

answered the description of Shaw riding away from the place. There were no traces of blood and it is almost certain that Shaw is uninjured.[15]

Just prior to Shaw's reported death, Marshal Foraker had requested approval to retain outgoing Chief Deputy Loomis as an office deputy for at least two months to work secretly on the Black Jack cases. In support of the request, William Burr Childers, New Mexico's U.S. attorney, wrote that the government has a "disadvantage when its officers are compelled to advertise their presence wherever they go in any effort to apprehend such desperate criminals as these and in the section of the country where these out-laws may be found and where they have sympathizers at almost every place." The Justice Department, always parsimonious, denied the request with costly results, as will be seen.[16]

On October 15, Texas Ranger Robert Ross of El Paso penned a letter to Foraker correctly asserting that George Musgrave, Van Musgrave, and Tom Anderson (Bob Christian) were secreted in the Mexican state of Chihuahua. Judge James R. Harper of El Paso verified Ross's news and informed New Mexico's Governor Miguel Otero that the governor of Chihuahua was aware of the presence of the fugitives and "promises an immediate arrest upon presentation to him of proper extradition papers." Governor Otero then learned from Secretary Joseph A. LaRue of New Mexico's Cattle Sanitary Board that the outlaws had been spotted near Corralitas, heading west from Tapiesitas in Chihuahua toward the state of Sonora. Foraker hastily relayed the information to Cipriano Baca. "I have reliable information that 'Black Jack' and Musgrave is in old Mexico at Musgrave's father's ranch, but don't let this information get out. I may have work for you soon." Although new to the office, it seems remarkable that Foraker was unaware of Black Jack's death. Moreover, by the time Baca received this news, Musgrave and his confederates were already on their way back to Arizona, eluding capture once again.[17]

On the evening of Sunday, October 24, three men quietly rode
into Fort Thomas, Arizona. Although twenty-year-old George Musgrave had recently trimmed his mustache, his face sported four or
five days of trail growth. His white hat covered his sandy-colored
hair, but his dark suit failed to conceal his revolver and cartridge
belt. Riding at his side was the only other surviving member of the
original band, Bob Christian, whose craggy face had not seen a
razor for a couple of months. He wore a white hat and a brown
canvas coat, under which could be seen two revolvers and two
belts of cartridges, one for the pistols and the other for his rifle. The
third man, riding behind the other two, was moody and morose
Sid Moore. Most people found him nondescript, save for his light
blue eyes and the bald spot that shone through his blond hair. Not
observed with the others was Van Musgrave, most likely riding in
the shadows nearby, acting as lookout for his companions.[18]

At Fort Thomas, the outlaws stopped at the mercantile and
bought one hundred and twenty pounds of barley, which suggested
that they were preparing for a long and arduous ride, and also
some red silk handkerchiefs, which implied a nefarious purpose.
Well-supplied with money, they tried to pay with a twenty-dollar
gold piece, but the clerk, suspicions aroused, pretended that he
could not make change for that amount. Without hesitation, they
replaced the gold with shiny new silver. They left the store and
crossed the street, and two of them entered Louis V. Voelckel's
saloon, while the third remained outside with the horses and supplies. Inside, the two cowboys treated the other customers to several drinks before they bought three quarts of whiskey for the road,
spending a total of about six dollars.[19]

Later that evening, all four gang members were seen outside of
Fort Thomas, traveling in a southerly direction. Two more days
passed before they were noticed with a newly acquired pack animal in the vicinity of the headquarters of the Norton and Stewart
Cattle Company, near Cedar Springs and Cottonwood Canyon. A
rider who had observed them on the trail later recalled that he had
seen three men with a pack animal turn off the road, while a fourth

man came forward and inquired as to the location of the Cottonwood ranch.

The following Friday in Geronimo, Arizona, Deputy Marshal
Andrew Alexander received word to come to Fort Thomas; another
suspicious character had been spotted in town. Alexander and a
dependable companion arrived just after dark and immediately
spotted the suspect. Convinced that the stranger was a member of
the High Five gang, Alexander placed men in strategic positions
where they could watch developments during the night. Nothing
happened.

The next morning, the suspect saddled up his horse and, when
questioned, told the deputy several suspicious, contradictory stories, adding that he was riding southeast to Solomonville. Alexander firmly believed that the man, who identified himself only as
Monk, was a spy connected with the gang and wrote to Marshal
Griffith that he was "satisfied something is in the wind and some
holdup is in sight." He was right; at that very moment the High
Fives were riding east into the Malpais country of New Mexico.[20]

Rugged and remote, the Malpais had long been a haven for outlaws and renegade Indians. Distinguished by vast lava flows and
forbidding mountains, its rocky terrain provided protection from
inclement weather as well as from pursuing lawmen. The two Musgraves, Christian, and Moore rode east, then north through the desolate region and arrived at Grants on Friday, November 5. George
Musgrave rode into town and bought some canned goods. At least
two of the gang visited the town the next day and were seen in a
saloon; Bob Christian walked into Colonel Solomon Block's general store, purchased a bottle of "Cowboy's Delight," and calmly
strolled out.[21]

At about 7:55 that evening, November 6, the gang's intentions
became clear when they held up the Santa Fe Pacific's eastbound
number 2 train near Grants, seventy miles (ninety-six rail miles)
west of Albuquerque.[22] The train, hauled by Santa Fe's locomotive
number 67, had departed Los Angeles the day before and arrived
about thirty minutes behind schedule to make its routine stop at

Grants Station, a desolate coaling site. When the fireman, Henry L. Abel, jumped off the engine with a can of water to cool a crank pin, Bob Christian and Sid Moore, wearing false beards, boarded the locomotive. Amid a fusillade of twenty to twenty-five shots, a number of stowaway tramps jumped to the ground and scattered in all directions.[23]

When one of the two outlaws on board the engine fired over Abel's head, the engineer, Henry D. McCarty, grabbed a torch and monkey wrench to use as a weapon. As McCarty jumped off the opposite side of the train into the darkness, the second robber fired over his head. With torch in hand, the engineer started to run back to the station house to get a gun, leaving the bandits in full control of the locomotive. Fireman Abel was forced back on board and ordered to pull the train ahead. As the train moved forward, Conductor Aldrich and McCarty "managed to catch the hind end of the Pullman sleeper." In fear of flying bullets, they hid under beds.[24]

Inside the express car, the train's messenger, C. C. Lord, seeing men fleeing in all directions and not realizing that a holdup was in progress, attributed the initial shots to a deputy sheriff's attempt to arrest the scattering tramps. However, when the train began to lurch forward, the station agent shouted and drew Lord's attention to an unknown man near the right side of the express car. Lord took a shot at him and missed. The Santa Fe's own McCarty, running for help, narrowly escaped being shot by his fellow trainman. As the train continued along the eastbound tracks, Lord, now aware that a holdup was in progress, took steps to safeguard the car's contents. He carefully hid the two through safes and the local safe containing cash, jewelry, and waybills. However, he was unable to conceal the combination portable safe.[25]

After traveling approximately two miles, Abel was ordered to bring the train to a halt near Saint's stockyards and water tank, where the gang demanded that Abel separate the locomotive, mail, baggage, and express cars from the rest of the train. As the fireman was uncoupling the passenger and Pullman cars from the train's forward cars, the conductor, Aldrich, emerged from his hiding place, jumped off the rear of the bisected train, and ran back down the tracks toward the station to telegraph Sheriff Thomas Hubbell at Albuquerque and Division Superintendent Hibbard at Gallup. Messenger Lord escaped out of the rear door of the express car into the day coach. He threw his telltale cap under one of the seats, borrowed a hat from a passenger, and waited, expecting each minute that the bandits would come back in search of him to open the car and the safe. He watched helplessly, and doubtless with relief, as the bandits forced Abel to move the detached front of the train farther down the tracks. Lord and the twenty-five passengers were left aboard the remaining cars of the train. One lady poked her head out of the window to see if the bandits were nearby. She heard the bark of a revolver and a western epithet; she hastily withdrew her head and slammed the window shut.[26]

Meanwhile, with a cocked revolver aimed at his head, fireman Abel continued to run the locomotive pulling the other three cars ahead into the darkness. Farther down the tracks, the short train came to a deep cut where George Musgrave was waiting with the gang's horses. Van Musgrave was likely hidden in the darkness, guarding the gang's supplies and the dynamite. Abel was ordered to bring the cars to a halt and then compelled to accompany the bandits back to the express car. Finding the car locked, and assuming that the messenger was inside, they riddled the door and sides with bullets. When this failed to give them access, they touched off three or four sticks of dynamite in an attempt to open the locked door. Two additional charges were required before the door finally gave way.[27]

Once inside the express car, the robbers immediately saw the large Wells, Fargo combination portable safe that was being routed east from San Francisco and Los Angeles. They mounted a dynamite charge onto the safe and sent Abel to the tender to gather some coal to place on top of the dynamite. The first charge blew open the safe to reveal six bags of coins and currency: one routed to Kansas City, three destined for Chicago, and the two remaining headed for New York. After opening a couple of the large bags, they took about one hundred pounds in gold coins, but "left some of the coin because the load was too heavy, and then dumped into their sacks bundles after bundles of paper money. They refused jewelry or silver, scattering such things over the car promiscuously."[28]

The outlaws took their time, spending nearly an hour filling their large sugar bags. While they worked, they pilfered three apples from the messenger's lunch basket, sharing one with the fireman. One of the outlaws pulled forth a bottle of whiskey and cordially offered Abel a sip. After sharing a round, they left the bottle for the engineer. The gang discussed going through the baggage and mail cars but decided they had enough.[29]

The bandits took Abel's name and address and promised to send him one thousand dollars (which they never did). They did tip him about fifteen dollars in coin and told him to get a good meal and have some fun. Shaking Abel's hand, Bob Christian facetiously instructed, "If anyone asks, tell them Old Bill Dalton has come to life again" (later press accounts erroneously substituted the name "Black Jack" for that of Dalton). Then George Musgrave, his brother Van, Bob Christian, and Sid Moore mounted their horses and rode off, serenading the stars with a rousing rendition of "Little Brown Jug." The now-wealthy desperadoes disappeared into the darkness of the Malpais.[30]

The dynamite blast that had opened the safe left express car number 661 afire. After the robbers fled, a badly frightened Henry Abel reversed the engines and opened the throttle. The engine pushed the mail and baggage cars, led by the still burning express car, back toward the remainder of the severed train, still parked near the water tank.[31]

The roar of the returning locomotive alerted the waiting passengers to flee the detached coach before the impending crash. The burning train raced toward the now-empty cars, and the resulting crash telescoped several of them and reduced others to kindling. Lamps and stoves toppled, and flames leaped from the wreckage, destroying two cars. Some baggage and mail were salvaged, and a sleeping car and a Pullman coach were detached from the burning wreckage and shoved out of danger.[32]

The Wells, Fargo express car compressed into a fiery mass when it ran into the day coach. The debris from the crash and refuse from the packages that had been torn open fueled soaring flames. Messenger Lord struggled in vain to remove the two unopened through safes and the still intact local safe from the inferno but the express car doors were partially blocked with burning wreckage, prohibiting their removal. Later, when the safes cooled and were opened, the contents of Lord's local safe were found to have been burned to a crisp. The contents of the messenger's through safe were also completely charred, except for a few pieces of jewelry. Likewise, the only items found in the La Junta and San Francisco through safe that could be salvaged from the ashes were some miscellaneous pieces of jewelry. General store owner Sol Block reported that the dawn's light revealed forty to fifty dollars in gold coins, some badly scorched, on the ground near the site of the robbery.[33]

Once they realized that the safes could not be removed from the burning express car, Abel, McCarty, and Lord, along with others who may have volunteered, worked through the night clearing the track. At eight o'clock the next morning, the crippled train departed, and limped into the Albuquerque station three and a half hours later. Sheriff Hubbell announced to the crew that Deputy Fred Fornoff and the Santa Fe's special officer, Cade Selvy, were following the outlaws' trail in the direction of the Mogollon Mountains. Hubbell reported to the press that Wells, Fargo had received an anonymous tip several days prior to the holdup warning that a train robbery would be attempted by the four members of the notorious Black Jack gang, specifically naming the two Musgrave brothers. Interestingly, the *San Francisco Chronicle* noted that "a peculiar feature of the case is that a tip was supposed to have been received and extra guards were put on. These have been on every train up to within a few days ago." The *Rocky Mountain News* revealed that after several weeks of vigilance, Wells, Fargo had concluded the warning was useless and ordered the extra guards removed.[34]

In Santa Fe, Foraker and a number of newspapers attributed the robbery to the Black Jack gang. The marshal informed the press that the gang had fled south toward the hills west of Magdalena, in Socorro County. He expressed his desire that this robbery, a case of aggravated interruption of the United States mail, would result in the Justice Department promptly providing the "necessary means to prosecute a vigorous and effective campaign against the border bandits." Much of the frustration experienced by law enforcement officers resulted from the nature of the crime. Train robbery, though a capital offense in New Mexico Territory, was not a federal offense and therefore did not fall within the jurisdiction of the U.S. marshal. In a letter dated December 28, 1897, Arizona's Marshal William Griffith asked the attorney general, "In case a railroad train is stopped by robbers, and a robbery of the express car attempted, the mail being unmolested beyond its detention, is it my duty to capture the robbers, or should I leave the matter entirely to local authorities?"[35]

Recently appointed Attorney General John W. Griggs replied, "You are advised that under the circumstances mentioned you should not undertake to make any arrest of such train robbers until you receive proper process commanding you to make the arrest, and that you should not employ a posse until specially authorized by this department."[36]

Foraker's only justification for pursuing the High Fives was therefore predicated upon outstanding federal warrants for mail robbery. The *Santa Fe Daily New Mexican*, unaware of the distinction, took this opportunity to inform its readers, "As it is now, strange as it may seem to the uninitiated, the United States marshal is not provided with any funds to meet such emergencies and must await authority from Washington before incurring the expenses to meet the same."[37]

Marshal Foraker further asserted his frustration with the Mexican government, which resisted any attempts to arrest the gang on its side of the border. He telegraphed the Justice Department, reported the robbery, and indicated that the suspects were the same men whose extradition was being sought from Mexico.[38]

A week later, El Paso newspaper reports commented: "Probably of all the noted gangs of train robbers in the country the Black

Jack Gang is now the most prominent. They are well organized and at their head they have an able man who directs their course and actions, but that man is not Black Jack. He is a man well known in New Mexico and El Paso, but his connection with the gang is known only to a few. He is now indicted and has been sought by the officers for over a year."[39]

Burrell Quimby Musgrave had arrived in Las Cruces six months earlier. It is uncertain whether any jurisdiction had Musgrave under indictment in November 1897, but he was indicted on April 1, 1898, on the charge of unlawfully selling mortgaged property. Tried on October 4, 1898, he was found not guilty by a jury. He also continued his real estate activities in El Paso. While proof is lacking of Burrell's relationship to the membership of the gang, his omnipresence certainly renders him suspect.[40]

Foraker left Santa Fe and traveled to Albuquerque, then on to Silver City where he learned that the gang had gone back into Arizona. Returning to Santa Fe, he surprisingly attributed the holdup to "two or probably three Arizona men whose names are known but cannot be given for the present." Incredibly, the names he withheld were those of James Shaw and Mason "Mace" Slaughter. It is difficult to conceive how Foraker arrived at this astonishing conclusion. One of his two principle suspects, Shaw, allegedly was dead; the other most certainly was: Mace Slaughter had been killed three years earlier. Foraker's opinion was not shared by Marshal Griffith, who informed Attorney General McKenna, "In November last, at Grant Station in New Mexico, a train was 'held up.' The robbers, a part of Black Jack's gang, were tracked directly across [New Mexico] into Arizona. Most of them crossed over the line in Old Mexico."[41]

Foraker contacted Charlie Paxton on November 21, seeking information about Shaw. In a second letter to Paxton written six days later, Foraker pleaded, "Write me if you know the whereabouts of Shaw, as I wish to close his account as soon as possible. Have you seen or heard of him since the late train robbery? Anything you write me will be kept in confidence." There is no evidence that

Foraker received any information from Paxton concerning Shaw. However, Shaw did reappear. He was arrested in Oregon in January 1899, on the charge of participating in the July 14, 1898, robbery of the Southern Pacific's train number 1 near Humboldt, Nevada.[42]

Paxton was concerned that his own involvement in Will Christian's death be rewarded. He had written directly to the Justice Department, noting that he had "not received one cent for [his] trouble," and demanded a reply. Eventually, he received $112.[43]

At the same time he wrote to Paxton, Foraker also wrote to the United States Marshal, District of Utah, and offered his belief that "James M. Shaw, alias J. J. Smith, alias James Stanley, whose real name is William Newberry, assisted by Jas. Bowie (alias Wagner), and one Maj. Riley perpetrated the deed." Foraker's assertion that Shaw's true name was William Newberry, a.k.a J. J. Smith, was not only incorrect but bizarre. On June 7, 1890, three men had robbed the eastbound Northern Pacific near New Salem, North Dakota. Lawmen captured one of the robbers, Newberry, near Philadelphia. Returned to Fargo, North Dakota, on November 12, Newberry was subsequently imprisoned where he remained. At the time of Newberry's arrest, J. J. Smith was behind the walls of the Arizona Territorial Prison at Yuma.[44]

In late November, while Foraker busily penned letters searching for Shaw, the *Winslow Argus* sarcastically commented: "The detectives who are out after the train robbers have returned to their respective headquarters to report to their chiefs. They failed to overtake the robbers, but claim to know who they are and about where they are located. They are experienced sleuths and we suppose know their business. To the uninitiated, however, their plan of action looks peculiar to say the least."[45]

Meanwhile, the newly enriched members of the High Five gang made their way south, gathering friends along the way. By the time they reached La Morita on Tuesday, November 23, reports suggest that the party had grown to thirteen strong. After taking a few drinks, the men continued into Mexico, leaving behind much conjecture concerning the precise amount of money that had been taken from the Santa Fe's eastbound number 2.[46]

Express companies such as Wells, Fargo routinely played down the dollar amounts they lost to discourage future robbery attempts. Additionally, a large portion of the records of Wells, Fargo and Co. were destroyed during the earthquake and subsequent fires in San Francisco in 1906. From the many opinions that were offered, some of the details can now be reconstructed.

The *Albuquerque Morning Democrat* and the *El Paso International Daily Times* labeled the robbery the most sensational in the history of railroading and the most successful holdup in the history of the Santa Fe. The *Democrat* added, "Recent money shipments from the west are known to have been heavy, one messenger estimating the average daily amount at $40,000." The *Santa Fe Daily New Mexican* presumed the amount to be large, "probably reaching thousands of dollars, as it is believed that the large express safes carried unusually heavy remittances from California to Eastern cities." The *San Francisco Chronicle* proclaimed, "It is known that recent money shipments from the Coast have been large, the safe containing about $57,000 a few nights ago." Marshal Foraker claimed ignorance of the amount stolen, but allowed that it was more than one man could carry. The *New York Times* maintained that the gang "helped themselves to a number of packages containing gold and silver coin," and later estimated the loss at $25,000 to $100,000. Yet express agents publicly placed the amount of the plunder at only a few hundred dollars.[47]

On November 22, 1897, Edward P. Ripley, the president of the Santa Fe Railway, learned that Wells, Fargo fixed its losses from the local safe at $1,716.64, this being money from the Arizona and New Mexico stations that was not taken by the robbers but rather was "burned to a crisp" in the fire, along with a considerable amount of jewelry. The railroad assessed the value of its loss, that of the "rolling stock," at five thousand dollars. Ripley, in turn, brought the matter to the attention of Aldace F. Walker, chairman of the board, and included a news clipping reporting the total loss at twenty-five thousand dollars. Walker expressed surprise that the dollar loss of the cars was pitched so low; his failure to comment on the reported amount of Wells, Fargo's monetary loss suggests that it was certainly not overstated.[48]

The primary witness to the robbery, fireman Henry Abel, told a reporter for the *Albuquerque Daily Citizen* that the filled sack was a big load for one man to carry; the highwaymen must have "struck a find amounting to $20,000 and $25,000." However, Abel also told a Santa Fe merchant that the total amount must have been at least $150,000. Forty-five years later, the fireman finally settled on $100,000, a good round number.[49]

Three weeks following the robbery, Sheriff Hubbell provided the press with what must rank as the closest approximation of an official statement of Wells, Fargo's loss. He fixed the sum at ninety thousand dollars, ranking the robbery among the most successful in the history of the West.[50]

While newspapers debated the amount of the booty and lawmen made excuses and wrote letters, the enriched robbers celebrated Thanksgiving Day by uncorking a number of bottles of "the brand of tanglefoot indigenous to the country," and hurrahed the community of Fronteras. Then, "amid a fusillade of shots they proclaimed their identity. When the shooting began the police fled with the other citizens, but after a time returned." Surrounded by over one hundred angry Mexicans, the celebrants were seized and bound hand and foot. When brought before the magistrate, they were found to be carrying more than nine thousand dollars in currency and coin. Undoubtedly, contributing most if not all of the loot to Mexican officials secured their release. However, with the most of the Grants robbery money safely secreted away, the very wealthy outlaws were still able to relax comfortably in Mexico.[51]

Cochise County Sheriff Scott White and his posse, including Wells, Fargo detective Fred Dodge, rode all night to take custody of the Grants robbers, only to learn of their absence. "There was not even convincing evidence that the outlaws had been arrested," bemoaned White, though he judged that they might have voluntarily paid a fine. The *Oasis* concurred, "The Fronteras authorities did not have the Black Jack gang in custody, and consequently did not let them go."[52]

Meanwhile, an outrageous report circulated that Constables Dayton "Date" Graham and William Long of Bisbee, by means of the liberal use of liquor, had lured the gang back, arrested them when they crossed the border, and jailed them in Bisbee. The source of the erroneous account appears to be none other than Constable Graham, who, on November 27, telegraphed Albuquerque's district attorney, Tom A. Finical: "Have effected capture of Jess Williams, Tom Anderson and unknown Grants station robbers. Send necessary papers, warrant and requisition."[53]

Marshal Foraker promptly revised his opinion and asserted that he had no doubt that the Black Jack gang was responsible for the robbery at Grants. In the meantime, Sheriff Hubbell of Bernalillo County traveled to Albuquerque and secured requisition papers to serve on the governor of Arizona. Deputy Sheriff Frank X. Vigil of Valencia County and Deputy Sheriff Fred Fornoff of Bernalillo County took the next train for Bisbee to return the wanted men to Albuquerque. But, unfortunately, Arizona's governor, Myron H. McCord, could not produce what Arizona did not have—the High Fives.[54]

On December 7, Marshal Foraker and a large posse, acting upon information of a pending holdup of the Southern Pacific, boarded a special train provided by the railroad at Deming. The *Silver City Enterprise*, mindful of past failures, quipped, "Let us hope—that the robbers won't capture the posse."[55]

Two days later, Tom Ketchum and associates made an abortive attempt to rob the Southern Pacific train at Steins Pass, resulting in the death of robber Edward H. Cullen. Ironically, many of the reporting journalists fortuitously placed the responsibility for the failed Steins robbery on the High Fives. This robbery attempt, as well as later depredations by the Ketchum band, quickly drew attention away from the true Black Jack gang. Tom Ketchum inherited both the Black Jack moniker and much of the gang's criminal record.[56]

CHAPTER TWELVE

ON THE LAM

Musgraves [sic] *had been guilty of more crimes than "Billy the kid" was ever accused of. These included cattle rustling, bank, train, stage, and post office robbery.*

CHARLES P. STERRETT

United States President William McKinley, in an extraordinary action, signed a warrant in early December 1897 for the arrest and extradition of George Musgrave from Mexico. The warrant also named three other members of the original High Five gang: Code Young, Robert Hayes, and Thomas Anderson (Bob Christian), all charged with the crime of post office robbery. Apparently, the Justice Department forgot, or at least overlooked, its own reports of the 1896 deaths of Young and Hayes. Noticeably absent from the list were Sid Moore and Van Musgrave (Theodore James), against whom there were no federal indictments. Secretary of State John Sherman forwarded the warrant to Attorney General John W. Griggs and authorized Texas Ranger Robert C. Ross to proceed to the state of Chihuahua, Mexico, and take the gang into custody.[1]

On March 9, Powell Clayton, envoy extraordinary and minister plenipotentiary of the United States of America to Mexico, forwarded the request for the arrest of the fugitives and their surrender to the

United States to Mexico's minister of foreign affairs, Ignacio Mariscal. Clayton received the Mexican government's response on March 22: it refused the request to arrest and extradite. Mariscal explained that the United States request lacked the proofs necessary to establish the fact that a crime had been committed, as required by Article I of the extradition treaty between the two countries. The only proof submitted, the testimony of postmaster Robert Milliken, failed to establish "the fact of the commission of the offense in such a manner that the accused parties could be tried had the crime been perpetrated in Mexico." Therefore, Mexico's Foreign Affairs Department would not order detention in accordance with the extradition treaty.[2]

Bob Christian and Sid Moore disappeared from the historical record, though Christian was later seen in Mexico. Musgrave probably remained in Chihuahua through April 1898, when Mexico refused to extradite him, and then roamed freely south of the border. It is equally probable that later that year Musgrave encountered Jim Lowe (Robert Leroy Parker, a.k.a. Butch Cassidy) and Will McGinnis (Elzy Lay) somewhere along the international line. Lowe and McGinnis had joined forces and participated in robberies at Montpelier, Idaho (August 13, 1896), and Castle Gate, Utah (April 21, 1897). In the fall of 1898, they headed for Cochise County where, contrary to the usual winter practice, the Erie Cattle Corporation was hiring hands. Intimate with this four-corners region, Musgrave certainly had opportunity to meet Lowe and McGinnis on the Sulphur Spring Valley range.[3]

About the same time, saloon owner James Herron of Naco, Sonora, began to purchase cattle in Mexico, importing them through Naco. In Naco, Mexican soldiers impounded a number of his best horses, maintaining that they had been smuggled into the country. The soldiers drove the remuda to La Morita. After a number of unsuccessful attempts to resolve the issue with local officials, Herron decided to take his case to the Mexican Federal Court at Nogales, Sonora.

On Saturday, September 9, Herron and his family, accompanied by a number of Mexican soldiers, set off for Nogales, about sixty

Elzy Lay (alias William
McGinnis). Courtesy of
R. G. McCubbin.

miles west. Herron's foreman, Bob Clayton, and Franco, a ranch
hand, followed close behind. After traveling south of the border
for about ten miles, Herron became suspicious when he could no
longer see his foreman and ranch hand. A few miles later he spotted three men riding toward him. Two of the riders stopped some
three hundred yards away while their companion, Harry Ramsey,
rode slowly toward the party. Ramsey, Herron's bartender, pulled
Herron aside. After telling of problems in Naco, Ramsey, lacking
any authority in Mexico, attempted to arrest the Mexican lieutenant in command of the soldiers. The lieutenant started to draw
his revolver, but Ramsey proved faster. He killed both the lieutenant
and the sergeant. The remaining soldiers fled the scene as Ramsey's two companions, George Astin and a stranger, rode up. When
Herron turned his team and whipped them north toward the border, four miles distant, the threesome followed.[4]

As Herron's team tired, the stranger suggested that they stop
and rest the horses. Looking back, Herron spied a column of Mexican soldiers in pursuit and again started the team forward, but the

stranger advised, "Don't get excited, just walk the team for a spell. As soon as those soldiers get in range I'll turn them back for you." When the stranger stepped down from his horse, withdrew a rifle, and steadied it on his saddle, the entire military column turned and headed back toward Naco. Harry Ramsey took the opportunity to introduce the stranger who called himself Burr. Herron's reminiscences later identified Burr as George Musgrave, a conjecture on the part of Herron's editor, a possibility but not a certainty.[5]

Ramsey and Astin, fearing for Herron's safety, offered more assistance. Burr spoke up, "I don't know this fellow, Jim Herron, but I'll tag along to keep you company. This is the sort of amusement I like, anyway." The next morning Burr helped Herron harness his team. He said that he had no special business, and that he would like to stick close to the Herron family to see that nothing happened to them. Herron accepted the offer and Burr stayed around as a self-appointed bodyguard. They drove into the Huachuca Mountains of Arizona and stopped at Tom York's ranch for several days. Satisfied that the Herron family was safe, the man thought to be Musgrave left after rejecting all offers of compensation.[6]

While George Musgrave remained secluded along the border, members of his family continued to make headlines. On March 4, 1899, Vollie Musgrave started his criminal career by rustling five neat cattle. Deputies promptly caught the inexperienced rustler, and he was indicted in Chaves County. On March 31, Vollie filed a motion to demur, alleging a flawed indictment, and subsequently filed a motion for continuance on April 3.[7]

Three weeks later, the Musgraves' brother-in-law, Dan Johnson (alias Thomas D. Mathes), with James Knight, Samuel Morrow, and Charles Ware, rustled six horses and two mules from John Eakin, J. H. Ussery, and Thomas and Sallie Fletcher in Eddy County. On April 26, Eddy County Sheriff Cicero Stewart and posse members Dee Harkey, D. D. Clark, and Silas H. Ussery (a brother of victim J. H. Ussery) set out from Carlsbad in pursuit. The posse trailed the rustlers to the old town of Turquoise, thirty miles south of Alamogordo in Otero County, on the path cut by the El Paso and Northeastern

Volney Campbell Musgrave, taken in Del Rio, Texas, ca. 1899. Courtesy of
the Martha Beth Walker collection.

Railroad line. There, the officers traded their spent horses for fresh
mounts. While there, they encountered Otero County Deputy Tom
Tucker, former foreman for Oliver M. Lee. Tucker, described by Sheriff George Curry as "a real gunman," joined the posse.[8]

Stewart telegraphed Sheriff George Curry at Alamogordo to be
on the alert. In response, Curry took four men and headed toward
Globe Springs, where he thought the outlaws might go for water.
Also notified was Doña Ana County Sheriff Pat Garrett at Las Cruces.
He led yet another posse into the San Andres Mountains in an effort
to head off the rustlers. Neither posse was successful in locating
the fleeing desperadoes. Meanwhile, Stewart and his men continued west across the southern part of the Tularosa Valley and into the
Jarilla Mountains.[9]

At the gold-mining camp of Jarilla (later renamed Brice after a mining supervisor), Stewart arrested a man identified only as Ross. Though Ross was known to have been in the company of the rustlers, Stewart had to release him because he could not be positively identified. The posse was unaware that he was probably Tom Ross (real name Hill Loftos/Loftis/Loftus), a one-time member of George "Red Buck" Weightman's gang and a fugitive from Indian Territory.

The posse left Jarilla, and followed the trail across White Sands to Parker's Well on the eastern slope of the Organ Mountains, near the entrance to San Augustin Pass. During the last days of the pursuit, the lawmen had the fugitives in sight much of the time.[10]

At sunrise on Tuesday, May 2, after six days and over 150 rugged miles on the trail, the Stewart posse closed in on the outlaws' encampment at Parker's Well. The *El Paso International Daily Times* for May 3, 1899, provided the following account of the resulting shootout:

> Sheriff Stewart's posse came up, and when within about 500 yards summoned them to surrender. A volley from the [rustlers'] rifles that came uncomfortably near the members of the posse was the outlaws' reply. While no one was hit several bullets came so close that the sheriff's men knew that the fugitives meant business.
>
> In an instant the fire was returned and continued until about fifty shots were fired, the deputies closing in on the outlaws all the time. The only living object hit was a horse, one of those stolen from Eddy. Seeing that they were cornered with no avenue of escape left open, the fugitives surrendered.

Posse member Dee Harkey, one of the most shameless tall-tale tellers in the history of the West, recalled almost a half a century later:

> The outlaws opened fire on me, using soft nose bullets and 30-30 Winchesters. Those bullets whizzed all around me, one through my clothes, one through my slicker, and another into my saddle horn.

Dee Harkey. Courtesy
Nita Stewart Haley
Memorial Library, Mid-
land, Texas.

When I dismounted, I noticed I was alone. None of my men
were in sight, and I supposed they were all killed. I piled all
my cartridges on the ground in front of me so I could get
them easily and I opened fire on the outlaws. Dan Johnson
and Nite [or Knight] left their bunch and walked toward me,
shooting as they walked. I decided I must kill them or else
they would kill me. I took aim at Nite and fired. Nite dropped
like he was killed. That scared the others, and when Nite got
up, he and Johnson ran back and got in the hole with the rest
of their gang.

Dan Johnson called out, "Dee, we will surrender if you won't
kill us."

Harkey claimed that the outlaws had fired over three hundred
rounds at him.[11]

Cis Stewart's recollection of events was in sharp contrast to Harkey's version:

> Well. [Harkey] made me out the damndest coward on earth over here at White Sands. He was off down there runnin' these boys' horses that they had hobbled out down there, afraid they'd get on some of these horses. And finally when he got through and come up there why me and Tom Tucker had these men already under arrest and disarmed.
>
> [Harkey] is just no good and if he's got ten friends in Eddy County I don't know who they are except his own family.[12]

The captured men were taken to El Paso, where the matter of their identities was the cause of much confusion. The *Daily Times* proclaimed:

> BLACK JACK CAPTURED.
>
> Black Jack, the noted outlaw, leader of the band of train robbers and cattle thieves that have so long terrorized the west is at last in the clutches of the law he so long defied.[13]

The *Daily Times* then went on to wrongly identify Black Jack as the long-sought outlaw George Musgrave. In the newspaper's erroneous judgment, arrested with Musgrave were his brother Vollie, their brother-in-law Dan Johnson, and Tom Ketchum. On May 3, the *El Paso Herald*, unwilling to allow itself to be scooped, agreed with its rival paper that one of the four was certainly Black Jack's brother-in-law, Dan Johnson, and added that the four men were "the remnant of the Dalton gang, noted throughout the west."[14]

The mistaken identification of George Musgrave as one of the outlaws at the Parker's Well shootout drew the attention of Enoch and Jonas Shattuck, principals of the Erie Cattle Company of Cochise County. They wrote to Sheriff Stewart that they, too, were victims of Black Jack's gang and urged him to watch out for three of their rustled horses. Stewart located the horses at Virgil Hogue Lusk's Chimney Wells ranch, twenty-five miles northeast of Carlsbad, and advised Lusk to be on the lookout for anyone coming to claim them. It is doubtful that Lusk, who had formed a friendship with the Ketchums, Dave Atkins, and Will Carver, and often traded horses with them, was startled by Stewart's discovery.[15]

Only one of the men was accurately identified—Dan Johnson, brother-in-law of the outlaw Musgrave brothers. Johnson correctly insisted that none of the captured men was Black Jack, whom he had known, and affirmed that Black Jack had been killed in April 1897. Johnson justified the shooting at Stewart's posse by arguing that, quite naturally, he and his party fired back when fired upon by strangers. He did allow that he had been in many jails, "But this one sets the best table and furnishes better accommodations than any I was ever in. The people in charge know how to treat a fellow right. If I had my choice I'd spend the rest of my life in the El Paso jail." Johnson's hopes were dashed a week later; he and his three colleagues, still misidentified, were transferred to the Eddy County jail in Carlsbad.[16]

When Chaves County authorities visited the neighboring jail, they recognized one of the captured men as Sam Morrow. The lawmen also identified Charles Ware, believed to be the right-hand man of the head of the gang. The leader, using the name Tom Thomas, carried scars that suggested that he had been in a number of desperate encounters. Chaves County officials confirmed that he was not George Musgrave, although Eddy County officials were convinced they were holding a man of some notoriety. At the preliminary hearing on May 11, Thomas waived examination and appeared as a witness for the other three men, testifying that he alone stole the horses, and the other three had merely been in his company. Bond for Johnson, Morrow, and Ware was set at $750; for Thomas, at $1,500.[17]

On May 17, Smith County Sheriff J. S. Robinson of Tyler, Texas, arrived in Carlsbad and positively identified Thomas as the notorious fugitive, James Knight (or Nite). A former member of the Bill Dalton gang, Knight had been convicted for his part in the 1894 robbery of the First National Bank of Longview, Texas, but escaped. Sheriff Stewart and Deputy D. D. Clark took Knight to the Texas State Penitentiary in Huntsville.[18]

Meanwhile, Van Musgrave had returned from Mexico to Texas and was arrested in Cotulla on an outstanding indictment of theft. Sam Morrow made bond in Carlsbad on May 15. The next day, Van, too, was released in Cotulla on bail set at three hundred dollars. Johnson and Ware languished in the Eddy County jail. Nearby, Virgil Lusk maintained his vigil over the horses allegedly rustled by the Black Jack gang.[19]

On August 15, two men rode up to Lusk's ranch house on two of the stolen horses and asked the whereabouts of the third animal. Advised that there was little chance of finding the horse in the darkness, the strangers camped out that evening on a high hill to the north of the house. When the two men settled in for the evening, Lusk rode to Carlsbad and notified Sheriff Stewart of the rustlers' presence. The next day, following a protracted gunfight, Will Carver escaped while Stewart and Deputies John D. Cantrell and Rufus Thomas captured the other outlaw—wanted for his participation in the Colorado and Southern Railroad robbery on July 11 near Folsom, New Mexico—who turned out to be none other than the elusive Will McGinnis (Elzy Lay). Ironically, the false report of Musgrave's capture had indirectly brought about the arrest and later conviction of his friend and future associate. McGinnis was incarcerated at the New Mexico Penitentiary at Santa Fe on October 10, 1899.[20]

On September 13, almost a month after McGinnis's arrest, Van Musgrave was again indicted in La Salle County, charged with the September 9 rustling of a horse belonging to John Dillard. The same day, the court jointly charged Van and Vollie with rustling another horse belonging to Dillard's son, Tom, on or about September 6.[21]

The next day in Carlsbad, the Eddy County Grand Jury brought in five indictments each against Johnson, Ware, and Morrow for larceny of horses, and one indictment each for larceny of mules. Perhaps fittingly, the grand jury also indicted Dee Harkey, one of their captors, for handling his pistol in a threatening manner. Arraigned that night, the defendants, represented by John Franklin and William W. Gatewood, entered pleas of not guilty and gave notice of their intention to file motions for a change of venue to Chaves County. Filed on September 16, the motions were agreed.[22]

In Roswell, the court set a trial date of October 6. Dan Johnson posted $500 bail and was released. On the scheduled date, the court heard the first case involving Charles Ware: theft of one horse (valued at thirty dollars) from Thomas Fletcher on April 25, 1899. The case was considered crucial by the prosecution as well as the defense because the outcome would directly affect not only the five remaining cases against the defendant but also the twelve indictments against Morrow and Johnson. Following two days of testimony, the jury took only thirty minutes to bring in a verdict of guilty. Ware was sentenced to five years in prison. The other five charges against him were dismissed.[23]

When the court called the first case against Johnson, it was discovered he had, in the words of one newspaper, "taken a change of venue and jumped bail," causing the bail of Sam Morrow to be raised to one thousand dollars. Unable to make the higher bail, Morrow, along with the convicted Ware, was returned to the Eddy County jail.[24]

When the case against Vollie Musgrave was also heard on October 6, the court dismissed the charges at defendant's cost. The next day in Texas, the La Salle County Court issued a *capias* (a writ ordering an arrest); Vollie was again taken into custody. A week later, Sheriff William Merrill Burwell of La Salle County formally received custody of Vollie at the state line, Reeves County, Texas, and conveyed him to the La Salle County Jail.[25]

On December 3, 1899, Morrow, Ware, Ed Clarkson, and several other prisoners escaped from the Eddy County jail by digging a hole through the walls. Surprisingly, the Eddy County jail remained vulnerable as only ten days later three additional prisoners also managed to escape. No more was heard of Ware. Morrow (alias Henry Sears) was later captured in Montana, brought back, and convicted in Chaves County on one count of horse rustling.[26]

On February 28, 1900, in La Salle County, Van and Vollie filed a joint motion for a continuance in the cases outstanding against them.

LaSalle County Sheriff William Merrill Burwell (1870–1918), taken in Amarillo, Texas, ca. 1905. Courtesy W. M. Burwell, Jr., collection.

The continuance granted, they posted bond of five hundred dollars each and rode to Del Rio on the Rio Grande to join their mother and their sister, Julia Doak. On March 22, Van filed for divorce from his long-separated wife, Ella; the court granted the decree on April 11. The next month Van married Mrs. Mary E. Remick of Del Rio. The Musgraves immediately moved on and, by June, Van, his new wife, Vollie, sisters Addie and Fannie, and mother Prudie had reached Sanderson, Pecos County (now Terrell County), Texas. Van, presumably using some of his Grants robbery proceeds, went into the hotel business. Van and Vollie failed to appear for the September term of the La Salle County court session and once again became fugitives. With Dan Johnson they fled to California where their brother, George, was now in hiding.[27]

Ed Roberts, George Musgrave's former employer, had sold his OH Ranch in 1897 and trailed a herd of cattle from Four Peaks (ten miles west of present-day Roosevelt Dam) to the Salt River Valley, and he remained in Phoenix at least through March 1898. Jim Herron later implied that Roberts had gone broke "because he couldn't handle the Mexican people." Roberts moved on to San Francisco, where he retired. George Musgrave reappeared with Roberts in San Francisco, where his presence served as a magnet for other male members of his family.[28]

By the time the three outlaws arrived in San Lucas, south of San Francisco, looking for work, almost a year had passed since Dan Johnson jumped bail. Van and Vollie secured jobs with a railroad gang, while Dan went to work for Herman Tompkins on his peach ranch.

On Saturday, September 15, 1900, Constable Joseph S. Dosh questioned the two men who worked for the railroad and became suspicious that they might be felons. After reviewing his papers, Dosh concluded that they might be two of the long-sought members of the Black Jack gang and arrested them both. Later, he released the one who used the name Collins (Vollie), and shadowed him to see what he might do. Vollie returned to work, but after about two hours he drew his wages and traveled on foot to the peach tree-growing country. Intercepting Collins and another man as they prepared to flee, Dosh, recognizing this third man, stopped him with, "Hold on, Dan, I want you." Dan Johnson, using the alias W. W. Wright, pulled his hat over his eyes and attempted to escape, but stopped when he caught sight of a revolver. Dosh was not fooled when the three claimed to be southern Californians and strangers to New Mexico.[29]

Dan Johnson was described as "42 years old, 5 feet 10 1/2 [actually 5 feet, 11 1/4] inches high, and of light complexion." Dosh identified Collins as Volney Musgrave, "21 years old [he was actually nineteen]," and appeared to have Indian blood. The third, James Taylor, was said to be about "28 years old [actually thirty-four], 6 feet 3 inches high, dark," and also looked Indian. Dosh failed to realize that James Taylor, alias Theodore James, alias Bob Lewis, was, in fact, Van Musgrave.[30]

On September 21, Sheriff Stewart and Sheriff Fred Higgins of Chaves County arrived from New Mexico at the jail in San Lucas. Johnson's cell was opened to exclamations of recognition. Johnson confessed to all.

> If I could have gone undetected I would soon have been across the ocean. You, Joe [Dosh], have treated me white, and I tell you everything. I would have killed you the night you arrested me, if I had had my gun. I fear nothing that walks or breathes under the broad heavens. No man dare stand against me single handed. I'm afraid of none of them.
> I stood off Sheriff Stewart for a hour and a half. I was shot at over thirty times, but escaped. I am Dan Johnson of Black Jack's gang.[31]

The next day, Sheriffs Stewart and Higgins left for New Mexico with Johnson in tow. As there were no known outstanding New Mexico warrants naming Volney Musgrave or James Taylor, they were released. Understandably, Stewart and Higgins were unaware that Van (Taylor) and Vollie were still wanted in Texas. [32]

In New Mexico, Johnson pleaded guilty to a single count of horse rustling. Sentenced to a two-year term, he entered New Mexico Territorial Prison on April 28, 1901.[33]

Two days earlier, northeast of Santa Fe in Clayton, Tom Ketchum was hanged. Authorities had captured the lone outlaw after his single-handed attempt to rob the Colorado and Southern Flyer, and he was convicted of felonious assault upon a railroad train, a

Dan Johnson (ca.
1859–1922). Courtesy of
the New Mexico State
Record Center and
Archives, New Mexico
Corrections Department
Records, neg. #1419.

capital offense. Reporters gathered at the hanging site and heard Ketchum insist, "There are a dozen men in southern Arizona who will swear that I and Black Jack are two different persons."[34] Ketchum continued in vain:

> I am not Black Jack and never was a member of the gang. Bill Ludley [Lutley], who lives in southern Arizona, in Cuchaza [Cochise] County, knows Black Jack. Ludley worked for Bert Cogsdale [Cogswell], and they know Black Jack well. John Bankey knows him, and I believe nearly all the Erie cowboys know him. The cowboys in south Arizona nicknamed him Black Jack. His name was Jack, and he was of very dark complexion, and they called him Black Jack to distinguish him from another party of the same name. I know his real name but I won't tell it. He held up the Wauchugle [Huachuca] Siding, and held up the Arizona [Atlantic] and Pacific, I think, a couple of times in 1897, I think. No; I am not Black Jack, and not the man who committed the depredations in the name of Black Jack.[35]

For once, Ketchum was telling the truth. They hanged him anyway.

With George, Van, and Vollie Musgrave in California, their sister Addie ran the hotel in Sanderson. Sister Fannie (Mrs. Dan Johnson) worked with her, cooking and waiting tables. On July 9, 1901, Fannie boarded the Galveston, Harrisburg and San Antonio train to travel to Santa Fe for a visit with her imprisoned husband. When the train stopped briefly at Marathon, Fannie moved to the top of the steps to stretch her legs. The train suddenly lurched; she fell to the ground, suffering serious injury. On August 27, 1901, she filed a successful lawsuit against the G.H. and S.A. Railway.[36]

Dan Johnson served five months of his two-year term before Governor Miguel Otero pardoned him on October 8, and Dan rejoined his recuperating wife in Sanderson. Van and Vollie also returned to Texas. Van took a job in El Paso working for the G.H. and S.A. Railway.[37]

L/r: Jerome McCowen "Roamie" Walker (1869–1960), Joseph Henry "Buddie" Walker (1866–1933). Courtesy of the Martha Beth Walker collection.

Adanna "Addie" Musgrave Parker (1868–1946). Courtesy Byrd Lindsey.

In 1902, Vollie and Addie Musgrave accompanied their mother to Arizona, along with their uncles, Joseph H. "Buddie" Walker and Jerome M. "Roamie" Walker (alias Billy Heywood), Buddie and Roamie's families, and an old ranch hand named Alexander. They drove roughly two hundred head of cattle from New Mexico to Cochise County and the San Bernardino ranch of John Slaughter.

Julia Musgrave Doak Rae. Courtesy of the Martha Beth Walker
collection.

Bennett remained behind for a short while to settle affairs. Burrell
Quimby Musgrave joined the family and became a major real estate
dealer, developing Douglas's Musgrave Addition.[38]

The Bennett Musgrave family continued west and leased some
land south of the Mustang Mountains near the Babocomari grant.
Nearby, Canelo rancher William A. "Uncle Billy" Parker, Jr., was a
widower in his early forties raising six children. Parker periodically moved his herd from Lyle and Korn Canyons south to Parker
Canyon on the border, and then north to grazing lands near the
Babocomari. Inevitably, in that sparsely populated country, the
widowed rancher met the Musgrave's daughter, Addie. Following
a brief courtship, the two were married on July 30, 1905. Addie's
new stepdaughter, Pearl, was married to Frank Bennett Moson,
nephew of Ed Roberts of the OH Ranch and stepson of Colonel
William C. Greene. Moson, manager of the Greene Cattle Company, provided employment for his brother-in-laws, Jim and John
Parker. He likewise exercised influence in securing positions for
some of the Musgraves with Greene's Cananea Cattle Company,
south of the line. Soon Van was working at the Cananea and resid-
ing in nearby La Bota, Sonora, Mexico.[39]

Fannie Musgrave Johnson Patrick and her second husband, John Patrick. Courtesy Byrd Lindsey.

George's sister Julia and her husband, Boyd Doak, were the next in the family to move to Arizona, settling in Bisbee. Soon after their arrival, on August 23, 1905, Boyd enlisted in the Arizona Rangers at Douglas. He lasted little more than a month before he was discharged for drunkenness and disobedience.[40]

Dan and Fannie Johnson also migrated to Arizona where, using the names Tom and Fannie Mathes, they settled in Santa Cruz County and bought the Rain Valley Ranch near Elgin.[41]

As his brothers and brother-in-law encountered trouble in the Southwest, and his family gathered in Arizona, George Musgrave returned from California and took advantage of the security offered by the border and Mexico.

CHAPTER THIRTEEN

SHACKLED

She cast an eye on Little Musgrave,
As bright as the summer sun;
And then bethought this Little Musgrave,
This lady's heart have I woonn.

"LITTLE MUSGRAVE AND
THE LADY BARNARD"

On his return from California, George Musgrave operated a large saloon in Chihuahua City. When Frank King met up with him there, Musgrave had assumed the name George Mason. The surname was one he used periodically during the first decade of the century, sometimes with George, at others times with Ed, R. W. (Bob), or Harry. King's recollection of the Mason alias gives credibility to his account, although he incorrectly placed the meeting in 1907, when in fact it must have occurred prior to the spring of 1906, after which Musgrave's whereabouts elsewhere are well documented.[1]

King's was not the only sighting of the outlaw. Also in the early 1900s, a childhood friend, Marvin Powe, found Musgrave working for the T4 outfit in Texas's Big Bend country. Neither of these meetings can be precisely dated, but it is evident that Musgrave, well aware that he was a federal fugitive, stayed in Mexico or close to the border.[2]

Thomas Hardee Walker
(1887–1957) and Pru-
dence Walker Musgrave
(1846–1923). Courtesy of
the Martha Beth Walker
collection.

Following his sister's marriage to Bill Parker in 1905, George's
parents moved to a secluded cabin in Korn Canyon, just north of
the border. Their home, located near the Parker's Canelo ranch
house, made it convenient for George to ride unobtrusively up the
rugged, overgrown smugglers' trail for frequent visits. In April
1906, Arizona Ranger Porter McDonald scrawled a letter to the
sheriff in White Oaks, New Mexico, to ask if there was a warrant
and, of course, a reward for Musgrave on the charge of murder.
McDonald had learned of George's furtive visits to Canelo.[3]

George Musgrave worked intermittently on Colonel Greene's
Mexican land holdings. Frank King claimed that Greene backed
Musgrave in stocking a ranch some four hundred miles west of
Chihuahua City. On June 1, 1906, dissatisfied miners walked out at
Greene's Cananea Consolidated Copper Company. Superficially,
the miners' wage demands appeared unjustifiable, as the Porfirio

Díaz government controlled Greene's pay schedule. However, it became evident that Mexican radical leaders in the United States led by Ricardo Flores Magón, Antonio I. Villereal, and Librado Rivera, founders of the Mexican Liberal Party and publishers of *Regeneración*, intended to use the Cananea protest as an excuse to launch the first revolutionary strike against the Díaz regime by attacking Greene's company.[4]

When he realized what was happening, Greene, in turn, vowed he would be no pushover. His stepson, Frank Moson, later related the specifics of the battle fought by him and by Greene and half a dozen cowpunchers, including George, Van, and likely Vollie Musgrave, along with Moson's brother-in-laws, Jim and John Parker (the Musgrave brothers' step-nephews).

> The two biggest fights took place when we turned the mob back the first time and when I and six other cowpunchers made our stand on the railroad at the end of the big bridge between the Mesa and Ronquilla.
>
> The governor of the state attempted to address the mob. His bodyguard had quite a tussle with some of the hombres who attempted to shoot the governor. When W. C. Greene started to talk, however they all listened, and abided by what he said. He told them of how he commenced as a common miner and had developed the property from a rock pile to the second largest camp in the world; that [as] he and the camp had advanced, their wages had likewise been advanced. His speech was what really decided them to go home and think it over. All of the fighting that was done was between the mob, W. C. Greene, myself and a half dozen cowpunchers after the fireworks at the lumber yards. Three whites and one hundred and ten Mexicans were killed.[5]

Soon after the Cananea battle, George Musgrave shifted his operations north. The South American adventurer Aimé Tschiffely wrote that Musgrave had a serious dispute with George Lewis "Tex" Rickard at Goldfield, Nevada. On July 30, Rickard was instrumental in the formulation of the Sportsmen Club, which on September 2 staged the world lightweight championship bout between Joe Gans and Battling Nelson. Swelling the community's fifty-four saloons, fifteen thousand outsiders came to Goldfield; perhaps Musgrave was among them. Aimé Tschiffely only reports that, as a result of the dispute with Rickard, Musgrave was "chased into a neighboring state by the police," and that he later "made a public vow that, if ever again he came across Tex, he would shoot him full of holes." The Goldfield press appears to have considered neither the circumstances of the dispute nor the threat itself newsworthy. However, a report that soon placed Musgrave gambling at Dalhart in Texas's Llano Estacado, again well removed from his traditional border haunts, lends credibility to Tschiffely's story.[6]

In February 1907, Creighton Foraker received a telegram signed by one J. A. Franklin, who claimed to be a deputy sheriff of Dallam County, Texas. Franklin informed the marshal that George Musgrave had been seen in and around Dalhart. Foraker promptly wrote to William Henry Harrison Llewellyn, United States attorney for the Territory of New Mexico, to seek an alias warrant and certified copy of the indictment in case number 1183, *The United States v. George Musgrave*. Interestingly, Llewellyn responded that "in 1901 the case was stricken from the docket with leave to reinstate." Having quickly moved to reinstate the case, Llewellyn filed a *praecipe* with the clerk of the Third District Court in Silver City, requesting an alias warrant and copy of the indictment.[7]

In the meantime, Foraker had advised George H. Green, United States marshal for the Northern District of Texas, of Musgrave's presence in Dalhart and of the federal charges outstanding against him. Green's deputy went to Dalhart and discovered that Musgrave had left town several days earlier. George had been working with several of the Rock Island section gangs along the railroad and, on paydays, had taken their money at the gambling tables. Green's response to Foraker's information must have shocked the New Mexico marshal. It appeared that J. A. Franklin was not a deputy sheriff, but was actually a relative of Musgrave's, more than likely George's cousin James A. "Gotch-eyed Jim" Franklin, who, together with Musgrave, had wired Foraker, evidently having a bit of merriment at Foraker's expense.[8]

Though he was long gone, Musgrave's name remained before the public in and along the border of Arizona. On July 19, 1907, Arizona Ranger Lieutenant William Olds and Ranger Sergeant Jeff Kidder believed they had George Musgrave trapped at the cabin of a man named Henderson, three miles from Patagonia in Santa Cruz County. After rushing the cabin, they found Willis Woods, recently extradited from Los Angeles to stand trial for the robbery of the Huachuca post office and currently free on bail. They also discovered the man who had been representing himself as George Musgrave crouched beneath a table, hiding under some saddle blankets. After investigating, the Rangers learned that they had Vollie Musgrave in custody; he was still wanted on the seven-year-old warrant from La Salle County, Texas. Apparently, not satisfied with his own reputation, the youngest Musgrave had been claiming that of his notorious brother. He was transported to Tombstone via Naco on July 26, and held in the Tombstone jail pending extradition.[9]

On August 2, alert guards thwarted Vollie's plan to break jail and to free fifty-five other prisoners, after discovering that the mortar surrounding the bricks under the barred window had been replaced by soap. The sheriff of La Salle County, W. T. Hill, delayed by bad weather and train schedules, did not arrive from Texas to take custody until August 18, just in time to block Vollie's release under a writ of habeas corpus. Returned to Cotulla on August 31, Vollie posted bond of $750 and promised to appear before the court on October 7. There is no disposition of the case, and it may be assumed that he again jumped bail and returned to Arizona and more misadventures. Meanwhile, officers still believed that the real George Musgrave was in Arizona, and they continued their search.[10]

Even as the Arizona Rangers sought him in southern Arizona, Musgrave left the Texas Panhandle, bound for Alma, New Mexico, and a reunion with Elzy Lay, who had permanently adopted the alias Will "Mac" McGinnis. New Mexico's Governor Miguel Antonio

Otero had commuted McGinnis's life sentence for the 1899 murder of Deputy Edward J. Farr. Released on December 15, 1905, Lay had returned to Alma before Christmas. Described as a "nice fellow to talk to and a nice fella to meet," Mac stayed with Lewis and Walter Jones of Jones Brothers general store for the next eighteen months.[11]

Musgrave arrived in Alma soon after his late February 1907 departure from Dalhart, Texas. The extent of their prior planning is unknown, but shortly after George's arrival in Alma, he and Mac bid good-bye to New Mexico and headed up the Outlaw Trail. A man using the name Jack Dempsey accompanied them. After traveling north along the banks of Utah's Green River, they reached Vernal, where McGinnis looked up his ex-wife, Maude, and his daughter, Marvel. When Mac learned that Maude had remarried Oran Curry, he, along with Musgrave and Dempsey, continued northeast through Brown's Park to the remote community of Baggs, Wyoming.[12]

In the summer of 1872, George Baggs had determined that the broad and well-watered valley of Wyoming's Little Snake River would be a fine place to winter a herd of cattle. The following spring he trailed two thousand head from New Mexico into the valley, registered his Double Eleven brand, and filed a homestead. Ranchers and settlers followed and soon founded the community of Baggs, four miles north of the Wyoming-Colorado border. The geographical features and climate made the valley attractive to stockmen; isolation made it a haven for outlaws. From the rugged country of western New Mexico, through Utah's Robbers' Roost, north through Brown's Park, and to Wyoming's Hole in the Wall, outlaws trekked largely unimpeded. Baggs lay along the Outlaw Trail, and, during the summer of 1907, Mac McGinnis introduced George Musgrave (using the alias Bob Cameron) and Jack Dempsey to the lively town.[13]

Mac went to work for Lycurgus "Kirk" Calvert on the latter's ranch along the Little Snake River, one mile east of Baggs. Later, he may have tended bar in town. During the winter of 1907–8, he contracted pneumonia, and Kirk Calvert's daughter Mary nursed him back to health. During McGinnis's convalescence, he and Miss Calvert became romantically involved. In spite of her parent's disapproval of the relationship, Mac and Mary eloped to Thermopolis, Wyoming, where Justice of the Peace J. W. Calloway married them on March 27, 1909.[14]

Meanwhile, Dempsey, a twenty-three-year-old native of California, joined a Carbon County gang of rustlers. On or about September 9, 1907, Dempsey allegedly stole a horse from Jake W. Hildebrand. He was jailed in Rawlins on February 1, 1908, but a jury acquitted him on March 12. Unreformed, Dempsey continued his larcenous ways.[15]

On August 15, he stole a horse from the Beeler brothers of Carbon County. Two weeks later, at Whiskey Gap near Independence Rock, he rustled eight horses from Albert A. Harper's 47 Ranch. Harper went after his stolen horses; their trail headed south toward the Bitter Creek desert. At Rawlins, Harper enlisted the aid of Sheriff E. M. Horton, and the two continued south toward Baggs. At Shell Creek, they caught up with Dempsey, and Horton arrested him. Harper recalled:

> We got our dinner and our man and all struck out for Baggs. We were halfway to Baggs when dark came on us. We found a cabin and stayed there all night. The next day we went to Baggs, and while eating dinner the sheriff was trying to get some pickles out of a jar, and was holding it up fishing for the pickle when Dempsey jumped up and says, "I'll quit you fellows," and dashed from the dining room into the kitchen. Horton, the sheriff, and I were right after him in the street and we shot at him. One bullet grazed his temple and knocked him down. He got up running, but we captured him right away.[16]

Two days later, Sheriff Horton and Harper reached Rawlins with Dempsey in custody. On October 5, 1908, Dempsey pleaded guilty to stealing a horse from the Beeler brothers and received a two-year sentence in the Wyoming State Penitentiary. With time off for good behavior, he was released on July 4, 1910. The day following his release, he was arrested for rustling Albert Harper's eight horses. A jury convicted Dempsey on December 2; he was

Jeanette "Jano" Magor
(1889–1976). Courtesy
The American Heritage
Center, University of
Wyoming, copyright
restricted.

sentenced to not less than three or more than five years. As Dempsey's fortunes waned, Musgrave's improved. Mary Calvert introduced George to her closest friend, Jeanette E. "Jano" Magor, the
orphaned daughter of Tom and Eliza Magor.[17]

Thomas H. Magor (1848–1898) and Eliza J. Edwards (1851–1903),
met, married, and had their first four children in their hometown
of Hazel Green, Wisconsin. They moved to Corwith, Iowa, about
1880, where their next three children were born. In 1887, Tom's
older brother, Richard C. Magor, a successful mercantile and liquor
entrepreneur in Rawlins, Wyoming, called upon Tom to assist him
in expanding business. Tom moved his family to Baggs, sixty miles
south of Rawlins, where Jano was born on February 24, 1889. The
Magors' last child, Harley, arrived the following year. Tom operated the Magor brothers' general store and ranched. Eliza founded
a boardinghouse on the west side of Penland Street between Via
and Howard Streets. The boardinghouse provided various tasks
for the Magor children.[18]

Jano's childhood was not all work. At the age of four or five
she took up singing at the local Episcopal Church. Her debut was

inauspicious. She commenced her song in the wrong key. Undaunted, young Jano backed up, bowed to the audience, and started over, in the proper key. As youngsters, Jano and her friend Mary Calvert demonstrated precocious entrepreneurial skills when they decided to found a laundry to serve some of the town's more unsavory visitors. The business was quickly forced to close when the girls encountered a pair of long-handled underwear "so black in the seat, [they] decided it was easier to trim away the offensive blemish than to scrub it away. Their customer took exception to his freshly ventilated underwear, and the girls abandoned their enterprise."[19]

Growing up in Baggs had its unique brand of excitement. During the winter of 1896–97, Harry Longabaugh (Harry Alonzo/Sundance Kid) and Robert Henry "Bert" Charter established their winter camp on the Lower Snake River. The next summer, Butch Cassidy and other members of the so-called Wild Bunch arrived in Baggs, making the new Magor boardinghouse their headquarters. While Jano's older sister Maude waited tables, and made eyes at Charter, Jano methodically calculated the sum of the outstanding rewards being offered for the family's nefarious guests. One of the town's most famous soirées unfolded during the summer when Butch Cassidy and some of his associates celebrated a recent misadventure with whiskey, women, song, and dance. The death of old Dick Bender during the festivities resulted in Cassidy forming a kangaroo court in which the gang tried a local physician on charges of malpractice and general moral depravity resulting in Bender's untimely demise. Other distractions brought the trial to a premature conclusion. The revelry ended, the outlaws acquitted the doctor, settled up all accounts, and rode out of Baggs.[20]

Tom Magor passed away on May 12, 1898, survived by his widow and all the children. When Eliza died on March 3, 1903, Jano became a fourteen-year-old orphan. Her brother William, ten years older, petitioned successfully for appointment as her guardian. Within a few years, Jano and Mary Calvert were off to Denver to attend business school. Eighteen-year-old Jano returned home, a five-foot, six-inch, auburn-haired beauty with dazzling green-eyes. When her friend Mary introduced her to George Musgrave, she quickly captured the affections of the handsome outlaw.[21]

Local history in Baggs indicates that Musgrave, having been given money by an unidentified local rancher for the purchase of cattle in eastern markets, departed the Wyoming community forever, neither returning the money nor purchasing the cattle. Although no evidence exists to confirm that rumor, one thing is certain: George did depart with one of Baggs's prizes—Jano Magor. Surviving legal documents suggest that the two eloped. They married in Denver on November 2, 1908.[22]

Possibly George and Jano would have chosen a different location for their wedding had they been aware of an event occurring more than two months earlier that put the law back on his trail. On August 25, 1908, John Bradley, alias John Brennan, shot and killed Denver policeman William H. Stevens in the fashionable University Park section of Denver. Before he died, Stevens killed his assailant's horse, and investigators traced the dead animal to its owner. After Bradley's arrest, a newspaper headline announced, "Slayer of Denver Policeman is Jeff Davis." The paper went on to describe Davis as the cowboy with the meteoric career as a badman, gunfighter, and outlaw in Sierra and Grant Counties who had left New Mexico some years previously.[23]

A United States deputy marshal asked Henry Brock of Apache Tejo whether he knew Jeff Davis. When Brock said yes, the deputy asked, "You'd know him if you saw him?" "Yes, I'd know him. I wouldn't forget him," Brock replied. "Well, you're the man we want," the delighted lawman announced. "We've got a man arrested up in Denver and we're pretty sure that's who it is but we want somebody to identify him." "Well, I dont know that fella," announced Brock. "You know I can take you up there," the irritated deputy threatened. "That's right, sure, but, by God, you can't make me know that that there's Jeff Davis," Brock fired back. The lawman blustered about for a while but received no further cooperation from Musgrave's former boss.[24]

In the end, it proved to be a case of misidentification. George Musgrave, alias Jeff Davis, was not implicated in the death of Stevens, a crime for which John Bradley was convicted and sentenced to thirty-five to forty-five years. Nevertheless, the deputy's death resulted in renewed efforts to capture Musgrave, and now the Pinkerton Detective Agency entered the hunt. Previously only mildly interested in Musgrave, the agency had misinformation on him in its Dalton Gang file. In response to an appeal by Denver's sheriff, the famed agency took up the pursuit, seeking Musgrave under the aliases of Bob Cameron, Bob Mason, and Bob Murray. Whether Musgrave ever employed the moniker Bob Murray is open to question, but the Pinkertons were getting warm—it was as George W. Murray that he married Jano in Denver.[25]

The Pinkerton hunt intensified. According to Jano's nephew, Boyd Charter, "When she left home, the Pinkertons were all over, many characters came to the ranches in Pinedale, [and] Jackson [Wyoming]." The Musgraves eluded the detectives; George took his bride to meet his sister Addie, who was then working at Hereford, Arizona. Following their return from Arizona, George and Jano settled in Grand Junction, Colorado, as Mr. and Mrs. R. W. "Bob" Mason. George became an upstanding member of the community and a member of the local Brotherhood of the Paternal Order of Elks #575.[26]

In October 1909, George, in town to dispatch a trainload of steers to Omaha, was recognized in Grand Junction by Frank Parks, a cattle buyer and the man who thirteen years earlier had brought the word to Roswell of the shooting of George Parker. Musgrave, aware that he was being watched, strolled up to Parks and said, "Got me spotted, ain't you?" "I'd a'knowed yore hide in a tan yard," responded Parks. According to Red Moon McBride of the Turkey Track outfit, Parks, who was then working for a Denver meatpacker, "was a one-eyed Irishman; but with that one eye he could see a brand plumb through a critter. He told me about recognizing Musgraves [sic]. If Parks said it was Musgraves, it was. He was the derndest cow thief I ever seen, but I never knowed him to be mistook."[27]

Having been spotted, Musgrave sent Jano back to Baggs for a temporary stay; the two made plans to reunite on his return trip from Nebraska. "Jano was followed by Pinkertons after she came back. She was watched in Baggs. She took a train east to Nebraska, doubled back, and met Cameron [Musgrave] on the train. They then caught him."[28]

Musgrave's old pursuer, Charlie Ballard, now sheriff of Chaves County, had learned of Musgrave's whereabouts and alerted police officials in Omaha. Somehow, Musgrave found out that Ballard had contacted the city's officials. Musgrave secured charity tickets for himself and Jano through the Omaha Elks, suggesting that he conned the local lodge into assisting him to leave town. The Musgraves boarded Union Pacific's train number 15 bound for Denver. Officers missed him in Omaha and telegraphed communities along the route to Denver, forewarning them.[29]

On Thursday, December 30, 1909, L. L. Miltonburger, sheriff of Lincoln County, Nebraska, accompanied by policeman Coates, arrested Musgrave aboard the train near North Platte, Nebraska. Musgrave had picked an inauspicious time to travel through North Platte. The city was welcoming sheriffs from throughout the state, gathering for their annual convention. Described by the North Platte newspaper as being over six feet tall and about two hundred and fifty pounds, Musgrave reluctantly identified himself as John Stoner, maintained that he was not wanted for any crimes, and otherwise had little to say. Jano was allowed to proceed on to Denver. Aware that he could share in a reward of approximately five thousand dollars, Miltonburger telegraphed Ballard to come get the fugitive.[30]

Ballard, his destination cloaked in secrecy, left Roswell for Nebraska the next morning. The *Roswell Daily Record* reported, "Sheriff C. L. Ballard left this morning for Colorado, where he has official business to look after. He will go to Denver and remain until after the National Live Stock Convention, which meets January 11." Ballard reached North Platte on January 2, 1910, and took custody of Musgrave, who now identified himself as R. W. Mason.

George Musgrave, alias Harry Mason, prior to assaulting *Rocky Mountain News* photographer Ralph Baird. *Rocky Mountain News*, January 4, 1910.

Declining to cause an extradition fight between Nebraska and New Mexico, he claimed that he wanted to return to Roswell to clear up his legal difficulties. Ballard and his prisoner boarded the train for the return trip to New Mexico.[31]

During a forty-minute stopover in Denver, as Ballard led the handcuffed Musgrave through the depot entrance, *Rocky Mountain News* reporter Ralph Baird moved forward and snapped Musgrave's photograph. A few minutes later, Baird strolled into the waiting room where Musgrave and police officials had gathered. Musgrave spotted Baird and suddenly, reaching out with his handcuffed wrists, grabbed Baird under the chin, lifting the news photographer completely off the ground. As Baird dangled frantically in midair, Musgrave kicked at the photographer's equipment in an effort to destroy the camera, the photograph, and quite possibly the photographer himself. Ballard and local police officials wrestled

Musgrave to the ground, sparing Baird and his accoutrements further harm. The photograph likewise survived. Ballard hustled Musgrave back onto the Fort Worth and Denver train, headed for Roswell, and the overdue trial of George Parker's killer.[32]

CHAPTER FOURTEEN

VINDICATED

Jury Instruction 43:
The character of the deceased is a proper matter for your con-
sideration, and you should give it such weight as you deem
proper in determining, under the evidence, defendant's knowl-
edge of deceased and in determining whether deceased by his
acts at the time of the alleged killing gave defendant reason-
able cause to apprehend danger such as to justify such killing
on the grounds of self-defense, according to the law upon that
subject as stated in these instructions. The mere fact, how-
ever, that the deceased was a man of bad character, if you
believe from the evidence he was of such character, will not of
itself justify the taking of his life.

JUDGE WILLIAM H. POPE,
Territory of New Mexico v. George Musgrave

Sheriff Charlie Ballard and his prisoner arrived in Roswell on Monday evening, January 5. As they neared the station, Musgrave
implored, "Charlie I want you to do me a favor. I wish you would
take these handcuffs and shackles off. I will give my word that I will
not try to escape. Let me go around the crowd and speak to my old
friends. This will help me at my trial." Demonstrating remarkable

trust in his prisoner, Ballard complied. In Roswell, the anticipated throng of Musgrave supporters had gathered to welcome their old friend. Those who met him, most of whom had not seen him in thirteen years, found that "the boy of thirteen years ago, [was] now a man of 29 [sic], over six feet tall, broad and heavy for his build, and, as many have said quite handsome." The unfettered prisoner circulated and greeted those he had not seen in many years before rejoining the sheriff to whom he expressed his thanks and announced, "I am ready to go to jail."[1]

Within twenty-four hours, public sentiment had begun to swing toward Musgrave. The *Roswell Daily Record* remarked that, up until this time, Musgrave's accusers had circulated all the information. Now, people heard new accounts of what might have led up to the shooting of George Parker. Many saw the issue in a different light, indeed "some even make him almost blameless in the affair." Roswell's other major newspaper, the *Register-Tribune*, concurred. "Since the killing, the smoke has had a long time to clear away, and the feeling against [Musgrave] is not near so bitter as it was immediately after the time the act was committed. The case was during the time of the cowboy days, when it was considered that a difficulty between men meant which one could get to his pistol the quickest, and this will be a strong plea by his attorneys, that it was done in self-defense."[2]

Taking advantage of the shift in public opinion, Musgrave agreed to be interviewed by a reporter from the *Daily Record*. He related that he had spent most of his years since leaving New Mexico headquartered in Denver, buying and selling cattle. He also noted his membership, under the alias R. W. Mason, in the Elks lodge of Grand Junction, Colorado. The reporter described the prisoner as a jolly fellow, adding that Musgrave claimed, "You would hardly believe it, but it is actually a pleasure for me to come back and see men I knew years ago, and talk of the others who were here in those days." Musgrave, obviously laying foundations for his defense, said that he was approaching his thirtieth birthday. In fact, he would turn thirty-three on May 27, but there was a reason for the untruth. If the people of Roswell, and ultimately a Roswell jury, believed that he was only twenty-nine, then they would presume that he had been only sixteen at the time of Parker's killing. The charming and deceitful George Musgrave concluded the interview insisting that he never had any connection with the Black Jack gang, had not carried a firearm or weapon of any kind for many years, had been living a square and honest life, and had always planned to return to Roswell to clear up this outstanding charge.[3]

For his defense, Musgrave employed William W. Gatewood of the firm of Gatewood and Graves. Gatewood enjoyed a successful career, along with a somewhat dubious reputation. Dee Harkey later maintained, "For a while, before law enforcement officers worked together, and before judges took to changing venue, the lawyers could clear nearly any criminal they defended. One W. W. Gatewood gave a lot of trouble. [He] was known by all criminals as being a lawyer who would frame his witnesses to testify in their behalf. He was as hard as nails and equally sharp." Musgrave also hired attorney O. O. "Ott" Askren for his legal team.[4]

While in jail awaiting the preliminary hearing, Musgrave entertained new friends and old. Frank Young, son of deputy sheriff and jailer C. R. Young, visited him a number of times, bringing with him Cecil Bonney, the son of C. D. Bonney (whom Musgrave had intended to kill, along with Parker). Once, when the issue of Parker's killing came up, Musgrave asked about the health of the elder Bonney and indicated that he would like to see and talk with C. D. When told of the invitation, the elder Bonney refused, saying, "I have nothing in common with George Musgrave, and I do not care to see him or talk to him."[5]

On January 24, in the absence of William H. Pope, judge of the Fifth Judicial District, the preliminary hearing was held in the judge's chambers with New Mexico's attorney general, James Madison Hervey, presiding. Chaves County prosecutor Louis O. Fullen represented the territory. Hervey set a trial date of May 27, and Gatewood filed a motion for bail. The Territory stipulated to bail in the amount of ten thousand dollars, which Judge Pope approved through telegraphic communication. Musgrave posted bail and returned to Denver to get Jano. The *Albuquerque Morning Journal* reported, "He will go at once to Denver and bring his family here to live." Diamond A cowboy Harry Aguayo more specifically stated, "In the meantime he had married and had a child one year old. His wife and child came with him to the trial."[6]

On April 18, the 1910 United States census taker in Chaves County enumerated George and Jano as childless and as renters of a home on South Kentucky Avenue. There is no evidence that they ever had a child. It is not outside the bounds of possibility that the wily Musgrave borrowed a child in order to evoke sympathy from the jurors.[7]

Concerned that Musgrave would disavow any association with the Black Jack gang, and that his defense would, in part, hinge upon his being portrayed as a legitimate businessman outside of New Mexico, the prosecutor, Fullen, took steps to undermine such a tactic. On February 22, he contacted the inspector in charge of the Denver Post Office Department to inquire whether he had any information that would definitely connect Musgrave with either the Separ or Steins robberies. The same day, Fullen wrote to Marshal Creighton Foraker seeking information that might assist the prosecution in connecting Musgrave with the 1896-97 operations of the Black Jack gang.[8]

Surprisingly, Foraker relayed his conviction that Musgrave was not involved in the only Black Jack matter of which he was aware, indictment no. 1183, the robbery of the United States mail at Separ on October 27, 1896. He overlooked indictment no. 1174 for the July 11, 1896, postal robbery at Separ and appeared to be unaware of the outstanding federal indictment no. 1255 for the November 2, 1896, San Simon postal robbery in Arizona. Foraker explained that the only Separ witness, Robert Milliken, had died. Astonishingly, he believed that the guilty party was Daniel "Red" Pipken, a member of Bronco Bill's band of train robbers. Fullen had to prepare a prosecution of Musgrave based solely upon the evidence; the jury would be precluded from considering a prior pattern of criminal behavior.[9]

Foraker's neglect proved a boon to Musgrave, but was countered by the March 8 death of prospective defense witness Hamp Collett, following an operation for stomach cancer at Hamilton, Texas. Formerly the foreman for the Circle Diamond outfit, Collett had testified at the original inquest that when Parker made a move for his gun, Musgrave beat him to the draw.[10]

Another witness to Parker's shooting, Austin Reeves of Chaves County, related that his brother-in-law, Frank L. Strickland, sold his cattle and ranch at the head of the Rio Felix, two miles above the big spring, as preparations for Musgrave's trial continued. The buyers? Charlie Ballard and George Musgrave! Reeves, who ran some cattle on Strickland's land, "got well-acquainted with George Musgrave while he owned that ranch." Although he described Musgrave as "one of the nicest men you ever saw to meet and talk with," his recollections also attest to a lack of trust. "I went over there and worked with George Musgrave for four or five days gatherin' my cattle. When I got 'em all gathered, why it was so late I didn't have time to cut 'em out and take 'em home and I sold 'em to George Musgrave and I figgered I'd be gettin' a bad check if I didn't get it cashed and the next morning I come to Roswell and cashed that check for my cattle."[11]

Although Chaves County records neither support nor refute Reeves's contention that Musgrave was Charlie Ballard's partner in the purchase of Strickland's ranch, they do suggest that something was afoot. Musgrave purchased a house at 410 Michigan Avenue from Lee and May Ella Fountain on April 5, but did not reside in the house. On April 18, the 1910 census enumerated them as renting a home on South Kentucky Avenue, four blocks east and a number of blocks south of the Michigan Avenue house. Three days later, George and Jano sold the property to the sheriff's brother, Chaves County probate clerk and recorder Richard Ballard, soon to be subpoenaed as a defense witness. The property sold for the same amount of money paid the Fountains, four hundred dollars.[12]

On May 10, seventeen days before the start of the Musgrave trial, Frank Strickland did, indeed, sell his 451-acre ranch to Charles

Ballard. That same day, Strickland also purchased twenty acres from Charles Ballard. The price for each of their acquisitions, one dollar and "other valuable considerations," strongly suggests that the exchange of two decidedly unequal parcels involved some other consideration of substantial value to someone, perhaps Musgrave. Eight days after the sales, a Chaves County deputy served Strickland with a subpoena as a defense witness.[13]

On July 8, 1910, despite the fact that he had sold the Michigan Avenue house to Richard Ballard, Musgrave borrowed six hundred dollars from Strickland, using the property as collateral. The following day, the county recorder, Richard Ballard, who did own the house, properly recorded the transaction. According to Reeves, "My brother-in-law was on [Musgrave's] note. He and Jack Browning [another defense witness] and Bruce Morris, I believe it was, was on his note and they had to pay it." On November 14, Ballard filed a quitclaim deed on the Michigan Avenue property in favor of Frank Strickland in return for one dollar. The Chaves County official record, in relating an obviously incomplete story of transactions involving Strickland, Musgrave, and the Ballards, and neglecting to specify the nature of "other valuable considerations," supports the essential correctness of Reeves's assertion. There is little doubt that Charlie Ballard and George Musgrave were partners in the acquisition of Frank Strickland's ranch prior to Musgrave's trial, at best an unusual connection between sheriff and accused.[14]

The trial, with Judge William H. Pope presiding, commenced with jury selection on May 27, 1910. Due to the razing of the old courthouse and the incomplete state of its replacement, the trial took place in the Malone Building, between 1st and 2nd Streets on the west side of Main Street. Of the thirty-six names drawn for a special venire, only three jurors were seated, necessitating the calling of a second venire. The next day, the court impaneled a jury of solid Chaves County citizens.[15]

The prosecution delivered its opening statement on Saturday afternoon, May 29. The jury was informed that Musgrave was being tried under an indictment which charged that on October 19, 1896, he did deliberately and with premeditation effect the death of George T. Parker, by inflicting upon him "three mortal wounds each of a depth of nine inches and of a width of one inch." At the conclusion of the defense's opening statements, Sam Butler, the cook for the roundup camp on the Rio Felix and the prosecution's first witness, took the stand.[16]

Butler recounted his version of the shooting, but admitted that he could not hear the conversation which had preceded it because he was peeling potatoes some distance away. However, when he continued with his testimony the next afternoon, Butler testified that after the shooting Musgrave admitted, "I came all the way from Mexico to shoot that son of a bitch." Butler's account provided the prosecution with the element critical to the foundation of their case—premeditation.[17]

Richard F. Ballard followed Butler to the stand, testifying that he had seen Musgrave the morning of the shooting but was out chasing stray horses at the time of the affair. Will Marable, next to be sworn in, also related that he was not present at the time, but that Musgrave and a stranger had stopped at the Marable ranch later that day. The visitors had cleaned their guns, and Musgrave, aware that his saddle might be recognized, said that he had traded it for Parker's saddle.[18]

At the conclusion of Marable's testimony, the trial "took a sensational turn" when the prosecution announced that it had located its key witness, William "Billy" Phillips, formerly of Roswell and currently working in the mines of Globe, Arizona. Phillips, who had accompanied Parker into camp, identified Musgrave as the aggressor and reiterated Butler's statement, attributed to Musgrave: "I came all the way from Mexico to shoot that son of a bitch." Again, the jury heard the crucial confirmation of premeditation.[19]

Ed Marable was on the stand when the judge adjourned the afternoon's proceedings. Following the jury's departure, Pope issued a startling ruling. Based upon the testimony of the prosecution's witnesses, Pope presumed the possibility of premeditation, revoked

Musgrave's ten-thousand-dollar bail, issued an alias warrant endorsed "no bail," and ordered Musgrave remanded to jail.[20]

Ed Marable returned to the stand on the morning of May 31 and confirmed Will Marable's testimony that Musgrave and a stranger had ridden to their ranch and had told them that he had traded for George Parker's saddle. Charlie Ballard, the sixth and final witness to be called by the prosecution, testified that Musgrave had been arrested in Nebraska using a different name, but had later admitted his real identity.

With the completion of the prosecution's case, Lycurgus "Curg" Johnson was called to the stand as the defense began its presentation. Johnson (sometimes referred to as Kirk Johnson) had come to Roswell just prior to the shooting and had worked for the Bloom Land and Cattle Company at the time of the incident.[21]

In the witness box, Johnson painted a picture completely at odds with that of the prosecution's star witnesses. He testified that, because he had been standing between the spot where Musgrave stood and the vantage point of Butler and Phillips, he was closer to the scene of the shooting. He said that he saw the quarrel between Musgrave and Parker, and Musgrave had not been the sole aggressor. Moreover, he said he did not hear Musgrave remark that he had come all the way from Mexico to kill Parker. The most important portion of his testimony came when he insisted that he saw Parker's hand drop to his pistol just before Musgrave shot. To the jury, this must have been particularly persuasive since Johnson had no apparent reason to favor Musgrave's cause. After all, it was his saddle, along with that of the deceased Parker, which Musgrave and Hayes had seized. At noon, as Judge Pope dismissed the jurors following Johnson's testimony, it was revealed the zealous Fullen had lost his voice due to acute laryngitis.[22]

At nine o'clock the next morning, June 1, eyewitness Les Harmon took the stand. Perceived by the press as a strong defense witness, Harmon confirmed most of Lycurgus Johnson's testimony, though he had not seen Parker's hand drop to his pistol just prior to Musgrave's shot. He too had not heard the defendant say that he had come all the way from Mexico to kill Parker. He had heard Musgrave state that he hated to kill Parker, but that he had to do it.[23]

Doubtless, at this point attorney Gatewood would have been more than delighted to call the late Hamp Collett to the stand to confirm Johnson's testimony that Parker had reached for a gun. Supernatural assistance being unavailable, the wily defense counsel nevertheless managed to place so much of Collett's presumed testimony before the jury that Judge Pope subsequently found it necessary to instruct them "that what any witness at this trial may have testified to what Hamp Collett may have told him as to the facts of the alleged killing is not evidence of such fact and may not be so regarded by you."[24]

The defense next put Lucius Dills into the witness box. Dills testified that the bullet hole in Parker's head was in the center of the forehead. J. A. Purviance and Dr. W. T. Joyner supported Dills's testimony, eliminating any suggestion of back-shooting.[25]

Continuing their effort to counter the prosecution witnesses, Gatewood called Mark Minter to the stand to impeach the testimony of Sam Butler. Minter, a member of Ballard's posse on the day of the killing, testified that Butler had told him that he had not heard Musgrave say that he had come all the way from Mexico to kill Parker. Minter's testimony was followed by that of Ed Bryant, who also addressed the location of Parker's wounds.[26]

The defense then called Jack Browning. Gatewood's questioning clearly sought to impugn the reputation of George Parker, and James M. Hervey, conducting the Territory's case while Fullen recovered from his bout with laryngitis, objected on the grounds of relevance. Judge Pope heard a long argument from the attorneys as to the admissibility of the evidence Gatewood was seeking to adduce. After a ruling for the defense, Browning's testimony continued.

Charlie Ballard, now appearing for the defense, as well as Frank Strickland and Joe Taylor, testified to Parker's reputation as a quarrelsome and dangerous man. Strickland further stated that one of Parker's hands rested under his body, near his gun. William T.

Arnold next attested that Parker had written a letter to Musgrave "telling Musgrave not to come back or he, Parker, would make it hot for him."[27]

When the trial resumed on the morning of June 2, the defense recalled Sam Butler and William Phillips. After posing accusatory questions to the prosecution's witnesses, Gatewood recalled Minter to further impeach Butler and Phillips. Taylor also returned to the witness box for recross examination on Parker's character. The defense then rested its case.[28]

Following the prosecution's recall of Sam Butler for rebuttal, the taking of evidence concluded at eleven o'clock in the morning. Musgrave did not take the stand in his own defense, though he had stated his defense through the press.

> I was only a boy of fifteen [actually seventeen] when Parker jobbed me. He traded me stolen horses for my cattle and then advised me to skip the country. I went away, returning in a year and a half to find that Parker had taken all my mother's cattle, telling her falsely that he had given me five hundred dollars to get out of the country, for which he was to receive the cattle. I heard the report that Parker had threatened to kill me. I went to see him, however, about my mother's cattle. As soon as I appeared Parker slid his gun belt around so it was handy. It was only when Parker dismounted and reached for his six-shooters, however, that I shot him.[29]

After the luncheon recess, the court reconvened at two o'clock. Judge Pope announced that each side would be allowed up to three hours to present its closing arguments. Ott Askren opened the summation for the defense, followed by attorney Gatewood. Musgrave's attorneys portrayed Parker as a dangerous man who had threatened to kill the defendant and given the defendant reason to fear Parker. Furthermore, they declared that the killing was done on "the spur of the moment in self defense," and closed by pointing out to the jury that Musgrave had lived an upright life during the years since the event.[30]

The next morning, Hervey began the summation for the prosecution, followed by Fullen, who argued that the killing was premeditated and without warrant, "a cold blooded deed." Judge Pope excused the jurors while the attorneys devoted much of the afternoon to argument over the judge's instructions to the jury. One of the more critical of these concerned the evidence that had been presented regarding Bob Hayes's presence at the shooting. If the jury decided that a conspiracy existed, then the acts by Hayes would be evidence against Musgrave. The instructions also said that the flight of the defendant could be considered in determining guilt and clarified the definition of justifiable homicide. Perhaps most significantly, the judge instructed the jury that the character of Parker was a proper matter for consideration when determining whether Musgrave had reason to believe that he was in such danger as to justify self-defense. Pope refused to include a defense-sought instruction that any motion of the hand constituted assault. Late in the afternoon, Judge Pope moved the case to members of the jury, and they retired to their deliberations.[31]

The jury returned to the courtroom at eight o'clock in the evening, after only thirty minutes of deliberation. Foreman Jake Cummins read the verdict of not guilty. Apparently the passage of time, the negative character of George Parker, and the testimony of Curg Johnson had convinced the jurors that Musgrave had acted in self-defense. Juror W. M Heitman related that the real evidence was not enough for conviction, "It was foolish to try Musgrave with no proof." Will McBride concluded, "If I'd been on that jury I'd of give George Musgrave a medal."[32]

An Albuquerque paper headlined the trial wrap-up with, "Plea of Self-Defense Wins Out in Case in Which Cowboy Was Charged With Killing Cowman." Observer Frank Jones agreed, "Any man who would get a boy into trouble and then rob his mother, 'orter be killed.'" Charlie Ballard later wrote, "It seemed to me that they had plenty of witnesses and evidence to convict him of murder in the first degree; however, the jury turned him loose."[33]

In his "Reminiscences," Ballard gave his family, who would neither understand nor approve, the impression that he believed Musgrave, his real estate and business partner, ought to have been convicted. However, the testimony of the sheriff, as well as that of
Browning, Strickland, and Taylor, along with Pope's instruction
that the jury could consider Parker's character, unquestionably
tilted the scales of justice in Musgrave's favor and facilitated his
acquittal. In the opinion of John Cox, "The sheriff, Charley Ballard,
I know Ballard pretty good, by god he taken the stand for him
[Musgrave] and, by god, they cleared him."[34]

Following acquittal, the *Roswell Register-Tribune* editorialized:

> No one had gained friends more quickly than [Musgrave]. The
> real cowboy days have gone from this part of the territory, and
> Musgrave but a youth of about sixteen [*sic*] and the large
> portly man that he has grown into are entirely two different
> characters. Those who considered him at that time a real ban-
> dit were the first to see what the outcome of such a character
> really was, and they were the first to go to his rescue to help
> him out. A sympathetic strain ran through the hearts of a large
> part of the citizens here and the verdict of the jury was a very
> satisfactory one to a large majority of the people.[35]

Press reports, editorials, and subsequent recollections do not
adequately substitute for the opportunity to sit in the courtroom,
to scrutinize the defendant, to listen to the witnesses, to evaluate
the attorneys' arguments, and to ponder the judge's instructions.
Nevertheless, two facts remain certain. One, regardless of whether
or not he stated that he "came a long way to kill this son of a bitch,"
Musgrave rode to the roundup camp on the Rio Felix to kill George
Parker, evidencing premeditation. Two, Parker was a son of a bitch,
an offense not punishable by death. In spite of the community's
obvious support for the acquitted outlaw, it remains difficult to
argue that justice was done.

Musgrave, in a statement published by the *Roswell Daily Record*,
thanked the people of Roswell for their kindness and sympathy,

which "was not undeserved." He thanked the jurors, "honest men who had the courage to render the verdict they did," adding, "it was impossible for me to avoid doing as I did, and that my conscience is clear in the sight of heaven." He allowed that he had done some things, "which any foolish frightened boy might have done under the same circumstances, and for these things I have been very sorry." He indicated his intention to live in Roswell and stressed his wish to be an honest, upright, law-abiding citizen as the deep-seated purpose of his life. He concluded by stating his regard "for law is second to no man's.[36]

Musgrave stayed with Drew Pruit the night following his release from jail and proposed heisting a train. Shortly before midnight on June 9, six days after Musgrave's acquittal, a lone robber held up the eastbound El Paso and Southwestern train number 2, seven miles east of Carrizozo, eighty-three miles west of Roswell. The bandit herded the passengers of the Pullman car into the private car at the rear of the train belonging to Superintendent G. V. Hawks and gathered some three hundred dollars in cash, along with a considerable amount of jewelry. He shot out the rear lights and rode south toward the San Andres Mountains. The railroad promptly posted a $2,500 reward. Time and place suggest that this may have been the heist to which Musgrave referred when, during a drinking spree in South America years later, he boasted to friends that he had once robbed a train single-handed.[37]

While George Musgrave had been caught up in the toils of Chaves County's legal system, Vollie Musgrave unleashed his own reign of lawlessness on the county. Presumably in celebration of his brother's acquittal, Vollie, on June 15, rustled six cattle valued at twenty-five dollars each. His deed not yet discovered, in early August Vollie turned to the production of a Wild West exhibition.[38]

Vollie left Roswell on August 9, for the Arroyo Seco, on the north side of the Capitan Mountains, where he obtained Block Ranch bucking stock for his exhibition. He returned with three well-known outlaw horses—Black Devil, Hightower Black, and the Block Sorrel. He also gathered horses from the Turkey Track Ranch and the Felix

Vollie Musgrave, 1912.
Courtesy of the New
Mexico State Records
Center and Archives,
New Mexico Correc-
tions Department
Records, neg. #2872.

ranch. The following Friday afternoon, over two hundred people
gathered at the Amusement Park to witness the roping and riding
of these wild horses, as well as five steers. Cowboys Ish Shields,
Johnnie Wilson, and Joe Foster delighted the crowd with their
skills, with only Foster being thrown by the horse Garnet. The exhibition drew a larger crowd on Saturday afternoon when Vollie joined
Shields, and Wilson, riding every animal on the grounds without
being thrown. Vollie repeated the show at Artesia the following
weekend. While he gathered stock for his exhibitions, he also sur-
reptitiously gathered additional stock for himself.[39]

On September 9, Vollie rustled nine head of cattle belonging,
variously, to the Capitan Live Stock Company, the Bloom Land and
Cattle Company, and James Shaw. Some might have concluded that
the two Musgraves were involved, but George had an alibi. He was
in Kansas City at the time, selling the cattle he had acquired from

Frank Strickland and Austin Reeves. Ballard, too, was in Kansas City, said to be "looking after cattle interests in the Ka market." The cattle were probably co-owned by the ranching partners.[40]

George returned to Roswell on September 18, as did Mrs. Ballard. Charlie Ballard remained behind in Kansas City for several more weeks. Two days following George's return, Vollie entered a horse race at the fairgrounds, only to be tied for first place with the Mills's brown colt, racing the 350-yard course in twenty-one and a half seconds. Bill Newman's sorrel ran third. The rules declared "one tie, all tie," and the prize money was withdrawn. Likely short of funds, having anticipated the winner's share, Vollie again resorted to larceny, rustling a horse from J. A. McPherson on October 24, and two mares from Breeb Hurst of Dexter on October 31.[41]

Vollie was arrested on November 10 and scheduled for trial two days later on the charge of rustling Breeb Hurst's two mares. On the evening of Saturday, November 12, after hearing the evidence and receiving instructions from the judge, the jury returned a verdict of guilty. On December 19, Judge Pope sentenced Vollie to four to five years in the penitentiary. Vollie appealed the case to the Supreme Court of the Territory of New Mexico. In the meantime, because he was unable to post the required five-thousand-dollar bail, and because the jail in Roswell was a temporary structure and not adapted to the safe keeping of the prisoner, he was transferred to the Territorial Penitentiary at Santa Fe to await the outcome of his appeal. As William H. Pope was both the presiding judge of the Fifth Judicial Court of Chaves County as well as chief justice of the Supreme Court of the Territory of New Mexico, the August 15, 1911, outcome of the appeal was a foregone conclusion. In the meantime, Vollie, described as having a bad reputation, bad habits, bad disposition, and bad associates, made two unsuccessful attempts to escape. Due to his poor record while in confinement, he remained imprisoned until October 16, 1915.[42]

Three days after his brother's conviction of theft of the mares, the Chaves County Grand Jury found evidence that on January 10, 1910, George Musgrave had attempted to persuade Noley Powell, a prospective witness in the Parker trial, to give false evidence. In truth, Noley Powell was not present at the killing of George T. Parker, and the Chaves County Grand Jury indicted Musgrave with inciting to commit perjury. George was not available to be arrested because he and Jano had already taken quick and permanent leave of Chaves County.[43]

George and Jano traveled to El Paso, where they met Joseph H. Nations, who presided over the J. H. Nations Meat and Supply Company and the Nations Packing Company. Nations, originally from Pecos, Texas, commissioned Musgrave to purchase cattle in Mexico. He deposited thirty thousand dollars in an account, and, naively, provided Musgrave with the checkbook. Reportedly, Musgrave concluded the transaction with a Mexican rancher's widow, and returned to the States. Some months later, when he realized that the check had not been presented for payment, the temptation proved too much. He withdrew the money and took the train south. "Well, then he got across into Mexico and throw in with old Pancho Villa killin' cattle for their hides and haulin' 'em in to those towns [El Paso and Carlsbad] and sellin' 'em," recalled Austin Reeves.[44]

By the onset of spring 1911, Francisco "Pancho" Villa, together with Pascual Orozco and José de la Luz Blanco, had emerged as the three principal leaders of Francisco Madero's revolutionary army. In April, Madero decided to seize Ciudad Juárez, the second largest city in the state of Chihuahua. Following weeks of vacillation and indecision on Madero's part, Orozco and Villa, in an act of insubordination, ordered their troops to fire upon the city. The resultant fighting forced Madero to commit all his forces to attacking the border community, and Juárez fell on May 10.[45]

Following the fall of Juárez, Villa established his headquarters in Chihuahua City, a town with which Musgrave had considerable familiarity. Certainly, an association between Musgrave and Villa, as revealed by Austin Reeves, would have been possible by midsummer. According to Jano's nephew, Boyd Charter, Musgrave took advantage of the revolutionary disruption extant in 1911 Chihuahua by pulling off a robbery or two in Mexico, but he and Jano got along with the rebels, being provided with a safe conduct pass for when they came across a "bad lot."[46]

Musgrave did not remain in Mexico for any length of time. He soon began a journey that would eventually take him to Paraguay, arriving there, probably, late in 1911. Circumstances suggest that Jano returned to Baggs sometime prior to mid-November 1911. On November 15, Jano received title to a lot in the Colfax Heights area of Denver as part of the settlement of her mother's estate. Although there is no direct evidence that Jano returned to Wyoming, estate records suggest that she did. The Carbon County District Court had ordered the lot to be sold as part of the estate's final distribution on April 27. At a time subsequent to April 27, but prior to November 15, Jano reached an agreement with her brothers and sisters that she would receive the property as partial settlement of her share of the estate. Within a matter of months, she, accompanied by Sarah Jebens of Baggs, traveled to New York, and then on to South America to join her husband.[47]

CHAPTER FIFTEEN

SOUTH AMERICA BECKONS

Paraguay contains more than half again as much land as the area of New York, New Jersey, and Pennsylvania. Almost none of the country has been carefully surveyed, and much of it has not even been explored.

FRANK CARPENTER

The first decade of the twentieth century marked a significant shift in America's policy toward the nations of Latin America. The Venezuelan debt struggle of 1902–3, the resolve to construct an Isthmian canal, and the Dominican Republic's fiscal crisis of 1904 captured public attention and preordained Theodore Roosevelt's 1905 "corollary" to the Monroe Doctrine, which contrived to thwart European intervention in Latin American affairs, and paternalistically sanctioned interference by the United States. A 1909 revolution in Nicaragua induced Roosevelt's successor, William Howard Taft, to modify the Roosevelt Corollary to preserve American investments in Nicaragua and, by implication, elsewhere. By 1912, the interventionism of the "Big Stick" and the business excesses of "Dollar Diplomacy" began to give way to "New Nationalism" and "New Freedom" and their calls for protection rather than intervention, responsible investment rather than plundering.

As America scrutinized the nations to the south for investment and profit, an increasing number of western outlaws looked to various South American republics for sanctuary. Robert Evans, William Wilson, Harry Nation, Dick Clifford, and, most memorably, Robert Leroy Parker (alias Butch Cassidy) and Harry Longabaugh (alias Sundance Kid), sought more congenial surroundings, although most met the untimely deaths they would have had every reason to expect in the Northern Hemisphere.

Cassidy and Sundance's friends at first discounted rumors of the North American *bandoleros'* deaths in Bolivia on November 6, 1908. Concern increased as months came and went with no word from the outlaws, and letters from their friends were returned unclaimed. Tales that several of Cassidy's cronies contributed to a fund to send an emissary to Bolivia to investigate do not bear up under scrutiny. In fact, George Musgrave's departure for Paraguay may well have provided the foundation for most, if not all, of them.[1]

According to Ann Bassett, the cattle queen of Brown's Park, Elzy Lay told her that he had sent an Afton, Wyoming, storekeeper named Burton to investigate the disappearance of the two Americans. In 1911, Lay tended bar in Shoshoni, Wyoming; his wife remained Jano Musgrave's closest friend. Undoubtedly, Lay knew of the Musgraves' plans to head south and may well have asked them to keep their ears open for news of Butch.[2]

Edmund Crabe, a pioneer resident of Shoshoni, related: "Billy Sawtelle, who in 1911 shot and killed a man on the main street of Shoshoni, pulled out and left for Buenos Aires. Some time later, when he returned, he brought word that Butch Cassidy had assuredly been killed down there in a skirmish with the police."[3]

Musgrave's brother-in-law, Bert Charter, and Cassidy prosecutor, Will Simpson, concurred that Sawtelle had gone to South America. Simpson maintained that a second man had accompanied Sawtelle. The significant family tie between Charter and Musgrave may explain Simpson's second-man recollection. On June 11, 1903, Charter had married Maude Magor (1882–1955), Jano Musgrave's sister. The Charters would certainly have had prior knowledge of the Musgraves' intention to leave for South America and likewise may have asked them to gather information on the missing bandits. If Sawtelle did go south to investigate, he may have learned of the December 1911 police killings of gringo bandits Robert Evans and William Wilson in Argentina and concluded the dead men were Butch and Sundance.[4]

Jano later related that her husband "had a set up in South America" before they married. There is no supportive evidence of this. Sarah Jebens, who accompanied Jano to Buenos Aires in 1912, believed that Jano had been in South America previous to settling there, but this seems unlikely. However, Jano could have had knowledge of South America from letters received from her husband and may have given Sarah Jebens the impression that she had been there herself. It is doubtful, but conceivably Musgrave could have ventured into South America prior to meeting Jano, and then told her about it.[5]

If Musgrave is the individual whose departure for the Southern Hemisphere spawned some or all of these yarns, certainly he did not act as an agent for a cabal of former outlaws. His relocation was otherwise motivated.

There is some evidence that he hired on to tend stock aboard a cattleboat bound for Spain, a relatively easy way for a cowboy to secure passage in pre-refrigeration days when livestock was shipped to Europe on the hoof. From Spain, Musgrave steamed for South America and reached Paraguay in late 1911 or early 1912. He adopted the alias Robert Steward, settled in the Paraguayan Chaco, and established a foothold during one of the country's numerous revolutions.[6]

In July 1910, with the backing of the army, Colonel Albino Jara, minister of war, had engineered an uprising against the government. During 1911, anarchy ruled. On March 23, 1912, Jara's forces secured a complete victory over the *Cívico* opposition in a battle at Asunción in which six hundred men were reported killed; interim President Pedro Peña took refuge in the Uruguay legation. The conflict was renewed on April 27, when four government warships bombarded the rebel positions of Col. Jara at Villa Encarnación, 174 miles southeast of Asunción. Jara's rebels successfully repelled the ships, but, on May 10, government troops finally prevailed; they imprisoned five hundred rebels, and killed many more. Five days later, the government announced that Col. Jara had succumbed to wounds received during the battle at Iturbicuary. Eduardo Schaerer emerged as president, and political calm settled over the country. Peace also brought renewed economic opportunities. Tex Rickard, Musgrave's one-time adversary from Goldfield, arrived in Paraguay to take advantage of them.[7]

Rickard had promoted the James J. Jeffries–Jack Johnson world heavyweight championship fight in Reno on July 4, 1910. Subsequently, the entrepreneur Percival Farquhar had summoned Rickard to New York to discuss the feasibility and profitability of raising cattle in South America. Farquhar, who had assembled a major syndicate of English bankers and French and Belgian investors, envisioned the creation of a cattle trade which would equal or surpass that of Argentina. After Farquhar explained to Rickard how he was to proceed as manager, he asked Rickard what salary he expected. Tex replied, "Salary be damned. This is a 50–50 deal, with your money and my savvy about cattle."[8]

On February 18, 1911, Rickard steamed from New York, aboard the Lampert and Holt liner *Vasari*, and arrived in Buenos Aires in mid-March. He checked into the Plaza Hotel, where he told the press that he and Mason Peters, his New York friend and partner, were planning to buy cattle and search for land. They intended to go west toward the Chilean boundary on the Transandine Railway. Lieutenant John S. Hammond, military attaché at the American embassy, suggested to Rickard that he consider the favorable leasing terms offered by the Paraguayan government.[9]

On June 21, 1912, accompanied by twenty Spanish-speaking cowboys, Tex Rickard, having wisely postponed his departure until the Jara revolution was over, sailed from Cherbourg, France, bound for South America and Paraguay. Press reports of the day do not indicate how Rickard found these cowboys in France. The most logical explanation is that they were Americans working the cattleships. In addition to those who accompanied him from France, "Rickard hired any American who turned up in Buenos Aires," including a number of colorful characters who lacked range skills. By all accounts, they were an incorrigible group.[10]

> They were an extremely tough crowd, gunfighters, gamblers, and hell raisers in the true tradition! It seems they used to spend a lot of their time plying up and down the River Paraguay on steamboats and their main relaxation was playing poker for high stakes and at which they would fleece anybody foolish enough to play with them. When not busy at the tables they used to expend revolver cartridges in drilling holes into oranges, tossed over the rail, before they touched the water.[11]

Mrs. Charles William Kent, the wife of Rickard's bookkeeper and storekeeper at Maroma, on the western part of the Paraguay Land and Cattle Company ranch, concurred. "Tex Rickard had brought over from America with him, a crowd of toughs, good cowboys all, but the majority on the run for killing, cattle rustling, or otherwise going contrary to the law."[12]

Rickard's use of North American cowboys proved less than successful as most of them had difficulties adapting to the Paraguayan environment. Moreover, the cowboys' wages were fifteen times greater than those earned by Paraguayan vaqueros. Sir Reginald Tower, British minister plenipotentiary to Paraguay and the Argentine Republic, described, with some irony, the problems Rickard encountered.[13] "This past year (1912) [Rickard] brought various Texas cowboys to Paraguay, but they deserted. He is now practically alone in this immense district, not knowing Spanish or the language of the indigenous Lengua, who are prevalent in the area, and he finds himself without indispensable work hands. The problem is to obtain efficient workers; it is a difficult problem to resolve."[14]

The New York and Paraguay Company, formed by the Farquhar syndicate, assumed ownership of the cattle-raising operation.

Managing partner Rickard, who planned to export meat to Great Britain, oversaw the stock-raising enterprise, across the Río Paraguay from Concepción, about 132 miles above Asunción. The ranch had some twenty-five miles of river frontage and extended westward across the Chaco to Bolivia. Farquhar's biographer later estimated its area at approximately four million acres. Rickard stocked the ranch with approximately forty thousand head of cattle. "Farquhar shipped purebred bulls and pigs from the States, and Tex ran the show."[15]

In 1913, the New York and Paraguay Company was reorganized as the Paraguay Land and Cattle Company, incorporated in Maine, controlled by the Farquhar syndicate, with the majority of its shares held by the Brazil Railway Company. Rickard continued to maintain an interest; Farquhar received reports of "Tex fearlessly riding through the Gran Chaco quebracho forests and grasslands of the Paraguay Land and Cattle Company, infested by hostile Indians who refrained from attacking the bold Texan." In truth, Rickard seems to have spent most of his time in Asunción and Buenos Aires.[16]

As Rickard had waited until the conclusion of the Jara revolution before moving to Paraguay, apparently Musgrave likewise hesitated to have Jano exposed to such danger. The precise time of her arrival in South America remains unclear. Papers held by Rickard's daughter, Maxine, indicate that Jano departed from New York on June 20, the day prior to Rickard's departure from France. Moreover, the steamship *Hyanthean* did embark from New York that day and docked in the Puerto Madero at Buenos Aires on July 19. However, a deed with accompanying notarized statement places Jano in Denver on November 19. Since it is unlikely that she arrived in Paraguay in mid-July and returned to Denver by mid-November, it is tempting to discount the Rickard account, but there are several troublesome issues associated with this transaction. Could Jano, in need of funds to finance her trip south, have used the property as collateral to borrow money from Denver's Armstrong-Williams Realty Company and subsequently, after her arrival in Paraguay, transferred the property to the company to clear the debt? This scheme would require that a cooperative, perhaps in-house notary falsify a statement as to her physical presence in Denver at the time of the transfer. Neither the deed whereby Jano acquired the property, nor the deed by which she disposed of it, were filed until May 15, 1913.[17]

Jano left for Paraguay accompanied by Sarah Jebens of Baggs (whose husband, Andrew, had also hired on with Rickard's cowboys) and the two Jebens daughters, Mary and Josephine. Upon their arrival in Buenos Aires, the four secured a riverboat to transport them up the Río Paraná and Río Paraguay to Concepción. Speaking no Spanish, they must have embarked upon the trip with some trepidation: they were the only Americans on board. The enormity of the muddy Río Paraná probably astonished them: only after leaving the estuary of the Río de la Plata could they have realized that they were not on an inland sea. Rarely could more than one bank of the river be seen at a time until they reached the Argentine city of Corrientes, after three days of travel. North of Corrientes, they reached the confluence of the Río Paraná with the clear waters of the Río Paraguay, along whose banks Jano would have seen scores of black *jacaras* (alligators) basking in the sunshine, the objects of constant plinking by river-going sportsmen.[18]

The riverboat continued north to Asunción. After five days on the river, it is unlikely that they would have bypassed the picturesque, though war-torn, provincial city perched on a high ridge sloping down to the river, without at least a brief respite before continuing their journey north. After another thirty-six hours on the Río Paraguay, Jano and the Jebens family reached Villa Concepción.

Situated on the Alto-Paraguay and described as a "hell fire town and hotter than the fictitious Hades," the community of Concepción, with some eight thousand inhabitants, served as the trade center in northern Paraguay and the local Brazilian districts for yerba maté, the leaves of which, when brewed, produce a strong, tea-like drink. A traveler described *Calle Ypané*, the main street, as "a miserable thoroughfare of one story brick and wood buildings plastered over." Nevertheless, with its low, flat-roofed houses and wide roads it was "more picturesque and less dirty than Asunción; but smaller and quieter."[19]

Reunited with her husband, Mrs. George Musgrave, alias Mrs. Robert Cameron, who by marriage had become Mrs. George W. Murray, now learned that she had become Mrs. Robert Steward. How did she recall which name they were using at any particular time? "Oh, we had to. He had to change his name lots of times. But Steward is the name we used in South America."[20]

Whatever Jano's expectations may have been concerning living conditions in the Gran Chaco, it is doubtful that she anticipated anything quite so primitive. "Flat, dreary, monotonous, repellent," in the opinion of Anglican Bishop Edward F. Every, "the whole country was covered with a waterproof sheeting, for the surface is of such a clayey substance that the water lies on it and cannot penetrate except very slowly." A hut, with open doorways and windows, served as home. Typically, these country huts were built from poles woven together, chinked with red mud, and covered with a gray thatch roof, not altogether unpleasant in appearance. The roof probably extended far out to one side, forming an open porch that also served as the kitchen. Mosquito netting abounded, and vinegaroons (scorpions), tarantulas, and numerous varieties of rattlesnakes, *mboy chumbies* (coral snakes), *yararás* (fer-de-lance), puff-adders, and the deadly and aggressive *ñanduriés* (small sticklike snakes) did little to add to the comforts of home. The natives also posed some danger and watched everything George and Jano did.[21]

In spite of the primitive housing and treacherous surroundings, Jano, "a real Western character," maintained her fine sense of humor. Adopting the local dress, she stuffed her *bombachas* (gaucho pants) into high leather boots and tucked a .22-caliber pistol into her *tirador* (wide leather belt), prepared for any untoward occurrence. George chided her, "If [you] shot someone with that it [would] make them awful mad." At least one native got the better of her when he appeared without pants while cattle buyers were present. She swiftly supplied him with a pair of Musgrave's. Thereafter, when-

Jano in Paraguay. Cour-
tesy Dennis Burchett.

ever he needed new pants, he repeated the ploy. But Jano proved
adaptable. She added Spanish to her already "highly stylized Western" tongue; she made friends with the natives; she organized a
household of three servants—cook, launderer, and maid—and she
took a hand in establishing their cattle business.[22]

Musgrave became the general foreman for Rickard's Concepción ranch. Just why he got the job remains unclear, but his initial
responsibility was to bring fence wire, tools, and supplies, all purchased in Buenos Aires, up the river to Puerto Pinasco. Musgrave,
however, had bigger plans.[23]

First, George and Jano began their own cattle business, renting
land east of the Río Paraguay at Carayá Vuelta, about twenty miles
north of Concepción, near the Brazilian border. They registered the
pigpen brand and began to supply cattle to the nearby San Salvador
packing plant.[24]

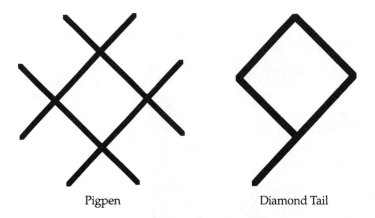

Pigpen   Diamond Tail

Rickard had previously registered the Diamond Tail brand. Significantly, Musgrave chose his brand with an eye to what a hot running iron could do with the Diamond Tail. When did Musgrave commence rustling cattle? "From the first day," according to his friend George Lohman. British adventurer Charles William Thurlow "Bill" Craig elaborated, "He had embarked on a careful course of refined skullduggery that left people gasping, so new it was, so suave, so devilishly effective. Against ordinary cattle-thieves, the time-honoured steps had nearly always been good enough, but [Musgrave] with his kid-glove approach was as dynamite to gunpowder."[25]

Once Rickard employee David Urquhart trailed cattle rustled by Musgrave north through the Chaco and reported having seen unhealed brands on six hundred head. A police patrol raided George's ranch. Forewarned, George and his men had fled. The patrol captured only Lorenzo Downing, Lohman's storekeeper who served as cook, probably the least larcenous of the bunch.[26]

As George rose from *jefe* to *patrón*, Jano Musgrave also herded and branded cattle. Furthermore, she handled all of the bookkeeping and correspondence for the Musgraves' ranch. Mrs. Constance Kent, the wife of the storekeeper at Rickard's Maroma settlement, credited Jano with much of the couple's success. English, and Victorian in character, Mrs. Kent confessed that, though he was a rough fellow, she thought highly of George as a friend. "There

Cattle branding on a Chaco estancia. *Pictureque Paraguay,* 1911.

was Bob Stewart [*sic*], known all over Paraguay, Brazil and the Argentine for his crookedness and his quickness with a gun, yet he was a fine friend although the last man to do business with."[27]

Musgrave, in turn, cherished Mrs. Kent's friendship, and confided to her that he had two .32-caliber bullets in his leg that he had to get removed as they bothered him when the weather turned bad. The Kent daughters adored George; he always brought them presents. Once, when Musgrave had the girls out for lunch, a row broke out and someone pulled a gun. Musgrave quickly and quietly twisted the gun away from the hand of the man who was holding it and rejoined the girls. They would have their lunch undisturbed.[28]

Musgrave's generosity extended beyond members of the Kent family. Dorothy Kent Eaton, a daughter, liked to recall the time that he came upon a barefoot boy, roaming the streets on a cold day.

Musgrave picked the boy up, marched to a clothing store and completely outfitted the child from head to toe with clothes and shoes. Later he shrugged off this charitable display as "just having fun."[29]

George and Jano temporarily left Paraguay in 1913. The trip north may have been prompted by the final distribution of the estate of Jano's mother. They arrived in Chihuahua on business, although it is uncertain what business. Perhaps it concerned the Chihuahua City saloon that George had once operated. Possibly it resulted from his association with Pancho Villa. Or then again, Musgrave simply might have decided that the Chihuahua region, a state with which he had long been familiar, offered gainful opportunity amid the revolution, particularly with Villa gaining the upper hand.[30]

Villa captured Torreón, an important rail center in the southwestern state of Coahuila, on October 2. He confiscated fifty thousand bales of cotton shortly thereafter. Ralph Vandewart, a wool and cotton buyer from Roswell, received a telephone call offering him the cotton. Villa next evacuated Torreón with his sights set on Chihuahua City, 288 miles to the northwest. Villa launched a surprise attack on Ciudad Juárez on November 15, and forced the Mexican federal forces to abandon Chihuahua City. He took the town on December 3.

After traveling to El Paso, and then to a meeting in Juárez with Enrico Purchase, Villa's purchasing agent, Vandewart set out on a harrowing trip by motorized handcar along the rebuilt railroad tracks from Juarez to Chihuahua City. He met Villa at the confiscated Terrazas hacienda, about five miles outside of Chihuahua. Villa demanded immediate payment for the cotton while Vandewart countered by offering to make a $250,000 advance on a consignment. After four days of negotiations, Vandewart, who had married a niece of Musgrave's former captor and real estate partner, Deputy Marshal Charles Ballard, broke off the talks and left Chihuahua City—but not before he encountered George Musgrave.[31]

Jano later spoke of their friendship with Villa. The Musgraves had experienced the revolution first-hand as they crossed a still-smoking battlefield, likely at Torreón, and saw dead men and animals strewn about. Her friend Bess Brown later related, "Her horse was stolen, and she wanted to protest and was warned to say nothing and she rode out of Mexico on a mule, and her husband also. I am not sure his mount was a mule."[32]

Tex Rickard's daughter placed the Musgraves back in Concepción in October 1914. Certainly the outbreak of World War I hastened their return. Soon after, Tex Rickard obtained a concession to build a meat-packing plant.[33] A. D. Hughes later related:

> My father and Rickard became involved [in 1914] in a scheme to build a packing plant which would freeze the carcasses which were to be shipped either down the Paraná River or over an ambitious railway building scheme known as the Farquhar Syndicate, which was proposing to drive a railway system right across South America. . . . Tex Rickard floated a company called Central Products Corporation which was going to put up the packing plant, dress the carcasses, etc. Both schemes foundered in the jungles of Paraguay and South American politics.[34]

Rickard and others also acquired a large minority interest in the San Salvador meat-packing plant on the east bank of the Río Paraguay just north of Carayá Vuelta. At the outbreak of World War I, the British government ordered $240,000 worth of canned beef from the San Salvador plant. Although the beef was delivered to, and eaten by, the British army, the British government refused to make payment to a company whose majority stockholders were Germans. The plant soon went out of business.[35]

A number of European adventurers who met George Musgrave during his years in South America later wrote accounts of his activities, often the only version of some particular misadventure, many of them were embellished to titillate the reader at the expense of fact. One such writer was Aimé Felix Tschiffely (1895–1954), a Swiss-born traveler and adventurer. Prior to World War I, he immigrated to England to take a position as assistant prep school master. It was he, it will be recalled, who maintained that Musgrave

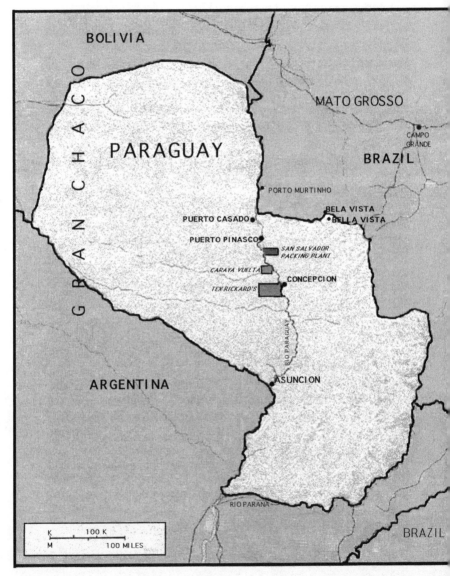

BOLIVIA

GRAN CHACO

PARAGUAY

MATO GROSSO

CAMPO GRANDE

BRAZIL

PORTO MURTINHO

BELA VISTA
•BELLA VISTA

PUERTO CASADO•

PUERTO PINASCO•
SAN SALVADOR
PACKING PLANT

CARAYA VUELTA

CONCEPCION

TEX RICKARD'S

RIO PARAGUAY

ARGENTINA

ASUNCION

RIO PARANA

BRAZIL

K   100 K
M   100 MILES

MAP BY KAREN HOLLIDAY TANNER

Paraguay

and Tex Rickard had earlier clashed at Goldfield, Nevada. Toward the end of the war, Tschiffely moved to South America.[36]

According to a colorful anecdote of Tschiffely's, when Rickard, the absentee manager, learned that Musgrave was foreman of the ranch in the Chaco, "he became very agitated." Upon hearing of Musgrave's presence at the ranch, Rickard quickly left South America.[37]

Allowing that Tschiffely's recounting is accurate, it seems improbable that Rickard, a director of the Paraguay Land and Cattle Company, presumably influential with the Paraguayan government, and living in Buenos Aires, would have to flee South America to avoid Musgrave's wrath. Moreover, Tschiffely had yet to reach South America at this time, which means that he picked up the story second-hand, casting further doubt on its believability. Its existence, however, makes more interesting the fact that in March 1915 Rickard did suddenly book passage for New York aboard the steamer ship *Verdi*. However, his departure could as easily be attributed to the growing economic difficulties then being experienced by the Farquhar syndicate.[38]

Meanwhile, an unusually large flood inundated the lands of the Paraguay Land and Cattle Company. As related by the none-too-reliable Tschiffely, Musgrave, whom the fleeing Tex Rickard had neglected to fire, began the task of transporting out salvageable materials that had any value. While freighting the materials overland by cart, he encountered Anglican Bishop Edward Francis Every on an inspection visit of Indian missions. The bishop later related his conversation to Tschiffely.[39]

> "Hell's bells and rattle-snakes! Guess I wasn't ordained to be no goddam navigator!" the tall, sun-burn't [*sic*] man who was perched on the rolls of wire drawled. Having finished airing his opinion on things in general, the grumbler inquired, "And who may you be, stranger?"
>
> "I'm Bishop Every, and I am on my way to the Chaco Indian Mission."

"My name's Bob Appin [an alias coined by Tschiffely]. Mighty glad to meet you. Shake, Bish," the other exclaimed, at the same time holding out a hand, which the liberal-minded Bishop shook with delight."[40]

The pioneer Paraguayan cattleman Robert Eaton heard of the Bishop's encounter with the irreverent cowboy, but the details he gave differ substantially from those related by Tschiffely. "That story about the American cowboy . . . was told me by my father-in-law [Tex Rickard's accountant/storekeeper], Charles Kent. 'I ain't no damned navigator' and he turned back after traveling two days in the water on horse back and near the Indian Anglican Mission. It was certainly not [Musgrave] on the ox cart."[41]

Rickard did not return to Paraguay, but he did maintain an active interest in the country. In the fall of 1921, representing the interests of a Texas oil company, he actively sought an oil concession in Paraguay. When he died in 1929, Rickard still held title to one hundred leagues (468,700 acres) in the interior of the Chaco, much of it in territory disputed with Bolivia.[42]

Whether Rickard's friend or foe, Musgrave seems to have been unaffected by the promoter's departure. For the immigrant outlaw, Paraguay remained a land of opportunity.

CHAPTER SIXTEEN

CHACO *ABIGEO*

Cu-cu-rru-cu-cu, Paloma!
Cu-cu-rru-cu-cu, no llores!
Las piedras jamás Paloma,
que van saber dea mores!

SEBASTIAN DE YRADIER

After Tex Rickard left the Chaco, George and Jano continued to prosper by both legal and illegal means. They trailed cattle, buying some from local ranchers and certainly rustling others from Chaco ranches. They brought most of their stock over the border from Brazil as contraband with little difficulty as few restrictions existed. It is doubtful that they rustled the Brazilian stock; the ranchers of Brazil "were unforgiving about rustlers." Moreover, it is unlikely they could have moved the volume of cattle supplied without being detected. Smuggling legally purchased Brazilian cattle across the sparsely settled international border into Paraguay, a practice that continues to the present day depending upon the exchange rate, involved less risk than rustling. Musgrave "practically owned the police at Concepción and he owned the Brasilian and Paraguayan border patrol."[1]

Don Enrique Saval, owner of the Casa Blanca Rancho, northeast of Concepción, commented sourly: "Here comes your friend, the dangerous Don Roberto Steward, a man I tolerate as an acquaintance but with whom I should hate to have business dealings. I wonder how and where did he pick up his present bunch of cattle, where he brought them across the frontier, and how much it cost him in bribes to the frontier patrols?"[2]

The Musgraves "operated in a big way, made money and there were apparently no incidents at [the] time." They became the main suppliers of cattle to the San Salvador packing plant.[3]

The war in Europe had greatly increased the demand for meat. Due to an inadequate canning industry, Paraguay could not meet the demand, and exportation of cattle to Argentina rose sharply. Shipments of live animals, unknown prior to 1912 when Argentina opened her border to Paraguayan cattle, peaked in 1917 at 67,000 tons. Jano claimed that she and George also shipped cattle down the river to Buenos Aires in sufficient numbers to warrant the purchase of a tugboat and barges.[4] Chaco cattleman Robert Eaton doubted it:

> I do not believe that [George] ever bought or had a tug boat and barges to ship cattle to Buenos Aires. The Paraná, Paraguay river is an international waterway and any boats are subject to control by two countries. From Concepción, Paraguay, to Buenos Aires, Argentina, is a long way. Cattle cannot survive such a trip without being unloaded along the way and rested and fed. It has been tried by others with no success. I have never heard of [Musgrave] trying to make such a move.[5]

Apparently, then, the Musgraves achieved success principally by selling cattle—mostly acquired or imported illicitly—to the San Salvador plant.

George and Jano's growing prosperity led them to seek more comfortable surroundings. Toward the end of the war, they moved to Asunción, where they could live like royalty for one hundred dollars per month. The picturesque, cosmopolitan—yet primitive—subtropical city, with its palm- and orange tree-lined streets and colorful flowers and plants, harmonized with the Spanish-style homes of light blue, pink, and yellow. In the marketplaces, the intermingling of the many tongues merged into a steady hum. Yet, Asunción lacked a public water supply, sewers, and, after the destruction of the exchange by fire in 1913, it had no telephone service.[6]

Soon after the end of the war, the Musgraves briefly returned to Texas and Arizona. Sam McCue of Roswell saw Musgrave in Texas, probably in the vicinity of Wichita Falls, during 1919. Musgrave is known to have been in that area during the oil boom. In Phoenix, they called upon Vollie and his new wife, Bessie. Surely, while in Arizona, they also visited with George's aging parents.[7]

George and Jano returned to Paraguay to find the economy in an uproar. The market for cattle had soured with the conclusion of World War I. Exports of livestock, dried and canned meat, and meat extract dropped 75 percent from their 1917 high. The Musgraves lost money on their last two shipments. Many other cattle ranchers, having borrowed on the cattle during the more prosperous war years, lost their herds to banks or other creditors.[8]

The acquisition of these four-legged assets likewise overburdened the banks. In the fall of 1920, the Bank of Spain suspended business in Paraguay. The Bank of Paraguay also closed its doors; in mid-November, the panic set off a run on the *Banco Mercantil*, which discontinued business under a two-month moratorium.[9]

While the postwar recession was an international phenomenon, in a country where revolution was almost a way of life, its effect was to doom the Gondra administration. On October 30, 1921, revolutionary followers of ex-President Eduardo Schaerer, supported by the police and the army, forced President Gondra from office. The Musgraves did not remain in Asunción to witness the fall of Gondra's regime; in late 1919 or early 1920 they moved their camp to Buenos Aires, the most cosmopolitan city in all Latin America.[10]

Fifteen times the size of Asunción, Buenos Aires must have seemed a huge urban setting for two people raised in the rural West. The British historian James Bryce, who had visited Buenos Aires only a few years earlier, described the city of "clear air" as "something between Paris and New York. It has the business rush and the luxury of one, the gaiety and pleasure-loving aspect of the other. Nowhere in the world does one get a stronger impression of exuberant wealth and extravagance."[11] With such an overt display of wealth, and with mutual wagering at the horse track the favorite pastime, the city must have been enormously attractive to Musgrave.

His constant need for funds required him to take frequent trips back to Paraguay, where he resumed rustling cattle and supplemented his income by gambling. He also sought to confirm his American citizenship and secure a passport and visa. According to a document executed by his friend Frank M. Hicks of Portalis and Company, Ltd., "Mr. Robert Steward . . . who has been living in Paraguay for the past nine years, has put in an application for registration for his American citizenship. Mr. Steward has made a half million dollars in land and cattle here [South America], and is about to sell out and come back to San Antonio [Texas] to make his home."[12] No evidence survives to indicate that Musgrave secured the passport and visa he sought.[13]

There was one story Musgrave later delighted in telling about his Buenos Aires years. He encountered a medical student who had failed his studies and, fronting for the would-be doctor, opened up a consulting office and hung out a sign: "Dr. Robert Steward." The ruse worked until Musgrave's lack of medical experience exposed him.[14]

Between gambling activities in Argentina, clandestine excursions back into Paraguay, and his short-lived medical career, Musgrave became a regular at "Dirty Dick's," the famed bar at the Criterion Hotel in Buenos Aires. It was here that Aimé Tschiffely, then a teacher at St. George's school for boys, first became acquainted with Musgrave, "a striking man I had seen there several times," as Tschiffely recalled. "The tall, broad-shouldered and handsome stranger—

who was about forty years of age—usually sat in a corner on his own, watching other clients, without speaking to them. He wore a large-brimmed sombrero, from beneath which protruded a rebellious tuft of black hair. Whilst with a firm grip he shook my hand, a friendly smile played round his penetrating eyes."[15]

Warned by headmaster J. T. Stevenson of Musgrave's reputation as a cardsharp, cattle rustler, bandit, and killer, Tschiffely, no doubt with more than a little trepidation, broached the subject to Musgrave. Was he all the things they said he was? George responded in his soft southern drawl, "Friend, let me tell you just one thing. Whatever you've heard about me ain't half the truth; but don't let that worry you. There's so many suckers about who think themselves smart, and take me for a greenhorn, that there ain't no need for me to pick on my friends."[16]

Musgrave, Tschiffely said, had developed into a consummate gambler; he had perfected his card-handling technique before a mirror placed upon a table. But danger walked hand-in-hand with gambling. Once, while he was playing with a number of tinhorns, and beating them at their own game, an observer pushed a gun into George's ribs and ordered that he continue playing. Unruffled, he continued his cheating ways; the observer left, astonished by Musgrave's beginner's luck. If Tschiffely's tale has any foundation, it would suggest that Musgrave, no longer content with fleecing railroad workers as he had done at Dalhart, Texas, twenty years earlier, had made a considerable effort to improve his gaming skills.[17]

George Lohman implied that, although Musgrave continued to gamble, perhaps he had not refined his skills to the extent suggested by Tschiffely. Musgrave had booked a room at the Hotel Tin-Tin in Concepción. So, too, had Lohman. That night Musgrave stopped by to check on the location of Lohman's room. He told Lohman that he had a poker game planned and asked Lohman to keep his door unlocked. About two in the morning, Musgrave stumbled in with a gun in one hand and a pile of money in the other. "If I couldn't win it one way," explained the outlaw, "I had to get it another way." Later, Lohman reflected, "I guess the other players were drunker than [Musgrave] as nothing was ever mentioned about the incident."[18]

Such adventures necessitated that Musgrave never go about unarmed; he generally carried a .44-40 Colt revolver. Invited to a picnic, Tschiffely claimed that Musgrave put on a shooting display with a number of revolvers he had brought, contained in a good-sized mahogany box.[19] "Oranges or empty tins, thrown into the air, were hardly ever missed, and coins, stuck into a barbed wire fence, he shot off from the hip as if by magic. There seemed to be nothing he could not do with six-shooters, from juggling to firing them upside-down, and among other tricks he showed us how to draw the weapon out of his holster and 'fan' six shots in rapid succession."[20]

Although it is unlikely that a range veteran like Musgrave normally carried six rounds in his single-action Colt, perhaps he did for this display. Fanning was not a common practice. However, the routine was associated on several occasions in connection with members of the High Five gang. Ed Wilson recalled, "Each member of the crowd [High Five gang], as soon as he bought a new 'six-shooter,' removed the trigger. When in a 'tight' place . . . they held the pistol in one hand and hit the hammer rapidly with the palm of the other."[21]

Carrying firearms also presented hazards. Tschiffely related that one night in Buenos Aires' renowned watering hole, Fanny's Tavern, the police entered and began to search the patrons for illegal firearms. A detective frisked George and found him, to Tschiffely's amazement, unarmed. Musgrave, with a sly wink, later told Tschiffely to look up under the table. Bending down, the writer saw a revolver, suspended under the table by a doubled-up jackknife, the blade driven into the table's underside.[22] Old-timer Bob Eaton didn't believe it:

> That episode of a heavy S.W. .44 stuck up under a table supported by a jack knife is enough to put me off. A .44 S.W. is a heavy gun. I do not believe that [Musgrave] could have hung it on a jack knife stuck in the under side of a table. Much less in a crowded restaurant where he obviously must attract no

attention. . . . [Musgrave] might have stuck a gun in his boot or in his belt in the middle of his back. These are areas generally over looked in a casual frisking.[23]

Women lavished attention on George. "My wife used to say, 'He looks like a handsome red Indian.' Yes, he was handsome and easy

Art Acord, Universal Studio's sad-eyed cowboy star of the silent motion picture era. Courtesy of Grange B. McKinney.

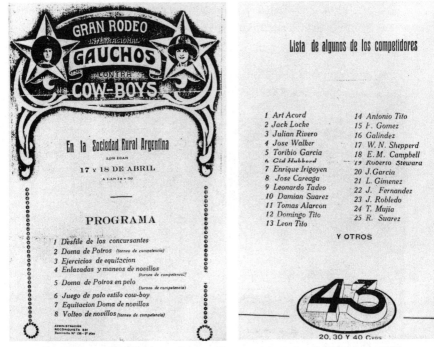

Gauchos versus Cowboys Rodeo, Buenos Aires, April 17 and 18, 1924.
From the authors' collection.

to talk to. I once commented 'He could turn the charm on and off like
a light,'" recalled Bob Eaton. "No wonder the girls fell for him in his
younger days." To Jano's growing dismay, Musgrave reciprocated
much of that attention. They were trying to sell their Chaco lease
when Jano decided to separate from George. She returned to Arizona
where George's sister, Addie Parker, advised her to divorce him.[24]

In April 1924, during Jano's absence, a troupe of American cowboys assembled by Hollywood silent film star Art Acord arrived in
Buenos Aires to compete in a Gauchos vs. Cowboys rodeo. Acord,
demonstrably a fine cowboy, had gathered friends from his rodeo
circuit days as well as studio cowboys for the trip. Among the latter was George's uncle, Joseph Henry "Buddie" Walker. Walker had
resettled in California and, with his brother Jerome, secured cowboy bit parts in Acord's movies. Walker prevailed upon his nephew

George, Jano, and Aime Tschiffely, ca. 1924. Courtesy Dennis Burchett.

to participate with the cowboys in the competition. During the April 18 and 19 performances, an astonished Tschiffely saw his friend ride into the arena in full cowboy regalia, then rope and throw a steer directly in front of the president's box.[25]

Musgrave was, of course, an old hand at handling stock and "as a cattleman was peerless." In Concepción, amid a boisterous group, Musgrave made a bet that, on an American stock saddle, he could rope and throw down a bull single-handedly. The crowd gathered outside the town to witness the feat. George roped a big bull, which he threw down and castrated, winning the wager. However, the next day the owner of the bull turned up demanding damages, claiming that the bull was of purebred lineage. Presumably, George paid up.[26]

Following their brief separation, Jano traveled back to Buenos Aires. George awaited her arrival with great anticipation. He introduced her to Tschiffely. Musgrave then learned of her desire for a divorce. Dismayed, he gave her money, and she returned to Carbon County, Wyoming.[27]

On June 28, 1926, Jano filed for divorce. She claimed that Musgrave "failed and neglected to provide the common necessaries of life" and that for a period of "more than three years" he had "drunk to excess and during that time [had] been quarrelsome and dangerous." Perhaps her vanity prevented her from citing the other women, but she recalled his womanizing with bitterness. The court finalized the divorce on September 10, 1926, and restored her maiden name. As Jano Magor she moved to Pine Ridge, Wyoming, where her sister and brother-in-law, Maude and Bert Charter, hired her to cook for the hands during the hay harvest. She loved to cook and took pride in it, but it was not all work and no play; she claimed that she would work all day and dance all night.[28]

In 1928, Jano moved to Tucson and managed the curio department of R. M. Bruchman's in the Congress Hotel Building. Later, she moved to California and reunited with Mary and Elzy Lay and another Baggs school friend, Myrtle Wedemeyer. After Lay's death on November 10, 1934, Jano worked as a housekeeper for a Los Angeles family and, later still, served as a nanny for two children in Michigan.[29]

Mary Lay moved to Tucson in 1935. In 1938, Jano joined her, and they ran a tuberculosis sanatorium. According to Jano's brother, Cornelius "Neil" Magor (1884–1956), they were out to bilk money from sick old men. When faced with exposure, the two women quickly left the state.[30] Before departing, Jano wrote to columnist Frank King of the *Western Livestock Journal*. King noted in his August 19, 1938, column:

> I was surprised to receive a letter the other day from the ex-wife of George Musgrave who was a member of the Black Jack gang when they held up the International Bank at Nogales, Arizona, at noon on August 6, 1896, at which time I shot an' wounded the hoss that George was riding. I am not at liberty to give the name she is using now, nor where she lives at the present time. She did not inform me what became of her former husband, but did say that she was with him in South

L/r: Jano and Mary Calvert Lay. Courtesy The American Heritage Center, University of Wyoming, copyright restricted.

America while he was hiding out down there, and that she learned a heap about Butch Cassidy, the Wyoming outlaw and others of the "wild bunch' down there and is writing the real facts about "Butch."[31]

However, a vow that she, her sister Maude Charter, and Mary Calvert Lay had taken never to speak of their husbands' nefarious activities apparently prevailed; no manuscript by Jano is known to survive. Even the lucrative offers of movie makers would not induce her to break her vow, though she considered most of "that Wild Bunch of outlaws" to be "socially detestable." Following a short-lived second marriage, Jano moved to Denver in 1955. She remained in good health until 1967, when she suffered a stroke. A second stroke in 1973 left her depressed and unable to cope with growing old and increasing incapacities. Jano pondered if strokes might be a punishment for things she had done wrong in her life, rather than just the result of old age. She stated that when people get like her, "They ought to just be shot." She passed away on November 6, 1975. It was evident to friends and family that her love for George Musgrave endured to the end.[32]

Musgrave, likewise, remained devoted to Jano. Following her departure, "It seems that he began to go down hill, get into all kinds of crooked deals." Musgrave warned Tschiffely to stay out of the way; he intended "to drown his disappointment in whiskey. This he proceeded to do with such determination that, whenever I saw him, he was in a terrible state." After a two-month binge, George temporarily abandoned the bottle and resumed his wanderings. He frequently remarked that he should have never sent Jano home, adding that "it was the mistake of his life."[33]

According to Tschiffely, Musgrave worked for a time as a corporate strikebreaker. As he strolled up and down outside of the company's headquarters, his presence proved sufficient to discourage the strikers. While strikebreaking offered monetary incentives, working for someone else was not to Musgrave's liking. He preferred self-employment and soon returned to Paraguay where he resumed a life of rustling cattle, mules, and horses, which he herded across the borders of various South American countries to sell to unscrupulous buyers. He needed a gang; Paraguay and Brazil provided a wealth of undesirables from which to select.[34] Bob Eaton recalled: "Handsome and always wearing a hat peaked like the northern cowboys, he took good care of his men. They did not consider themselves 'outlaws' but rather like kids stealing water melons. Cattle rusting is considered a 'crime' by cattle ranchers but the general public may take it as a joke (especially if a big company is the victim)."[35]

Musgrave soon came to enjoy notoriety as "the most famous of gringo cattle-rustlers [*abigeos*] in South America."[36]

He recalled one occasion when he had contracted to sell cattle to International Products Corporation. He rode to IPC's ranch at Pinasco and met Charles Campbell, the haughty English ranch manager and the company's vice-president. To gain an insight into Campbell's management habits, Musgrave plied him with drink; his men did likewise with the ranch hands. By the time the liquor had been consumed, Musgrave had the operation figured out.[37]

Some days later, Musgrave returned with more liquor; the thirsty Campbell heartily welcomed him. The next morning George's cowboys drove the first lot of cattle up to Pinasco, some five hundred according to the oft-told tale. Some of the IPC cowboys recalled that Musgrave supplied demijohns of water for his men, but water pails of rum for IPC's hands. The cattle passed through the chute to receive their brands, but as the alcohol warmed up the cowboys, the branding irons cooled off. After the count, Musgrave claimed that he and the manager returned to the house to drink to the arrival of the first lot. Three to four hours later, the second bunch arrived. After the count, the two men again retreated to the house to celebrate, as they did following the arrival of the third. After counting the fourth batch, and confirming the count, Musgrave received a check in payment, drawn on an Asunción bank. After sending his men back to Brazil, he took the next boat down to Asunción and presented the check for payment the next morning, pocketing the cash.[38]

> That son of a bitching manager never found out for six months that I had sold him five hundred head for the two thousand he had paid me for. He was half pie-eyed or he might have known, an' his men were plumb riotous with th' liquor my boys had given 'em. When we counted th' first herd in, it was took out again immediate, travelled round some, then brought up again, counted in, took out, counted in again, re-took out and recounted again, two thousand head barrin' a few fallers by th' wayside, which were duly discounted from th' total.[39]

Doubtless, Musgrave's story grew with the telling. Indeed, in some accounts the figure swelled to three thousand, almost the size of IPC's entire herd. More accurately, Musgrave's men unquestionably managed to run a number of cold-branded cattle through the chute more than once. Campbell, it is recalled, had agreed to buy Musgrave's entire herd, including his pigpen brand, on the condition that George not be present. IPC officials later learned of the shortage and called Musgrave to task. His rebuttal? He could hardly be held responsible when it was Campbell who had sent a bunch of drunken cowboys to receive his herd. IPC would never again have official dealings with the Chaco rustler.[40]

Another swindle story that Musgrave liked to tell concerned IPC's mandioca crop. The company cultivated mandioca, the cassava plant, used for making bread. With the sale of the cattle, Musgrave had contracted to sell mandioca plants at a fixed price per plant. The day before delivery, he claimed he stuck two hundred stalks into the ground and thereby artificially increased his delivered total by a like amount.[41]

The beginning of George Musgrave's transformation from rustler to modern-day mobster began with Jano's departure. This transformation is unique among the West's outlaw personalities. While a few of his 1890 contemporaries retired, and many more met violent ends, Musgrave adapted as the years passed and continued with his nefarious activities throughout his entire life. His crimes became increasingly organized, aided by the liberal use of influential contacts.

Musgrave also took a common-law wife, Zulema Montania, from Porto Murtinho on the east bank of the Río Paraguay in Brazil's Mato Grosso do Sul, and they had a son, Roberto. Still later, George and Zulema had a daughter named for his mother, Prudence. Yet all was not well. About 1928, Musgrave's incessant womanizing again got him in trouble. "His wife shot him, the bullet intended for his heart, but the gun, in the hands of his furious spouse, wavered; he was struck in the foot." The wound did not stop Musgrave from continuing both his personal and business exploits. About this time, he met a fledgling cowboy, Bill Craig.[42]

Born in England on September 4, 1901, Craig had served with the Royal Navy during World War I, then he migrated to Argentina,

Bill Craig. *A Rebel for a Horse*, 1934.

determined to become a cowboy. In 1924, following a six-month visit to England, he hired on as undermanager of the British-owned estancia Santa Inez in Argentina. Four years later he reached Paraguay. Craig "could write a story about anything and make it interesting." But the accuracy of many of Craig's stories, like Tschiffely's, is open to question.[43]

Craig boarded an old stern-wheeler cattleboat up the Río Paraná for Paraguay, and encountered the vessel's only other passenger, Musgrave. George praised the virtues of Paraguay, "Yeah, this heah is a mighty fine country for any one like myself who needs somewhere to be inconspicuous in from time to time. When you're in Paraguay," Musgrave elaborated, "you are within easy jump of Argentina, Uruguay, Bolivia and Brazil, which can sometimes be very useful."[44]

For the next two days the men drank *cóctel Guaraní*, smoked cigars, and fired pot shots at alligators. George slyly proposed that

Craig seek employment with International Products Corporation. The two men could pool their talents to mutual benefit, "For I am bringing in stock from Brazil without paying no tax. You buy 'em for the company and we split the tax and profits. Can't go wrong, it's a genuine business deal."[45]

Craig took Musgrave's advice and left the stern-wheeler at Villeta to apply for a job with IPC's packing plant in nearby San Antonio. As the vessel pulled away from the wharf, Musgrave "fired a salvo of shots in the air and waved adios with a caña bottle from his chair on the upper deck."[46]

Stories of Musgrave's exploits circulated throughout the region. George would board the Mihanovitch company's luxurious side-wheelers that steamed up and down the Río Paraná and the Río Paraguay and make them wait in port until he finished drinking and cavorting. Yarns indicated that when asked what type of whiskey he desired, he would pull out his gun and shoot the neck off a bottle of White Horse. There were tales of him shooting out the lights in his stateroom while lying in bed. The boat captains bore his escapades good-naturedly; Musgrave always made good on the damages.[47]

After he had served some months as stockyard foreman with IPC, the company appointed Craig one of its cattle buyers. One day, bound for the ranch of Enrique Saval near the Brazilian frontier, he boarded a plush side-wheeler to Concepción. Craig claims to have again encountered Musgrave, lounging in the big saloon amid blaring American music and blazing electric lights. Musgrave called for a bottle of White Horse and the best *Flor de Cuba* cigars on board, then told Craig that he had heard about Craig's new job with IPC. Musgrave had just acquired a large number of Brazilian steers, "bought and paid for," which he planned to import, contraband. He would, of course, be willing to sell them to IPC cheap, for cash, no check. Craig said he could do nothing without the permission of the company. He wired his boss when the vessel anchored at Concepción. Musgrave rented a car to drive to Brazil;

Craig accompanied him as far as the Saval ranch, one hundred and eighty miles to the northeast.[48]

As they drove, Musgrave told Craig about a fine string of horses that he also intended to bring in from Brazil. Craig wanted one, less than five years of age and no less than fifteen hands high.[49] After Musgrave left, Don Enrique entertained Craig with stories of the outlaw and his capabilities as a cattleman: "You know that when you are trooping a herd, after about a week you know the cattle; if any escape during the night you can generally tell which are missing when day comes? [Musgrave] goes further than that. I'll guarantee that if he was to take this herd you have just bought, nine hundred head, before he'd had it twelve hours on the road he'd know every individual steer."[50]

Musgrave returned to Saval's ranch a week later. Bill Craig, ever the romantic, related that in the evening while they sat on Saval's verandah, Musgrave played a guitar and tearfully sang the old Spanish song, *La Paloma*. Musgrave described the herd of cattle and horses that he had acquired, including, according to Craig, a large iron-gray bronco bearing the brand of Don B. Castado de Miranda of Mato Grosso. Craig bought the horse and named him the Bobby Horse. However, Bob Eaton insists, "The Bobby Horse was a great animal as I can attest from riding and working him but it did not come from [Musgrave]."[51]

When they reached Concepción, Craig received IPC's response to his inquiry regarding the cattle purchase. Craig revealed the contents of the telegram to Musgrave—on no account should he buy cattle from Musgrave. George contended: "Hell's flames, I might of been able to stole 'em ten years ago, but this country's getting so damned civilised that a man cain't do nothin' without cash. These heah cattle of mine are smuggled, but that don't mean I didn't have to pay nothin' to th' customs; I sure did. And they ain't stole, I paid for every mother's son of 'em. Had to."[52]

Musgrave and Craig took rooms that evening at the Hotel Frances. The next morning, they encountered a number of Paraguayan Army officers in the hotel's saloon. A drunken officer, Lieutenant Evan Evans of Welsh extraction, introduced himself, and Captain Arturo Bray, of English descent, sauntered over. When Evans began to fire his .32 revolver into the floor near Musgrave, George let out a yell, pulled his gun, and shot a row of bottles off the shelf behind the bar. The four then ran for their horses and galloped down the street, shooting as they rode. They reached the top of a hill, turned, and raced back. They found the street empty, save for one pig in front of the hotel. "This pig we unanimously percolated before dismounting and going into the bar," claimed Craig. They dined that night on pork loin and joked with the officers. When the siren then announced the departure of Craig's boat, Musgrave saw him off. It was the last Craig saw of George, though he would hear of many exploits in the future.[53]

Bill Craig effectively captured the lighthearted side of Musgrave's character in these yarns; he certainly found Musgrave memorable. What truth there may be in his tales is another matter: Musgrave later told Bob Eaton, "This guy Craig is said to have written about me but I never saw him in my life."[54]

After Craig's departure, Musgrave did manage to sell his contraband herd at a good price. Predictably, the company that bought it found itself in an international legal entanglement over ownership, and the legal fees involved in cutting the Gordian knot proved considerably more expensive than the savings on the herd. Of course, Musgrave was no longer around. He had become a twentieth-century crime boss.[55]

CHAPTER SEVENTEEN

CRIME BOSS

You'd never think [George Musgrave] was what he was to look at him. You'd be ready to bet he was a senator or some-one high up in Tammany at the very least. Tall, big, suave, soft-spoken and invariably well-dressed. He's about the most famous man who ever hit this part of the world.

CHARLES WILLIAM THURLOW CRAIG

Between 1919 and 1933, organized crime in the United States flourished against the backdrop of Prohibition. The age of the classic western outlaw passed as the old-style bandit gave way to the gangster, racketeer, and mobster, and the automobile replaced the horse. Among the lawless element, the Thompson submachine gun and the semiautomatic pistol succeeded the Winchester rifle and the Colt six-shooter.

The grip of depression seized the industrialized world in the 1930s. Non-industrialized but laissez-faire Paraguay, her economy largely dependent upon foreign investment, likewise suffered. The outbreak of a devastating war in 1932 further threatened her fiscal resources.

Musgrave could have become a relic of the past, as did most of his desperado generation. He did not. More individualistic than

George West Musgrave.
Courtesy The American
Heritage Center, Univer-
sity of Wyoming, copy-
right restricted.

nationalistic and in favor of a government that took a laissez-faire
attitude toward his occupation, Musgrave diversified his illicit
operation. Cattle-rustling remained the leitmotiv, but smuggling,
assassination, even counterfeiting also became common activities.
Although Musgrave never developed a crime network compara-
ble to those of American crime bosses, he—the contemporary of Butch
Cassidy, the Sundance Kid, and Black Jack Christian—entered, and
survived, the era of Al Capone, Dutch Schultz, and Bonnie and
Clyde.

> Elegantly dressed in a white suit of heavy tropical silk that
> had obviously been made for him by a good tailor, he wore
> no weapons in sight and the only things that might have sug-
> gested that he was a cattleman were his well-cut, high-heeled
> boots, which he wore under his trousers. He looked more like

a senator than a cattle rustler. He had a presence that would have instilled confidence into the most suspicious mind, and a personality that fitted his appearance.[1]

Selling and delivering contraband, he appeared monthly at Puerto Casado, always with a new señora. "Doing good business, [he was] thinking about returning to the States and buying a castle in Beverly Hills." It was perhaps with that goal in mind that, near the end of the 1920s, he contracted to deliver a large herd to a Brazilian ranch on the frontier, north of the Río Apa. Continuing his long tradition of preying upon Paraguayan ranches, he rustled a herd from the English-owned Liebig Ranch. Undoubtedly, Musgrave and his men had previously pillaged this extremely large, but poorly managed, concern. The caper should have unfolded without incident, but Musgrave's wife, Zulema, weary of his infidelities and determined to get even, evidently found some officials not on his payroll and reported his plan to them.[2]

As George and a dozen of his tough Brazilian cowpunchers drove the last of the stolen Liebig herd at a leisurely pace across the huge ranch of the *Societé Foncière du Paraguay* and into the Río Apa, they had no reason to expect an ambush. In his inimitable style, Bill Craig recounted, "There was a nice moon and plenty of light. He sent his point riders over first so as to hold them on the other side, and then started to let the cattle down nice and gentle, the boys rolling cigarettes, sitting sideways on their saddles, talking about this and that and generally taking things easy."[3]

Suddenly, gunfire erupted.

> [Musgrave] was about halfway across the river at the time, the water about belly-deep to his horse, which was shot from under him at the first volley. He landed on his feet and took a slug through the shoulder. He saw his men falling all around and decided that it was no battle and just floated downstream in the night. Fortunately for him that's a fast running little river and he didn't get attacked by pirañas or alligators. He drifted a mile or so, then came ashore and walked to the hut

of a hunter who was a friend of his. When he was fit to travel he rode home, gave [Zulema] some money and told her to get the hell out. It wasn't for himself, he told her, but he didn't like losing all his best men.[4]

According to Craig, Musgrave lost the entire herd and two of his men died in the brief battle. Bob Eaton, however, contends that there was no shooting and Musgrave and his men fled from the police. The Liebig corporation might have been poorly managed but it enjoyed considerable political influence, which it now brought to bear. With his reputation in Paraguay completely tarnished, Musgrave fled to Brazil and settled at Porto Murtinho in the Mato Grosso, on the east bank of the Río Paraguay.[5]

Primarily a forested region, the Mato Grosso also contained hundreds of thousands of acres of grassy rangelands; cattle raising was the principle industry. In 1913, former President Theodore Roosevelt had described the small Brazilian town of Porto Murtinho as being home to some twelve hundred inhabitants: "Some of the buildings were of stone; a large private house with a castellated tower was of stone; there were shops, and a post-office, stores, a restaurant and billiard-hall, and warehouses for matte, of which much is grown in the region roundabout. Most of the houses were low, with overhanging, sloping eaves; and there were gardens with high walls, inside of which trees rose, many of them fragrant."[6]

In Porto Murtinho, Musgrave was removed from troubles that were brewing in Paraguay. However, he maintained his connections there. Although many of the exploits attributed to him rely purely on anecdotal sources, an assassination plot that attracted modest international attention, is partially documented and therefore deserves examination.

The target was Canadian-born John H. Scott, general manager of the IPC facility at Puerto Pinasco. Craig recalled that "he was a dictator manager and made many enemies amongst the workers. He liked to think they were afraid of him." To fatten his wallet, Scott entered into a partnership with Musgrave and Enrique Fox of

Asunción. Aware of Musgrave's incorrigible reputation, he should
have had enough sense to sidestep the deal, but greed overcame
wisdom. Using ten thousand dollars invested by Scott, Musgrave
acquired cattle. He may have purchased the herd legally in Brazil
and smuggled it into Paraguay, or he may have rustled at least some
of the stock from IPC, then shipped the cattle to Fox, who sold them
profitably. Before any division of the profits could be made, Fox
died of a heart attack and Musgrave disappeared. So, too, did the
money. Out ten grand, not to mention the anticipated profit, the
enraged Scott sought revenge. No doubt, Musgrave now saw Scott
as a dangerous enemy, an enemy that he needed to eliminate.[7]

Late in 1929, Craig, still employed at the company's packing
plant at San Antonio, traveled to Puerto Pinasco to conduct a count
of the herd at the company's port ranch. Arriving at the port ranch,
Craig received some bad news. Although the company's main
ranch, eighty kilometers west, should have thirty thousand head of
stock, he was told its manager believed the count would be no more
than twenty-seven thousand head. The manager of another of IPC's
outlying estancias sorrowfully reported an even worse shortage—
12 percent—while at the company's port ranch, where Craig would
conduct the count, manager John Francis Wright hesitatingly pre-
dicted that his count would be worse still. He attributed the pro-
jected shortfall to jaguars, Indians, and rustlers.[8]

Although Craig secretly believed Wright to be a former member
of Black Jack Ketchum's gang, in fact he came from Lansing, Michigan; had settled in Pennsylvania; was a veteran of World War I and
a member of the American Legion. He had worked for IPC for ten
years and knew that the expected shortage would put his job in jeop-
ardy. Bob Eaton recalled that Scott was "a hard fellow to deal with"
and would "heckle Wright over the most childish subjects." Wright
confided to Craig that he believed Scott suspected him of rustling
and anticipated that the eighteen thousand head of cattle, uncounted
for two and a half years, would fall short by four thousand.[9]

After nine days of counting, the final tally proved Wright's fore-
cast correct. Scott angrily threatened to fire Wright, and to replace

him at the port ranch with Duncan McDonald, a sheepman from Patagonia who had arrived to assume management of the main ranch, if he did not come up with at least fifteen hundred head of missing cattle.[10]

It is apparent that Scott had decided to make Wright a scapegoat to cover his own indiscretion. Any large shortfall in the count would indicate rustling, which, in turn, would surely suggest Musgrave's involvement. Scott could hardly afford to have his own name linked to the American rustler. Scott and Wright, each without the knowledge of the other, could have been in collusion with Musgrave. The vehemence with which Scott subsequently condemned Wright suggests strongly that he did believe Wright to be Musgrave's agent, yet nothing suggests that Musgrave conspired with Wright to rustle IPC stock. Indeed, it could be inferred from Wright's personality that he lacked the grit for such an undertaking. Only when Wright was faced with dismissal, would Musgrave evidently find him a useful ally. In spite of his later protestations, as well as the findings of the court, events implicate Wright as a figure caught within Musgrave's web.

Wright fled from Scott's wrath, encountered Craig, and, to Craig's surprise, insisted, in spite of his concern for his job, that everything was fine. Wright asked if Craig had an old, unwanted revolver he would sell. Craig had a nearly worn-out Colt single-action Frontier for which he wanted one thousand pesos. Wright pulled out a roll of five thousand pesos and handed a thousand to Craig.[11]

Wright pocketed the six-shooter and invited Craig to ride some miles out of Pinasco to meet with Antonio Dos Santos, one of the company's line riders. Possibly, Wright explained, Dos Santos could shed light on the rustling activities. That afternoon, Wright and Craig rode to see Dos Santos. Craig later claimed that he took an immediate dislike to the dark, evil-looking Brazilian who came from Murtinho, in itself indicative of a link to Musgrave. The presence of an obviously battered wife only magnified Craig's hostility toward Dos Santos. After a discussion that touched on many topics, but curiously failed to bring up the subject of rustling, Wright and Dos Santos slipped outside for a private conversation. Craig stayed inside, listening to the wife's tales of woe. As Craig and Wright returned to Pinasco, Wright displayed mixed emotions: a measure of elation, but also a touch of nervousness.[12]

Craig rode to the Radio Club that evening. Inside, he spotted Duncan McDonald, sitting alone drinking a glass of beer. Craig introduced himself, ordered a drink, and joined the Scotsman. Craig soon learned that Scott planned to give McDonald a tour of the IPC facility the next afternoon.

Craig arose late the next morning, November 29, and soon encountered Wright, who mentioned that he had to go to the office to draw some money. Although curious about what happened to the rest of the five thousand pesos Wright had flashed only the day before, Craig remained silent.[13]

About three o'clock in the afternoon, Scott and McDonald climbed into a rail-car mounted on the narrow-gauge tracks leading west out of Pinasco. The square boxlike car, with the engine and gearshift in the center, had two seats in front and a bench seat in back. A chauffeur took the left front seat and Scott the right. McDonald sat behind. The driver fired up the engine; the rail-car chugged out of town.[14]

Near kilometer nine, they rounded a sharp bend and discovered a heavy branch lying between the tracks, small enough for the logging train to pass over, but large enough to stop the rail-car. The driver got out to move it. As he leaned over to grab the branch, a shot rang out from the heavy vegetation to the north. The bullet just missed; he fell flat and lay still. Scott reached for a .44-caliber Winchester, locked in the toolbox under the seat. A second shot killed McDonald; his body tumbled out of the car. As Scott turned to look back at McDonald, the rifle barked a third time. A bullet tore into Scott's side. The driver, frightened but unwounded, crawled back to the car, threw it into reverse, and pulled away, the car continuing in reverse until it reached a maintenance crew working on the track. With the workmen as reinforcements, the driver and the wounded Scott returned for McDonald's body.[15]

In the brush, assassin Antonio Dos Santos's rifle jammed after the third shot. His orders were to kill all three men, place their bodies into the car, and then set it on fire. He had failed, but believing that he had killed Scott, the primary target, he left the scene and rode back to his house. Scott, however, was not dead. The bullet had struck his bottom rib and deflected forward, stopping just under the skin.

A telegram from Pinasco arrived at the company's packing plant at San Antonio informing John Tippett, IPC president, of Scott's shooting. Tippett and the newly hired Robert Eaton immediately traveled up river. "The evening of our arrival I met John Scott for the first time. He was tightly bandaged as the wound was on the right side where the bullet had hit a rib and glanced off leaving a painful but not dangerous wound. I heard his report of the incident as made to the president."[16]

Meanwhile, Pinasco Police Commissioner Vincinte Silveira hurriedly formed a posse of seven or eight men. Bill Craig, eager to participate, invited himself along. The posse soon located the spot where the assassin had lain in wait. From where Dos Santos had tied his horse, a Toothli Indian tracker led the posse five miles to Dos Santos's house. When they confronted him, the frightened Brazilian protested that he had not left the house. Craig later credited himself with being the one who alertly called attention to the line rider's horse, covered with fresh sweat. A couple of men in the posse led Dos Santos outside and mercilessly battered a confession out of him. The posse also searched the house and found four thousand pesos and a Colt Frontier revolver.[17]

They took the badly beaten suspect to Pinasco and subjected him to further questioning in Commissioner Silveira's custom-built, water-filled, electrified bathtub. After only a few jolts, Dos Santos named John Wright as his contact. He did not mention Musgrave. Evidently, Dos Santos feared Musgrave's wrath even more than Silveira's torture. He claimed that Wright offered him five thousand Paraguayan paper pesos to "liquidate" Scott, and continued to pester him to commit the murder, even calling Dos Santos a "coward and a bum" if he refused do it.[18]

On the evening of the shooting, the Puerto Pinasco justice of the peace ordered the formation of a *sumario* (inquest). Dr. Eusebio Rios, criminal judge of the second Judicial District, traveled to Pinasco and took charge of the inquest on December 5. Brought before the *sumario,* Dos Santos cold-bloodedly related, point by point, how he planned and carried out the assassination. He boasted that the McDonald shooting was not his first murder for hire. In his native Brazil (at Murtinho and Corumba), he had committed similar assassinations for others. "This hardened criminal sees himself as a veteran at this sort of crime, a *cebado* [a man-killer], reported one of Asuncíon's newspapers." The *sumario* had no difficulty in identifying Dos Santos as the *autor material* (killer). In the opinion of Judge Rios, Dos Santos's testimony "gravely implicated" John Wright as the *autor moral* (instigator). Musgrave's name was not mentioned. On December 10, Rios ordered the preventive detention of Wright and the removal of Wright and Dos Santos to the jail at Asunción.[19]

Located on Calle Comuneros, the overcrowded old jail held all manner of felons. Craig visited the former manager there, bringing a bottle of rye whiskey and a carton of cigarettes. He listened to Wright's claim of innocence: "Come close and I'll tell you who's really responsible." Craig heard Wright whisper the name of notorious "badman" George Musgrave.[20]

Two decades after the killing of McDonald and the wounding of Scott, and seven years following Musgrave's death, Craig wrote of the event: "It is not really a closed book even today [1954], for although the two protagonists are long-since dead, there are those who stoutly maintain that Bob Steward [George Musgrave], was the driving force behind the whole thing. He died peacefully in bed in Asuncion several years ago, and although he was far away in Brazil at the time could possibly have been the driving force."[21] Undoubtedly, Craig would have been less equivocal had he known of the business partnership between Scott and Musgrave.

Scott recovered from his wounds. Dos Santos's trial date was repeatedly postponed, as was Wright's. Dos Santos contracted pneumonia in January 1930. Convinced that his death was at hand, on January 24 he retracted that portion of his testimony implicating Wright. Nevertheless, Wright remained in jail with no trial scheduled.[22]

In August, Post Wheeler, America's minister to Paraguay, arranged Wright's removal from the jail to more comfortable quarters in one of the police stations, a routine transfer for a prisoner of "some position." At the end of the quarter, the police returned such prisoners to the jail for one or two days for inspection by the judicial authorities, then brought them back to the police stations.

Certain that Scott had bribed police officials to keep him in jail, Wright became convinced that, as an American, he would not get justice. In fact, Scott had brought pressure upon the British Legation to delay the trial in order to find more evidence against Wright.[23]

Scott's pressure paid dividends. The British chargé d'affaires, Herbert Ashley Cunard Cummins, complained to the Paraguayan Foreign Office that Wright, implicated in the murder of a British subject (McDonald), received "unwarranted liberty and may take the opportunity to escape."[24]

In December, the American chargé d'affaires, John B. Faust, notified Secretary of State Henry W. Stimson:

> By what right the British Chargé d'Affaires presumes to indicate to the Paraguayan Government where it shall keep its prisoners I am unable to say but, since it appears that Mr. Wright was removed to the police station as a personal and unofficial favor to Mr. Wheeler and, of course, with no indication that it would result in a protest from Mr. Cummins, it does not appear expedient at the present time for me to request that [Wright] again be placed there in spite of the objection.[25]

Faust reconsidered and submitted a request that Wright be allowed to remain at the police station. Paraguayan officials agreed to the request, but the first time Faust took a leave "some attempt was made to have Wright transferred from the police station back to the jail." Faust considered the British chargé the likely culprit.[26]

The American consulate was not alone in alleging intrigue. Bill Craig later claimed that the U.S. vice consul offered him five thousand dollars not to testify against Wright, but he refused the bribe. "Five thousand dollars then was worth easily 6,000 English pounds now [1965]. Particularly in that country. And I've often wondered why I didn't accept it. A sense of loyalty to Scott, I suppose. Or Musgrave."[27]

There is no question about Craig's loyalty to Scott. "Craig felt very involved in this incident and had letters from John Scott thanking him for his support as witness." Does Craig's claim of a bribe have merit? Acting U. S. Consul V. Harwood Blocker, Jr., was posted as foreign service officer to Asunción on March 28, 1930, and assumed position as vice consul on October 22. Pioneer Chaco cattleman Robert Eaton recalled, "Blocker, my friend and best man at my wedding, was upset that Wright, a U.S. citizen could not get a fair trial." However, as far as his offering a bribe was concerned, "I know this is not true. Craig never met Blocker." Moreover, while Blocker did express his view concerning Wright's predicament, Faust, as chargé d'affaires, handled the matter. Finally, there is not the slightest indication within the State Department's confidential file on the affair that the government instructed any American official to tender a bribe to Craig or anyone else.[28]

Nine months following the killing, Minister Post Wheeler summed up the circumstances:

> The testimony assembled during this prolonged period appeared extremely weak. There was no indication of motive shown. The Brazilian murderer, on whose first statement Mr. Wright had been charged, a month later retracted it when he believed himself to be at the point of death from pneumonia, making a sworn declaration in the presence of the hospital authorities (which he confirmed without solicitation five months later before Judge [Clemeco] Fernandez) that he had

implicated Wright to satisfy a personal grudge, and that his accusation made in Pinasco was a falsehood. And without motive shown, allegation of premeditation was valueless.[29]

Throughout this time, the inquest remained uncompleted, in direct violation of Paraguay's Penal Law limiting the duration of any inquest to two months.[30]

In late 1930, Wright's attorney, Dr. Luis Raffinelli, filed a petition with the *Tribunal Inferior* for the discharge of his client on the ground of insufficient evidence. When the *Tribunal* rejected the petition on May 25, 1931, Raffinelli promptly appealed the decision to the Appellate Division.[31]

Days later, at the Asunción jail, a knife fight broke out between Dos Santos and Valentín González. González plunged his dagger into Dos Santos's stomach. Dos Santos dropped his knife and retreated, grasping his abdomen. The guards intervened and restrained González, also wounded.

Quickly responding to an urgent summons from the prison authorities, Dr. Rogelio Alvarez determined the gravity of Dos Santos's condition and ordered him rushed to the hospital, where careful examination revealed that Dos Santos had suffered multiple perforations of the intestines. He died of peritonitis on Saturday, June 6. Bill Craig maintained that "someone had made certain that he would not testify again." If there was any connection between González and Musgrave, evidence of it remains undiscovered.[32]

John Wright complained to Chargé Faust about the court's lack of action: "Now, with the Brazilian at rest, the only question that concerns my end of the case is, did I tell or order the Brazilian to do the shooting. Whether he did it or not has no bearing on my end of the case."[33]

"The legal shenanigans, dragged on for a couple of years," recalled Bob Eaton. Throughout, Wright staunchly maintained his innocence. Eaton "met Wright in the Consul's office. He was obsessed about convincing any one who listened, of his innocence."[34]

On September 5, 1931, the American minister, Post Wheeler, requested that the Paraguay minister of foreign affairs, Dr. Gerónimo Zubizarreta, give the case his personal attention. Two days later, the judges of the Court of Appeals in Commercial and Criminal Cases adjudged that:

1) The accusation against Wright and Dos Santos was brought at an improper time.
2) There was a failure to follow leads suggesting involvement by others.
3) Dos Santos retracted his deposition naming Wright as "moral instigator."
4) Dos Santos had died.

The Court of Appeals quashed the case and Wright walked out of jail after twenty-three months of imprisonment. Although the ruling gained Wright his freedom, it certainly did not exonerate him. A number of unresolved matters still suggest that he was Musgrave's pawn.[35]

And, what of Musgrave, the actual *autor moral*? His involvement remained shrouded in mystery, discussed only in whispers. John Scott had sought to profit from a business proposition he knew to be unlawful. Although an experienced ranchman, he was not in the same league as Musgrave, who was "very bad and even dangerous company." IPC's President John Tippett best summarized the relationship and its outcome, "I do not believe there is any reason to take measures against Scott as this has been a tough lesson for him."[36]

Craig related that within the next two years, things became too hot for George in the Mato Grosso of Brazil. Certainly Musgrave saw the 1930 Revolution, begun by Governor Getulio Dorneles Vargas of Río Grande del Sul, as a further opportunity for his specialized talents. It would appear, however, that the Vargas administration failed to fully appreciate those talents.[37]

One day during his Brazilian interlude, Musgrave and others were shooting at alligators from the deck of a passenger boat at Isla

Margarita in front of the Murtinho port. The vessel's captain offered some sarcastic remarks about the quality of the shooting. George handed his revolver over to the captain and challenged him to do better. Without warning, the captain shot him in the face and neck. Unconscious, or perhaps feigning unconsciousness, Musgrave was dumped into a canoe, and the captain ordered the canoe's owner to "take this Gringo and bury him." Later in relating the incident to IPC President John Tippett, Musgrave joked, *"Yerba mala no muere"* [You can't kill a bad weed].[38]

Bill Craig exercised ample literary license in describing Musgrave's actions after the shooting:

> He sat back in his chair and laughed at the captain with blood a'running down out of his mouth and nose, and got to work extracting his own gun.
> Aboot the time they was planting the captain, [George] was at the beginning of a ten days' drunk, laughing fit to bust every time he emptied his mouth. Thet bullet had ricochetted off a tooth root and come out through his cheek. He suffered powerful from the toothache until the drink cured him, and now he ain't got but two little round scars to show thet it happened, one in his upper lip and the other on the side of his cheek, like little beauty spots.[39]

Musgrave later did bear "impressive" scars from the shooting on his right cheek and throat. However, the ship's captain survived the incident unscathed. It is tempting to attribute the captain's salvation to Musgrave's jocular nature. Being shot in the face would tend to strain even the finest sense of humor. Musgrave's decision not to retaliate was based, however, upon cold reality. The ship was under the Paraguayan flag in Paraguayan waters. As a resident of Brazil and persona non grata in Paraguay, he did not need added difficulties with Paraguayan officials.[40]

For decades, a dispute had been brewing between Paraguay and Bolivia over boundaries in the Chaco Boreal (that portion of the Gran Chaco lying north of the Río Pilcomayo). Bolivia, after losing its seacoast in the War of the Pacific (1879–1883), desired to secure a port on the Río Paraguay and thereby an access to the sea. Paraguay, in turn, sought to retain the region because two-thirds of its foreign exchange came from Chaco revenues. When the dispute over ownership escalated into hostilities in July 1932, the *New York Times* observed that the Chaco territory being fought over "includes immense stretches of fine pasture land," but quoted John Foster Frazer, the English journalist, as remarking that "when our ancestors invented hell they had no knowledge of the Chaco."[41]

In September 1932, as the Paraguayan army prepared to launch its initial offensive thrust against Boquerón, elements of the Fourth Cavalry stationed themselves at George Lohman's Chaco ranch at Pozo Colorado, a short distance east of *fortín* Nanawa. The army requisitioned large numbers of his cattle and took possession of some of his corrals in which it confined the cattle until required at the front.[42]

Following months of bloody encounters, Paraguay officially declared war on Bolivia on May 10, 1933. With larger, well-schooled, well-equipped forces, and a German-trained officer corps, Bolivian General Hans Kundt had adopted a strategy of advancing toward Concepción and was already focusing attention upon *fortín* Nanawa. "Our fort was bombed, and we could hear artillery fire," recalled Robert Eaton. "We had all the discomforts of war and none of the glories." At ten o'clock on the morning of May 8, two days prior to the declaration of war, four Bolivian planes bombarded George Lohman's ranch. The planes dropped ten bombs in the thirty-five minute attack, destroyed one house, and seriously damaged three others (a loss valued at one hundred thousand Paraguayan paper pesos). The bombs also killed a number of cattle and horses, damaged one steel water tank, and additional ranch equipment (worth an additional fifty thousand pesos). A second air raid on August 25 killed a ranch worker by the name of Kelly. The ranch itself suffered no material damage, although two bombs fell close to the house. When a new truce was accepted on June 12, 1935, Paraguay occupied nearly all of the disputed territory. The Chaco Peace Conference formally declared the war concluded on October 28.[43]

Whatever Musgrave's activities were during the Chaco War, they remain undocumented. His friend Aimé Tschiffely noted only that he profited from the subcontinent's frequent revolutions. Indeed, during one, according to Tschiffely, he was responsible for providing the winning side with so many mules, rustled from a neighboring republic, that he became something of a hero to the country where previously he had been an outlaw. Tschiffely may very well have exaggerated this story, but it is more than likely the Chaco War provided Musgrave with profitable opportunities.[44]

Throughout all these turbulent years in South America, George kept in contact with his family. A number of times he invited his sister Adanna to fly down for a visit, offering to pay her way. He wanted her to see his ranch "that he couldn't cover in a day on horseback." Then, about 1938, Musgrave returned to the United States, bringing his son and daughter to Arizona and California to meet members of his family.[45]

By the end of the 1930s, the brief and notorious careers of John Dillinger, Charles "Pretty Boy" Floyd, and George "Machine Gun" Kelly were things of the past. Alphonse "Scarface" Capone, born two years after the Grants train robbery, languished in Alcatraz, his brain rotted by syphilis. But George Musgrave remained alive, well, and active. Again using the alias Bob Cameron, he moved his residence to São Paulo. Serving as the business center of Brazil's rich coffee lands, São Paulo exhibited a prosperity exceeding anything Musgrave would have seen during his years in Paraguay and the Matto Grosso. Most of his activities there remain unknown, but he later told Robert Eaton a story about some Brazilians who had counterfeited money but were afraid to pass the bogus notes. Musgrave went into partnership with them, handled the distribution, and undoubtedly profited.[46]

On one occasion, rancher George Lohman contracted with Musgrave to supply horses from Brazil, and advanced him the money. Musgrave headed toward one his familiar haunts, Bela Vista, on the north bank of the Río Apa separating Paraguay from Brazil. Bill Craig labeled the "little dual-nationality town very cosmopolitan and interesting. I remember once seeing a well-known and highly respected rustler [Musgrave] passing the night in a state of paralysis, side by side on the verandah of a saloon with an unfrocked Irish priest, also incapably drunk."[47]

Outside Bela Vista, Musgrave and a Paraguayan confederate waylaid and held up a messenger carrying the payroll to one of the large ranches of the Matto Grosso. Although his horse was shot, the employee managed to escape on foot. Celebrating, the bandits proceeded to get very drunk and collapsed in a stupor near the site of the robbery. Meanwhile, moving quickly, the messenger contacted the police, who swiftly took up the trail, captured Musgrave and his associate, and jailed them at Bela Vista. Later, while exercising in the patio of the police station, the Paraguayan escaped and carried word to George Lohman that Musgrave needed to see him.

Putting spurs to horse, Lohman rode to Bela Vista. He learned from Musgrave that a police sergeant had been sent from Campo Grande, the capital of Mato Grosso, ostensibly to take the outlaw back as prisoner. Moreover, the sergeant enjoyed a reputation for administering *ley fuga*—that is, liquidating habitual criminals and undesirables, then maintaining that they had been killed while attempting to escape. Lohman agreed to carry a letter from Musgrave to the outlaw's attorney, along with ten thousand pesos. George told Lohman that the reason he was sending the money and letter was to ensure that his family would be looked after. In fact, they both had quite another purpose. As soon as it reached him, the attorney forwarded the letter to Musgrave's men. Evidently, it instructed them to remedy the situation.

Two days later, a pair of gunmen entered the Bela Vista cantiña where the sergeant and several troopers were drinking. As one of them kept the infamous policeman's fellow troopers covered, the other walked up to the sergeant, shouted "You bastard, you killed my brother," and shot him dead. The two then casually strolled the short distance to the border and crossed back into Paraguay. Significantly, Brazilian authorities immediately released Musgrave and deported him to Paraguay. Lohman remained forever convinced it was the ten thousand pesos that had purchased the sergeant's death. However, Musgrave's men demonstrated their loyalty on many occasions, and it seems unlikely that he would have had to pay them to help him on this one. More probably, the money purchased Musgrave's freedom.[48]

CHAPTER EIGHTEEN

END OF THE TRAIL

"Yerba mala no muere" *[You can't kill a bad weed].*

GEORGE WEST MUSGRAVE

"This is the West. When the legend becomes fact, print the legend."

DOROTHY M. JOHNSON

No longer welcome in Brazil, Musgrave returned to Paraguay about 1940 and, probably to secure residential status, quickly took another wife, the Paraguayan-born Carmen González. They settled into a home on Calle Mayor Cassianoff, Villa Morra, Asunción. A new baby, Edison Steward, soon entered the household.[1]

The aging Musgrave met Bob Eaton, a native of South Royalton, Vermont. After high school graduation, Eaton entertained dreams of becoming a cowboy. He packed up and headed for Flagstaff, Arizona, and a job with the Arizona Land and Cattle Company. On Black Thursday, 1929, Eaton signed a three-year contract with the International Products Corporation as a ranch foreman in Paraguay. "I came to South America in search of a frontier, to be another Kit Carson, or a Daniel Boone, or at least a Charles Goodnight. I often wonder why I didn't stop to look at an atlas."[2]

Robert "Bob" Eaton. *Black Jack's Spurs,* 1954.

Musgrave, now in his early sixties, began to slip. His drinking increased; he began to dwell on past glories. One night at George Lohman's Chaco ranch, Musgrave, Lohman, and William F. "Billy" Lewis, another native of Texas and the owner of the neighboring Estrella Sola Ranch, sat around swapping stories. When Lewis recalled that he had known George in Tombstone, Musgrave urged him to remain silent. Later in the evening, and drinking heavily, Musgrave became loquacious. He regaled his small audience with a tale of a Tombstone jailbreak. With the help of a smuggled revolver,

he escaped, stole a horse from a local livery stable, and, riding bare-
back, fled to Mexico. Or so he claimed. As no records or accounts
exist in Cochise County documenting Musgrave's incarceration in
Tombstone, this almost certainly is an elaboration of the story of
his release from jail in Fronteras in 1897, colored with details borrowed from the Christian brothers' breakout in Oklahoma City. He
continued with a story of a single-handed train robbery, likely the
June 9, 1910, heist of the El Paso and Southwestern train no. 2, and
concluded by detailing his efforts to smuggle some Chinese into
the United States. Perhaps the liquor did some of the talking, or
maybe nostalgia caught up with Musgrave. Bob Eaton reflected,
"Picturesque as [George] was, I believe he liked to tell about his
'smart' operations and present them as a big joke. He was his best
publicity agent in many respects. All agree that he could be charming or he could be low down tough."[3]

Carmen gave birth to a second son, Buck Jones Steward, about
October of 1945. Perhaps actor Buck Jones's exciting adventures on
the silver screen had appealed to Musgrave, and he conjured up
memories of his youthful days with the High Five gang. The sad
fact was that there was little else but memories left for the aging outlaw. He no longer had big money to throw around. George Lohman
gave Musgrave enough to live on just to keep him out of trouble.[4]
Musgrave's friend Eaton philosophized:

> I am impressed that none of these apparently successful rob-
> bers seems to have saved any loot or to have done any good
> for themselves. Or maybe that is the case of all outlaws,
> mafia, etc. Easy come, easy go. Live rich and die poor. For 21
> years I was President of the Chaco Vigilante Committee. My
> observation is that these rustlers who worked in a big scale,
> lived harder, worked more, and made less than they would
> have with the same effort as honest ranchers.[5]

Late in his life, George learned of the possibility of an inheritance
in Texas. Under the impression that he and his children might come
into some two hundred thousand dollars, Musgrave discovered

George Musgrave's Colt .44-40, which he gave to Bob Eaton in 1940 with the observation, "You're the only man in Paraguay who will appreciate it." As a gun's front sight will wear down when carried in a holster on horseback, this revolver sports an Enfield-like sight guard. Photograph from the authors' collection.

that to claim it he would have to legally establish his true identity. Ironically, having spent most of his life employing aliases and covering tracks, Roberto Steward now had difficulty establishing that he was George Musgrave. He appealed to the American embassy in Asunción for assistance in establishing his claim. On May 29, 1947, he gave his niece, Ora F. Skelton, a power of attorney so that she could handle his interest in his grandfather's estate. Clearly, he lacked specific details of the legacy.[6]

On May 9, 1873, Musgrave's grandfather, Joe Walker, had filed a claim against Mexico with the Robb Commission. Employing optimistic calculations, Walker maintained that between 1866 and 1873 he lost to raiding Mexican and Indian bands, with the consent of Mexican authorities, 12,328 cattle and 752 horses. Based upon those losses, Walker calculated that Mexico owed him $153,360 plus interest. Joseph Walker died in 1888 with his claim unsettled. His widow, Amanda, pursued the claim throughout the remainder of her life; she died December 19, 1929. Under Section 7 of the Settlement of Mexican Claims Act of 1942, on December 11, 1946, the United States General Claims Commission granted to Walker's estate an award of $11,816.00 with interest. Musgrave's portion of his mother's share amounted to $110. However, George died prior to distribution. He had hoped that the proceeds would provide for his children. In fact, each of his children was entitled to receive only $22.[7]

Musgrave had sound reason to be concerned about his children's future. He suffered from hardening of the arteries. Bob Eaton's wife, Dorothy, believing that he also had throat cancer, kept him supplied with fruit because he had difficulty swallowing hard food.[8]

During the first week of March 1947, when President Higinio Morínigo, a hero of the Chaco War, formed a de facto alliance with his Colorado Party hard liners and their *Guión Rojo* (Red Standard) paramilitary group, full-scale civil war broke out in Paraguay.

Toward the end of July, as the factional struggle continued, Musgrave's wife, Carmen, gave birth to their last son, George Steward. On the last day of July, the government's First Army Corps captured Concepción from the rebels. It was an empty victory since the rebel capital had been largely evacuated. Boatloads of rebels steamed south toward Asunción.[9]

On August 5, a rebel plane dropped several bombs upon the capital, and cannon fire could be heard within the city. The American Embassy offered to evacuate all American women and children, and President Morínigo called upon all residents of Asunción capable of bearing arms to mobilize into the Second Army Corps. Even had he wished to, George Musgrave could not respond to the call. With his arterial sclerosis worsened by acute bronchitis and probable throat cancer, his health failed rapidly.[10]

On August 9, rebel forces captured the airport—*Hernando de la Morris*—isolating the city from the rest of the country. The next day, the rebels fought their way into the capital's suburbs. When the revolt reached the Asunción Navy Yard, and the rebels seized a strategic working-class neighborhood, Lieutenant Colonel Alfredo Stroessner, a member of the Colorado Party, assumed command of the government forces in that area of the fighting.[11]

On August 14, the rebels captured the southern and eastern portions of the city; fighting was continuous, particularly on Olimpio and Pettorosi Streets, which led into the heart of the city and the government-held barricades. The full-scale battle for Asunción began the following day. "The gun fire during the last attack was impressive by any standard," recalled Bob Eaton. Rebel planes, for no apparent military purpose, haphazardly bombed the city, barely missing the Mexican embassy. Due to the fierce fighting, Asunción's banks and shops closed, mail service stopped, and food became increasingly difficult to obtain. The old outlaw missed the excitement.[12]

Amid the heaviest fighting of the war, George West Musgrave, alias Robert Steward, died on August 15, seventy years old, at his home on Calle Mayor Cassianoff. In addition to his personal effects at home, Musgrave's other possessions were, "'horses, a revolver, saddle, etc.' said to be scattered among various places in Argentina, Brazil and Paraguay."[13]

Citing Musgrave's 1912 arrival in Paraguay, his obituary stated that he "from then on has lived in the country dedicated to dealing in cattle, a business at which Mr. Steward enjoyed fame." He was "very well known in all circles." Amusingly, at the time of his death the American embassy allowed that it had heard rumors that Steward was an assumed name.[14]

The morning after his death, following both Protestant and Catholic funeral services, the last of the old-time southwestern outlaws was buried in *Cementerio de la Recoleta*. In the midst of the four-day struggle for Asunción, the government clashed with the rebels for control of the city and of Paraguay. Only two people attended Musgrave's service, Mrs. Eaton and the United States consul. "Bullets were whistling over the walls of the cemetery," according to Dorothy Kent Eaton. "[George] would have liked that send off."[15]

Although modern society teaches and accepts Pericles's admonition that respect for authority and the law provides the bulwark against lawlessness, American tradition applauds courage, self-reliance, endurance, and preserves an ingrained disrespect for government. Perhaps in this dichotomy rests the foundation of America's love affair with the outlaw. Selfish, violent, and unscrupulous, the western badman is eulogized for his Robin Hood qualities, his code among thieves, his chivalry toward women. Yet, history provides us with precious few examples of badmen who embodied this mythic ideal.

George Musgrave rustled, robbed, and killed. George Musgrave was a badman. In 1896, while Democratic presidential candidate William Jennings Bryan campaigned for free silver, the High Fives helped themselves to it. Musgrave participated in the first bank robbery in the history of the Arizona Territory, he held up a previously unrobbed stage line four times in two weeks, he joined in the largest heist in the history of the Santa Fe railroad, and he killed a former Texas Ranger in cold blood. Yet crimes against banks, railroads, and express companies were forgivable felonies in the opinion of many westerners.

In spite of the fact that he was tough, hard, and cold-blooded, it was Musgrave's jovial nature that stood out most in the recollections of oldtimers. The Steins Pass postmaster, Emma Rodgers, witnessed the High Fives' chivalry; the Kent daughters attested to Musgrave's gallantry.

A bandit with staying power, Musgrave distinguished his outlaw career by his adaptation to twentieth century circumstances. Handsome and rugged, charming yet obdurate, affable but incorrigible, George Musgrave, the last of the old-time badmen, came close to possessing the almost impossible list of qualities that exemplify America's legend of the western outlaw.

NOTES

Collections and sources frequently cited have been identified by the following abbreviations:

AHS   Arizona Historical Society
ASA   Arizona State Archives
BT   Louis Bradley Blachly Transcripts
NAB   National Archives Building, Washington, D.C.
NACP   National Archives at College Park, Maryland
NMSA   New Mexico State Archives and Records Center
NSH   Nita Stewart Haley Memorial Library and J. Evetts Haley History Center
TSA   Texas State Archives
UNM   University of New Mexico
WSA   Wyoming State Archives

INTRODUCTION

1. John Cox, ca. June 10, 1952, BT; C. W. Thurlow Craig, *River of Diamonds*, p. 93; Charles P. Sterrett, "Sam Butler—Cowboy Lawman," p. 9.

2. Located on a hill overlooking West Metate Creek, the house stood eight miles south of Pleasanton.

CHAPTER 1: *LA BRASADA*

1. Numerous deeds for the properties of Joseph W. Walker (George Musgrave's maternal grandfather) are filed in Atascosa and McMullen Counties.

2. Martha Beth Walker, interview with the authors, July 1, 1997. For further information see Joseph Walker, Conditional Certificate, Mgl. 10412, August 13, 1838; Headright Certificate #485, 2nd Class, Mgl. 10413, July 12, 1847, file 347—both in TSA, Austin.

3. Rose, *The Texas Vendetta: The Sutton-Taylor Feud,* p. 13, quoted in C. L. Sonnichsen, *I'll Die Before I'll Run*, p. 35.

4. Day Book of Joseph Walker. Walker's second son, Thomas Ira Walker, was tall, with black hair and blue eyes. Texas Ranger Sergeant James B. Gillett wrote of him, "He stands straight, steps firm, is lightning with a pistol." Walker drifted to Abilene after two 1875 acquittals on charges of assault with intent to commit murder in Atascosa County. Following a July 4, 1879, altercation with J. W. Carter in Taylor County, Walker fled Texas with a five-hundred-dollar reward on his head. He reached Lincoln County in the New Mexico Territory in the midst of the Lincoln County War. He died in a gunfight at Seven Rivers, New Mexico, on November 23, 1879 (see Gillett, *A List of Fugitives from Justice*, pp. 258–59; Taylor County, Texas, District Court, *State of Texas v. Tom Walker,* cause #24A; Ferguson, ". . . *and they laid them to rest in the little plot beside the Pecos,*" pp. iv–210). A review of Joseph Walker's purchases for the eighteen months from January 1870 to July 1871, reveals the acquisition of 14 pounds of lead, 8 boxes of revolver caps, and 9 pounds of gun powder, not to mention 247 bottles of whiskey (Live Oak County, Texas, District Court, *James Lowe v. Joseph Walker*, cause #180).

5. *McMullen County History*, p. 449.

6. Live Oak County, Texas, Marriage Book 1, p. 34. A native of Gilmer County, Texas, Prudie was born on February 1, 1846, the second of Joe and Mary Walker's seven children (Day Book of Joseph Walker, Dogtown, Texas, 1869).

7. Musgrave's English Quaker ancestors, likely from the shire of Cumberland, first settled in Lancaster, Pennsylvania. Several of the family branches later migrated to Wayne County, North Carolina. Calvin Musgrave settled in that portion of Gonzales County that was later organized as Caldwell County (Calvin Musgrave's headstone, Bonita Cemetery [located within what is now San Ysidro Cemetery], Pleasanton, Texas; Musgrave Family Bible, owned by Danna Crump, Redding, California, hereinafter Family Bible). Bennett Musgrave was born in Hardeman County, Tennessee, on August 14, 1837. List of names of Captain Levi English's Co. of Mounted Men, organized Aug. 1855 at their own expense for the protection of the Western Frontier within the Western portion of Bexar County, Texas, Nov. 13, 1855, TSA, Austin. This region of Bexar County was organized into Atascosa County in 1856.

8. Cortina led a group of one hundred followers into Brownsville, killed at least four men, released prisoners being held in the Brownsville jail, seized the recently vacated Fort Brown, and launched the Cortina War. See Capt. Peter Tumlinson's Company of Mounted Volunteers in the Service for the State of Texas for the suppression of the Cortina Disturbances on the Rio Grande Frontier on the 12th of November, 1859 thru Feb. 10, 1860, Muster Roll, TSA, Austin.

9. Ford, *Rip Ford's Texas*, pp. 282–83.

10. He was mustered in at Camp McCord on January 24. About May 2, Duff's Battalion was increased to regimental strength and redesignated Thirty-third Texas Cavalry Regiment (Muster Rolls, Co. D, Thirty-third Texas Cavalry Regiment, NAB).

11. Atascosa County, Texas, Deed Book A–1, p. 572. Bennett and Prudie Walker had ridden to neighboring Live Oak County to secure a marriage license (Live Oak County served as the administrative center for McMullen County until 1877). Unaware of Mariah's death, they married the following day, on November 19, 1863.

12. March 12 (United States Post Office Appointments, Texas, vol. 35 [ca. 1867–77], p. 562, also vol. 55, p. 20, [microfilm], U.S. National Archives—Pacific Southwest Region, Laguna Niguel, California). The following year, on November 19, 1868, Calvin married Mary Anderson, the widow of John Augustus Anderson (Atascosa County, Texas, Marriage Book 1, p. 291.)

13. Family Bible. Samuel died on September 23, 1866. Van's first name honored his grandfather; his middle name, his uncle, Texas Ranger Aaron Van Buren Oden. Aaron married Martha Jane Walker, Prudie Musgrave's older sister, on March 17, 1862 (Day Book of Joseph Walker, Dogtown, Texas, 1869). On July 22, 1863, soon after their first anniversary and only four months following the birth of their son, Alonzo Van "Lon" Oden, outlaw Julian Gonzales shot Aaron, about twenty miles south of Eagle Pass. Before expiring, Aaron returned the gunfire and Gonzales also died (George Hindes, Pearsall, Texas, to Laura Oden, El Paso, Texas, October 12, 1925, reproduced in Richards, *The Rest of the Diary and Scrapbook of Alonzo Van Oden*, attachment A). Lon Oden (1863–1910) grew up with his Musgrave cousins, but he followed a strikingly different path as he, like his father, later joined the Texas Rangers (Tanner and Tanner, "Lon Oden, The Rhymin' Ranger," pp. 10–14). The twins were born on March 14, 1868. Burrell Musgrave died at the age of three on September 1, 1871.

14. Bell, *Memories of Peter Tumlinson Bell*, p. 39.

15. Brite, "When He Got Big Enough to Fight, The Indians Were Gone," in Hunter, *Trail Drivers of Texas*, p. 685.

16. March 26, 1869 (Atascosa County, Texas, Deed Book B–1, pp. 262–63). Three years earlier, Prudie's father had provided her with one hundred head of stock cattle and a horse (Atascosa County, Texas, Will of Joseph Walker, Will Book A, p. 609). She filed her brand, PW, in Atascosa County on February 16, 1863 (Atascosa County, Marks and Brands Book 1, p. 150). On April 9, 1867, following her marriage, she registered the SAM brand (Atascosa County, Marks and Brands Book 1, p. 170). There are forty-one real estate entries for the Bennett Musgraves in the Atascosa County Deed Books (B-1 through J-1) between 1869 and 1883. Born on January 2, 1870, and named for a neighbor, LeRoy died one and a half years later on June 14, 1872 (Family Bible). A single stone in Bonita Cemetery, in the town of Pleasanton, marks the graves of the three infant Musgrave boys.

17. Family Bible. Julia was born on June 18, 1872. See J. W. Driskill, "Helped Drive the Indians Out of Brown County," *Trail Drivers of Texas*, p. 707; Gard, *Chisholm Trail*, pp. 190–91. It is difficult to determine the herd's size. West's contribution appears to be the 778 head that he checked through Tilden on April 15, 1872. Later Musgrave occasionally loaned his trained steers to other drivers (Lauderdale and Doak, *Life on the Range and on the Trail*, p. 11).

18. Stock Record Book of Atascosa County, Book #6, pp. 97–106, 155–56, 170–78; Marks and Brands of Atascosa County, Texas, Book 1, pp. 150, 170, and 210. Musgrave later registered the inverted dK brand (Ibid., p. 42).

19. Dykstra, *Cattle Towns*, pp. 76–77; Musgrave secured a loan for some five thousand dollars from W. A. Bennett of San Antonio (Atascosa County, Texas, Index of Mortgages, Book 1, pp. 20–21; Atascosa County Deed Book E-1, p. 413). By 1890, Musgrave's indebtedness had grown to twelve thousand dollars (Atascosa County, Texas, Index of Mortgages, Book 1, pp. 204–5, 207, 326, 398, 400, 410–11, 432; Atascosa County Deed Book M-1, pp. 355–58).

20. Family Bible; Lauderdale and Doak, *Life on the Range and on the Trail*, p. 35; Atascosa County, Texas, Deed Books B–1 through F–1. One additional child, Volney Campbell "Vollie" Musgrave (of whom more later), was born on May 6, 1881 (Family Bible).

CHAPTER 2: AN OUTLAW'S EDUCATION

1. May 13, 1884, Atascosa County, Texas, Marriage Book 1, p. 118; Atascosa County, Texas, District Court, *State of Texas v. Van Musgrave*, case no. 372. Ella West Musgrave was born at Seguin, Texas, on November 17, 1860 (Texas Department of Health, Bureau of Vital Statistics, Certificate of Death, Bexar County, File no. 2150). Van obtained a divorce on April 11,

1900, complaining that on or about December 28, 1884, "[she] voluntarily abandoned [his] bed and board and went to her father's residence with the expressed intention of permanently living separate and apart" (Val Verde County, Texas, District Court, *Van Musgrave v. Ella Musgrave*, case no. 426). In 1900, Ella and her son Frank were living in San Antonio, where she was employed as a public school teacher and referred to herself as widowed. She remained a resident of San Antonio, never remarried, and died there on June 14, 1948 (1900 U.S. Census, Bexar County, Texas, vol. 7, E.D. 89; Texas Department of Health, Bureau of Vital Statistics, Certificate of Eath, Bexar County, file no 2150).

2. Culley, *Cattle, Men and Horses*, pp. 51–57.

3. Colonel Ike Prior, quoted in Dobie, *Cow People*, p. 18.

4. Guy Edward Scogin, nephew of Bennett Musgrave, Tilden, Texas, interview with the authors, April 10, 1982; Atascosa County, Texas, District Court, *State of Texas v. Bennett Musgrave*, Minute Book B, case no. 200, pp. 396, 415, 419–21.

5. Frio County, Texas, District Court, *State of Texas v. Van Musgrave*, Criminal Docket Book B, case nos. 320, 322, 331, pp. 24, 47, and 98; Criminal Docket Book 3, p. 9. Frank Howard Musgrave, the only child of Calvin Van and Ella West Musgrave, was born in Atascosa County on April 4, 1885. He died on December 16, 1946, in San Antonio, Texas (Texas Department of Health, Bureau of Vital Statistics, Certificate of Death, Bexar County, file no. 3901).

6. Criminal Docket Book 3, pp. 9, 31.

7. William Cowley had homesteaded in the western portion of Atascosa County, near Chiltipin Creek (Atascosa History Committee, *Atascosa County History*, p. 120); Atascosa County, Texas, Minutes of the District Court, *State of Texas v. Calvin V. Musgrave*, case no. 625, Book 3, pp. 390, 391 and 397.

8. As early as March 15, 1886, Bennett commenced the disposal of his Atascosa County holdings with the sale of 320 acres (Atascosa County, Texas, Deed Book L-1, pp. 70–71). On July 30, 1886, following Van's failure to appear to face charges in Frio County, Bennett Musgrave sold a lot in Pleasanton (Ibid., pp. 178–79).

9. Calvin S. Musgrave died August 18, 1888. He is buried at the Bonita Cemetery in Pleasanton, (Family Bible). Joseph W. Walker died on June 30, 1888. He is buried at Hilltop Cemetery in Tilden (Day Book of Joseph Walker, Dogtown, Texas, 1869).

10. Atascosa County, Texas, Deed Book M-1, pp. 355–58, 410–12, 452–53, and pp. 494–95).

11. Frio County, Texas, District Court, *State of Texas v. Van Musgrave*, Criminal Docket Book B, case no. 322.

12. Cox, June 10, 1952, BT. Coincidentally, on October 16, 1919, the Musgrave brothers' uncle, Thomas Hardee Walker, married Jim Upton's niece, Hertha Upton. It was Walker's second marriage (Martha Beth Walker, San Antonio, Texas, letter to authors, June 24, 1997).

13. Daughter Julia remained behind. She had married Boyd M. Doak (born 1864), the son of Jonathan A. and Mary Elizabeth Zumwalt Doak, on November 28, 1888 (Atascosa County, Texas, Marriage Book 3, p. 206); Frank M. Hicks, Buenos Aires, to Hon. Carlos Bee, Washington D.C., December 6, 1920, File 130 ST 4211; United States Department of State, Record Group 59, NAB.

14. Marvin Powe, August 3, 1953, BT.

15. Ibid. The Estado Land and Cattle Company, an eastern syndicate, owned the G4 Ranch. The brand was registered on August 30, 1888 (Brewster County, Texas, Record of Marks and Brands, vol. 1, pp. 32–33).

16. Thompson, *They Were Open Range Days*, pp. 100–102, 107. In 1891, Musgrave's personal property was assessed at $577. Passed over from 1892 through 1894, he was assessed in 1895 on $100 in property improvements, $452 in cattle, and $1,175 in personal property. He would not be assessed in Chaves County again (Chaves County Assessment Rolls, NMSA, drawer 17, no. 1).

17. Chaves County, N.Mex., Marriage Book A, p. 24; Byrd Lindsay, Canelo, Ariz., interview with the authors, July 31, 1997; Nancy McCuistion, Lochiel, Ariz., interview with the authors, August 24, 1997. In the *Roswell Record* (July 25, 1894) the groom appears as Thomas Mathews [*sic*]. He is called Dan Johnson in the *Roswell Register*, July 25, 1894. J. J. Cox orginally used the Bar V brand on his ranch along the west bank of the Pecos River. Following his death in the spring of 1889, the Cass Land and Cattle Company, which owned the adjacent range to the east side of the Pecos, purchased the ranch and its well-known brand from Mrs. Cox. Organized in 1883 in Pleasant Hill, Missouri, the Cass Land and Cattle Company was represented in New Mexico by G. R. Urton, W. G. Urton, and J. D. Cooley (Shinkle, *Fifty Years of Roswell History*, pp. 51–53; Thompson, *They Were Open Range Days*, p. 99; Hinkle, *Early Days of a Cowboy on the Pecos*, pp. 1, 2, and 8).

18. *Roswell Record*, October 23, 1896. By consensus, at the age of nineteen, Musgrave stood six feet tall, weighed two hundred pounds, had a sandy complexion with brown hair and blue-gray eyes (*Albuquerque Morning Democrat*, November 3, 1896). On September 1, 1887, Parker enlisted as a private in Captain George H. Schmitt's Company C of the Frontier Battalion of the Texas Rangers. He was discharged three months later, at Pena, Texas, on November 30 (George T. Parker Enlistment Papers, TSA).

Parker had served as a Chaves County deputy sheriff, appointed by Sheriff William M. "Billy" Atkinson in 1892.

19. These accounts are almost certainly correct, judging from later Musgrave and Johnson civil suits brought against Parker's estate and C. D. Bonney, serving as a surety for Johnson (Bonney, *Looking Over My Shoulder*, pp. 7–8; Cox, April 11, 1953, BT; Austin Reeves, July 2, 1953, BT. Chaves County, N. Mex., Fifth Judicial District Court, *Territory of New Mexico v. George Musgrave*, Criminal Records, case nos. 127 and 128 [rustled on September 26, 1894], indicted March 30, 1895). The Diamond A Ranch was founded when Billie Anderson from California bought out the Rafter T and the Boot Bars about 1881. In 1883, when William E. Anderson, Frank G. Bloom, John A. and M. D. Thatcher organized the Anderson Cattle Company of Pueblo, Colorado, they filed on 160 acres along the banks of the Rio Hondo and turned Colorado cattle loose to graze. For the next few years, many small ranches were purchased and consolidated by the Anderson Cattle Company, until the Diamond A holdings amounted to several hundred sections of land, including the Circle Diamond farmlands, along the Rio Hondo. Burton C. Mossman, later the first captain of the Arizona Rangers, initially became associated with the company in 1893. In 1895, all of the property of the Anderson Cattle Company, as well as the Diamond A brand, was transferred to the newly formed Bloom Land and Cattle Company. In 1907, Captain Mossman incorporated the Diamond A Cattle Company in South Dakota, which then merged with the Bloom Land and Cattle Company. Mossman continued as president and manager of the Diamond A Cattle Company until its sale in 1942 to James Phelps White interests (Charles Ballard, Luna, New Mexico, to J. Evetts Haley and Hervey Chesley, June 9, 1939, NSH; Ernestine Chesser Williams, "Diamond A Ranch," in Fleming and Williams, *Treasures of History II: Chaves County Vignettes*, p. 33).

20. Reeves, July 2, 1953, BT; Chaves County, N. Mex., Fifth Judicial District Court, *Territory of New Mexico v. George Musgrave and Dan Johnson*, Criminal Records, case no. 143, rustled on September 26, 1894, indicted November 5, 1895. Bennett and Prudence Musgrave later filed suit against the estate of George T. Parker in the amount of $1,400. The complaint was dismissed when the Musgraves failed to post sufficient bond to cover payment of costs (Chaves County, N. Mex., Fifth Judicial District Court, *Prudence Musgrave v. The Estate of George T. Parker*, Civil Records, case no. 147, filed March 6, 1897, dismissed May 12, 1897). Nonetheless, it appears clear that Parker fraudulently acquired a portion of the Musgraves' herd, an offense deserving punishment by George Musgrave's code.

21. *Roswell Daily Record*, January 6, 1910.

22. Chaves County, N. Mex., District Court, *Territory of New Mexico v. Dan Johnson and George Musgrave*, case no. 143; J. Smith Lea, Nogales, Ariz., to Edward L. Hall, Santa Fe, N. Mex., May 24, 1897, United States Department of Justice, General Correspondence of the United States Marshals, Arizona, MS 820, series 1, AHS, hereafter Marshals' Correspondence. The court later dismissed the charge against Johnson on March 22, 1897. Significantly, C. D. Bonney and James Sutherland (manager of the Block Ranch) posted Johnson's bail. Clearly, Bonney suspected that Parker was the ringleader and that Johnson would testify against him. What else could explain Bonney acting as surety for Johnson's bail? Almost certainly Dan Johnson also had an agreement with Parker. On March 1, 1897, Johnson sought asumpsit damages against Parker's estate (Chaves County, N. Mex., District Court, *Dan Johnson v. Estate of George T. Parker*, civil case no. 152). The case was later dismissed.

23. Cox, ca. June 10, 1952, BT. The Double S Ranch was located on Cuchillo Negro Creek, west of Hot Springs. Born about 1878, the six-foot-tall Cox died in Albuquerque on July 14, 1954 (Bryan, *True Tales of the American Southwest*, p. 107). John T. Cox's rustling activities were well evidenced by his, and Charles Shinn's, arrest on September 1, 1896, by U.S. Deputy Marshal H. Will Loomis for smuggling stolen cattle in from Mexico. Initial reports included them within the High Five gang (Edward L. Hall, Santa Fe, N. Mex., to Judson Harmon, U.S. attorney general, September 2, 1896, Justice File; *Globe-Democrat*, September 3, 1896; *Tombstone Prospector*, September 10, 1896; *Silver City Enterprise*, September 4, 1896). That same year, Cox rode into Arizona intending to join the High Five gang, but he could not locate them.

24. Johnny Longbotham, July 19, 1952, BT. James Newton Upton, born in Tyler, Texas, came to Deming in 1887 and purchased the old Mimbres River Ranch.

25. Henry Brock, June 15, 1952, BT; *Albuquerque Daily Citizen*, October 3, 1896. Henry Brock was born near Cincinnati, Ohio, on June 24, 1867. In 1888 he went to work for a cattle-feeding ranch in Kansas, and in October 1890, he left Kansas and arrived in New Mexico. He soon hired on at the Diamond A as a horse wrangler and rose through the ranks to superintendent. Brock later served as McKinley County undersheriff (1912–16), and as a security officer in Gallup and Gamerco for the Gallup-American Coal Company (1917–44). He died April 15, 1960 (Bryan, *True Tales of the American Southwest*, pp. 74–75, 89–91). The origin of the ranch familiarly known as the Diamond A in southwestern New Mexico traces to the 1882 contract to purchase the Gray Ranch by California mining investor George Hearst, for himself and associates James Ben Ali Haggin, Addison Head,

and Lloyd Tevis. A number of additional purchases quickly followed. At the turn of the century, due to the death of Hearst and the withdrawal of Head, the holdings were registered in California and New Mexico in 1899 as the Victorio Land and Cattle Company, solely owned by Haggin and Tevis's Kern County Land Company of California. This ranch in southwestern New Mexico should not be confused with the Bloom-owned Diamond A Ranch near Roswell, New Mexico. For a history of the ranch, see George Hilliard, *A Hundred Years of Horse Tracks*.

26. Longbotham, July 19, 1952, BT; Brock, June 15, 1952, BT; Brock and Montague Stevens, April 8, 1953, BT; Bryan, *True Tales of the American Southwest*, p. 83. A letter of inquiry received by *Tombstone Prospector* on December 3, 1896, from F. A. Tate of La Porte, Iowa, explained that "An incorrigible young man named Hayes some years ago left his home at La Porte and drifted westward, and the belief is entertained that he was the outlaw who met his death at Deer Creek." Grant County Sheriff Baylor Shannon later learned the description of Bob Hayes perfectly corresponded with that of Sam Hassells, formerly a resident of Gonzales County, Texas. He had been convicted about 1889 and sentenced to five years' imprisonment for horse rustling. As there may have been another charge awaiting his discharge from the penitentiary, he escaped the Texas State Penitentiary when he had only four months to serve (*Albuquerque Morning Democrat*, December 24, 1896). There were several Hassell families in Gonzales County, Texas, and the 1880 census for that county enumerated two Samuel Hassells: Alexander Hassell, who had a son Samuel, born ca. 1866 (line 20), and Jesse Hassell, who had a son Samuel, born ca. 1860 (line 32), vol. 13, E.D. 71, sheet 59. However, the authors' inspection of the Docket Books for Gonzales County revealed no charges filed against Sam Hassell(s), John West, or Bob Hayes. Moreover, these two accounts appear to be mutually exclusive, though Lorenzo Walters essentially, and inaccurately, combined them into one individual, Sam Hassells, born at La Porte, Iowa, who came to Gonzales County, Texas (Walters, *Tombstone's Yesterday*, p. 144).

27. Brock and Stevens, April 8, 1953, BT.

28. *Sulphur Valley News*, March 31 and August 4, 1896.

29. Axford, *Around Western Campfires*, pp. 15, 254–55; Lemmon, *Boss Cowman*, pp. 170–73. Lemmon, in error, also indicated that William C. Greene later married Roberts's widow. In fact, he married Roberts's sister, Ella. Born about 1848, Roberts was a member of a prominent Tulare County, California, family. By 1880, Roberts and his family had settled near Roseburg, Oregon, where he engaged in cattle buying. Two years later, Roberts and his family, accompanied by his divorced sister, Ella Roberts

Moson, and her two young children, Frank and Virginia, arrived in Cochise County in search of a desirable site for a cattle ranch. Frank Moson later married Pearl Parker, stepdaughter of Adanna Musgrave Parker, George Musgrave's sister (Sonnichsen, *Colonel Greene and the Copper Skyrocket*, p. 23; Axford, *Around Western Campfires*, p. 8; *Great Register of the County of Cochise, Territory of Arizona, For the Year 1884*, p. 20; "1890 Great Register of Cochise County, Territory of Arizona").

30. *Albuquerque Daily Citizen*, October 3, 1896; Alverson, "Reminiscences of Leonard Alverson," p. 8, hereafter "Reminiscences." Born in California in 1868, Alverson came to Arizona in 1885 or 1886 and settled first in Prescott. Moving on to Cochise County, he cowboyed for Henry Clay Hooker, then ran his own herd in Tex Canyon, at the southeastern end of the Chiricahua Mountains. Alverson died on February 28, 1939. Newspaper accounts invariably used the name "Cole." Deferring to Alverson and Wilson, who knew him, the authors have chosen to refer to him as Code Young (Alverson, "Reminiscences," p. 8; Wilson, *Exciting Days of Early Arizona*, p. 52).

CHAPTER 3: THE CHRISTIAN BROTHERS

1. Identified as Mark Christian at the time of his first arrest in Indian Territory, he was referred to as William M. by subsequent documents in the case file. He signed one document as "William M. [his X mark] Christian" indicating illiteracy. Although there are no documents indicating a transposition, it is possible that early in the proceedings "his X mark" transposed with M. to become Mark (*United States v. Mark Christian and one Christian*, case no. 2059, Defendant Jacket File no. 241, Records of the U.S. District Court for the Western District, Fort Smith Division, Record Group 21, National Archives and Records Administration—Southwest Region [Fort Worth], hereafter Fort Smith Records). Ed Wilson knew Bob and Will in Arizona, and believed them to be half–brothers (Wilson, *Exciting Days of Early Arizona*, p. 53). Sam Hayhurst thought Will Christian was three-fourths Cherokee, while Capt. William French labeled him a half-breed ("Recollections of Sam J. Hayhurst [September 27, 1937]," MS 419, AHS, hereafter "Recollections"; French, *Some Recollections of a Western Ranchman*, p. 204). Round Timber was a mile from the east bank of the Salt River in Baylor County and about a mile north of the boundary of Throckmorton County, where the 1880 census enumerated the family (1880 United States Government Census, Throckmorton County, Texas (T773 no. 15), vol. 30, E.D. 180, sheet 8, line 24). There were children born after 1880. According to Jim Herron, who, as a youngster, had been a neighbor of the Christians at Round Timber, there were eight in the family (Chrisman, *Fifty Years*

on the Owl Hoot Trail, p. 247). Bill Deister remembered a daughter Rosie, born ca. 1882 (Deister, "Outlaws I Have Known": 9).

2. *Daily Oklahoman,* July 23, 1895; Deister, "Outlaws I Have Known": 10; Newsom, *The Life and Practice of the Wild and Modern Indian,* p. 209. Writing in 1923, Newsom erred by approximately five years with respect to most dates concerning the Christian family.

3. *Eddy Current,* January 9, 1897. Herb Brogden remembered attending school with Will Christian in the mid-1880s. Dee Harkey believed Herb and his brother Jack to be cousins of the Christians (Harkey, Carlsbad, New Mexico, interview by Haley, February 27, 1945, NSH). It is possible they did not move. By present standards, Round Timber would not be considered part of the Texas Panhandle. However, the term enjoyed broader usage in the 1880s. Regional records indicate that a William S. Christian was indicted on August 14, 1886, for larceny of three head of cattle (subsequently found not guilty) and arrested again on October 19, 1888, for larceny of three hogs (discharged November 8, 1888). It is apparent from the record that this William S. Christian had a brother, James—establishing that he and Will Christian are not one and the same. Perhaps this William S. Christian was the son of George R. Christian of Jack County, Texas, almost certainly a relative of William M. Christian. Author Ed Bartholomew confused this Will Christian with the subject of the chapter. "Will Christian died in a cowboy accident while doing an honest day's work. Struck by lightning while holding a dozen head on the rise in the Palo Duro country, a hill about a dozen feet elevation. The other cowboy killed by lightning with Will was Warner Reid, . . . Mrs. Adair buried them in the same grave with proper respect at Silverton, Texas. I write this from memory but I have proof in my files." Bartholomew confused the two Christian families and erred with respect to which Christian was killed by lightning. George R. Christian's son Bob was the victim, struck by lightning on October 23, 1895 (*United States v. William Christain* [*sic*], Defendant Jacket File no. 92, Fort Smith Records; Harman, *Hell on the Border,* pp. 259–60; Shirley, *Law West of Fort Smith,* p. 85; *United States v. William S. Christian,* case nos. 1139 and 1563, Defendant Jacket File no. 39, Fort Smith Records; Horton, *History of Jack County,* p. 94; Ed Bartholomew, Houston, Tex., to Howard Bryan, Albuquerque, N. Mex., ca. 1991, typescript provided to authors by Howard Bryan; Doshier, "Lone Prairie Graves": 38).

4. *United States v. Mark Christian and one Christian,* case no. 2059, Defendant Jacket File no. 241, Fort Smith Records; Burton, *Dynamite and Six-shooter,* p. 195; Burton, "Jottings in the Margin [pt. 2], Frank and Flavius Carver: A Pretty Pair of Scoundrels": 5. William Christian was living "20 miles up creek at the Muskogee Nation" when he was taken to Fort Smith

for trial on May 2, 1891 (ibid.). The Trade and Intercourse Act of July 9, 1832, forbade the introduction of "ardent spirits . . . into the Indian country" (Burton, *Indian Territory and the United States, 1866–1906*, p. 10).

5. *United States v. Jim Castleberry, William M. Christian and Isaac Trett*, case no. 1358, Defendant Jacket File no. 287, Fort Smith Records, hereafter Case no. 1358; Newsom, *The Life and Practice of the Wild and Modern Indian*, p. 209. Bill Deister concurred with Newsom, relating that they rented a house about one–half mile from Sacred Heart Mission and later moved back on the Seminole County line—likely to the earlier residence (Deister, "Outlaws I Have Known": 10).

6. Bob Christian was the more formidable of the brothers in Oklahoma. Newsom, not good with chronology, stated that Christian was about twenty when he began his outlaw life (*Daily Oklahoman*, July 12, 1895; Newsom, *The Life and Practice of the Wild and Modern Indian*, pp. 210–11).

7. *Daily Oklahoman*, July 12, 1895; Deister, "Outlaws I Have Known": 10. Criminal behavior was not limited to Bob and Will. On February 22, 1893, brother Ben Christian was charged with assault with intent to kill and a warrant issued. He was arrested two days later and bail was set at $750 (*United States v. Ben Christian*, case no. 7018, Defendant Jacket File no. 241, Fort Smith Records). The outcome is unrecorded.

8. June 27, 1894, Jacket no. 287, Fort Smith Records; *Daily Globe-Democrat*, April 3, 1894, September 15, 1888, June 26, 1895; *Indian Citizen*, April 12, 1894; *Daily Oklahoma State Capitol*, April 5, 1894; *Guthrie Daily Leader*, April 5, 1894. It has traditionally been believed that George "Bitter Creek" Newcomb died following the May 2, 1895, shooting at the Dunn ranch on the Cimarron River of Oklahoma. Recent research by Herman Kirkwood and Nancy B. Samuelson has established that the Newcomb killed at the Dunn ranch was Alfred, a much younger man. It is now believed that George Newcomb died in February 1894 as a result of wounds suffered during the September 1, 1893, Ingalls fight (Nancy B. Samuelson, Sacramento, Calif., June 29, 2001, letter to the authors).

9. *Elevator*, April 27, 1894; *Guthrie Daily Leader*, April 3, 1894.; *Indian Citizen*, April 12, 1894. The partner was reportedly wounded in the left shoulder. The report is subject to question. A reporter for the *St. Louis Globe Democrat* who later viewed Bill Dalton's corpse noted (on June 9, 1895) that exclusive of his fatal wound, "not a scar or mark is visible on the body." (Quoted in Samuelson, *The Dalton Gang Story*, p. 140).

10. Case no. 1358.

11. *Daily Oklahoman*, May 24, 1894.

12. Burton, to authors, July 21, 1997. A dispatch from Paul's Valley, I.T., indicated that Bob Christian was implicated in the Longview robbery (*Daily*

Globe-Democrat, July 11, 1895). Although this does not indicate that he was a participant, it surely suggests aiding and abetting.

13. Case no. 1358.

14. Ibid.; *Daily Globe-Democrat,* June 26, 1894.

15. *United States v. Jim Castleberry, Bill Christian and Isaac Trett,* case no. 347, Defendant Jacket File no. 287, Fort Smith Records; *Indian Chieftain,* February 21, 1895. Why was a warrant issued at Fort Smith as the charge was being submitted to the grand jury at Paris? There was an obvious jurisdictional issue. Wewoka was in the Western District of Arkansas. Guthrie was in the Oklahoma Territory, where horse stealing was not a federal offense. The deputies were attached to the court of the Eastern District of Texas; the Paris officers certainly believed that other horses of unknown provenance were pastured/corralled at the Christian place, perhaps stolen from the nearby Chickasaw or western Choctaw Nation, within their jurisdiction. That could be the answer; perhaps not. Commissioner H. H. Kirkpatrick, who submitted the case to a grand jury at Paris, certainly knew the jurisdictional boundaries. Deputy Mynett might have carried the case to Fort Smith on his own volition. Based upon the contention which existed between Eastern Texas and Western Arkansas Districts at the time, it would seem unlikely that Kirkpatrick would submit it to a Paris grand jury on June 28, then submit it to Fort Smith to be referred by June 30. Jeffrey Burton makes the point that in capital cases, Paris grand juries were demonstrably more inclined to follow Texas custom than the common law, with fewer resultant convictions (Burton, *Indian Territory and the United States, 1866–1906,* p. 195). Perhaps Mynett believed the odds for conviction for lesser felonies were better at Fort Smith. Moreover, there was a certainty of jurisdiction; Mynett had evidence for two definite Fort Smith cases.

16. *United States v. Bob Christian, West Love, John Champion and Two Others,* case no. 2916, Defendant Jacket File no. 287, Fort Smith Records. The amount taken included $1.50 from George Nelson. On January 9, 1895, Joe Criner, of mixed Choctaw, Chickasaw, and Cherokee blood, was a citizen of the Chickasaw Nation and resided about twelve miles outside of Purcell. His mother was a Love, and he was likely the cousin of West Love. Possibly he and the unidentified fifth party also participated in the Rockett robbery, lurking outside the store (*United States v. Joe Criner and Bob Christian,* case no. 47, Defendant Jacket File no. 352, Fort Smith Records).

17. Burton, "Bob Hall, Politics, and the Law": 7. In 1893, Hall had shot and killed John Lowrey, but the jury was unable to reach a unanimous finding (*United States v. Robert H. Hall; Elevator,* January 19, 1894).

18. Burton, "Bob Hall, Politics, and the Law": 8.

19. On September 12, 1895, Criner pled guilty to the charges (Jacket nos. 287 and 352, Fort Smith Records). Interestingly, a year and a half later, the *Fort Smith Elevator* reported that the case against Joe Criner for his complicity in the Riddle robbery was discontinued by the prosecution (April 16, 1897). Apparently more than one charge had been filed against Criner. South McAlester is present-day McAlester (since 1907), county seat of Pittsburg County. McAlester of the 1890s is now North McAlester. Both bear the name of James J. McAlester, merchant, entrepreneur, and eventual U.S. marshal (Burton, to authors, September 18, 1998).

20. *Indian Chieftain*, January 16, 1896; *Elevator*, January 17, 1896; quotation from Burton, "Bob Hall, Politics, and the Law": 11.

21. Walters, *Tombstone's Yesterday*, p. 127. Proceedings against Childers, Young, and Bob Christian were held before the Atoka division of the U.S. District Court for the Central District of Indian Territory. Although the disposition is unknown, the case was continued, likely following a series of continuances, on April 19, 1897. Bob Christian had long since left Indian Territory (*Indian Citizen*, March 25, 1897).

22. Newsom, *Life and Practice of the Wild and Modern Indian*, p. 215. Newsom actually wrote, "You may go to a hotter climate." One reasonably suspects that while the good minister protected the eyes of his readers, Bob Christian's response was decidedly more direct. Another version relates the dialogue as, "The deputy told Christian he had a warrant for him, when Christian said, 'd—— you, you had better keep it' (*Herald*, April 27, 1895). Newsom attributed the fatal shot to Will Christian. However, Bob Christian assumed responsibility (*Daily Oklahoman*, May 23, 1895).The site of the encounter has been placed variously at "Burnett," "during a running fight in the south part of Pottawatomie county," "at Violet Springs," "near Violet Springs." Deputy Turner's name also appears as Turney (*Daily Oklahoman*, May 31 and May 7, 1895; *Herald*, April 27, 1895; *Leader*, April 26, 1895). Elmer Lewis, alias Foster Holbrook, Younger Lewis, "the Mysterious Kid," was born in Neosho, Missouri, in March 1876. He has been, and should not be, mistaken for the much older Foster Crawford. Following his adventures with the Christian gang, Holbrook, Joe Beckham (the former sheriff of Motley County, Texas, who had killed his successor, Sheriff Cook) and the deadly Hill Loftus (or Loftis) joined with Red Buck Weightman to form a gang in western Oklahoma. Following a December holdup of the post office at Waggoner's, northeast of Wichita Falls, Texas, Holbrook (now using the alias Younger Lewis) and Loftus teamed up with Foster Crawford. On February 25, 1896, Holbrook and Crawford attempted a holdup of the City National Bank at Wichita Falls, killing Frank Dorsey,

the cashier. That night they were cornered and captured by a force of Rangers led by Captain Bill McDonald. The following day the two men were lynched by the town's irate citizens (*Daily Times-Journal*, March 5, 1896; *Daily Globe-Democrat*, March 4, 1896; Burton, "Jottings in the Margin, pt. 3: "The Mysterious Kid" [with addenda, corrigenda, amplifications, and comment– September 1998]: pp. 4–10; Burton, to authors, August 15, 1998). Mackey and Holbrook's preliminary hearing was April 25, 1895.

23. Alverson, "Reminiscences," p. 7.

24. Jacket no. 287, Fort Smith Records. John Fessenden's name is spelled variously Fessington and Fessender. The authors have employed the spelling commonly found; *Daily Oklahoman*, May 23 and 31, 1895; *Democrat* (Tecumseh), reprinted in *Daily Oklahoman*, June 9, 1895.

25. She slipped him the gun on Monday, June 24. Frank Rensberger's surname is also given variously as Renzberger and Rantzberger. Could Newsom be Christian family friend J. A. Newsom, later ordained and reformed? *Daily Oklahoman*, November 26, 1895. Fessenden and Reeves smuggled two revolvers to the brothers (Ibid., July 30, 1895). "Bob Christian seems to have a superfluity of sweethearts. Up to date Jessie Findley, Emma Johnson, Kate Grayson and Irene Champion are in evidence, with several precincts to hear from" (*Weekly Oklahoman*, September 12, 1895). On April 30, 1895, the Welch brothers, Tullis and Henry, had robbed one Ross of about seven dollars. Springfield arrested them about a week later. They were apparently out on bond when prevailed upon to aid in the escape of the Christians, Casey, and Cox (Burton, to authors, July 21, 1997, September 18, 1998). Newsom maintained that Emma Johnson of Sasakwa, Oklahoma, was another girl friend of Bob Christian's. He attributed several of the revolvers to her (Newsom, *Life and Practice of the Wild and Modern Indian*, p. 216). The *Weekly Oklahoman*, September 12, 1895, also mentioned her relationship with Bob. Other press accounts linked her to Will Christian.

26. Twenty-year-old Casey was awaiting an appeal on his conviction for the May 21, 1894, murder of Canadian County Deputy Sheriff Sam Farris at Yukon, Oklahoma. Garver was later charged and convicted of negligently permitting the escape of the prisoners (*Daily Oklahoman*, November 24, 26, 27, and 28, 1895).

27. The *Daily Oklahoman* initially (June 30) placed Bob in the buggy and Will on the horse. It corrected the error in the revised story (July 2, 1895); *Weekly Oklahoman*, July 25, 1895.

28. *Daily Oklahoman*, July 24, 1895.

29. *Weekly Oklahoman*, July 25, 1895. Gus White survived wounds in the abdomen and right leg by the fusillade.

30. Deister, "Outlaws I Have Known": 10.

31. *Daily Oklahoman*, July 6 and 12, 1895; *Daily Oklahoma State Capitol*, July 13, 1895. According to the *Daily Globe-Democrat* of July 5, "Will Christian, the most desperate of the two was shot in the neck while escaping, but was not dangerously wounded."

32. *Daily Oklahoman*, July 12, 1895; *Indian Citizen*, July 25, 1895.

33. *Daily Oklahoman*, July 12 and 18, 1895. Louis (Lonie) Miller was also arrested as an accessory because he had frequently visited the prisoners and talked privately with them. In early August 1896, Pottawatomie County Deputy Sheriff B. F. Owens with a posse encountered Miller at Old Man Christian's home in Seminole County. Miller reached for a shotgun over the door; Owens shot him in the back (*Herald*, August 8, 1896). The back shooting of Miller by a deputy outside of his jurisdiction suggested murder to some residents.

34. *Daily Oklahoman*, July 21. 1895; *Daily Times-Journal*, July 22, 1895. Tullis Welch, Frank Rensberger, George Yott, George Fernell, George McCraner, and Jim Castleberry had also joined Watts, Carr, Miller, and Christian in custody.

35. *Daily Times-Journal*, July 30, 1895.

36. Ibid.; Burton, *Bureaucracy, Blood Money, and Black Jack's Gang*, p. 2. Following her testimony, Jessie Findley remained confined in the Oklahoma City jail; the court continued the case to the following spring. In late April 1896, she took an overdose of cocaine, but survived (*Indian Citizen*, April 30, 1896). She was released on bond the following September. There appears to be no final disposition to the case. The Christians robbed Brown's store on July 26, 1895 (Burton, "Jail-Break": 11; *Daily Globe-Democrat*, July 28, 1896). Glenn Shirley dates the robbery as July 28, citing a dispatch from Eufaula in the *Daily Times-Journal*, July 30, 1895 (*West of Hell's Fringe*, pp. 295, 459). The *Daily Globe-Democrat*'s report, also citing the Eufaula dispatch (received July 27) appears to have been the first account published. The *Daily Times-Journal* received a similar dispatch on July 29, accounting for its erroneous assumption that the robbery transpired on July 28.

37. *Indian Arrow*, August 2, 1895. Author Lorenzo Walters placed the sighting on July 27, in nonexistent "Milburton" on the Missouri, Kansas and Texas Railroad (Walters, *Tombstone's Yesterday*, p. 127). Walters erred, the line near Wilburton was the Choctaw, Oklahoma and Gulf Railroad. It is possible that the South McAlester dispatcher may have repeated exactly what had come from Wilburton the previous evening, which would make Walter's date of July 27 correct. It is unlikely that the entire gang could have been sighted. The Missouri, Kansas and Texas Railroad crossed the South Canadian some thirty-five miles from the Wewoka Trading Company.

It was robbed that same evening by the Christian brothers and one other man. Observers likely spotted a number of the gang's members on their way to join the Wewoka robbers, bringing the group to full strength.

38. *Muskogee Phoenix,* quoted in *Daily Oklahoman,* August 11, 1895; *Daily Oklahoman,* August 4 and 9, 1895; *Daily Globe-Democrat,* August 3, 1895.

39. Burton, "Bob Hall, Politics, and the Law": 9; *Hartshorne Sun,* reported in *Indian Citizen,* August 22, 1895; Burton, "Jail-Break": 11; *Daily Times-Journal,* August 6, 1895. The most reasoned account of the gunfight insists that only a single volley was fired. "The *Sun* is not advised as to which party did the running; but certain that there was no fighting after the fatal volley" (*Hartshorne Sun,* reprinted in *Indian Citizen,* August 22, 1895).

40. Burton, "Jail-Break": 10; *Edmond Sun-Democrat,* August 16, 1895; Burton, *Bureaucracy, Blood Money, and Black Jack's Gang,* p. 2; *Daily Globe-Democrat,* August 20, 1895; *Indian Citizen,* August 22, 1895; *Weekly Oklahoman,* August 29, 1895. The *Daily Globe-Democrat* placed the robbery thirty miles west of Atoka. The *Indian Citizen* identified the site as beyond Coalgate. Seemingly, the location was northwest of Atoka, very near the Christian house, and along the line of travel between Wilburton and Paul's Valley.

41. Tried at El Reno (on a change of venue) in December 1896, for his role as an accessory in the murder of City Marshal Milt Jones, he was sentenced to life in prison. His conviction was upheld on appeal (*Reeves v. Territory of Oklahoma,* Supreme Court of Oklahoma, June 30, 1900, *Second Decennial Edition of the American Digest*). He was released early in October, 1907, by gubernatorial order, as part of a pre-statehood amnesty (Burton, to authors, September 12, 1998).

42. *Daily Times-Journal,* August 23, 1895; *Daily Oklahoman,* August 25 and September 15, 1895. The *Weekly Oklahoman* of August 29, 1895, identified some of the members of the posse as: "Deputy Marshals [W. E. "Jake"] Hocker, Miller, Minor, Randall, and others, with Deputy Sheriffs Jim DeFord and Jesse Graham." Additionally, there was the man named Martin (whose rifle shot the Christians mistook as an all-clear signal), along with Benjamin H. Goode, and Thomas Noel (Burton, to authors, September 12, 1998).

43. August 25, 1895, September 15, 1895, reprinted from the *Paris (Texas) Advocate;* The *Weekly Oklahoman,* August 29, and September 15, 1895. This scenario was first presented by Jeffrey Burton (*Black Jack Christian: Outlaw,* pp. 5–6). The *Weekly Oklahoman* for August 29, 1895, placed Nuckells and Edwards in the company of the Christian brothers. Moreover, the *Daily Oklahoman* reported, "There were only two of them, the other two [Nuckells and Edwards] having left before the brush with the officers occurred" (August 25, 1895). By process of elimination, the two

involved outlaws were Nuckells and Edwards. Hocker survived his wounds and fully recovered (*Weekly Oklahoman*, October 1, 1895).

44. *Daily Times-Journal*, October 8, 1895. Jeffrey Burton contended that the brothers probably led the gang that held up a train at Curtis, Oklahoma, on September 12, 1895 (*Dynamite and Six-shooter*, p. 195). However, it now appears definite that George "Red Buck" Waightman and Elmer "Kid" Lewis were involved, and several others, including Joe Beckham and George Miller were far more likely than the Christians to have been their associates (Burton, letter to authors, April 1, 1998; Butler, *Oklahoma Renegades*, pp. 174–75). Flave Carver, one of Old Man Christian's drinking cronies, encountered the post office inspector, W. P. Houk, and fingered Thomas Harless and the Draper brothers—Alfred, Hugh, and George—as the robbers. All were convicted on Carver's testimony and sentenced as accessories after the fact, suggesting that even Judge Isaac Parker remained unconvinced of their guilt. George Draper soon secured a new trial and the United States attorney promptly entered a *nolle prosequi*, basically overturning the jury's conviction. In July 1896, Carver was tried on a charge of horse theft. Sentenced to twelve years, he got his term commuted to expire on April 1, 1904. He was killed on his farm near Muskogee in November 1912 (Burton, "Frank and Flavius Carver: A Pretty Pair of Scoundrels," pp. 6–8).

45. Burton, Addenda and Corrigenda to *Bureaucracy, Blood Money, and Black Jack's Gang*, photocopy in possession of the authors; *Daily Oklahoman*, December 10 and 12, 1895.

46. *Atoka Indian Citizen*, January 23, 1896. Although the Christian brothers were linked to the Savanna, Coalgate, and Kiowa robberies, the identifications were more tenuous than in previous holdups. Assuming that the sightings are correct, the brothers would have had to leave the Territory almost immediately following the Kiowa robbery in order to reach New Mexico, tarry for two months, and reach Arizona by April. On the other hand, if these robberies were not attributable to the brothers, then they would have had to go into hiding in the late fall of 1895, not to resurface in Arizona until the following spring. It does not seem credible that they could have avoided public notice for that many months (Burton, letter to authors, April 1, 1998).

47. Debo (*The Rise and Fall of the Choctaw Republic*) and Carter (*McCurtain County and Southeast Oklahoma*) both describe the prevalence of "thief runs."

48. *Eddy Current*, January 9, 1897; Cicero Stewart, Carlsbad, N. Mex., December 20, 1953, BT; Harkey, interviews with Haley, February 24, 1945, December 16, 1947, NSH. Harkey also maintained that the Christians were

cousins of the Brogdens. Harkey cannot be considered a completely reliable source.

49. Deister, "Outlaws I Have Known": 10–11; Chrisman, *Fifty Years on the Owl Hoot Trail*, p. 246.

50. Hayhurst to J. Evetts Haley, December 17, 1946, in Haley, *Jeffrey Milton: A Good Man with a Gun*, pp. 267–68.

CHAPTER 4: THE HIGH FIVES

1. Longbotham, July 19, 1952, BT; Axford, *Around Western Campfires*, p. 255; Wilson, *An Unwritten History*, pp. 51–52, 255; Potter and Hayhurst to Haley, December 17, 1946, in Haley, *Jeff Milton*, p. 268; Sam Hayhurst, Recollections, p. 1; Hughes, *South from Tombstone*, p. 72; Alverson, "Reminiscences," p. 8. As the Christian brothers settled into Cochise County, five hundred miles away at Liberty, New Mexico, Tom and Sam Ketchum robbed the post office and store belonging to Levi and Morris Herzstein on June 10, 1896. During the pursuit, the Ketchums killed Levi Herzstein and Merejildo Gallegos. In St. Louis, the *Globe-Democrat*, in error, later credited the killings to the Christian brothers (*Globe-Democrat*, February 7 and April 30, 1897). Mrs. Ed Roberts informed Jeff Milton that Black Jack had worked for them (Jeff Milton, December 2, 1942, Haley interview, NSH). Will Christian was identified as Ed, Frank, and Jack Williams by Hayhurst, Wilson, and Hughes, respectively. Alverson and Axford both mistook Black Jack for his brother Bob. Hayhurst likewise mistook Black Jack for Bob Christian and ascribed to him the alias Jack Anderson, confusing it with Tom Anderson. In 1888, in partnership with William Lutley and Charles E. Stewart, McNair, an original stockholder in the Erie Cattle Company, founded the Swisshelm Cattle Company (Bailey, *"We'll All Wear Silk Hats,"* pp. 12, 60, 112).

2. Hayhurst, "Hayhurst Was with Arizona Rangers," *Douglas Daily Dispatch*, May 4, 1941, sec. 5, 1–2. Born in Bastrop County, Texas, in 1871, Hayhurst spent his first nine years in Atascosa County, then moved with his family to Abilene. He later described Will Christian as "the genuine Black Jack of the Southwest." Hayhurst continued, "The Oklahoman [Will Christian] was an 18-carat bandit and lived up to that rating all the time." The 7UP ranch had been founded in July of 1883 by Milt Joyce, one–time proprietor of Tombstone's Oriental Saloon, his bartender "Buckskin" Frank Leslie, and John J. Patton (Bailey, *"We'll All Wear Silk Hats,"* pp. 36, 87–88).

3. Axford, *Around Western Campfires*, p. 255. Alverson, Ballard, Birchfield, and Cox all referred to the gang by the name High Five (Alverson, "Reminiscences," p. 8; Ballard, "Autobiography of Charles L. Ballard," p. 33,

hereafter Ballard, "Autobiography"); Walter Birchfield, El Paso, Texas, to Haley, Midland, Texas, November 2, 1939, NSH; Cox, June 10, 1952, BT).

4. During the month of May, there had been several skirmishes in the area between troopers of the Seventh U.S. Cavalry and Apaches (*Sulphur Valley News*, April 14 and June 30, 1896; *Tombstone Prospector*, May 23 and June 27, 1896).

5. *Silver City Enterprise*, July 24, 1996; *Western Liberal*, July 24, 1896; *Santa Fe Daily New Mexican*, July 23 and 27, 1896; *Sierra County Advocate*, July 31, 1896; *Graham County Bulletin*, July 31, 1896; Robert C. Milliken, Separ, N. Mex., to William K. Meade, Tucson, Ariz., September 7 and 13, 1896, Meade to Milliken, September 8, 1896, Marshals' Correspondence; United States Post-Office Department, *Annual Report of the Postmaster General, 1897*, p. 62. The report in the *Silver City Enterprise* on July 24, 1896, described the three men as follows: "One was tall and slender, with thin dark mustache, and wore a light brown and white plaid shirt[,] had a new belt with a double row of cartridges and carried a revolver [Christian or Musgrave]. Another of the trio [Code Young] was a man of medium size with light mustache, wore a black hat, black coat and black pants and carried a rifle. The third man kept in the background and was masked so as to render identification difficult [Christian or Musgrave]." This contradicts other reports that all three men were masked. John Weems and his father had settled at Separ, where they founded a general store, post office, and hotel. The younger Weems also operated a mine near Hachita (Anna Owenby, March 15, 1952, BT; Charles Holson, June 6, 1957, BT; *Silver City Enterprise*, April 30, 1897).

6. *Western Liberal*, July 24, 1896; *Graham County Bulletin*, July 31, 1896. Cox, June 7, 1952, BT. Cox identified Behmer, a German, as Alamo Hueco Dutch. The Alamo Hueco Mountains are in the southeast corner of present-day Hidalgo County. The *Silver City Enterprise* gave Dutchy's name as Burman (November 27, 1896).

7. *Western Liberal*, July 24, 1896.

8. Cox, June 10, 1952, BT.

9. *Silver City Enterprise*, July 31, 1896.

10. Ibid.; *Tombstone Epitaph*, reprinted from the *Western Liberal*, January 20, 1897.

11. *Western Liberal*, July 31, 1896. The *Silver City Enterprise* later erroneously reported that the gang members had fled from the Bisbee camp into Mexico and were imprisoned by Mexican authorities (August 7, 1896).

12. Byrd Lindsey, Canelo, Arizona, interview with the authors, November 23, 1996.

13. *Oasis*, August 8, 1896. The precise amount remains in question. The *Border Vidette* fixed the amount at $30,000, which would indicate a herd

valued at $150,000, while the *Oasis* reported on August 8, 1896 that the sum was $10,000, the duty on a herd worth $50,000. A herd of one-, two-, and three-year-olds, averaging six dollars a head, would place the size of the herd at five thousand head if the *Border Vidette* is accurate. The authors believe that the *Oasis*'s figure is the more accurate.

14. For a descriptive account of the region through which the High Fives traveled, see Egloff, "Circle Z Ranch and the Sonoita Valley": 65–72."

15. *Denver Rocky Mountain News*, August 7, 1896. Frank King, a special deputy collector of customs at the time, provided a first-hand, though somewhat erroneous, account of the robbery to the *Border Vidette*. Almost four decades later, he wrote an elaborate and even more inaccurate account of the same event. His 1935 determination as to the identity of the bandits included "Black Jack Muskgrave [*sic*], or Christian as some call him, Jess Williams [George Musgrave], Bob Hay [Hayes], George Muskgrave, and an outlaw known as Three Finger Jack." It is self-evident that King remained totally befuddled regarding the true identity of the culprits (King, *Wranglin' the Past*, pp. 242–43).

16. *Oasis*, August 7, 1896. The bank encompassed the downstairs, southern one-third of the two-story building. About 130 yards north of the border, it had approximately 23 feet of frontage on the east side of Morley Avenue and extended 73 feet to the rear. Entering, one saw a staircase to the left (north) leading upstairs, necessitating that a forward-placed robber maintain an eye upon it lest someone descend. The upstairs was a single room over all three downstairs businesses. Forty-six feet to the rear of the entry, and attached to the south wall, was the vault (approximately eight feet square). To the left and beyond the vault was the meeting room at the rear.

17. Ibid., August 8, 1896; *Sulphur Valley News*, August 11, 1896.

18. *San Francisco Chronicle*, August 7, 1896; *Oasis*, August 8, 1896. Knowing the Christian family's penchant for the Winchester, and considering Will Christian's instinctive reach for it in subsequent events, he appears to have been the most likely of the three to have carried a rifle into the bank. Major A. O. Brummel was a Washington, D.C. financier with the ambition of organizing the Calabasas Irrigation Land and Water Company (*Arizona Silver Belt*, September 3, 1896).

19. *Border Vidette*, August 7, 1896; *Oasis*, August 8, 1896. King reported that wind caused a door to slam, which distracted the robbers (King, *Wranglin' the Past*, p. 243). However, both the *Border Vidette* and the *Oasis* of August 8, 1896, reported that in order to hold the men discovered meeting in the back room, one of the robbers (by implication, Musgrave) slammed the door shut, alarming his associate. Neither version is satisfactory. More

likely, once Dessart fled from the bank, Hayes and Musgrave's control within the bank quickly eroded and any door that may have slammed was inconsequential. Robert Ekey stated that Herrera's bullet struck Musgrave. Later statements indicated that Musgrave's right knee bent backward when standing or walking. However, the disability was not permanent (Robert J. Eaton, Asunción, Paraguay, to authors, January 26, 1998). Musgrave did have some small, bothersome .32-caliber bullets removed from his leg (Eaton, letter to authors, August 6, 1999).

20. King, *Wranglin' the Past*, p. 244; King, Los Angeles, California, to J. Haley, November 2, 1947, NSH. King afterwards maintained that he was under-gunned with a short-barreled Colt's .41 double-action revolver. King recalled that in later years Musgrave would chide him when introducing people to King, remarking that King "made the robbers drop the money by throwing rocks at them" (King to Mrs. Jeff Milton, Tucson, Ariz., November 17, 1947, NSH).

21. *Rocky Mountain News*, August 7, 1896; *Oasis*, August 8, 1896; *Arizona Daily Star*, August 9, 1896. Outdistanced by the robbers, Hambleton soon gave up the hunt.

22. Arthur M. Peck, "In the Memory of Man," MS 652, AHS, p. 369; *Graham County Bulletin*, November 20, 1896; *Border Vidette*, August 7, 1896; *Oasis*, August 8, 1896.

23. King, *Wranglin' the Past*, pp. 245–46; King to Haley, November 2, 1947, NSH; *Border Vidette*, August 14, 1896; Sam F. Webb, Nogales, Ariz., to Secretary of the Treasury, Washington, D.C., August 14, 1896, File 13.065 for 1896 Confidential Correspondence, 1896–1898; Central Files, United States Department of Justice, Record Group 60, NACP, hereafter Justice File. Webb provided the Justice Department with the list of the suspects. King later wrote that Jim Speedy, the town constable, organized the posse. His name is not mentioned elsewhere. Likewise, the *Oasis* of August 8, 1896, maintained that the posse was formed by Deputy Sheriff John W. Roberts. Again, his name is not mentioned elsewhere. Critics later questioned the efficacy of customs agents participating in the posse. However, Musgrave and Hayes were known to have rustled Mexican stock, and to have brought them north of the line, which technically justified the agents' involvement. (*Tombstone Prospector*, August 24, 1896). Musgrave's wounded mount had followed the fleeing gang out of town before dying, while Black Jack's horse, badly wounded in the thigh, had been abandoned when the robbers came upon a Mexican driving a team. King, in error, placed the San Antonio Pass in the Sierra de los Pajaritos, which are west of Nogales.

24. King, *Wranglin' the Past*, p. 246; *Daily Globe-Democrat*, August 8, 1896, report provided by Frank King. Albert Behan was the son of Cochise

NOTES TO PAGES 48-49   283

County's first sheriff, John Harris Behan (Boyer, "Johnny Behan of Tombstone," *Frontier Times:* 6–9, 55–57).

25. White to Meade, January 2, 1897, Marshals' Correspondence; *Daily Globe-Democrat*, August 8, 1896. A number of individuals associated with the Nogales adventure appear to have been involved in dubious activities. Reuben George, vice consul, was concerned about "irregularities in the United States Customs office." He particularly suspected Sam F. Webb and Frank King. On one occasion, he reported to Thomas C. Hannum, a special inspector of customs, that bricks exported from Mexico had been used to construct a brick building within three hundred feet of the Customs House in Nogales, Arizona, without the duty having been paid. To George's astonishment and chagrin, Hannum promptly divulged George's information to Webb, and the exporter soon presented an invoice for authentication. George complained, "I have tried hard to bring Mr. Webb's utter unfitness as Collector of Customs before the Treasury Department; but, when Special Agents will carry important information to those whose official acts they were sent to investigate, the investigation amounts to nothing more than an official burlesque" (George to Quincy, October 27, 1893, Despatches). Webb and King, the former a member of the Democratic Central Committee of Arizona, and the latter its secretary, lobbied for the removal of George (a Republican). Their activities culminated with a fiery editorial, "Fire Him Out" (*Arizona Gazette*, September 28, 1895). Webb attempted to get Tucson's *Arizona Daily Star* to mount a similar attack, but failed (Frank W. Roberts, consul, to Uhl, October 17, 1895, Despatches). John Dessart was later arrested in 1904 and charged with embezzlement. The court committed him to the territorial lunatic asylum. He subsequently escaped and fled to South America (*Border Vidette*, April 2 and June 11, 1904; "The Recollections of Arcus Reddock," Peck Collection, AHS). It would seem that the High Five gang members were not the only crooks in Nogales.

26. *Tombstone Prospector*, August 10 and 11, September 13 and 23, 1896; *Sulphur Valley News*, August 18, 1896. On September 12, Forrest was discharged in Cochise County due to lack of evidence, but was rearrested by Pima County authorities and transported to Tucson the next day. A week later, he was discharged in Pima County, again due to lack of evidence.

27. *Border Vidette*, August 14, 1896; *Sulphur Valley News*, September 8, 1896; *Arizona Daily Star*, September 9, 1896. The *Vidette* failed to indicate whether "Deputy Doyle" was Tombstone City Marshal Michael Doyle or U.S. Deputy Marshal O. P. Doyle of Tucson. Leatherwood, since January 9, 1895, was also a U.S. deputy marshal (United States Marshals Service: Appointment Bonds and Oaths, U.S. Marshals for the Territory of Arizona, hereafter U.S. Marshal's Service).

28. *Tombstone Prospector,* August 11, 1896. Burt Alvord and his cohorts, William Downing, Matt Burts, and William "Billy" Stiles, soon commenced their own reign of lawlessness (*Tombstone Epitaph,* September 11, 1899; February 15 and 25, April 8, 1900; December 21, 1903).

29. Milton, interview with Haley, December 2, 1942, NSH; *Bisbee Orb,* reprinted in the *Arizona Daily Star,* August 18, 1896.

30. Milton, interview with Haley, December 2, 1942, NSH.

31. *Arizona Daily Citizen,* August 14, 1896.

32. *Bisbee Orb,* reprinted in the *Arizona Daily Star,* August 18, 1896; King, *Wranglin' the Past,* p. 247. Frank Robson of Mesa, Arizona, a twenty-four-year-old customs official, left a wife and a two-year-old child (*Tombstone Epitaph,* August 19, 1896; *Tombstone Prospector,* August 14, 1896). Alvord alleged the horse to be Black Jack's, of which more later (*Tombstone Prospector,* August 18, 1896).

33. *Sulphur Valley News,* August 18, 1896.

34. Milton, interview with Haley, Tucson, Arizona, March 1, 1945, NSH.

35. Hovey, "Black Jack Ketchum Tried to Give Me a Break!": 10–11; *Bisbee Orb,* reprinted in the *Arizona Daily Star,* August 18, 1896.

36. *Bisbee Orb,* reprinted in the *Arizona Daily Star,* August 18, 1896; White to Meade, August 19, 1896, Marshals' Correspondence.

37. *Tombstone Prospector,* August 14, 1896; *Bisbee Orb,* reprinted in the *Arizona Daily Star,* August 18, 1896.

38. Horn, foreman of Burt Dunlap's ranch at Aravaipa, had been lured away "at a very fancy salary" to participate in the army's summer campaign (*Sulphur Valley News,* June 16, 1896).

39. *Bisbee Orb,* July 22, 1896, reprinted in the *Sulphur Valley News,* August 4 and September 1, 1896.

40. *Santa Fe Daily New Mexican,* August 25, 1896; Hall to Harmon, August 24, 1896, Justice File. The incoming Cleveland administration appointed Hall, a rancher in Grant County, New Mexico, and a Democrat, on May 16, 1893 (Ball, *The United States Marshals of New Mexico and Arizona Territories,* p. 137).

41. *Santa Fe Daily New Mexican,* August 26 and 27, 1896; *Rio Grande Republican,* August 28, 1896; *New York Times,* August 28, 1896; *Silver City Enterprise,* September 4, 1896. Joseph B. Doe, acting secretary of war, ordered that the troop not be used as a posse comitatus (Joseph B. Doe, Washington, D.C., to Brig. Gen. Frank Wheaton, Denver, Colo., August 26, 1896, Justice File).

42. *Western Liberal,* September 4, 1896; *Santa Fe Daily New Mexican,* March 21, 1895, and August 31, 1896; Geo. B. Waterbury, Bowie Station, Ariz., to Wm. McMechen, Denver, Colo., Nov. 11, 1896; Letter Book, Sept 2, 1896–July 1, 1897, Records of the Inspector's Office, Denver, 1879–1907,

Records of the Post Office Department, Record Group 28, NAB, hereafter Special Reports; *Roswell Register,* April 10, 1897. Grant County records indicate two arrests of Burrell Musgrave for violating Sunday law in May 1895 (Grant County, N. Mex., *Territory of New Mexico v. B. Q. Musgrave,* case no. 3981 [case dismissed] and no. 4002 [not charged], Grant County, N. Mex., Docket Book G, pp. 511 and 522). B. Q. Musgrave paid off an outstanding debt on March 27, 1897, apparently at the time of his departure for Las Cruces (Grant County N. Mex., Misc. Deed Record Book 32).

43. *Western Liberal,* September 4, 1896; *Santa Fe Daily New Mexican,* August 31 and September 1, 1896.

44. *Western Liberal,* September 4, 1896.

45. *Arizona Daily Star,* August 22 and 24, 1896; *Tombstone Prospector,* August 21 and 24, 1896. Robert Hill's first name was also reported as John (*Tombstone Prospector,* August 21, 1896). The San Simon Cattle Company, founded in 1883 by Texans Claiborne Walker "Clabe" Merchant (1836–1926) and James Harrison Parramore (1840–1917), with Parramore's brother-in-law, Hugh Lewis, as a minor partner, controlled the largest portion of the San Simon Valley. Merchant and Parramore had each put up fifteen hundred head of cattle in 1885. In 1897, the San Simon Cattle Company moved about five thousand head to a second ranch of the same name near Carlsbad, one of southeast New Mexico's largest. In 1902, the two ranches separated ownership, with Parramore taking the Arizona holdings and Merchant the New Mexico. The Arizona San Simon Company ceased operation in 1920 (Oscar Cochrane, interview with Haley, March 11, 1945; D. D. Parramore, interview with Haley, September 26, 1946, NSH; Grant County, New Mexico, Deed Book 24, pp. 313–17, Deed Book 28, p. 5). Merchant and Musgrave's mother were first cousins (Martha Beth Walker, San Antonio, Tex., interview with the authors, June 30, 1997). Doubtless this provided George with a certain sense of security.

46. White to Meade, August 19, 1896, Marshals' Correspondence; *Tombstone Prospector,* August 26, 1896; *Sulphur Valley News,* September 8, 1896.

47. *Tombstone Prospector,* September 1, 1896.

48. Ibid., August 29, 31; September 4, 8, 14, 1896.

49. *Globe-Democrat,* September 3, 1896; Daniel Robert Williamson, Recollections, AHS.

50. *Western Liberal,* September 18, 1896.

51. *Tombstone Prospector,* September 18, 1896; *Sulphur Valley News,* September 22, 1896 A visit to Tombstone would seem most unwise, particularly as the outlaws' presence in Cochise County was well reported. Nonetheless, the very audacity of the act lends it credence.

52. *Silver City Enterprise,* September 11, 1896.

53. United States District Court, Third Judicial District, Territory of New Mexico, case file no. 1174, *United States v. Jesse Miller, alias Jesse Williams, alias Jeff Davis, Code Young, alias Code Estis [sic], Robert Hoy, alias Robert Hayes, Thomas Anderson, and "Black Jack"*; Records of the District Courts of the United States; Record Group 21; National Archives, Rocky Mountain Region, Denver, Colo., hereafter case file no. 1174; George P. Money, assistant U.S. attorney for New Mexico, Silver City, to Meade, September 19, 1896, in Marshals' Correspondence; *Santa Fe Daily New Mexican,* October 3, 1896.

CHAPTER 5: DEATH AT RIO PUERCO

1. Longbotham, July 19, 1952, BT.
2. Clark, "William Christian, Alias Black Jack," pt. 2, p. 22.; Burton, *Dynamite and Six-shooter,* p. 67.
3. Charles Ross, Albuquerque, N. Mex., to Richard English, Albuquerque, October 3, 1896, and Wells, Fargo & Co.'s Express, "Attempted Robbery Report for October 2, 1896," both in Rio Puerco File, Wells Fargo Bank History Room, San Francisco, California, hereafter Rio Puerco File; *Albuquerque Morning Democrat,* October 3, 1896. Charles Ross correctly numbered the robbers as five, three who covered him from the engine's tank and one on each side of the engine.
4. Train number 802 included the engine (number 72), one mail car, two baggage and express cars (numbers 705 and 706), one day coach, three tourist cars, and two Pullmans.
5. *Albuquerque Daily Citizen,* October 3, 1896; *Albuquerque Morning Democrat,* October 3, 1896; *Santa Fe Daily New Mexican,* October 3, 1896; L. J. Kohler, Albuquerque, N. Mex., to G. H. Young, Albuquerque, October 3, 1896, Rio Puerco File. Will Loomis put the time of the robbery at 7:45 P.M. (H. W. Loomis, Magdalena, N. Mex., to Edward L. Hall, Santa Fe, N. Mex., October 3, 1896, Justice File).
6. Ross to English, Rio Puerco File.
7. T. G. Hutchinson, Albuquerque, N. Mex., to G. H. Young, Albuquerque, October 3, 1896, Rio Puerco File; *Albuquerque Daily Citizen,* October 3, 1896; Ross to English, Rio Puerco File; *Albuquerque Morning Democrat,* October 3, 1896.
8. *Western Liberal,* October 9, 1896. *Albuquerque Daily Citizen,* October 3, 1896; *Albuquerque Morning Democrat,* October 3, 1896. The *Daily Citizen* reported that Reed simply argued that he did not know how to uncouple the cars.
9. Kohler to Young, Rio Puerco File; *Albuquerque Daily Citizen,* October 3, 1896. Henry Brock labeled Cole Estes (Code Young) the dynamite man

(Brock and Cox, April 11, 1953, BT). Officials later discovered three dyna-mite bombs near the scene of the attempted robbery. The first was com-posed of four sticks of Giant no. 2 dynamite with cap and a one-foot fuse. The second was constructed from seven sticks of Giant no. 2 dynamite with the fuse pulled out of the cap and thereby likely inert. The third con-tained nine sticks of Hercules no. 2 dynamite, firmly bound within a flour sack with a four-foot fuse (*Tombstone Prospector,* October 24, 1896).

10. Kohler to Young, Rio Puerco File. Selvey was a special agent for the Atlantic and Pacific. Bay, returning from a family vacation in southern Cal-ifornia, was a route agent for Wells, Fargo & Co. Express (*Albuquerque Daily Citizen,* October 3, 1896).

11. *Albuquerque Morning Democrat,* October 3, 1896; Kohler to Young, Rio Puerco File.

12. Hall to Harmon, October 3, 1896, Justice File.

13. *Santa Fe Daily New Mexican,* October 3, 1896.

14. Loomis to Hall, October 3, 1896, Justice File.

15. Ibid.; *Albuquerque Morning Democrat,* October 3, 1896. An attempted robbery would prove the least of the difficulties faced by the Atlantic and Pacific's train. As it continued on its way east after the attempted holdup, the locomotive boiler exploded near Osage, Kansas, killing the engineer, fireman, two passengers, and three tramps (*Silver City Enterprise,* October 9, 1896).

16. *Santa Fe Daily New Mexican,* October 3, 1896. On July 17, 1896, the United States District Court, Third Judicial District of the New Mexico Ter-ritory, had reissued warrants for the members of the High Five gang. Loomis returned Code Young's to the court with the notation: "I hereby certify that on the night of October 20, 1896, I served this writ on the within named Cole [sic] Young, alias Cole Estes, with a shotgun. . . ." (E. L. Hall, U.S. marshal, by H. W. Loomis, deputy, case no. 1174). Young had $1.45 in his pocket (*Albuquerque Daily Citizen,* October 3, 1896).

17. *Santa Fe Daily New Mexican,* October 3, 1896.

18. *Albuquerque Daily Citizen,* October 5, 1896; *Albuquerque Morning Democrat,* October 6, 1896; Hall to Harmon, January 21, 1897, Justice File. Fornoff maintained that they followed the gang's trail from the camp for forty miles, without water, before turning east to the Rio Grande and Sabi-nal. Had the posse, in fact, followed that route, it would have reached the river near Socorro, thirty-five miles south of Sabinal. Hubbell and his posse returned to Albuquerque on the afternoon of October 4, with Code Young's horse (*Albuquerque Daily Citizen,* October 5, 1896).

19. Hall to Harmon, January 21, 1897, Justice File; *Santa Fe Daily New Mexican,* October 5 and 7, 1896. Serving in Loomis's posse were: James

Osburn, Thomas Bowlen, Gus Grossett, Alfredo Gallegos. Gabriel Montoya, and J. J. Sfier (Hall to Harmon, December 9, 1896, Justice File). Loomis did not specify where the horses were captured. If the capture took place in Lake Valley, the horses possibly had been left by the High Fives on the way to Rio Puerco. They certainly were not left by the gang following the abortive holdup.

20. Hall to Harmon, November 2, 1896, Justice File; *Albuquerque Morning Democrat*, October 6, 1896. The men from Hillsboro were Pink Murray, J. P. Mitchell, H. B. White, H. A. Ringer, Tomas Abeyta, John Dissenger, and Blas Chaves (Hall to Harmon, January 21, 1897, Justice File). By February 1882, Holm Olaf Bursum reached San Antonio, New Mexico, where he went to work for his uncle, Agustus Holver "Gus" Hilton. "Olaf" Bursum was later elected to the United States Senate to replace Albert Fall upon the latter's appointment to President Harding's cabinet (Donald R. Moorman, "A Political Biography of Holm Bursum: 1899–1924"; Bursum, Papers, 1873–1936, MSS 92 BC, box 1, UNM).

21. *Santa Fe Daily New Mexican*, October 5, 1896; *Albuquerque Morning Democrat*, October 6, 1896. Read continued, "I am of the opinion that Estes took the name of Young when he was in the vicinity of Deming several months ago, and he had two companions with him, calling themselves 'Tom' and 'Jim.' They passed through Head & Hurst's [sic] cattle ranges on Aug. 5 last [impossible], and the cowboys of that outfit heard of them later, on the Atlantic & Pacific" (*Morning Democrat*). Although Read's recollection as to the date is in error, Young, Tom Anderson, and Jim (Bob Hayes) had passed through the Head and Hearst range in the Animas Valley following their flight from Skeleton Canyon on August 12.

22. *Albuquerque Daily Journal*, April 6, 1881; *Independent Democrat*, October 14, 1896; Hall to Harmon, October 13, 1896, Justice File. The line was founded in 1879 by Gus Hilton. For a detailed examination of the 1886–95 era, see Hart, "'She'll Be Comin' Round the Mountain': The Ozanne Stage to White Oaks and Lincoln, 1886–1895," pp. 29–41. Aaron Hollenbeck held the mail contract in October 1896.

23. *Albuquerque Morning Democrat*, October 10, 1896; A. P. Frederick, Post Office Inspector, to William M. McMechen, Inspector-in-Charge, Denver, Colo., November 3, 1896; pp. 478–81; Special Reports 1894–1897, Records of the Inspection Office, Denver, Colorado; 1879–1907, Record Group 28, NAB, hereafter Special Reports, RG 28; McMechen to M. D. Wheeler, Chief Inspector, Washington, D.C., undated; Letters of the Inspection Office, Denver, Colorado, 1896–1898, p. 334, RG 28, NAB, hereafter, Letters, RG 28; Hall to Harmon, October 9, 1896, Justice File.

24. *Albuquerque Morning Democrat,* October 9 and 10, 1896; *Socorro Chieftain,* October 8, 1897; McMechen to Wheeler, no dates; Letters, pp. 328–333, RG 28. Five letters, which contained from one to twenty dollars in cash, produced the sum, as itemized: Hattie E. Parsons, Parsons, N. Mex., to Montgomery Ward, Chicago, October 7, 1896, $2; Hattie E. Parsons, Parsons, N. Mex., to Golden Eagle Dry Goods House, Denver, Colo., October 7, 1896, $6.20; A. C. Storm, Bonito, N. Mex., to Eliza Pool, Moody, Tex., October 7, 1896, $20; Attie Minter, Bonito, N. Mex., to George Buente, St. Louis, October 7, 1896, $3.40; Chloe Bourne, Bonito, N. Mex., to Publishing House, M. E. Church, Nashville, Tenn., October 7, 1896, $1.00. "Strange to say," one registered letter was not opened. Another registered letter, which was opened, contained $56 in checks, which were recovered.

25. United States Post Office Department, *Annual Report of the Postmaster General, 1897,* p. 800; *Santa Fe Daily New Mexican,* October 9, 1896.

26. Wiley Sidwell, June 20, 1952, BT; Mayer, "Pioneer Story, 1938," *Old Lincoln County Pioneer Stories,* p. 17; Hall to Harmon, November 2, 1896, Justice File; *Eddy Current,* January 9, 1897. Many years later, according to Sidwell, Guy Nix, a cowboy with the Block ranch, dug in the ruins and uncovered two large Dutch ovens and claimed that he could see the prints of dollars in those ovens (Sidwell, June 20, 1952, BT).

27. *Sierra County Advocate,* November 20, 1896; Hall to Harmon, November 2, 1896, Justice File; William Kidder Meade, Tucson, Ariz., to Harmon, November 3, 1896, Justice File. William Kidder Meade (1851–1818), a native of Virginia, came to Tombstone, Arizona Territory, in 1879 and engaged in mining and also commenced a political career. Elected as a Democrat to the territorial legislature from Pima County in 1881, he was appointed marshal in 1885 by President Cleveland. Replaced in 1889 by the Republican, Robert H. "Bob" Paul, Meade served briefly as the warden of the Arizona Territorial Prison at Yuma. The return of Cleveland to the White House in 1893 brought the marshalcy back to Meade (*Tombstone Prospector,* March 14 and 18, 1918).

CHAPTER 6: REVENGE

1. *Roswell Register,* October 24, 1896; From Karnes County, Texas, Parker, described as a "sonofabitch" by John Cox, had tried his hand at land speculation. He first bought land in Chaves County on March 23, 1893, and last owned land on May 24, 1894. Having invested $130, his profit from the three deals amounted to $120, a 92 percent return in fourteen months (Chaves County, N. Mex., Deed Book E, pp. 313, 386, 387, 455, 458, 530).

2. Reeves, July 2, 1953, BT; The camp was jointly operated by the El Capitan Cattle Company's Circle Diamond Ranch and James F. Hinkle's CA Ranch.

3. Aguayo, "The Murder of George Parker by George Musgraves [sic] in Sept. 1897 [sic]," hereafter Reminiscences. For information on Butler, see Sterrett, "Sam P. Butler: Saga of a Lifetime Cowboy," in As We Remembered It, pp. 107–15).

4. Reeves, July 2, 1953, BT; Livingston, "Musgraves Own Law and Slew a Defender," newspaper clipping (likely the Roswell Daily Record, c. 1927), Files, Historical Center for Southeast New Mexico, Roswell, New Mexico; Aguayo, Reminiscences; Roswell Record, October 23, 1896. Carl Livingston, who had served as assistant attorney general of New Mexico, secured most of his information from Charles Ballard and Fred Higgins.

5. Roswell Record, October 13, 1896; Roswell Register, October 24, 1896; Rocky Mountain News, November 3, 1896; Bonney, Looking Over My Shoulder, p. 7; Aguayo, Reminiscences.

6. Gladys Wheeler, Tilden, Texas, interview with the authors, July 23, 1996; Roswell Record, October 24, 1896.

7. Reeves, July 2, 1953, BT; Aguayo Reminiscences. Significantly, thirteen years later Curg Johnson would prove the strongest witness in Musgrave's defense (Bonney, Looking Over My Shoulder, p. 10).

8. Aguayo, Reminiscences; Reeves, July 2, 1953, BT. Curg Johnson, Frank Parks, and Will Tucker were identified by one newspaper (Roswell Record, October 23, 1896). The other Roswell newspaper named Franks Parks and Curg Johnson as the riders (Roswell Register, October 24, 1896). Harry Aguayo wrote that Frank Parks assumed command of the Diamond A outfit and sent Dick Ballard and Tom Perry to Roswell to notify the sheriff (Aguayo, Reminiscences). Reeves agreed, naming Ballard, Perry, and someone else (Reeves, July 2, 1953, BT). Deputy United States Marshal Charles L. Ballard named Frank Parks as bringing the news of Parker's killing (Ballard, Autobiography, p. 33). Charles Haynes had been only recently appointed sheriff—on July 23.

9. Rocky Mountain News, November 3, 1896. The Roswell Register reported the comment as, "There are three or four more I'll get before I leave" (Roswell Register, October 24, 1896).

10. Theodore T. Sutherland, interview with Eve Ball, June 1, 1965, in Ball, "Charles Ballard: 'Lawman' of the Pecos," English Westerner's Brand Book 7 (July 1965): 3.

11. Bonney, Looking Over My Shoulder, pp. 7–8.

12. Cox, April 11, 1953, BT; Reeves, July 2, 1953, BT; *Roswell Register,* July 15, 1894.

13. Cox, ca. June 1952, BT.

CHAPTER 7: PURSUED

1. The *Eddy Current,* reprinted in the *Santa Fe Daily New Mexican,* November 3, 1896. Charles Littlepage Ballard was born in Hayes County, Texas, on October 11, 1866. In 1878 the family left Texas and traveled to Fort Sumner, New Mexico Territory, and in 1879 to Roswell, where Ballard went to work for Captain J. C. Lea. Leaving Lea's employment in 1892, he became a cattle inspector as well as a law enforcement officer. He was later commissioned a second lieutenant in the First U.S. Volunteer Cavalry Rough Riders. Returning from Cuba in 1899, he accepted a commission in the Eleventh U.S. Volunteer Cavalry and served in the Philippines. In 1905 he was elected to the New Mexico Territorial Senate and in 1906 was elected sheriff of Chaves County. He died at Duncan, Arizona, on April 17, 1950 (*Roswell Daily Record,* December 25, 1955; Laura Ballard Lodewick, et. al., "Allan J. Ballard Family," *Roundup on the Pecos,* pp. 128–30; Rickards, *Charles Littlepage Ballard: Southwesterner,* Southwestern Studies 4 [1966]).

2. Ball, "Charles Ballard: 'Lawman' of the Pecos," p. 2. The court issued the formal indictment on March 24, 1897 (Chaves County, New Mexico, Criminal Records, Fifth Judicial District, *Territory of New Mexico v. George Musgrave,* hereafter Case no. 153).

3. Georgia native Frederick Higgins (1860–1941) served both as a Chaves County deputy sheriff and as a New Mexico deputy marshal. He later served three terms as sheriff of Chaves County.

4. Frederick to McMechen, November 3, 1896, Letters, RG 28; Mayer, "Pioneer Story: 1938," *Old Lincoln County Pioneer Stories,* pp. 19–20. The Roswell paper indicated that word was sent to Sheriff Emil Fritz, at Lincoln, and by him to Deputy Tate, at White Oaks, and posses started from these points as soon as notice was given (*Roswell Record,* October 23, 1896).

5. *Roswell Register,* October 30, 1896; Ballard, Autobiography p. 34; *Santa Fe Daily New Mexican,* November 4, 1896. Three squares resembling a block became the brand of the El Capitan Cattle Company, owned by investors from New York and Missouri.

6. *Albuquerque Morning Democrat,* October 25, 1896; Ibid., October 27, 1896, reprinted from the *White Oaks Eagle; Albuquerque Daily Citizen,* October 26, 1896; McMechen to Wheeler, March 3, 1897, Letters, RG 28; *Santa Fe Daily New Mexican,* October 26, 1896. The letter containing the check

was from Sirilis Aragon, Richardson, N. Mex., to Pedro José Sedillo, Tome, N. Mex., and was returned to the sender. The five dollars in currency was sent by Emma E. May, Bonito, N. Mex., to Montgomery Ward & Co., Chicago. The gold dust was mailed by the Taliferro Brothers, White Oaks, addressed to W. J. Pucket, Denver (McMechen to Wheeler, March 3, 1897, Letters, RG 28).

7. *Rocky Mountain News*, November 3, 1896.

8. Aguayo, Reminiscences; *Rocky Mountain News*, November 3, 1896.

9. The package (registered #1713, R.P.E. #1425), contained merchandise shipped by the White S. M. Co., Cleveland, Ohio, and addressed to Juan Taliferro of White Oaks. The contents were repackaged and sent on to Taliferro (McMechen to Wheeler, no date, p. 489, Letters, RG 28); *Rocky Mountain News*, November 3, 1896. A fifth horse, deemed unfit, was shot (*Albuquerque Morning Democrat*, October 25, 1896).

10. *White Oaks Eagle*, reprinted in the *Albuquerque Morning Democrat*, October 27, 1896.

11. Morris B. Parker, *White Oaks*, p. 45; copy in Hall to Harmon, January 21, 1897, Justice File; *Albuquerque Morning Democrat*, October 24, 1896; *Albuquerque Daily Citizen*, October 25, 1896.

12. *Silver City Enterprise*, November 13 and 20, 1896. The horse was recovered on November 10. Musgrave evidently had released the horse near the west entrance to Rhodes Canyon, and it had meandered in a due west direction. Fowler abandoned the hunt on November 18 and returned to Albuquerque (*Albuquerque Morning Democrat*, November 19, 1896).

13. Hall to Harmon, October 24, 1896, Justice File; *Albuquerque Morning Democrat*, October 28, 1896; *Tombstone Prospector*, October 28, 1896.

14. *El Paso Daily Times*, November 29, 1896. Ballard, "Autobiography," pp. 34–35. Highly regarded by Ballard, Dow was viewed variously by some of his contemporaries. Charles Hansen, later sheriff of Otero County, believed that Dow attempted to frame Oliver Lee and James Gililland for the murder of Albert J. Fountain. Following Dow's death, a newspaper stated that Dow "was a typical Texas cowboy, brave, quick in a quarrel, a hard fighter and exceedingly gun handy. He . . . had earned a reputation of a gun fighter, which he seemed to enjoy" (Hansen, *Harrowing Adventures of an Old-time Cowboy and Sheriff*, pp. 53–56; *Santa Fe Daily New Mexican*, February 19, 1897).

15. *Sulphur Valley News*, October 27, 1896; *Silver City Enterprise*, November 20, 1896; Powe, August 2, 1953, BT.

16. *Rio Grande Republican*, October 30, 1896; *Globe-Democrat*, October 29, 1896; Hall to Harmon, November 2, 1896, Justice File; *Sierra County Advocate*, November 6, 1896; United States District Court, Third Judicial

District, Territory of New Mexico, *United States of America v. George Mus-grave, alias Jeff Davis, alias Jesse Williams, and Robert Hayes,* case no. 1183, indictment of February 11, 1897, Justice File; *Silver City Enterprise,* May 7, 1897; *Tombstone Prospector,* September 3, 1896; United States Post Office Department, *Annual Report of the Postmaster General, 1897,* p. 62. Several individuals later related that the Black Jack gang singled out Weems and Milliken as objects of attention: "[Weems] was tryin' to catch 'em all the time and they'd go out of their way to rob him" (Longbotham, July 19, 1952, BT). Reportedly, they took offense at the fact that Weems and Milliken identified the gang to the authorities after the first holdup at Separ (Cox and Brock, April 11, 1953, BT).

17. Waterbury to McMechen, November 11, 1896, Letters, RG 28; *Santa Fe Daily New Mexican,* November 2, 1896; *Sierra County Advocate,* November 6, 1896; *Tombstone Prospector,* November 20, 1996.

18. *Silver City Enterprise,* October 30, 1896; Hall to Harmon, November 2, 1896, Justice File.

19. Waterbury to McMechen, November 11, 1896, Letters, RG 28; *Tombstone Prospector,* November 19, 1896; *Santa Fe Daily New Mexican,* November 10, 1896; *Arizona Daily Star,* November 20, 1896; Joe Schaefer, interview by Haley and Chesley, February 28, 1945, NSH; J. S. Lea to Hall, May 24, 1897, Justice File; *Graham County Bulletin,* November 12, 1896. Adolph Solomon served as postmaster. Wickersham took over as Bowie's postmaster on August 21, 1897 (Theobald, *Arizona Territory Post Offices and Postmasters,* p. 131). The precise relationship between Pruit and Mus-grave remains undetermined, but it was apparently through the Mer-chant family (Joe Schaefer, interview by Haley and Chesley, February 28, 1945, NSH).

20. United States Post Office Department, *Annual Report of the Postmas-ter General, 1897,* p. 62; *Sulphur Valley News,* November 10, 1896; *Albuquerque Morning Democrat,* November 17, 1896.

21. *Tombstone Prospector,* reprinted from the *Western Liberal,* November 6, 1896.

22. Oscar Cochrane, interview with Haley, March 11, 1945, NSH. Cochrane became the San Simon's foreman in 1902.

23. *Western Liberal,* November 6, 1896; *Silver City Enterprise,* November 6, 1896; *Sulphur Valley News,* November 10, 1896.

24. Cochrane, interview with Haley, March 11, 1945, NSH; United States Post Office Department, *Annual Report of the Postmaster General, 1897,* p. 62. Post Office Inspector George Waterbury reported that "they brutally pounded the postmaster over the head with a revolver, and when done— kicked him insensible" (Waterbury to McMechan, November 11, 1896,

Letters, RG 28). There is no other report suggesting that the gang physically abused Brandt.

25. *Bisbee Orb*, reprinted in the *Sierra County Advocate*, November 20, 1897; *Western Liberal*, November 6, 1896; *Sulphur Valley News*, November 3, 1896.

26. *Tombstone Prospector*, November 7, 1896.

27. Meade to Harmon, November 3, 1896, Marshals' Correspondence.

28. *Albuquerque Daily Citizen*, November 7, 1896; United States Post Office Department, *Annual Report of the Postmaster General, 1897*, p. 44.

29. *Silver City Enterprise*, November 13, 1896.

30. George L. Bugbee, Bowie, Arizona, to Grover Cleveland, Washington, D.C., November 6, 1896, Justice File; *Arizona Silver Belt*, January 28, 1897.

31. *Albuquerque Daily Citizen*, November 16, 1896; telegram from Meade to Horn, cited in Tom Horn, Aravaipa, Ariz., to Meade, November 7, 1896, Marshals' Correspondence; *Sulphur Valley News*, June 3, 1896.

32. *Tombstone Prospector*, November 9, 1896; *Graham County Bulletin*, November 20, 1896. Identified as Joseph Temple in the *Tombstone Prospector*, he was also Huachuca's postmaster (Theobald, *Wells Fargo in Arizona Territory*, pp. 118 and 175).

33. *Tombstone Prospector*, November 12, 1896.

34. Ibid.

35. *Arizona Daily Star*, November 20, 1896; *Sulphur Valley News*, November 17, 1896; *Silver City Enterprise*, November 13, 1896.

36. Horn to Meade, November 7, 1896, Marshals' Correspondence. See also Larry Ball, ed., "'No Cure, No Pay,' A Tom Horn Letter": 200–202.

37. Nat Hawke, Tombstone, Arizona, to Meade, November 12, 1896, Marshals' Correspondence; Nolt E. Guild, Willcox, Ariz., to Meade, November 28, 1896, Marshals' Correspondence. Nathaniel E. Hawke was the Tombstone city auditor. Rumors, clearly false, also suggested that the gang was in the Pinos Altos range north of Silver City at this time (*Silver City Enterprise*, November 13, 1896). That day Post Office Inspector George Waterbury reported the gang's presence twenty miles south of Separ, heading for Deming (George Waterbury, Bowie Station, Ariz., to McMechen, November 11, 1896, Letters, RG 28. Hawke's information was that "Black Jack and one other" was at Pearce. The *Sulphur Valley News* placed the number as "at least two of them" (November 17, 1896). The *Silver City Enterprise* reported that three of the gang went into Pearce (November 20, 1896).

38. Waterbury to McMechen, November 11, 1896, Letters, RG 28.

39. *Sulphur Valley News*, November 17, 1896; W. M. Breakenridge, Willcox, Ariz., to Meade, November 16, 1896, Marshals' Correspondence. Crump, a Rucker Canyon stock raiser, had recently had his difficulties with ammu-

nition. As he entered a tack room on August 27, he adjusted his pistol and it accidently discharged, the bullet entering his right leg, just above the knee. He discarded his crutches on September 21 (Ibid., September 1 and 22, 1896). Joe Schaefer later related that "a fellow by the name of Sherman Crump was a great friend to them. He kept them mounted on horses and packed chuck to them" (Joe Schaefer, interview by Haley and Chesley, February 28, 1945, NSH). A .50–82-caliber was not chambered by Winchester. Probably Crump purchased the .50–95.

40. *Tombstone Prospector*, November 16, 1896; Breakenridge to Meade, November 16, 1896, Marshals' Correspondence; *Sulphur Valley News*, November 17, 1896; Joe Schaefer, Bowie, Ariz., interview by Haley and Chesley, February 28, 1945, NHS. The *Prospector* reported that the rancher sought anonymity and therefore did not identify him. However, the circumstances dictate that the rancher was Stark. Musgrave was likely the "loquacious" bandit. An Alabama native, Brannick K. Riggs (1828–1907) came to Arizona in 1877, via Texas and Colorado, and ultimately settled in the Sulphur Spring Valley in 1879, at the mouth of Pinery Canyon at the juncture with Bonita Canyon, approximately thirty miles south of Willcox and west of the present-day Chiricahua National Monument. Riggs's daughter Mary married Bill Stark (*Arizona Range News*, July 12, 1907; *Tombstone Epitaph*, April 17, 1925, and October 15, 1929; *Arizona Daily Star*, March 22, 1936). The horses were left in the south end of the Animas Valley of the New Mexico Territory, and Riggs recovered his stock. Schaefer explained, "These cow punchers in winter camp, all they had to do was play poker and, yes, plan some hold-up. And they was honorable buggers in a way, wouldn't molest any small ranchers and they took those big rancher's horses and would notify them when they made changes" (Schaefer, interview by Haley and Chesley, November 17, 1945, NHS).

41. Schaefer, interview by Haley and Chesley, November 17, 1945, NHS; *Tombstone Prospector*, November 16, 1896.

42. *Silver City Enterprise*, November 20, 1896; *Arizona Daily Star*, November 20, 1896; *Santa Fe Daily New Mexican*, November 20, 1896; United States Post Office Appointments, New Mexico, (National Archives Microfilm Publication M841, roll 84); Records of the Post Office Department, Record Group 28; United States National Archives—Pacific Southwest Region, Laguna Niguel. Somewhere along the way they may have met up with Cal Cox and Sherman Crump to receive the ammunition, and perhaps other supplies purchased at Willcox. More likely, having been found out and in fear of legal retribution, Cox and Crump spilled, rather than delivered, the beans, which would explain Les Dow's later statement that the posse *knew* the outlaws were out of supplies and

would likely head for the Diamond A horse ranch (*El Paso Daily Times,* November 29, 1896).

CHAPTER 8: DEER CREEK

1. *Rio Grande Republican,* November 27, 1896.

2. Telegram, Harmon to Hall, typescript in Hall to Harmon, January 21, 1897, Justice File; *Arizona Daily Star,* November 20, 1896; *Sulphur Valley News,* November 24, 1896; William M. Breakenridge, Willcox, to Meade, November 16, 1896.

3. *Rio Grande Republican,* November 27, 1896; *Western Liberal,* November 20, 1896.

4. *Rio Grande Republican,* November 27, 1896; Charles Martin, ca. 1952, BT; Brock and Stevens, April 8, 1952, BT.

5. *Rio Grande Republican,* November 27, 1896; *Silver City Enterprise,* November 27, 1896; *Western Liberal,* December 18, 1896. Although reported throughout the Southwest, the primary source for details concerning the shootout at Deer Creek is eyewitness Henry Brock, from whom this account of the battle is derived unless otherwise noted (June 12 and 15, 1952; Brock and Stevens, ca. April 8, 1953, BT; Bryan, *True Tales of the American Southwest,* pp. 83–86).

6. *Albuquerque Daily Citizen,* November 20, 1896; Birchfield to Haley, November 2, 1939, NSH; Meade to Hall, ca. November 27, 1896, Marshals' Correspondence; Cox, ca. June 1952, BT.

7. Walter Birchfield numbered the shots from Hayes as three (Birchfield to Haley, November 2, 1939, NSH).

8. Cox, ca. June 1952, BT; *Western Liberal,* November 27, 1896.

9. Ballard, Autobiography, p. 35; Birchfield to Haley, November 2, 1939; *Albuquerque Morning Democrat,* November 22, 1896. Bob Hayes was buried in Deming.

10. *Western Liberal,* November 27, 1896.

11. *Arizona Daily Star,* November 20, 1896; *Santa Fe Daily New Mexican,* November 20, 1896; *Albuquerque Morning Democrat,* November 21, 1896; *El Paso International Daily Times,* November 29, 1896; *Western Liberal,* December 18, 1896; *Eddy Current,* January 2, 1897. Charlie Ballard later confirmed Les Dow's assertion to Dow's son: "Shannon and his deputies never followed us out as we thought they would. They stayed in the house until the fight was over" (Ballard to Hiram M. Dow, ca. 1947, quoted in Burton, *Bureaucracy, Blood Money and Black Jack's Gang,* p. 25).

12. *Western Liberal,* November 27, 1896.

13. *Silver City Enterprise,* November 27, 1896.

14. Ibid.; Meade to Harmon, November 23, 1896, Justice File; *Tombstone Prospector*, November 24, 28, and December 1, 1896. Scott White served as sheriff of Cochise County in 1894 and 1894, and again from 1897 to 1901.

15. Meade to White, November 26, 1896, and Meade to Hall, ca. November 27, 1896, Marshals' Correspondence; Ballard, "Autobiography," p. 36.

16. Brock and Stevens, April 8, 1953, BT ; Cochrane, interview with Haley, March 11, 1945, NSH; *Western Liberal*, December 4. 1896; Cox, ca. June 1952, BT; Milton, interview with Haley, December 2, 1942, NSH; *Arizona Daily Star*, December 20, 1896.

17. *Albuquerque Morning Democrat*, December 9, 1896; White to Meade, December 28, 1896, Marshals' Correspondence.

18. D. M. [Deputy Marshal White] to Meade, December 16 and 31, 1896, and White to Meade, December 19 and 28, 1896, in Marshals' Correspondence; *Albuquerque Morning Democrat*, December 9, 1896; *Tombstone Prospector*, December 4, 1896; *Roswell Record*, December 18, 1896.

19. White to Meade, January 2, 1897, Marshals' Correspondence.

20. *Santa Fe Daily New Mexican*, January 6, 1897.

21. Alverson, "Reminiscences," p. 6.

22. Ibid.

23. Cox, June 10, 1952, BT.

24. Anna Zona Liggett, no date, BT.

25. Cochrane, interview with Haley, March 11, 1945, NSH.

26. *Tombstone Prospector*, December 16, 1896; Marshal Hall expended $1,500 of the government's money and requested an additional $1,200 to continue the pursuit (Hall to Harmon, December 29, 1896, Justice File). Marshal Meade submitted expenses amounting to $1,993.70 (Meade to Harmon, January 9, 1897, Justice File).

CHAPTER 9: MAYHEM AND MURDER

1. White to Meade, January 11, 1897, Marshals' Correspondence.

2. Ibid.; J. H. Thompson, Globe, Arizona, to Meade, January 15, 1897, and Daniel R. Williamson, Globe, Arizona, to Meade, January 27, 1897, in Marshals' Correspondence.

3. Ballard, "Autobiography," p. 36.

4. Axford, *Around Western Campfires*, p. 14; "Great Register of the County of Cochise, 1890," p. 28; Livingston, "Rounding-up the 'Black Jack' Gang," pt. 3: 53–54; Ballard, Autobiography, p. 36.

5. Thompson to Meade, January 15, 1897, Marshals' Correspondence.

6. Longbotham, July 19, 1952, BT; *El Paso Daily Herald*, March 12, and 25, 1897; *Silver City Enterprise*, March 19, 1897; *Albuquerque Morning Democrat*,

March 23, 1897; Hall to Meade, May 31, 1897, Marshals' Correspondence; Hughes, *South from Tombstone*, p. 75. Longbotham described Van Musgrave as "a great, big man and I guess he was just as tough as they made 'em." Weathered was referred to variously as Weathered, Weatherford, and Weatherhead.

7. Drake's cousin, Lenora Franklin, had married the Musgrave boys' uncle, Joseph Henry Walker. In 1902, following a number of rustling raids on the Diamond A Ranch, Drake was convicted of one charge of larceny of a horse and sentenced to three years in the New Mexico Territorial Penitentiary (*Silver City Independent*, March 18, 1902).

8. Hall to Meade, May 31, 1897, Marshals' Correspondence; Ringgold, *Frontier Days in the Southwest*, p. 152; Creighton Foraker, Albuquerque, N. Mex., to Fred J. Dodge, Kansas City, Mo., September 2, 1897, United States Marshals' Service, General Correspondence of the United States Marshals, New Mexico, MS 322 BC, The Center for Southwest Research, UNM, hereafter Foraker Correspondence. The Eagle Creek region had long been a haven for outlaws and rustlers from both sides of the border.

9. McCauley, *A Stove-up Cowboy's Story*, p. 35; Hughes, *South from Tombstone*, pp. 75–78. Colin Rickards wrongly opined that Bill Traynor had previously teamed up with Volney Musgrave, who, Rickards believed, ran the horse-rustling ring. Later employed by the Arizona Cattleman's Association as an undercover agent, Traynor accused Bill Downing of altering brands. Downing shot and killed Traynor at Tom Fulghum's Saloon in Willcox in May 1899 (Rickards, "There Were All Kinds of Gunfighters": 22–23, 60–62; Ringgold, *Pioneer Days in the Southwest*, p. 152).

10. *Sierra County Advocate*, February 5, 1897.

11. Lewis Jones, June 31, 1952, BT.

12. *The Santa Fe Daily New Mexican*, February 6, 1897. Significantly, the *Arizona Range News* of February 9 reported the capture and claimed, almost accurately, that Black Jack's real name was Christianson.

13. *El Paso Daily Herald*, February 9, 1897; *Silver City Enterprise*, February 9 and 10, 1897; *Albuquerque Morning Democrat*, February 12 and 19, April 1, May 11 and 15, 1897; United States District Court, Third Judicial District, Territory of New Mexico, case no. 1183, *United States of America v. George Musgrave, alias Jeff Davis, alias Jesse Williams, and Robert Hayes*, Justice File.

14. Chrisman, *Fifty Years on the Owl Hoot Trail*, pp. 246–47. Herron isolated the incident merely to the spring of 1897. Christian's movements in March and April within Arizona and New Mexico suggest that the meeting with Herron took place prior to those two months.

15. Hayhurst, "Hayhurst Was with Arizona Rangers"; Chrisman, Denver, to Colin Rickards, London, October 17, 1965, Burton Miscellaneous

Papers; Chrisman, *Fifty Years on the Owl Hoot Trail*, pp. 247–49. Dan de Lara Hughes likewise saw the outlaw in Mexico (Hughes, *South from Tombstone*, p. 72). Although Chrisman used the family name Christian in his recounting, Herron withheld the name in his manuscript. He did make it clear to Herron that both he and his brother were members of the gang (Chrisman to Rickards, October 17, 1965, Burton Miscellaneous Papers). Chrisman also inserted into the conversation reference to the forthcoming robbery at Cliff, New Mexico, thereby suggesting that the trip into Mexico took place after March 22. However, Herron made no such reference in his original account (Burton, to authors, October 28, 1999).

16. Chrisman, *Fifty Years on the Owl Hoot Trail*, p. 248.

17. Ibid., p. 249; Hayhurst, "Hayhurst Was with Arizona Rangers."

18. *Silver City Enterprise*, April 2, 1897. The *Enterprise* incorrectly stated that the party crossed from Sonora, Mexico, to New Mexico. This is not likely. They would have crossed into Arizona.

19. Hall to Joseph McKenna, March 23, 1897. *El Paso Daily International Times*, May 4, 1897; William A. Pinkerton, *Train Robberies and Train Robbers*, p. 42; *El Paso Daily Herald*, March 12, 15, and 25, 1897; *El Paso Daily International Times*, March 13, 1897; *Silver City Enterprise*, March 19, 1897. Weathered and Rios were charged in El Paso with bringing stolen property into the state. O'Brien was released due to a lack of evidence (*El Paso Daily Herald*, March 25, 1897).

20. Ringgold, *Pioneer Days in the Southwest*, p. 152. On March 20, 1889, the eastbound express of the Atlantic and Pacific was held up in Canyon Diablo, Yavapai County, Arizona. Several days later, four men were overtaken at Cannonville, Utah: John Halford, William D. Stiren, Daniel M. Harvick, and J. J. Smith, subsequently identified as James Madison Shaw. Shaw was convicted and sentenced to thirty years at Yuma. On July 25, 1893, Dr. P. G. Cotter wrote to Superintendent Thomas Gates that Shaw suffered from consumption. Shaw received Gates's support, and, on August 12, 1893, Governor Louis C. Hughes pardoned Shaw. Years later, his confederate, Dan Harvick, claimed that he, Harvick, conceived of the idea and posed it to Shaw. Shaw replied, "I'm your huckleberry. Name the place, and I'll go with you" (Third Judicial District Court, Yavapai County, *Territory of Arizona v. John Halford, William D. Stiren, Daniel M. Harvick, and J. J. Smith*, case file no. 36, AHS; Territorial Prison at Yuma, Arizona, James Madison Shaw, no. 621, AHS; Records, Secretary of the Territory, Parole of J. J. Smith, Record Group 6, AHS; Harvick, "Canyon Diablo Train Robbery": 40).

21. *Silver City Enterprise*, April 2, 1897; *Albuquerque Morning Democrat*, March 16, 1897; *Rocky Mountain News*, March 19, 1897; *Albuquerque Daily Citizen*, March 13, 1892; *El Paso International Daily Times*, March 17, 1897.

22. Clark, "William Christian, Alias Black Jack," pt. 1: 25; Livingston, "Rounding-up the 'Black Jack' Gang," pt. 3: 54.

23. *Albuquerque Daily Citizen*, March 26, 1897; *Graham County Bulletin*, March 26, 1897; *Silver City Enterprise*, April 2, 1897.

24. United States District Court, First Judicial District, County of Pima, Territory of Arizona, Minute Book Volume N, pp. 195 and 198, *United States v. Black Jack, George Musgrave, and Tom Anderson*, case no. 1255.

25. *Albuquerque Daily Citizen*, March 26, 1897; *Chieftain*, April 2, 1897; French, *Some Recollections of a Western Ranchman*, p. 204.

26. *Chieftain*, April 2, 1897.

27. French, *Some Recollections of a Western Ranchman*, pp. 204–9; *Chieftain*, April 2, 1897. French wrote that Baca claimed that he was Clifton's town marshal. Whether it was a false assertion of Baca's or an error on the part of French is uncertain. In either case, Baca was not an Arizona town marshal. There are no other reports of a captured associate of Black Jack and his gang.

28. *Silver City Enterprise*, March 26, 30, and April 2, 1897; *Annual Reports of the Post-Office Department, 1898*, p. 77; *Black Range*, March 26, 1897, in Stanley, *No Tears for Black Jack Ketchum*, p. 38. The *Enterprise* reported that the party that rode to Cliff consisted of four men. Although it is possible that one remained behind, more likely all five rode to Cliff. The *Silver City Independent* judged the men to be "Black Jack and his desperate confederate Musgrave" from their descriptions (March 30, 1897). The *Enterprise* identified the robbers as Black Jack and Van Musgrave (March 26, 1897). Van's name recently had been in the news and perhaps the reporters now believed that George, whom they had identified on several occasions as William Musgrave, was Van. A dispatch from Silver City to the *El Paso Herald* identified the robbers as Black Jack and Anderson (March 23, 1897). It is doubtful that Heather could positively identify the robbers. Will Christian and either of the two older Musgrave brothers would fit the same general description. The nature of the banter between the outlaws and Heather suggest that the two were Black Jack and George Musgrave. Neither Van nor Anderson (Bob Christian) enjoyed a jovial reputation. It is apparent that the other members of the gang were present, hidden in the darkness.

29. *Silver City Independent*, March 30, 1897; *Silver City Enterprise*, March 26, 1897.

30. *Silver City Enterprise*, March 26, 1897.

31. Ringgold, *Frontier Days in the Southwest*, pp. 152–60. Ringgold was the sister of Sheriff John D. Parks. Many years later, Charlie Williams sold his goat ranch and moved to the mining town of Winkelman, in Gila County. On March 14, 1940, he was committed to the state insane asylum in Phoenix.

He never spoke of Black Jack Christian or the High Five gang (Ibid.). The cave on Williams's ranch had two compartments. The gang kept their horses in the larger compartment, which was about fifteen-by-twenty-five feet, while they lived in the smaller (Charles Martin, no date, BT).

32. Hall to McKenna, July 13, 1897, Justice File.

33. Ibid.; Ringgold, *Frontier Days in the Southwest*, pp. 152–53. Ringgold's depiction of Shaw conforms to his description as found in Shaw's prison record (Records, Secretary of the Territory, Parole of J. J. Smith, Record Group #6, AHS).

34. Clark, "William Christian, Alias Black Jack," pt. 1: p. 25.

35. *Roswell Register*, April 3, 1897; Hall to McKenna, July 13, 1897, Justice File.

36. White to Meade, March 31, 1897, and April 20, 1897, and Hall to Meade, May 31, 1897, Marshals' Correspondence; Longbotham, July 19, 1952, BT.

37. White to Meade, April 20, 1897, Marshals' Correspondence

38. *Sierra County Advocate*, reprinted from the *Bisbee Orb*, April 2, 1897; *The Black Range*, April 23, 1897.

39. Breakenridge, *Helldorado*, pp. 395–406.

40. Henry Graham, ca. July 7, 1952, BT; *Albuquerque Daily Citizen*, April 8, 1897. Smith, who had previously contracted to purchase cattle from rancher Fred Ruch of the San Simon Valley, had only recently returned (*Arizona Range News*, February 2, 1897). A variation of his conversation with his killer went, "I thought I left you in Arizona?" "You did, but I thought I would come over her and look around for awhile" (*Albuquerque Daily Citizen*, April 21, 1897).

41. *Graham County Bulletin*, April 16, 1897.

42. Stevens, ca. June 7, 1952, BT.

43. *Albuquerque Daily Citizen*, April 8, 1897.

44. Ibid., April 30, 1897.

45. *Santa Fe Daily New Mexican*, April 30, 1897.

CHAPTER 10: BLACK JACK CASHES IN

1. Alverson, "Reminiscences," p. 22; *Graham County Bulletin*, May 7, 1897. It is apparent that Ben Clark provided the *Bulletin* with its information.

2. Clark, "William Christian, Alias Black Jack," pt. 2: 20; *Western Liberal*, reprinted in the *Sierra County Advocate*, May 14, 1897; *Graham County Bulletin*, May 7, 1897. No Winchester was chambered in a .35-caliber until 1903. Introduced by Winchester in 1886, the .45-90 was a popular sporting cartridge and remained in production until 1919. Chambered in the

Winchester "Centennial" Model 1876, the .50–95 Winchester Express was introduced in 1879 and had a relatively short sales life (Barnes, *Cartridges of the World*, pp. 127 and 131). A Willcox clerk had recalled the purchase of .50–82-caliber ammunition (*Sulphur Valley News*, November 17, 1896). Probably Cox and Crump purchased .50–95s.

3. Clark to Meade, May 2, 1897, Marshals' Correspondence; *Roswell Register*, April 17, 1897. In his later account, Clark related that a Mexican brought word to him that Shaw would meet him secretly that evening (Clark, "William Christian, Alias Black Jack," pt. 1: 24). Experiencing a convenient loss of memory in this later account, Clark was unable to recollect even Higgins's name (Ibid. pt. 2: 20). It is apparent that Shaw and/or Paxton first contacted Higgins and indicated that, should a posse lie in wait between the cave and the Cole Creek ranch house, it would have an opportunity to take the gang. Jennie Parks Ringgold identified the posse members as Clifton city marshal and merchant Bill Hagan, Charles Ballard [certainly not there], Ben Clark, Clifton deputy and jailer Billie Hart, Charlie Paxton, William "Crookneck" Johnson, Billie Hamilton, Fred Higgins, and Jim Shaw (*Frontier Days in the Southwest*, p. 153). Hagan and Hamilton are not mentioned in other accounts and were likely not part of the posse.

4. Hall to McKenna, July 13, 1897, Justice File; *Graham County Bulletin*, May 7, 1897.

5. Clark, "William Christian, Alias Black Jack," pt. 2: 20; Clark to Meade, May 2, 1897, Marshals' Correspondence; Hall to McKenna, July 13, 1897, Justice File.

6. Clark to Meade, May 2, 1897, Marshals' Correspondence; *Graham County Bulletin*, May 7, 1897; *Western Liberal*, reprinted in the *Sierra County Advocate*, May 14, 1897. The *Silver City Eagle* later published a response to the *Liberal's* article, calling it a falsehood that "reflects on the Marshal's office." The *Liberal* replied, "What 'reflects' the most on Marshal Hall's office is the way he has managed the campaign against these marauders, and, excepting Loomis and Dow, the class of deputies he has put in the field" (*Western Liberal*, reprinted in the *Sierra County Advocate*, May 28, 1897).

7. Clark to Meade, May 2, 1897, Marshals' Correspondence; Ben R. Clark, "William Christian, Alias Black Jack," pt. 2: 20. Clark wrote in both accounts that three of the gang were in full view of the posse. Ringgold believed that only one member of the gang was in view of the posse when it opened fire, the others being hidden by the shadows (Ringgold, *Frontier Days in the Southwest*, p. 154).

8. Clark to Meade, May 2, 1897, Marshals' Correspondence; Clark, "William Christian, Alias Black Jack," pt. 2: 20; *Sierra County Advocate*, May 14, 1897; *Western Liberal*, reprinted in the *Graham County Bulletin*, May 7, 1897.

9. Harkey, December 16, 1947, to Haley, NSH. Harkey was being interviewed by J. Evetts Haley.

10. Ringgold, *Frontier Days in the Southwest*, p. 154; Jim Parks, Duncan, Ariz., interview by Haley and Chesley, February 27, 1945, NSH. Ed Wilson named Bert Farmer, a cowboy, as the man who came upon Christian (Ed Wilson, *An Unwritten History*, p. 58). The *Western Liberal* published a similar account, except it reported that Jones, not Farmer, discovered Will Christian (*Western Liberal*, reprinted in the *Sierra County Advocate*, May 14, 1897).

11. Clark, "William Christian, Alias Black Jack," pt. 2: 20.

12. *Santa Fe Daily New Mexican*, April 28, 1897.

13. Alverson, "Reminiscences," p. 22; Ballard to Hall, copy to Meade, May 28, 1897, Marshals' Correspondence.

14. Ringgold, *Frontier Days in the Southwest*, pp. 155–56. New Mexico's Sacaton Creek flows south from the Mogollon Mountains into Duck Creek at Buckhorn, eight miles northwest of Cliff. Three of the four—George Musgrave, Bob Christian, and "Pal"—were spotted in the San Simon Valley (J. Smith Lea, Nogales, Ariz., to Hall, copy to Meade, May 24, 1897, Marshals' Correspondence). As Moore subsequently was known to be in the cave with one or more of the others, the "Pal" is likely Moore. Van Musgrave is absent from the quartet.

15. Ringgold, *Frontier Days in the Southwest*, pp. 155–56.

16. *Globe-Democrat*, April 29, 1897.

17. See note 34 below.

18. J. Smith Lea, Nogales, Ariz., to Hall, copy to Meade, May 24, 1897, Marshals' Correspondence. Lea numbered John Vinnadge (alias John Cush) and Bill Warderman among the friends, who, along with Walter Hoffman, were arrested soon after the Ketchum gang's December 9, 1897, robbery of the Southern Pacific train near Steins Pass.

19. Ballard to Hall, copy to Meade, May 28, 1897, Marshals' Correspondence.

20. Hall to McKenna, May 1, 1897, Justice File.

21. The *Western Liberal*, reprinted in the *Sierra County Advocate*, May 14, 1897.

22. Clark, "William Christian, Alias Black Jack," pt. 2: 20–21.

23. W. E. Beck, Morenci, Ariz., to Meade, May 31, 1897, Marshals' Correspondence.

24. Clark to Meade, May 2, 1897, Marshals' Correspondence; *Western Liberal*, reprinted in the *Sierra County Advocate*.

25. *Sierra County Advocate*, May 7, 1897; Hall to McKenna, May 1, 1897, Justice File.

304 NOTES TO PAGES 127–30

26. Hall to Meade, May 31, 1897, Marshals' Correspondence; Hall to McKenna, April 30, 1897, Justice File; Clark, "William Christian, Alias Black Jack," pt. 2: 21. In 1897, Clark confirmed his own stupefaction: "Body arrived in Clifton next morning at 6 ock [sic] when an inquest was held and the dead body was positively identified to be Tom Ketchum, alias Black Jack" (Clark to Meade, May 2, 1897, Marshals' Correspondence).

27. Wilson, *An Unwritten History*, p. 59; Alverson, "Reminiscences," p. 21; White to Meade, May 6, 1897, Marshals' Correspondence; Axford, *Around Western Campfires*, p. 255.

28. Clark to Meade, May 2, 1897, Marshals' Correspondence; French, *Some Recollections of a Western Ranchman*, pp. 218–19; *Silver City Enterprise*, May 21, 1897; Hall to Meade, May 31, 1897, Marshals' Correspondence.

29. Hall to Meade, May 31, 1897, Marshals' Correspondence; Hall to Harmon, November 2, 1896, January 21, 1897; Hall to McKenna, March 25, 1897, Justice File; United States District Court, Territory of Arizona, First Judicial District, case no. 1255, and United States District Court, Territory of New Mexico, Third Judicial District. case no. 1174; *Santa Fe Daily New Mexican*, January 5 and April 9, 1897.

30. White to Meade, May 5, 1897, Marshals' Correspondence.

31. Hall to Meade, May 31, 1897, Marshals' Correspondence. Ed Wilson commented on the single photo: "The picture taken of him, after he was dead, hung in the Solomonville jail. It was as natural as could be of Black Jack" (Wilson, *An Unwritten History*, p. 59).

32. Meade to J. W. Slankard, Phoenix, December 8, 1896; Meade (telegram) to Brannick Riggs, Willcox, Ariz., May 29, 1897; White to Meade, May 6, 1897; unsigned telegram (Brannick Riggs) to Meade, May 29, 1897, Marshals' Correspondence. Ed Wilson later, in referring to a previous wound, confirmed Christian "had been shot on the end of the little finger and the bullet followed the bone, stripping the flesh clear. From lack of medical attention it never grew back, leaving the finger half bent and stiff and it has the appearance of being flat and thin" (Wilson, *An Unwritten History*, p. 60).

33. White to Meade, May 6, 1897, Marshals' Correspondence; *El Paso Daily International Times*, May 4, 1897.

34. Ballard to Hall, copy to Meade, May 28, 1897, Marshals' Correspondence. The surviving typescript of Ballard's longhand note either incorporated errors of transcription or, written hastily, Ballard's report skewed the chronology. In the typed copy, Ballard reported that George Musgrave had been at his father's camp and, with James (Van Musgrave) and Moore, was headed, on May 10, for a rendezvous with Bob Christian in the Graham Mountains. It is unlikely that the Musgrave brothers and

Moore rode to Bennett Musgrave's camp, over 125 miles distant, only to return to Arizona by May 10.

CHAPTER 11: THE GREAT GRANTS CAPER

1. Hall to Meade, May 31, 1897, and Ballard to Hall, copy to Meade, May 28, 1897, in Marshals' Correspondence.

2. *Border Vidette* May 2, 1897, reprinted from the *Tucson Citizen*.

3. Lea to Hall, copy to Meade, May 24, 1897, Marshals' Correspondence.

4. *Globe-Democrat*, July 3, 1897.

5. White to William M. Griffith, Tucson, July 5 and July 27, 1897, Marshals' Correspondence. Griffith, formerly the operator of the Texas and California Stage Company and a Republican Party national committeeman, assumed the marshalcy on June 15, 1897 (Ball, *The United States Marshals of New Mexico and Arizona Territories*, pp. 214–25).

6. *Santa Fe Daily New Mexican*, August 21, 1897; *Chieftain*, August 20, 1897; *Silver City Enterprise*, August 20, 27, and October 8, 1897.

7. Creighton Foraker, Santa Fe, to McKenna, August 19, 1897, Justice File. Born in Hillsboro, Ohio, May 8, 1861, Foraker was a brother of Joseph B. Foraker, a powerful Republican senator (Ball, *The United States Marshals of New Mexico and Arizona Territories*, pp. 190–95).

8. *Silver City Enterprise*, August 20, 1897; Agnes Meader Snider, ca. March 1952, BT.

9. Quoted in *Silver City Enterprise*, September 3, 1897.

10. Foraker to McKenna, August 18, August 23, and October 26, 1897, Justice File; Foraker to Cipriano Baca, Dry Creek, N. Mex., August 29, 1897, Foraker Correspondence; *Santa Fe Daily New Mexican*, August 21, 1897.

11. *Silver City Enterprise*, October 1, 1897; Agnes Meader Snider, ca. March 1952, BT. John Davis (apparently Tully's true name), a twenty–one-year-old native of Bastrop County, Texas, was convicted of murder in Socorro County and was admitted to the penitentiary on December 24, 1897. He was released on September 14, 1902 (New Mexico Territorial Penintentiary Record Books of Convicts, November 2, 1884–April 20, 1904).

12. *Graham County Bulletin*, August 20, 1897, reprinted from the *Deming Searchlight*; White to Griffith, August 24, and Augsut 25, 1897, Marshals' Correspondence.

13. Foraker to F. [Fred] J. Dodge, Kansas City, Missouri, October 5, 1897, Foraker Correspondence.

14. *Silver City Independent*, October 19, 1897; *Sierra County Advocate*, October 22, 1897.

15. *Silver City Enterprise,* October 22, 1897.

16. Foraker to McKenna, October 9, 1897; W. B. Childers, Santa Fe, to McKenna, October 16, 1897, Justice File.

17. Rob Ross, El Paso, Texas, to Foraker, October 15, 1897, Justice File; James R. Harper, El Paso, to Miguel Otero, Santa Fe, November 2, 1897, and Otero to Foraker, November 10, 1897, all in Miguel Otero Papers, Letter Box 2, NMSA; Foraker to Baca, n.d., Letterpress Book (Misc. Letters) (August 1, 1897–August 25, 1898), p. 188, Foraker Correspondence.

18. A. C. Alexander, Fort Thomas, Arizona, to Griffith, October 30, 1897, Marshals' Correspondence.

19. Ibid.

20. Ibid.; *Rocky Mountain News,* November 8, 1897

21. *Albuquerque Daily Citizen,* November 15, 1897.

22. Interestingly, Marshal Foraker first expressed his opinion that Black Jack had not been killed in the Cole Creek shootout the day of the holdup (Foraker to McKenna, November 6, 1897, Justice File).

23. *Grant County Democrat,* November 13, 1897.

24. *Albuquerque Morning Democrat,* November 8, 1897; *Albuquerque Daily Citizen,* November 8, 1897.

25. Statement of C. C. Lord, Wells, Fargo & Co's Express, "Robbery Report for November 6, 1897," Wells, Fargo Bank History Room, San Francisco, California, hereafter Grants Report; *Rocky Mountain News,* November 8, 1897.

26. *Rocky Mountain News,* November 8, 1897; *San Francisco Chronicle,* October 3, 1897.

27. *Albuquerque Daily Citizen,* November 8, 1897; *Albuquerque Morning Democrat,* November 8, 1897; *Santa Fe Daily New Mexican,* November 8, 1897; *San Francisco Chronicle,* November 8, 1897; *Rocky Mountain News,* November 8, 1897.

28. *San Francisco Chronicle,* November 8, 1897; Grants Report; *Rio Grande Republican,* November 26, 1897.

29. *Rio Grande Republican,* November 26, 1897; *Rocky Mountain News,* November 8, 1897.

30. *Albuquerque Daily Citizen,* November 8, 1897; *Grant County Democrat,* November 13, 1897. Later accounts, like the one in Silver City's *Grant County Democrat,* indicated that the parting remark was "to tell anyone who said that 'Black Jack' was dead that they were 'liars' as he was that much-sought-for individual" (November 13, 1897).

31. Express car no. 661 was completely destroyed (*Albuquerque Daily Citizen,* November 8, 1897).

32. *Santa Fe Daily New Mexican,* November 8, 1897; *Albuquerque Daily Citizen,* November 8, 1897. Chair car no. 418 and day coach no. 133 were also destroyed by fire (*Albuquerque Daily Citizen,* November 8, 1897). Santa Fe President Edward Payson Ripley placed the value of the loss of equipment at five thousand dollars (N. G. Flinn [?], Los Angeles, to Edward Payson Ripley, November 22, 1897, MS, Santa Fe Railway Archives, Kansas State Historical Society, Topeka, hereafter Santa Fe Report).

33. Grants Report; *Albuquerque Daily Citizen,* November 8, 1897.

34. *Albuquerque Morning Democrat,* November 9, 1897; *San Francisco Chronicle,* November 9, 1897; *Rocky Mountain News,* November 8, 1897.

35. *New York Times,* November 8, 1897; *Santa Fe Daily New Mexican,* November 8, 1897; Griffith to McKenna, December 28, 1897, Marshals' Correspondence.

36. John W. Griggs, Washington, D.C., to Griffith, February 16, 1898, Marshals' Correspondence.

37. *Santa Fe Daily New Mexican,* November 8, 1897.

38. Foraker to McKenna, November 7, 1897, Justice File.

39. *Eddy Argus,* November 13, 1897, reprinted from the *El Paso Herald.*

40. Dona Ana County, N. Mex., *Territory of New Mexico v. Burrell Q. Musgrave,* case no. 2583.

41. *Santa Fe Daily New Mexican,* November 12, 1897; Foraker to McKenna, November 12, 1897, and Griffith to McKenna, December 22, 1897, Justice File. Mason Lee "Mace" Slaughter (1863–1894) had an airtight alibi. Unbeknownst to Foraker, Slaughter had been killed over three years previously, shot by "Cap" Smith near Morenci, Arizona, on July 2, 1894 (Clarke, *Slaughter Ranches and Their Makers,* pp. 193–98; *Arizona Daily Citizen,* August 7, 1894).

42. Foraker to Charles M. Paxton, Clifton, Ariz., November 21, 1897, and November 27, 1897, Letterpress Book (Misc. Letters), (August 1, 1897–August 25, 1898), p. 220, Foraker Correspondence. In April 1899, a jury found Shaw and codefendant Leslie Bowie not guilty (*Elko Free Press,* April 29, 1899).

43. Paxton to Justice Department, September 2, 1897, Justice File. Paxton was paid four dollars a day for twenty-eight days service on February 4, 1898 (Foraker to McKenna, February 11, 1898, Justice File).

44. Foraker to U.S. Marshal, District of Utah, Salt Lake City, n.d., Letterpress Book (Misc. Letters), (August 1, 1897–August 25, 1898), p. 230, Foraker Correspondence; Burton, to authors, January 5, 1998. Gambler and fight promoter Tex Rickard, of whom more later, gave a convoluted account of the Northern Pacific robbery in which he named Newt Gibson, Mat Shaw, and William Newberry as the robbers (Samuels, *Magnificent*

Rube, p. 24). However, only two robbers were identified, Newberry and Charles E. Bailey.

45. *Winslow Argus*, reprinted in the *Arizona Republican*, November 24, 1897.

46. *Rocky Mountain News*, December 10, 1897.

47. *El Paso International Daily Times*, November 7, 1897; *Santa Fe Daily New Mexican*, November 8, 1897; *Albuquerque Morning Democrat*, November 8, 1897; *San Francisco Chronicle*, November 8, 1897; Foraker to McKenna, November 12, 1897, Justice File; *New York Times*, November 8 and 29, 1897.

48. Flinn to Ripley, November 22, 1897, Santa Fe Report; Grants Report.

49. *Albuquerque Daily Citizen*, November 8, 1897; *Rio Grande Republican*, November 26, 1897; J. Wesley Huff, "Malpais Mystery": 37.

50. *San Francisco Chronicle*, November 30, 1897.

51. Ibid.; *Santa Fe Daily New Mexican*, November 29, 1897; *Arizona Daily Star*, December 2, 1897.

52. *Graham County Bulletin*, December 3, 1897; *Oasis*, December 4, 1897.

53. Ibid.; *Silver City Independent*, November 28, 1897; *Rocky Mountain News*, November 28, 1897.

54. Ibid., November 29 and 30, 1897; *Silver City Independent*, November 30, 1897.

55. *Silver City Enterprise*, December 10, 1897.

56. *Arizona Daily Star*, December 10, 1897; *Santa Fe Daily New Mexican*, December 10, 1897. However, both the *Arizona Republican* and the *Arizona Daily Star* properly reported under a December 10, Deming dateline that the robbers were not the original Black Jack gang that was thought then to be hiding in the Sierra Madre in Mexico (*Arizona Republican*, December 11, 1897; *Arizona Daily Star*, December 11, 1897). On the morning of his April 26, 1901, hanging, Tom Ketchum regaled reporters with an explanation of his Black Jack nickname. Black Jack, "was the cause of my becoming an outlaw. Lee [*sic*] Dow, the officer, saw Black Jack [Christian] at the Deer Creek tank affair, and in 1898 [*sic*] he told me that if I was ever tried for Black Jack's crimes I would never get free, for I looked too much like him. I thought if I was going to be hanged for Black Jack's crimes I might as well have some of my own" (*San Francisco Chronicle*, April 27, 1901; a variation appeared in the *Rocky Mountain News*, April 27, 1901). Ketchum's self-serving rationalization is, at best, improbable. Any conversation with Dow had to occur after November 18, 1896 (date of the Deer Creek shooting), but prior to February 18, 1897 (Dow's death), and would have had to take place in the Carlsbad area, judging by Dow's prompt departure following Hayes's killing. During these three months, Ketchum, along with Dave Atkins and Will Carver, appears to have returned to southwest Texas.

In truth, once Ben Clark confused Will Christian with Tom Ketchum, Ketchum assumed Black Jack's nickname and claimed credit for some of the High Five's depredations for one reason—notoriety.

CHAPTER 12: ON THE LAM

1. John Sherman, Secretary of State, Washington, D.C., to John W. Griggs, Attorney General, Washington, D.C., December 16, 1897, Justice Department. Article II of the existing Treaty between the United States of America and the United Mexican States for the Extradition of Criminals (1861) made it unecessary, and therefore unusual, for President McKinley to sign the warrant and make the formal requisition request. Envoy Extraordinary and Minister Plenipotentiary Powell Clayton also received instructions to request the Mexican Government to simply surrender the fugitives to Ross, though it was well publicized that the governor of Mexican Sonora would not deliver the gang without extradition papers (Sherman to Powell Clayton, Mexico City, December 16, 1897, File 239, Despatches from the U.S. Ministers to Mexico 1823–1906, November 1, 1897–May 14, 1898 [National Archives Microfilm Publication M–97, rolls 126–28]; State Department Central File, Record Group 59, National Archives at College Park, Md., hereafter: Despatches, U.S. Ministers; *Arizona Republican*, December 2, 1897).

2. Clayton to Ignacio Mariscal, Mexico City, March 9, 1898, Mariscal to Clayton, March 22, 1898 File 356, Despatches, U.S. Ministers. On April 15, 1898, Assistant Secretary of State William R. Day notified Attorney General Griggs of the Mexican government's refusal to surrender (Day to Griggs, April 15, 1898, Justice Department). Article I specifically stated, "That this [deliver upon requisition] shall be done only when the fact of the commission of the crime shall be so established as that the laws of the country in which the fugitive or the person so accused shall be found, would justify his or her apprehension and commitment for trial if the crime had been there committed." The Extradition Law of Mexico, promulgated May 19, 1897, required a minimum of two proofs (Ibid.).

3. Livingston, "Rounding up the 'Black Jack' Gang," pt. 3: 55; Axford, *Around Western Campfires*, p. 41. During the winter of 1898–99, Perry Tucker, sometime straw boss of the Erie, received a letter from Colonel French of the WS Ranch requesting that he come to the WS to help stifle rustling. Perry agreed to take charge of the WS outfit and invited Lowe and McGinnis to join him. Accompanied by Mack Axford, Jim James, and Clay McGonegal, they rode to Alma, New Mexico (French, *Some Recollections of a Western Ranchman*, pp. 257–58 and 275; Axford, *Around Western*

Campfires, p. 41; French, *Some Further Recollections of a Western Ranchman,* p. 513).

4. Chrisman, *Fifty Years on the Owl Hoot Trail,* pp. 212–20.

5. Ibid., p. 220. Harry Chrisman learned that George Musgrave had had an older brother named Burrell (1868–1871). Given Musgrave's familiarity with the name, and knowing he was hiding out within the vicinity, it was suggested to Chrisman that Burr, as named by Herron, must be an alias used by George Musgrave. It was presented as fact in Chrisman's edition of Herron's reminiscences (Burton, to authors, January 18, 1997).

6. Chrisman, *Fifty Years on the Owl Hoot Trail,* pp. 222–23.

7. Chaves County, N. Mex., Fifth Judicial District, *Territory of New Mexico v. Vollie Musgrave,* case no. 198.

8. *El Paso Herald,* May 2, 1899; Curry, *George Curry,* pp. 91 and 94; Eddy County, N. Mex., Fifth Judicial District. Criminal Records, *Territory of New Mexico v. Charles Ware,* case nos. 224–28 and 241; *Territory of New Mexico v. Samuel Morrow,* case nos. 229–33 and 242; *Territory of New Mexico v. Dan Johnson,* case nos. 234–38 and 243. Hereafter, Eddy County Criminal Records.

9. Garrett and a posse went out into the mountains to head off the rustlers but the gang did not come their way (*El Paso Herald,* May 6, 1897).

10. *El Paso International Daily Times,* May 3, 1899.

11. Harkey, *Mean as Hell,* pp. 191–201.

12. Cicero Stewart, Carlsbad, N. Mex., December 20, 1953, BT.

13. *El Paso International Daily Times,* May 3, 1899.

14. Ibid.; *El Paso Herald,* May 3, 1899.

15. Livingston, "Rounding-up the 'Black Jack' Gang," pt. 2: 471–76; *Carlsbad Argus,* August 18 and 25, 1899; Axford, *Around Western Campfires,* p. 259.

16. *El Paso Herald,* May 3, 1899.

17. *Pecos Valley Argus,* May 5, 12, and 19, 1899. Less than three weeks later, on May 23, the citizens of Eddy, New Mexico, changed the name of their community to Carlsbad. The *Pecos Valley Argus* quickly followed suit, becoming the *Carlsbad Argus.* The Morrow brothers—Sam, Bill, and Archie—originally from near Fort Worth, had moved to the Pecos Valley with their divorced mother. Sam and Archie took to rustling. William King "Bill" Morrow went to work for rancher J. C. Lea of Roswell, where he met Charlie Ballard and later married Eva Corn, a younger sister of Ballard's wife, Arminta (Fleming and Huffman, *Roundup of the Pecos,* pp. 185–86; Alden Hayes, *A Portal to Paradise,* pp. 219–20).

18. Two years earlier, Jim, his brother Jourd, Jim Crane, and Jim Pettigrew had rustled cattle and horses from John Gardner and Peter Patterson

of Kimble County, Texas. On February 6, 1897, Kimble County Sheriff John L. Jones and his deputies located the rustlers at Rust Ranch, twenty–one miles northwest of Junction City (later Junction). Jourd Knight and Crane were killed in the ensuing fight, while Pettigrew escaped, and Jim Knight (using the alias John Underwood), badly wounded in the thigh, left leg, and right hip, was arrested. Former Frio County Sheriff Joseph Walter Durbin identified the wounded rustler and reported that the outlaw's father was then living in Atascosa County (*The Daily Light*, April 13, 1897). Knight was tried and convicted on five counts of rustling and sentenced to seven years imprisonment (Kimble County District Court, *State of Texas v. John Underwood*, nos. 630–34). He was next taken to Kerr County, and from there he was returned to Longview to stand trial for murder committed during the First National Bank robbery. After securing a change of venue from the Gregg County Court to the Smith County Court in Tyler, Knight was given a life sentence. Ordered to the state penitentiary at Huntsville, he began serving his term for rustling while his attorney appealed the murder conviction. Granted a new trial on appeal, he was returned to the Tyler jail, where he had sawed his way out on February 18, 1899 (*Pecos Valley Argus*, May 19, 1899; *Carlsbad Argus*, May 26 and June 30, 1899). Following his return to Texas, on a change of venue, Knight was removed to Henderson, Rusk County, Texas, where his new trial commenced on July 27. Convicted and sentenced to a life term, he was returned to Huntsville on August 14, and was later transferred to the state prison facility at Rusk, Cherokee County. Knight was conditionally pardoned on December 20, 1914. He moved to Oklahoma and, in January 1920, was killed while attempting to rob a drugstore in Tulsa (*Tulsa Tribune* January 25, 1920, and *Tulsa World*, January 25, 26, and 27, 1920, cited in Nancy Samuelson's "Who Really Robbed the Longview Bank?": 33).

19. La Salle County, Tex., District Court, *State of Texas v. Van Musgrave*, theft by conversion of horse held under bailment, case no. 844. The case, dating back to June 14, 1894, was eventually dismissed due to insufficient evidence.

20. Livingston, "Rounding–up the 'Black Jack' Gang," pt. 2: 471–76; *Carlsbad Argus*, August 18 and 25, 1899. For a detailed account, see Jeff Burton's "'Suddenly in a Secluded and Rugged Place . . .'."

21. La Salle County, Tex., District Court, *State of Texas v. Van Musgrave*, case nos. 859 and 871, and *State of Texas v. Volney Musgrave*, case no. 858.

22. *Carlsbad Argus*, September 15, and 22, 1899; Eddy County, N. Mex., Fifth Judicial District, Criminal Records.

23. Chaves County, N. Mex., Fifth Judicial District, Criminal Records, *Territory of New Mexico v. Dan Johnson*, case nos. 218–23, and 224; *Roswell Record*, October 13, 1899. Ware was convicted in case no. 225.

24. *Roswell Register,* October 13, 1899. Johnson had been noted missing as of October 9 (Ibid.).

25. Chaves County, N. Mex., Fifth Judicial District, *Territory of New Mexico v. Vollie Musgrave,* case no. 198. Burwell (1870–1918), a native of Jackson County, Texas, and a former Texas Ranger, served as chief deputy of La Salle County in 1897, and sheriff from 1897 to 1900. In 1901, he returned briefly to the Rangers before accepting the office of sheriff under appointment by the district court of Potter County, Texas. Elected sheriff of Potter County in 1910, he remained in the office until his 1918 death in Amarillo. At the time of his death, he was a nominee for the post of U.S. marshal for the northern district of Texas (William M. Burwell, Jr., Corpus Christi, Tex., interview with the authors, November 12, 1998; Burwell, to authors, January 5, 1999).

26. *Roswell Register-Tribune,* December 8, 1899; Chaves County, N. Mex., Commitment to Penitentiary, December 11, 1907, NMSA; New Mexico Territorial Penitentiary, Admission Records (Record of Convicts), Prisoner #2233, NMSA. The Eddy County escapees were Frank Carper, Charlie Drain, and Tom Roberts (*Roswell Register,* December 15, 1899). Sentenced to a one-year term, Morrow entered New Mexico Territorial Prison at Santa Fe on December 17, 1907. Governor Curry pardoned Morrow less than two weeks later. Locals credited Charlie Ballard with securing Morrow's early release. Sam later joined his brother Bill in Paradise, Arizona, and worked as a carpenter (Hayes, *A Portal to Paradise,* p. 220).

27. Val Verde County, Tex., District Court, *Van Musgrave v. Ella Musgrave,* case no. 426; Val Verde County, Tex., Marriage Book 2, p. 7. Divorce proceedings were filed on March 22, 1900; the court granted the divorce on April 11. Van remarried on May 9, 1900. Evidently, Mrs. Remick had been married to a Mr. Taylor prior to her marriage to Remick, as Van acquired two Taylor surnamed stepdaughters: Lulu (b. 1888) and Ludy (b. 1892) (1900 U.S. Census, Pecos County, Texas). Bennett Musgrave and his daughter Addie temporarily moved to Cloudcroft (in newly formed Otero County) New Mexico in 1899. Addie worked there as a telegrapher. Bennett began prospecting in the Capitan Mountains around Lincoln. He filed on his first location on November 4 (Lincoln County, N. Mex., Book S of Mining Records, p. 434). Victimized by sunstroke, he sold his claims on December 18, 1900 (Lincoln County, N. Mex., Deed Book S, p. 161). Meanwhile, during the summer of 1899, Prudie moved from Cedar Hill to her daughter Julia's home in Del Rio, Texas.

28. King, *Pioneer Western Empire Builders*, pp. 73–74; White to Griffith, March 11, 1898, Marshals' Correspondence; Chrisman, *Fifty Years on the Owl Hoot Trail*, pp. 188 and 324, n. 7. Jeff Burton recalled, "Mrs. Frank Moson told us that Ed Roberts moved to California circa 1900 and that, she believed, George Musgrave visited him not long afterwards" (Burton, to authors, January 5, 1998). Addie Musgrave Parker's grandson, Byrd Lindsey, also related that Musgrave went to California at this time (Lindsey, interview with the authors, November 23, 1996). Musgrave's journey to California was confirmed by non-family source Mack Axford (Axford, Tombstone, Ariz., to Colin Rickards, London, England, June 29, 1965, Burton, Miscellaneous Papers). Charlie Ballard was also aware of Musgrave's sojourn to California. Unfortunately, numerous errors crept in when Earnest Mathews recounted Ballard's story to James Shinkle (Ernest Mathews, Trabuco Canyon, Calif., to James D. Shinkle, Roswell, N. Mex., June 13, 1966, in Shinkle, *Reminiscences of Roswell Pioneers*, p. 257).

29. *San Francisco Chronicle*, September 19, 1900.

30. Ibid., September 22, 1900. Certainly Van Musgrave was known to be very large and dark. Having previously grown accustomed to the James alias, he now linked it to his step-daughters' surname and was James Taylor.

31. Ibid., September 23, 1900.

32. Ibid.

33. New Mexico Territorial Penitentiary, Admission Records (Record of Convicts), Prisoner #1419, NMSA.

34. *San Francisco Chronicle*, April 27, 1901.

35. *Rocky Mountain News*, April 27, 1901.

36. Brewster County, Tex., District Court Minute Book #2, pp. 78, 111, 112, and case file #396, *Fanny M. Mathis [sic] et. ux. v. The Galveston, Harrisburg & San Antonio Railroad*. On September 11, 1902, Fannie was awarded $7,500.

37. New Mexico Territorial Penitentiary, Admission Records (Record of Convicts), Prisoner #1419, NMSA. Van was employed in El Paso as a car repairman for the G.H. & S.A. railroad (*Buck's Directory of El Paso, Tex. for 1902*, p. 292).

38. Velma Thornton Walker, Benson, Ariz., interview with the authors, March 31, 1999. Raised by Calvin Musgrave, Slaughter's sister-in-law, Rebecca Wallen Slaughter, though Bennett's cousin, was treated as a sister. Buddy Walker, born at Yarbrough Bend, McMullen County, Texas, on November 8, 1866, cowboyed in south Texas prior to moving to Arizona. He later served as a deputy sheriff in Gila County for a number of years, then resettled his family to southern California in 1924. He died in Burbank

on September 17, 1933. Roamie Walker, born at Yarbrough Bend on September 20, 1869, settled in Safford, Arizona. He also moved to Burbank, where he died on November 4, 1960. Both Walkers were veterans of the Kansas and Colorado trail drives. Burrell Q. Musgrave began selling blocks and lots, transferring several blocks to his daughters, Mary and Timor (Cochise County, Ariz., Deed Book 25, p. 31, and Deed Book 38, p. 274).

39. Eunice Parker Lindsey, Tombstone, Ariz., interview by Barbara J. Wincn, August 13, 1987, transcript provided to authors by Mrs. Wincn; Santa Cruz County, Ariz., Marriage Book 1, p. 396. Frank Moson married Pearl Parker on New Year's Day, 1902. His mother, Ella Roberts Moson (sister of Ed Roberts), had married Greene on June 9, 1884 (Cochise County, Ariz., Marriage Book 1, p. 67). Van Musgrave later appeared on Greene's behalf somewhat out of character as a witness for the prosecution in a cattle rustling case, *The State of Arizona v. B. H. Behrends* (case no. 1653) on June 21, 1909. Behrends was found not guilty (Reel No. 10, Cochise County, Ariz., Superior Court, Criminal Judgment Terr.; Axford, *Around Western Campfires*, pp. 131–37).

40. Arizona Territory, Enlistment Papers, Boyd M. Doak, Arizona Rangers, Record Group 42, ASA. The Doaks has left Atascosa County and settled in Del Rio in 1898, They sold their Del Rio residence to Doak's brother, John (deed not dated, but recorded April 3, 1905 [Val Verde County, Tex., Deed Book 12]).

41. Dan Johnson died in Santa Cruz County on August 14, 1922 (Arizona Death Records, State Index #297; County Record #2117; Local Reg. #1, ASA).

CHAPTER 13: SHACKLED

1. Frank King, Los Angeles, Calif., to Mrs. J. D. Milton, Tucson, November 24, 1947, NSH. In another recollection he placed the meeting in 1908, which was equally in error (King, "Mavericks," *Western Livestock Journal*, April 25, 1935).

2. Powe, August 2, 1953, BT; King, "Mavericks," *Western Livestock Journal*, April 25, 1935. It was briefly thought that postal authorities had arrested Musgrave, along with his gang, in March 1902 near Alamogordo, New Mexico (Jane Adler, Pinkerton archivist, to authors, May 16, 1997). It proved to be a false report. Those arrested were George R. Massagee and other members of the Mesa Hawks gang. See: Burton, *Dynamite and Sixshooter*, pp. 212–13.

3. Porter McDonald, Tombstone, Ariz., to Sheriff, White Oaks, N. Mex., April 25, 1906, NMSA.

4. King to Mrs. Milton, November 24, 1947, NSH.

5. King, "Moson Tells Own Story," *Western Livestock Journal*, May 6, 1933.

6. Tschiffely, *Bohemia Junction*, p. 148; Samuels, *Magnificent Rube*, p. 93; *Goldfield Daily Sun*, July 30, 1906.

7. Foraker to W. H. H. Llewellyn, Silver City, New Mexico, March 1, 1907; Llewellyn to Foraker, March 2 and 21, 1907, Foraker Correspondence. Franklin's telegram does not appear to have survived. Foraker references it in other correspondence—see Foraker to George H. Green, Dallas, Texas, February 26, 1907, Letter Book (August 1, 1897–January 17, 1911), Foraker Correspondence.

8. Foraker to Green, February 26, 1907; Green to Foraker, March 6, 1907, Foraker Correspondence. James A. "Gotch-eyed Jim" Franklin, born in Texas about 1855, was a double first cousin of Musgrave's aunt, Nora Franklin Walker (Mrs. Joseph Henry Walker), and of another aunt, Melvina Walker, who had married Nora's brother, Frank Franklin.

9. *Tombstone Prospector*, July 22 and 23, 1907; *Tucson Citizen*, July 23, 1907; *Arizona Daily Star*, July 23, 1907; *Albuquerque Morning Journal*, July 25, 1907; La Salle County, Tex., District Court, *State of Texas v. Volney Musgrave*, case no. 858, hereafter indicated as case no. 858.

10. *Tombstone Prospector*, August 3 and 18, 1907. Sureties were Miles E. Williams (married to Vollie's cousin, Mary E. "Mamie" Musgrave), Thomas D. Mathes (alias Dan Johnson, Vollie's brother-in-law), and J. C. Black (case no. 858).

11. William H. McGinnis, prisoner number 1348, Penitentiary Record Book of Convicts, November 2, 1884–April 20, 1904, pp. 89–90, NMSA; Ben Avery, no date, Lewis Jones, no date, John Allred, no date, in BT. Farr was killed during the chase that followed the robbery of the Colorado and Southern Railroad on July 11, 1899. Will McGinnis was admitted on May 4, 1900. Governor Miguel Otero commuted his sentence to ten years on July 4, 1905. Due to be freed on January 10, 1906, Lay was actually released, with "good time and extra leave allowed, 15 Dec 1905." For full details see: Tanner and Tanner, "Elzy Lay: New Mexico Prisoner #1348": 14–20. H. A. Hoover correctly wrote that Lay remained at Alma for eighteen months (Hoover, "The Gentle Train Robber": 45).

12. Lewis Jones, no date, John Allred. no date, in BT; speech delivered by Harvey Murdock (grandson of Elzy Lay) at the Ninth Annual Convention of the Western Outlaw-Lawman History Association, Buffalo, Wyoming, July 22, 1999. Maude had been widowed in 1903.

13. Burroughs, *Where the Old West Stayed Young*, pp. 78–80; Carley Jebens, Baggs, Wyo., interview with Larry Pointer, May 25, 1974, Larry

316NOTES TO PAGES 176–78

Pointer Papers, no. 10345, Box 5, American Heritage Center, University of Wyoming, Laramie, hereafter Pointer Papers. Jebens was called as a witness during Dempsey's 1910 trial. Certainly the three arrived prior to September 1907, when Dempsey began to rustle horses (see following).

14. Dullenty, "The Farm Boy Who Became a Member of Butch Cassidy's Wild Bunch": 7; Kelly, *Outlaw Trail*, p. 259; Pointer, "Jano," p. 12, Pointer Papers. Between 1895 and 1898, Calvert had pieced together a ranch of four hundred acres along the Little Snake River (Carbon County, Wyo., Deed Books no. 28, p. 525; no. 38, p. 151; and no. 41, p. 359). There are several reports that McGinnis purchased a ranch near Baggs. Carbon County deed records refute these reports.

15. Carbon County, Wyo., District Court, District Number Three, *State of Wyoming v. Jack Dempsey,* case no. 645, WSA; *Rawlins Republican,* March 14, 1908; *Carbon County Journal,* March 14, 1908.

16. Beebe, *Reminiscing along the Sweetwater,* p. 95; *Carbon County Journal,* October 3, 1908; *Rawlins Republican,* October 3, 1908. According to the press, Dempsey made two attempts to escape.

17. Carbon County, Wyo., District Court, District Number Three, *State of Wyoming v. Jack Dempsey,* case nos. 664, 726, and 735, WSA; Wyoming State Penitentiary Records, Jack Dempsey, Convict #1311, WSA. The parents of both Thomas and Eliza Magor were born in England and migrated to Wisconsin. In 1879 the Thomas Magor family moved from Wisconsin to Amsterdam Township of Hancock County, Iowa, where they resided in 1880. They moved to Baggs, Carbon County, Wyoming some time after 1884 but before 1889 (U.S. Census, 1880, Hancock County, Amsterdam Twp., Iowa; U.S. Census, 1900, Carbon County, Wyo.).

18. Pointer, "Jano," p. 3, Pointer Papers; Carbon County, Wyo., Deed Book No. 41, p. 151. Children of Thomas and Eliza Magor: Thomas, Jr. (July 3, 1873–January 5, 1901), Mabel E. (c. 1875–1920), Elizabeth J. "Lizzie" (October 14, 1876–April 23, 1958), and William (c. 1879) were born in Wisconsin. Maude L. (December 29, 1882–March 5, 1955), Ethel (died in infancy), and Cornelius I. "Neil" (December 23, 1884–January 19, 1956) were born in Iowa. The name was originally Meaghor. Richard C. Magor was born about 1847 in England (U.S. Census, 1880, Rawlins, Carbon County, Wyo.). Harley S. Magor was born in November of 1890 (Ibid.).

19. Jeanette Magor, Denver, interview with Larry Pointer, October 13, 1974, Pointer Papers; Pointer, "Jano," Ibid., p. 6. Mary Calvert, six months older than Jano, was born in Baggs in July 1888 (1910 U.S. Census, Carbon County, Wyo.).

20. Burroughs, *Where the Old West Stayed Young,* pp. 129–30.

21. *Craig (Colo.) Courier,* reprinted in Charter, *Cowboys Don't Walk,* p. 49; Pointer, "Jano," Pointer Papers, p. 5; District Court of Carbon County, District Number Three, Guardianship Record no. 240, Jeanette E. Magor, WSA; Jeanette Magor, September 24, 1974, Pointer Papers. Bert Charter was born at Delhi, Iowa, June 14, 1873, and died in 1939. Maude L. Magor later married Charter on June 11, 1903, at Rawlins, Wyoming (Charter, *Cowboys Don't Walk,* pp. 6, 46, and 61).

22. Jebens, May 25, 1974, Pointer Papers; District Court of Carbon County, Wyo., District Number Three, Estate Record no. 233, Estate of Eliza J. Magor, WSA; Denver County, Colo., Marriage Record no. 44651. The family does not, initially, appear to be aware of her marriage or new name. A March 15, 1909, Decree of Settlement and Final Distribution still refers to Jano as Jeanette Magor, as does a June 14 petition for the removal of William Magor as administrator and guardian of the minor heirs, Jeanette and Harley Magor. On October 15, 1914, the court issued a Decree and Order of Settlement of Accounts and Distribution of the Estate. In it, Jano is referred to as Jeanette Magor, now Mrs. Musgrove [*sic*], and subsequently as Jeanette Magor Musgrove.

23. *Albuquerque Morning Journal,* September 21, 1908.

24. Brock and Cox, April 11, 1953, BT.

25. State of Colorado, Denver District Court, Second Judicial District, *State of Colorado v. John Bradley,* case no. 18620; Jane Adler, Pinkerton archivist, to authors, May 16, 1997.

26. Boyd Charter, interview with Larry Pointer, December 1, 1973, Pointer Papers; Byrd Lindsay, Canelo, Ariz., telephone interview with the authors, November 23, 1996; *Albuquerque Morning Journal,* January 7 and May 28, 1910. In these reports he is identified as Mason and Ed Mason. The *Rocky Mountain News* of January 4, 1910, identified him as Harry Mason. The *North Platte Semi-Weekly Tribune* of January 4, 1910, identified him as R. W. Mason. This is the name under which he joined the Elks lodge (Dorothy Inscho, Grand Junction, Colo., to authors, April 19, 1997).

27. Shinkle, *Reminiscences of Roswell Pioneers,* p. 248; Ball, "Charles Ballard: 'Lawman' of the Pecos": 4; Ball, "Lawman of the Pecos": 68.

28. Carley Jebens, January 22, 1974, Pointer Papers.

29. *North Platte SemiWeekly Tribune,* December 31, 1909. Case no. 153 for the murder of George Parker had been dismissed, with leave to reinstate, on October 31, 1903. On November 3, 1909, following the sighting of Musgrave, a court order to reinstate and an alias warrant was issued. On December 30, a certified copy of indictment was issued for Sheriff Ballard.

30. *North Platte Semi-Weekly Tribune,* December 28, 1909, and January 4, 1910; *Roswell Daily Record,* January 4, 1910; *Albuquerque Morning Journal,*

January 4, 1910. Any reward was contingent upon Musgrave's conviction and therefore never was paid.

31. *Roswell Daily Record,* December 31, 1909; *North Platte Semi-Weekly Tribune,* January 4, 1910.

32. *Rocky Mountain News,* January 4, 1910.

CHAPTER 14: VINDICATED

1. *Roswell Daily Record,* January 6, 1910; Mathews to Shinkle, May 3, 1966, in Shinkle, *Reminiscences of Roswell Pioneers,* p. 257.

2. *Roswell Daily Record,* January 6, 1910; *Roswell Register-Tribune,* January 25, 1910.

3. *Roswell Daily Record,* January 6, 1910; *Albuquerque Morning Journal,* June 4, 1910.

4. Harkey, *Mean as Hell,* pp. 89, 163–66. Askren, a native of Bolivar, Missouri, moved to New Mexico in 1907, and in 1910 he was practicing law in Roswell. He went on to become one of New Mexico's most distinguished attorneys and New Mexico state attorney general.

5. Bonney, *Looking Over My Shoulder,* p. 9.

6. *The Roswell Register-Tribune,* January 25, 1910; Chaves County, N. Mex., Fifth Judicial District Court, *Territory of New Mexico v. George Musgrave,* case no. 153, murder of George T. Parker, October 19, 1896, hereafter case no. 153; *Albuquerque Morning Journal,* January 13, 1910; Aguayo Reminiscences. Pope was attending the supreme court in Santa Fe. Born in Indiana in 1872, Louis Fullen came to New Mexico in 1886, and cofounded the *Pecos Valley Register* in 1888. Admitted to the bar in Carlsbad, New Mexico, he was appointed district attorney of the Fifth Judicial District in 1908 and resettled in Roswell (Bonney, *Looking Over My Shoulder,* pp. 180–82). Texas native James M. Hervey also came to New Mexico in 1886. He practiced law in Lincoln for a number of years before moving to Roswell, where he formed a partnership with Granville A. Richardson (Ibid., p. 85).

7. U.S. Census, 1910, Chaves County, New Mexico.

8. Louis O. Fullen, Roswell, N. Mex., to Inspector in Charge, Post Office Department, Denver, Colo., February 22, 1910, Foraker Correspondence.

9. Foraker to Fullen, February 26, 1910, Foraker Correspondence.

10. *Albuquerque Morning Journal,* March 9, 1910 (this issue is misdated 1909); Ball, "Charles Ballard: 'Lawman' of the Pecos": 2.

11. Reeves, July 2, 1953, BT.

12. U.S. Census, 1910, Chaves County, N. Mex. On May 2, Musgrave's attorneys subpoenaed Lee Fountain as a defense witness. Musgrave paid

four hundred dollars for the home. Located on the west side of Michigan Avenue (then 410 Michigan and now 410 and 412), the purchase was not recorded until November 22, 1910, after Musgrave's departure from Chaves County (Chaves County, N. Mex., Deed Record Book 35, pp. 291–92).

13. Frank Strickland to Charles Ballard—total of 451 acres, consideration: one dollar and other valuable considerations (Chaves County, N. Mex., Deed Book 33, p. 516). May 10, 1910: Charles Ballard to Frank Strickland—20 acres, consideration: one dollar and other valuable considerations (Ibid., p. 545); case no. 153. The court issued the subpoena on May 2, eight days prior to the sale, but it was not served until May 18.

14. Reeves, July 2, 1953, BT. The promissory note was in the amount of six hundred dollars, due sixty days from the transaction, and bearing interest at 10 percent (Chaves County, N. Mex., Record of Mortgage Deeds, Book 31, p. 109). On September 16, 1921, Strickland filed a reconveyance indicating that the note, with interest, had been fully paid (Chaves County, N. Mex., Satisfaction of Mortgage Record, Book Q, p. 213). The quitclaim deed was filed November 14, 1910 (Chaves County, Deed Book 37, p. 36).

15. *Roswell Daily Record,* May 27, 1910; *Albuquerque Morning Journal,* May 28, 1910. The ground for the new courthouse was broken in February (*Roswell Daily Record,* February 3, 1910).The jury was comprised of Roswell butcher Burke B. Dietrich; Charles W. Shephard, later a partner with Cyrus M. Fransworth in the Roswell Auto Company; Lake Arthur blacksmith James S. Talley; James S. Kennedy, secretary and treasurer of a hardware company; Edward S. Mundy, manager of a transfer company; Jake Q. Cummins, a director of the Roswell Building and Loan Association and Roswell's first elected city treasurer; rancher Lark B. Craig; J. Harvey Hall, an employee of the Pecos Valley and Northeastern Railway; Roswell's fire chief, Charles S. Whiteman, who served for thirty-two years; salesman Ernest Burns; dairyman E. B. Evans; and W. M. Heitman, a resident of Dexter (*Roswell Daily Record,* May 28,1910). "Competent and conscientious," Heitman, of German descent, came from Ohio, had been a schoolteacher, and had studied law (Charles P. Sterrett, Dexter, New Mexico, to Jeff Burton, London, March 27, 1967, Burton, Miscellaneous Papers.)

16. True Bill of Indictment, March 24, 1897, case no. 153.

17. *Roswell Daily Record,* March 30 and 31, 1910.

18. Ibid., March 31, 1910.

19. Ibid.

20. Ibid., May 31, 1910; *Roswell Register-Tribune,* May 31, 1910; case no. 153.

21. *Roswell Daily Record,* May 31, 1910; Fleming and Huffman, *Roundup on the Pecos,* p. 265.

22. *Roswell Daily Record,* May 31 and June 1, 1910; *Albuquerque Morning Journal,* June 1, 1910.

23. *Roswell Daily Record,* June 1, 1910.

24. Instruction 43a, case no. 153.

25. Dills arrived in Roswell in 1887 where, for the next three years, he served as foreman of Pat Garrett's ranch. He was the son-in-law of Judge Frank Lea, who had conducted the inquest into Parker's killing (Lucius Dills, "Retrospects on Early Roswell," in Shinkle, *Reminiscences of Roswell Pioneers,* pp. 109–11).

26. *Roswell Daily Record,* June 1, 1910.

27. Ibid.

28. Ibid., June 2, 1910.

29. *Albuquerque Morning Journal,* January 7, 1910.

30. *Roswell Daily Record,* June 2, 1910; *Roswell Register-Tribune,* June 3, 1910.

31. *Roswell Daily Record,* June 3, 1910; case 153.

32. *Roswell Register-Tribune,* June 7, 1910; Sterrett, "Sam P. Butler, Saga of a Lifetime Cowboy," *As We Remembered It,* p. 110; Sterrett to Burton, March 27, 1967, Burton, Miscellaneous Papers); Ball, "Lawman of the Pecos," p. 69. The jurors acquitted Musgrave on their second ballot, the first ballot had resulted in nine votes for acquittal, three votes for conviction (*Roswell Daily Record,* June 3, 1910).

33. *Albuquerque Morning Journal,* June 4, 1910; Ball, "Lawman of the Pecos": 69; Ballard, Reminiscences, p. 36.

34. Cox, April 11, 1953, BT.

35. *Roswell Register-Tribune,* June 4, 1910.

36. *Roswell Daily Record,* June 3, 1910.

37. Ora Carlton Schrader, Roswell, N. Mex., to Jeff Burton, London, England, October 25, 1966, Burton, Miscellaneous Papers. *Santa Fe Daily New Mexican,* June 10, 1910; Robert J. Eaton, Asunción, Paraguay, to authors, August 7, 1997.

38. Chaves County, N. Mex., Fifth Judicial District, *Territory of New Mexico v. Vol Musgrave,* case no. 1167.

39. *Roswell Daily Record,* August 10, 13, and 16, 1910.

40. Chaves County, Fifth Judicial District, *Territory of New Mexico v. V. C. Musgrave,* case nos. 1147, 1168, 1169, and 1170; *Roswell Daily Record,* September 16, and 19, 1910. There is no evidence that this James Shaw was one and the same with James Madison Shaw.

41. *Roswell Daily Record,* September 19 and 21; Chaves County, Fifth Judicial District, *Territory of New Mexico v. V. C. Musgrave,* case nos. 1177 and 1237.

42. *Roswell Daily Record,* December 12 and 19, 1910; case no. 1170; New Mexico Territorial Prison Records, no. 2872, New Mexico State Records Center, Santa Fe. On December 19, 1910, all other outstanding charges were dropped with leave to reinstate.

43. *Roswell Daily Record,* December 19, 1910; The court issued a warrant for Musgrave's arrest on November 16. The case was continued on May 1, 1911, and at subsequent sessions of the Superior Court until it was dismissed with leave to reinstate in 1920 (Ibid.); *Roswell Daily Record,* May 12, 1911.

44. Livingston, "Rounding-up the 'Black Jack' Gang": 52–53; Reeves, July 2. 1953, BT.

45. Friedrich Katz, *Life and Times of Pancho Villa,* pp. 103–11.

46. Charter, interview with Pointer, December 1, 1973, Pointer Papers. It is doubtful that Musgrave and Villa encountered each other prior to the summer of 1911. Musgrave's association with Chihuahua City and regions north apparently concluded early in 1906, while Villa, who fled to the state of Chihuahua from Durango in 1902, remained along the southern Chihuahua-Durango border at Parral before moving to Chihuahua City near the end of the decade.

47. Frank M. Hicks, Buenos Aires, to Hon. Carlos Bee, Representative, 14th District, Texas, Washington, D.C., December 8, 1920, file no. 130 STATE 4211, Administration Correspondence, 1920–1929, State Department Central File, General Records of the Department of State, Record Group 59, NAB, hereafter file no. 130 STATE 4211; Denver County, Colo., Deed Book 2347, pp. 196–98; Carbon County, Wyo., District Court Records, Estate Record no. 233, Eliza J. Magor, WSA; Jebens, Baggs, Wyo., interview with Pointer, January 22, 1974, Pointer Papers.

CHAPTER 15: SOUTH AMERICA BECKONS

1. For a well-reasoned argument that no one went looking for Butch and Sundance see: Buck and Meadows, "Did Butch Cassidy Return? His Family Can't Decide": 34 n. 86, 48.

2. Kelly, *Outlaw Trail,* pp. 35, 314–15.

3. Edmund Crabe, Shoshoni, Wyo., interview with Ludwig Stanley Landmichl, ca. 1937, WPA File #1806, WSA.

4. Charter, interview with Pointer, December 1, 1973, Pointer Papers; William L. Simpson, Jackson, Wyo., to Charles Kelly, Salt Lake City, May 5, 1939, Charles Kelly Papers, Marriot Library, University of Utah, Salt Lake City; Pointer, interview with the authors, October 30, 1996; Pointer, *In Search of Butch Cassidy,* pp. 51, 120, 253; Daniel Buck and Anne Meadows,

"Did Butch Cassidy Return? His Family Can't Decide": 34 n. 86. Bert Charter allegedly assisted Cassidy, Matt Warner, and Warner's brother-in-law, Tom McCarty, in the 1889 Telluride bank robbery, staking out the relay horses used by the bandits during their getaway. He is thought to have done likewise following Cassidy and Lay's holdup of the Pleasant Valley Coal Company payroll at Castle Gate, Utah, on April 21, 1897. Warner asserted in *The Last of the Bandit Riders* (p. 323) that a man he identified only as Walker went south (certainly not Wild Bunch member Joe Walker, killed in 1898). Could Musgrave, a man of numerous aliases, have passed himself off under his mother's maiden name? Even Musgrave's uncle, Joseph Henry Walker, and his family, believed that George intended to search in South America for his friend Jim Lowe, which was Cassidy's alias in Arizona and New Mexico (Leonore "Pat" Walker Hornback, Stanton, Calif., interview with John D. Tanner, Jr., July 20, 1984).

5. Jeanette Magor, interview with Bess Brown, Denver, Colo., January 8, 1974; Josephine Jebens Barnett, Pleasant Grove, Utah, telephone interview with Pointer, January 23, 1974, Pointer Papers.

6. Robert J. Eaton, Asunción, Paraguay, to authors, May 21 and July 6, 1997. Musgrave related to Frank Hicks that he had been in Paraguay nine years, suggesting a 1911 arrival. However, his obituary reports that he had been a resident since 1912 (Hicks to Bee, file no. 130 STATE 4211; *La Tribuna*, August 18, 1947).

7. *Times* (London), January 19 and 17, 1911; *New York Times*, March 24, April 28, and May 14, 1912. The calm was shattered in 1922.

8. Hanson, "The Farquhar Syndicate in South America": 315, 317, and 325; John F. Benitt, St. Augustine, Florida, 1957, quoted in Gauld, *The Last Titan*, p. 221.

9. *New York Times*, February 18, 1911; *Buenos Aires Herald*, March 18, 1911; Samuels, *Magnificent Rube*, p 176. Peters, born in 1878, developed New York real estate and produced Broadway plays at this time. Peters served on Herbert Hoover's public relations staff during the latter's 1928 campaign. Still later, he served as an assistant to Secretary of Commerce Robert P. Lamont (*New York Times*, March 22, 1965). Rickard was not the first American to be attracted by Paraguay's potential as a cattle-raising region. Granville Stuart, who served as America's minister to Uruguay and Paraguay from 1894 to 1898, had investigated the economic possibilities as early as 1896. He painted a rosier picture than in truth existed. For instance, his assertion that Paraguay lacked cattle disease was demonstrably untrue: hoof and mouth disease existed and persists to this day. Nevertheless, the relative underpopulation of the country, occasioned by the tremendous loss of life during the 1864–70 Great War, had encouraged

NOTES TO PAGES 205–206

the Paraguayan government to adopt a policy of making liberal cattle land concessions to enhance government revenue. Moreover, as Stuart had pointed out, cattle were less troubled by drought and cold, and the luxuriant grasses provided excellent graze (Dahl, "A Montana Pioneer Abroad": 356–57; Dr. Jerry W. Cooney, Castle Rock, Wash., to authors, October 2, 1999; Kleinpenning, *Rural Paraguay*, pp. 148–49).

10. *Buenos Aires Herald,* June 21, 1912; Robert J. Eaton, Asunción, Paraguay, to Daniel Buck and Anne Meadows, Washington, D.C., February 22, 1988, hereafter Eaton-Buck Letters. Farquhar spent almost all of 1912 in Paris, which explains Rickard's departure from France. The cowboys with Rickard in Paraguay included William Archerd from Lynn, Oklahoma; James B. Howard from Bernet, Texas; Hye Carrell (born Peoria, Illinois, December 17, 1887); and Glen Cunningham from Henrietta, Texas, Rickard's hometown (Maxine Texas Rickard Halprin, Miami, Florida, to Dan Buck and Anne Meadows, Washington, D.C., April 4, 1988). A pair of brothers named Helpmann also signed on. One was murdered by a "peon." The surviving brother undertook a year-long chase to track down the murderer and extracted his revenge (A. D. Hughes, Argentina, to Colin Rickards, London, July 2, 1965, Burton, Miscellaneous Papers). Thurlow Craig added Cacique, Monté the Mexican, Billy Williams, and Billy Lewis (Craig, *Black Jack's Spurs,* p. 58). Craig's information is always questionable. William F. "Billy" Lewis, for example, was not one of Rickard's cowboys.

11. Hughes to Rickards, July 2, 1965, Burton Papers.

12. Kent, *Life in Paraguay,* pp. 115–16.

13. Kleinpenning, *Rural Paraguay,* p. 189.

14. Sir Reginald Tower, Buenos Aires, to Sir Edward Grey, London, August 27, 1913, Confidential no. 113 [authors' translation], in Juan Carlos Herken, *Ferrocarriles, Concpiraciónes, y Negocios en el Paraguay,* p. 106. Tower (1860–1939) was posted to Argentina in 1910 and served in both posts from 1911 to 1919.

15. Gauld, *The Last Titan,* p. 241; Eaton, to authors, July 26 and September 20, 1998; Benitt, quoted in Gauld, *The Last Titan,* p. 208. Mrs. Rickard placed the number of cattle at 44,000 head (Rickard, *Everything Happened to Him,* p. 244). More precisely, Gauld provided the figure of 1,687,000 hectares.

16. Kleinpenning, *Rural Paraguay,* p. 189; *Buenos Aires Herald,* June 21, 1912; Gauld, *The Last Titan,* p. 221. At the time of his death in 1929, Rickard maintained title to close to one-half million acres (Eaton, to authors, May 28, 1998). In later years, Jeanette Magor denied that Musgrave had worked for Rickard, but did recall that the Rickards were neighbors of the Musgraves (Bess Brown, Denver, Colorado, to Larry Pointer, February 19, 1974,

Pointer Papers). Rickard's biographer related that Rickard could live in Buenos Aires in a suite in the city's finest hotel for less than a stable owner charged him for maintaining three tigers he had acquired (Samuels, *Magnificent Rube*, p. 177). In December 1914, Rickard stated that he was domiciled at the Grand Hotel, the most luxurious in Asunción (G. L. Rickard, Asunción, "Request for Concession for Refrigeration Plant," December 16, 1914, File 834.6582 [National Archives Microfilm Publication M1470, roll 12, frames 0958-0962], State Department Central Files; Record Group 59, NACP, hereafter R.G. 59, File 834.6582; Cooney, to authors, October 2, 1999).

17. Halprin to Buck and Meadows, April 4, 1988; Denver County, Colo., Warranty Deed Book 2279, p. 350. The *Hyanthean* was the only vessel steaming out of New York for Argentina on June 20. The vessel arrived at Montevideo, upon her return, on July 23 (*New York Times*, June 20 and July 23, 1912). Information held by the Charter family likewise dates Jano's departure as 1912 (Anne Charter, Shepherd, Mont., January 19, 2000, to authors). The deed indicates that Jano sold property in Denver on November 19, 1912, to the Armstrong–Williams Realty Company, Inc., for "one dollar and other valuable considerations," without indication as to what the other valuable considerations may have been. The property was worth over six hundred dollars, judging from the growing property tax bill. In spite of transfer, the estate paid the 1911 taxes on March 27, 1912, and a special fee on August 10 (District Court of Carbon County, District Number Three, Estate Record no. 233, Estate of Eliza J. Magor, WSA; Denver County, Colo., Trust Deeds and Manuscript Book 2347, pp. 196–98).

18. Jebens, interview with Pointer, January 22, 1974; Josephine Jebens Barnett, telephone interview with Pointer, January 23, 1974; Charter, interview with Pointer, December 1, 1973, Pointer Papers.

19. MacDonald, *Picturesque Paraguay*, p. 451; Stephens, *Journey and Explorations in Argentina, Paraguay, and Chile*, pp. 197–98; Decoud, *Geographia de la Republica del Paraguay* (Asuncion: 1901); Kent, *Life in Paraguay*, p. 23. Yerba maté (*Ilex Paraguayensis*) is a species of the Holly genus.

20. Magor, interview with Pointer, October 13, 1974, Pointer Papers. William G. Burris related to Lou Blachly that a member of the Black Jack gang went to South America—Argentina—and used the alias Leander Butler (William G. Burris, October 25, 1952, BT). None of Musgrave's known adventures in South America have been associated with that alias.

21. Every, *Twenty-five Years in South America*, p. 148; Carpenter, *Along the Paraná and the Amazon*, p. 39; Frances Cheney, interview with Pointer, December 30, 1973; Josephine Barnett Jebens, interview with Pointer, January 23, 1974, Pointer Papers. The bite of an insect under her toenail, and

the resultant infection, caused Jano to lose the nail (Magor, January 1, 1974, Pointer Papers).

22. Pointer, interview with the authors, April 28, 1997; Magor, January 1, 1974, Charter, December 1, 1973, Magor, January 8, 1974, Pointer Papers. Jano suffered a stroke in May of 1967, "when she came out of it she was speaking Spanish—swearing!" (Charter, December 1, 1973, Pointer Papers). Jano also had an inimitable way of expressing herself in English. She would refer to a plate of chicken breasts, for example, as a "mess of chicken bosoms" (Pointer, interview with the authors, April 28, 1997).

23. Tschiffely, *Bohemia Junction*, pp. 143. Will Greene, owner of the Cananea Cattle and Consolidated Copper Company, had failed to secure financial backing when he conceived the idea of extending the railroad in Chihuahua, Mexico, to exploit the region's potential. In early 1909, Farquhar's associate, Fred Pearson, formed the Mexican Northwestern Railway Company in Canada to take over and extend the railroad as well as Chihuahua's lumber industry (*New York Times*, August 7, 1910, and September 22, 1912). Perhaps through Greene, Musgrave first ingratiated himself with Pearson and later came to Farquhar's attention.

24. Eaton, to authors, May 21, 1997. The Saldero San Salvador, located north of Concepción, near the Río Apa, began producing jerked beef for export in 1903. In 1909, Dr. Guillermo Kemmerich converted the *saldero* to a *frigorífico*, or packing house, producing meat extract, the first such plant in Paraguay. About 1910, Hermann Krabb and Compagnons of Hamburg, Montevideo, and Buenos Aires, acquired the plant (Diego Abente, "Foreign Capital, Economic Elites and the State in Paraguay during the Liberal Republic [1870–1936]: 69; Kleinpenning, *Rural Paraguay*, pp. 167–68).

25. Eaton, to authors, July 6, 1997; C. W. Thurlow Craig, *Black Jack's Spurs*, p. 111. George Lohman (1890–1950), a Texas cowboy from El Dorado, near San Angelo, arrived in Paraguay in 1912. A close friend of Musgrave's, he later acquired much of the Rickard ranch.

26. Eaton, to authors, May 21, 1997.

27. Charter, December 1, 1973, Pointer Papers; Kent, *Life in Paraguay*, p. 116. Jano and her friend Mary Calvert had attended business school in Denver prior to their respective marriages to Musgrave and Elzy Lay (Magor, September 24, 1974, Pointer Papers). Maroma, the westernmost outpost on Rickard's ranch, was thirty-six miles from the Río Paraguay. Several missionary families lived there as well (Eaton, letter to authors, January 13, 2001).

28. Eaton, February 22, 1988, Eaton-Buck Letters; Eaton, letter to authors, May 21 and August 7, 1997, May 28 and July 26, 1998. Dorothy Kent (later

Mrs. Robert Eaton) particularly prized a small silver ring with amethyst stone that he gave her (Eaton, to authors, May 28, 1998).

29. Eaton, to authors, May 28 and July 26, 1998.

30. The District Court of Carbon County, Wyoming, agreed to the final settlement of the estate on October 15, 1914 (Final Report of John Irons, Administrator de Bonis Non of Said Estate, District Court of Carbon County, Wyo., District Number Three, Estate Record no. 233, Estate of Eliza J. Magor, WSA); Ralph Vandewart, "Autobiography," MS pp. 21-24, transcribed by Joanna White, 1983, photocopy provided by Mrs. Blanche Vandewart White, El Paso, Texas; Magor, September 24, 1974, Pointer Papers. Jano claimed that they met Butch Cassidy in Mexico, an assertion that is questioned by many. Jano had known Cassidy since 1897, when, as a young girl, she met him at her mother's boardinghouse in Baggs (Pointer, *In Search of Butch Cassidy*, p. 217).

31. Vandewart, "Autobiography," pp. 22-24.

32. Magor, January 1, 1974, and Brown, February 19, 1974, Pointer Papers.

33. Halprin to Buck and Meadows, April 4, 1988. On July 14, 1915, the Congress granted the concession as Law 144 (R.G. 59, file 834.6582). Law 144 freed Rickard from taxes for twenty-five years (art. 1), but established a minimum capitalization (art. 2), a requirement that 25 percent of the capital be subscribed from Paraguay (art. 2), a minimum production level of three hundred animals daily (art. 4), and a time limit of two years to get established (art. 5) (*El Diaro*, December 15, 1914).

34. A. D. Hughes, Argentina, to Colin Rickards, London, July 2, 1965, Burton, Miscellaneous Papers.

35. Stephens, *Journey and Explorations in Argentina, Paraguay, and Chile*, p. 198. In early 1912, Farquhar had begun construction of Brazil's first *frigorífico* at Osasco, near São Paulo. The plant opened in 1914 (Gauld, *The Last Titan*, pp. 219-20). Rickard envisioned a logical extension of Farquhar's activities in Brazil. Stephens noted that Americans owned nearly one-half of the stock, and were badly hurt by the British actions. In 1919, the concession was transferred to the South American Land and Cattle Company, a Swift meat-packing concern (Abente, "Foreign Capital, Economic Elites and the State in Paraguay during the Liberal Republic": 69; Kleinpenning, *Rural Paraguay*, pp. 167-68, 177). Although European markets might have been closed to the plant due to the British Maritime System, and although the possible failure of the British government to pay its debts would necessarily affect the plant adversely, general economic difficulties were mounting for the Farquhar syndicate "in consequence of the financial dislocation caused by the war." On October 15, 1914, with liabilities totally $118 million, the Paraguay Central Railway Company

went into receivership (Hanson, "The Farquhar Syndicate in South America" p. 325 n. 30).

36. Tschiffely, *Bohemia Junction*, p. 120.

37. Ibid., pp. 147–48.

38. In 1912, Farquhar had bought stock unceasingly in his effort to gain control of the Brazilian railroad. "Early in 1913, after the first Balkan war jolted Europe's financial structure, Farquhar bought more to bolster the railroad, but W.W. I and Brazil's defaulting on much of her debt, including a $10 million debt to Farquhar, ruined him" (Gauld, *The Last Titan*, p. 273).

39. Born on April 3, 1862, The Rt. Rev. Edward Francis Every, D.D., became Bishop of Argentina and eastern South America in 1910. He served there until 1937, and died on January 16, 1941.

40. Tschiffely, *Bohemia Junction*, p. 149. Tschiffely referred to Musgrave as "this man—whom I shall call Bob Appin" (Ibid., p. 143). The selection of the Appin surname proved a clever ruse on Tschiffely's part. The Stewarts of Appin form the West Highland branch of the royal family of Stewart. Through marriage with the family of Lorne, they became Lords of Lorne and received a grant of lands at Appin, where they built the family seat, Castle Stalker, on the Cormorant's Rock at Loch Linnhe. Tschiffely took a small leap from Stewart to Steward.

41. Eaton, to authors, July 26, 1998. Eaton continued, "I rather doubt that [Musgrave] ever rode in an ox cart. I certainly never have. The land of the Paraguayan Land and Cattle Co. extended all the way across the Chaco to Bolivia. The plan was to ride clear across the territory. After about five days the expedition was abandoned. It was the rainy season."

42. Samuel Dickson, chargé d'affaires ad interim, Asunción, to Charles Evans Hughes, secretary of state, Washington, D.C., January 18, 1922, File 834.6363/7, State Department Central Files, Record Group 59, NACP. At that time, *La Critica*, Asunción's radical newspaper, feared that Rickard's heirs would exploit the land in quest for oil, thereby serving as the "Yankee capitalist vanguard of the dominion of those same Yankees (*La Critica*, June 12, 1929; File 834.00/27; State Department Central Files; Record Group 59; NACP). A number of writers, including Carpenter, *Along the Paraná and the Amazon* (p. 57); J. Gonzales and Ynsfran, *El Paraguay Contemporaneo* (pp. 167–68); and Kleinpenning, *Rural Paraguay* (p. 176), have incorrectly asserted that the Paraguay Land and Cattle Corporation reorganized as the International Products Corporation, owned by the Farquhar interests. In fact, substantial back taxes had accrued. George Lohman paid the back taxes, got the titles in order, purchased much of the land (including the name Paraguay Land and Cattle Company), and arranged to sell the rest for Rickard's widow (Eaton, to authors, April 9 1998). Sir Herbert

Gibson and his family later acquired the land and company from Lohman (Ibid., May 28, 1998). When the company disbanded in 1959, Robert Eaton purchased some of the land and cattle, along with the old Rickard brands—the Ostrich Track and the Diamond Tail (Ibid., February 21, 1998).

CHAPTER 16: CHACO *ABIGEO*

1. Eaton, April 1, 1988, Eaton-Buck Letters; Eaton, to authors, May 21, 1997, May 28 and September 20, 1998, August 6, 1999.

2. Craig, *Black Jack's Spurs*, p. 114.

3. Eaton, April 1, 1988, Eaton-Buck Letters; Eaton, letter to authors, May 28, 1998. The packing plant closed temporarily in 1916. The South American Land and Cattle Company acquired it from Rickard, the principal investors being Edward and Ira Nelson Morris, brothers and Chicago meat packers (Daniel F. Mooney, American minister to Paraguay, to Robert Lansing, secretary of state, September 2, 1918, File 834.6582/7, State Department Central Files, Record Group 59, NACP; Albert Marquis, *The Book of Chicagoans* p. 491).

4. Kleinpenning, p. 169. Stock, valued at $8.50 in gold a head rose to $40–67 gold in 1919, but plunged in 1920 (Abente, "Foreign Capital, Economic Elites and the State in Paraguay during the Liberal Republic," p. 66). Charter, interview with Pointer, December 1, 1973, Pointer Papers.

5. Eaton, letter to authors, July 6, 1997.

6. Cheney, interview with Pointer, December 30, 1973, Pointer Papers; Stephens, *Journey and Explorations in Argentina, Paraguay, and Chile*, p. 8; MacDonald, *Picturesque Paraguay*, pp. 81–82; Carpenter, *The Paraná and the Amazon*, pp. 25–26; Parker, *Casual Letters from South America*, pp. 491, 511–12.

7. Shinkle, *Reminiscences of Roswell Pioneers*, p. 259; Danna Musgrave Crump, to authors, October 24, 1997. Volney Campbell Musgrave and Bessie Buckner Killingsworth were married at Tolleson, Arizona, the license issued November 1, 1917 (Maricopa County, Arizona, Marriage Book 15, p. 347). Ora Schradle wrote, "I have seen him many times, when he would go to my father's office [in Wichita Falls] for legal advice—he often asked advice, but seldom abided by it—if he had, he would have kept out of court many times" (Ora Schradle to Burton, October 7, 1966, Burton, Miscellaneous Papers). Bennett Musgrave died of influenza in Phoenix, at the home of his daughter Julia, on February 26, 1920, and is buried in the Greenwood Cemetery. He was eighty-three years old (Arizona State Board of Health, Certificate of Death). Prudence Walker died on July 14, 1923, at Canelo, Santa Cruz County, Arizona, and is buried in Black Oak Cemetery, Canelo (Records, Marsh Mortuary, Nogales).

8. Kleinpenning, *Rural Paraguay*, p. 169; Frances Cheney, December 30, 1973, Pointer Papers.

9. Cambell, "The Cattle Industry in Paraguay," September 15, 1922, File 834.62221/orig., Internal Affairs, Paraguay, 1910–1929 (National Archives Microfilm Publication M–1470, roll 5), United States Department of State, Record Group 84, NACP; *New York Times*, September 17, 1920.

10. *New York Times*, October 31, 1921; File no. 130 STATE 4211. See also: Cheney, interview with Pointer, December 30, 1973, Pointer Papers.

11. Bryce, *South America: Observations and Impressions*, p. 318.

12. Hicks to Bee, December 8, 1920, File no. 130 STATE 4211.

13. "In the 1912–1948 period the records for many posts in classes 0–2 and file 811.11 (visas) have been destroyed" ("State Department Records in the National Archives; Post Files," Finding Aid, NACP). "I do not believe that he ever had a passport. When he returned to Paraguay in 1940 with no papers, my wife had the idea that he married here to a Paraguayan in order to get resident police papers" (Eaton, letter to authors, May 21, 1997).

14. Eaton, to authors, November 6, 1999.

15. Tschiffely, *Bohemia Junction*, p. 143.

16. Ibid., p. 144.

17. Ibid., pp. 145–46; Green to Foraker, March 6, 1907, Foraker Letters.

18. Eaton, to authors, August 7, 1997.

19. Musgrave was known to use a long–barreled, double action .44 Smith and Wesson, but he favored his Colt .44–40. Upon leaving Brazil in 1940, and in dire need of money, he sold his .44–40 Colt to rancher Robert Eaton for twenty dollars. He maintained that Eaton "was the only man in Paraguay who would appreciate a Single Action Colt" (Eaton, to authors, May 21, 1997).

20. Tschiffely, *Bohemia Junction*, p. 146.

21. Wilson, *Exciting Days of Early Arizona*, p. 53.

22. Tschiffely, *Bohemia Junction*, pp. 146–147.

23. Eaton, letter to authors, August 7, 1997; July 26, 1998. If the story has veracity, the knife must have been large as well as very sharp to penetrate the underside of the table, unnoticed, and to securely hold the approximately forty-four ounces of a loaded .44 Smith & Wesson revolver, likely the .44 Hand Ejector Second Model, constructed on Smith & Wesson's N-Frame, introduced in 1908 (Jinks, *History of Smith & Wesson*, pp. 195–96).

24. Eaton, letter to authors, August 7, 1997; Pointer, *In Search of Butch Cassidy*, p. 272 n. 6; Magor, January 1, 1974, Charter, December 1, 1973, and Cheney, December 30, 1973, Pointer Papers; Martha Beth Walker, San Antonio, Texas, letter to authors, June 19, 1996.

25. Program for the *Gran Rodeo International Gauchos Contra Cow-boys En la Sociedad Rural Argentina*, April 17 and 18, 1924, photocopy in possession of the authors; Tschiffely, *Bohemia Junction*, p. 144. Musgrave related the steer-roping incident to George Lohman (Eaton, April 1, 1988, Eaton-Buck Letters). For additional information on Artemus "Art" Ward Acord (1890–1931), see *Variety*, January 7, 1931; McKinney, *Art Acord and the Movies*.

26. Craig, *Paraguayan Interlude*, p. 106; Eaton, to authors, November 6, 1999.

27. Tschiffely, *Bohemia Junction*, p. 149. Tschiffely placed the length of separation at several years. However, this does not concur with the recollections of friends and family members. Robert Eaton makes it clear that Musgrave sent Jano back to the States (Eaton, to authors, July 6, 1997).

28. Pointer Papers.

29. 1928 *Tucson Directory*, p. 307; Helen Bingston (niece of Mary Calvert Lay), Lander, Wyo., interview by Larry Pointer, October 1, 1973, Pointer Papers. Located at 311 E. Congress, Bruchman's was across the street from the Rialto Apartments (314 E. Congress), where Jano resided.

30. Burchett, "They Called Her Jano": 46. In 1936, Mary Lay lived at 717 N. 6th Avenue and worked at the Southern Methodist Hospital and Sanatorium (1936 *Tucson Directory*; Pointer, "Jano," pp. 25–26, Pointer Papers). Postcards to her family were postmarked from Willcox, Arizona (Dennis Burchett, telephone interview with the authors, February 6, 1998).

31. King, *Western Livestock Journal*, August 19, 1938. Jano also returned from Paraguay with a silver-mounted riding crop allegedly once owned by Cassidy. She gave it to her brother Neil, who, in turn, passed it on. By 1939, the crop had come into the possession of Mrs. Elsie Hunt, wife of Wyoming Secretary of State L. C. Hunt (*Wyoming State Journal*, June 29, 1939, quoted in Larry Pointer, "Jano," p. 28).

32. Charter, December 1, 1973, and Magor, January 8, 1974, Pointer Papers; Wright, "Dad Rode with the Wild Bunch": 21; Charter, *Cowboys Don't Walk*, p. 58; Burchett, "They Called Her Jano": 46; Magor, January 1, 1974, Pointer Papers. Neither would Jano view the motion picture *Butch Cassidy and the Sundance Kid*, arguing that it "wouldn't be true to life" (Magor, January 8, 1974, Pointer Papers).

33. Eaton, April 1, 1988, Eaton Letters; Tschiffely, *Bohemia Junction*, p. 149; Eaton, letter to authors, July 6, 1997. Eaton concurred with Tschiffely's assessment (August 7, 1997). George, with determination, attempted to "drown his disappointment in whiskey."

34. Eaton, to authors, July 6, 1997; Tschiffely, *Bohemia Junction*, p. 150. Tschiffely failed to state whether Musgrave's corporate strikebreaking activities took place in Paraguay or in Argentina.

35. Eaton, letter to authors, November 6, 1999.

36. Craig, *Paraguayan Interlude*, p. 12.

37. With wealthy friends such as Minor Cooper Keith (1848–1929, founder of the United Fruit Company) and Theodore Newton Vail (1845–1920, president of American Telephone and Telegraph), Percival Farquhar had organized International Products Corporation (IPC) as a holding concern (Hanson, "Farquhar Syndicate in South America": 325; Gault, *Last Titan*, p. 221; *New York Times*, April 17, 1920, and June 15, 1929). At Puerto Pinasco, International Products, destined to become Paraguay's largest industrial company, extracted tannin from the quebracho tree, developed a model program for enhancing pasture lands, and continued to raise beef cattle.

Rickard failed to meet the terms for the establishment of the second packing plant concession (Law 144 of July 14, 1915). Under the terms of Law 241 of May 30, 1917, Rickard's guarantees were transferred to Central Products (American Legation, Asunción, Despatch no. 266, November 16, 1917, State Department Central Files, Record Group 59, NACP). The resultant *Campañia Paraguaya de Frigorífico y Carnes Conservadas* secured the concession on April 1, 1917 (Construction and Engineering Finance Company, Asunción, to Lansing, Secretary of State, December 18, 1918, State Department Central Files, Record Group 59, NACP). In November 1919, Central Products Company and International Products Company jointly incorporated in Paraguay as the *Campañia Internacional de Productos* (CIP). Musgrave's friend George Lohman took over the management of IPC's herd of 150,000 cattle (Weller, "American Cowboy in a Wild New Land," pp. 31, 59–61).

38. Eaton, letter to authors, February 18, 2000.

39. Craig, *Black Jack's Spurs*, pp. 117–18.

40. Eaton, to authors, April 9, 1998, November 6, 1999, and February 18, 2000. On April 9, he wrote, "I expect that affair of running cattle through the corral four times is exaggerated. He might have got away with 20 or 30 head in the count. Campbell was before my time but some of the [pigpen branded] cattle were still in the herd [in 1929]." Musgrave's pigpen brand is presently owned by Bob Eaton.

41. Eaton, to authors, November 6, 1999.

42. Eaton, April 1, 1988, Eaton-Buck Letters; Craig, *Paraguayan Interlude*, p. 119; *Black Jack's Spurs*, pp. 64, 112; United States Department of State, American Foreign Service, Report of the Death of an American Citizen, Robert Steward, 334.113, NACP, hereafter Report of Death. Prudy, in later years, lived briefly with the Kent family. She had been in a convent school in Brazil and was bilingual. A beautiful girl, she married a Brazilian

diplomat and lived several years in Rome before returning to Brazil. Roberto (Jr.) also lived in Brazil (Eaton, letter to authors, May 21, 1997).

43. Eaton, to authors, July 6, 1997. "He was trying to make romance out of his years in South America. As my wife said when I met him in 1972 in London carrying a [Webley] .455 revolver and a Bowie knife, 'Bill has never grown up'" (Eaton, to authors, May 21, 1997).

44. Craig, *Paraguayan Interlude*, p. 19, and *Black Jack's Spurs*, p. 64.

45. *Black Jack's Spurs*, pp. 63, 65. *Cóctel Guaraní* is made from white rum, lemon juice, and sugar.

46. Craig, *Paraguayan Interlude*, p. 22. *Caña* is the Paraguayan version of rum.

47. Ibid., p. 100; Eaton, February 22, 1988, Eaton-Buck Letters.

48. Craig, *Paraguayan Interlude*, pp. 100–101; *Black Jack's Spurs*, p. 110. During this trip Craig had a Colt .38-40 single action, which he believed had belonged to Musgrave. He offered to sell it back to George. "Later, when Craig's book (*Paraguayan Interlude*) came out, [Musgrave] could not remember Craig or the incident" (Eaton, February 22, 1988, Eaton-Buck Letters). "The problem [with the .38-40] was ammunition which was used very little in South America" (Eaton, to authors, July 6, 1997).

49. Craig, *Black Jack's Spurs*, p. 112.

50. Craig, *Paraguayan Interlude*, p. 106.

51. Ibid., *Paraguayan Interlude*, pp. 110, 101–8, and *A Rebel for a Horse*, opposite p. 320; Eaton, February 22, 1988, Eaton-Buck Letters.

52. Craig, *Black Jack's Spurs*, p. 116. "Musgrave did not talk in that 1880 dialect that Craig tries to present. After all Craig was upper class British and had never been in the US. I presume his Texas slang sold well in England" (Eaton, letter to authors, March 26, 2000).

53. Craig, *Paraguayan Interlude*, p. 121–22; Craig identified the officer as Robert ———. "The Paraguayan army officer that Craig had problems with who had also served in the British Army in WWI was Arturo Bray, born in Paraguay of English parents, officer in Brit army, general staff Paraguay, served in Chaco War, and politically involved. He is not identified by name in Craig, but no other Paraguayan officer of the time fits the description" (Dr. Jerry Cooney, to authors, June 4, 1997).

54. Eaton, to authors, August 6, 1999.

55. Craig, *Black Jack's Spurs*, p. 118.

CHAPTER 17: CRIME BOSS

1. Craig, *River of Diamonds*, p. 93. A novel, Craig's *River of Diamonds*, unlike *Paraguayan Interlude* and *Black Jack's Spurs*, "doesn't pretend to be

strictly factual; but fact—said Craig—is woven into it" (Burton, to authors, March 24, 1999). Identified by the pseudonym "Jim" in *Paraguayan Interlude* (1935), Musgrave in *River of Diamonds* (ca. 1944) becomes the character "Jim Palgrave." Only after Craig became aware of Musgrave's 1947 death did he reveal George's actual identity—Bob Steward/George Musgraves [*sic*]—in *Black Jack's Spurs* (1954).

2. Alejandro Langer, Costa Brava, Spain, to Rickards, November 5, 1965, Burton, Miscellaneous Papers; Craig, *Paraguayan Interlude*, p. 119; Eaton, letter to authors, July 6, 1997. Craig mistakenly wrote that the theft was from the French-owned cattle company *Societé Foncière du Paraguay*, on the east bank of the Alto Paraguay (Craig, *Paraguayan Interlude*, pp. 118–19). The tradition of cattle smuggling across the Río Apa from Paraguay into the Brazilian Mato Grosso traced back to colonial times (Cooney, to authors, October 1, 1999).

3. Craig, *River of Diamonds*, pp. 79–80.

4. Ibid.

5. Craig, *Black Jack's Spurs*, p. 112; Eaton, to authors, August 6, 1999; Craig, *Paraguayan Interlude*, pp. 118–19; Eaton, February 22, 1988, Eaton-Buck Letters.

6. Roosevelt, *Through the Brazilian Wilderness*, pp. 56–57.

7. Eaton, to authors, August 6, 1999, and April 9, 1998.

8. Gavilan [C. W. Thurlow Craig], "The Ambush": 210–19 (the participant's true names are used in this recounting, rather than the altered names used by Craig); Craig to Rickards and Burton, November 3, 1965, Burton Collection; *Philadelphia Public Ledger*, May 24, 1931; Norman Garrett, commander, Henry H. Houston, 2nd, Post no. 3, American Legion, Germantown, Penn., to Henry W. Stimson, secretary of state, Washington, D.C., May 8, 1931, File 334.1121 (Wright), Confidential Correspondence, 1930–1931; Records of the State Department, Central Files, Record Group 59; NACP, hereafter State Department file 334.1121.

9. Eaton to authors, April 9, 1998. Robert Eaton later managed the port ranch and had access to all files. "There was a container of letters to and from Scott. Obviously there was no love between them but I never found anything to be taken too seriously" (Ibid.). The American minister to Paraguay, Post Wheeler, agreed. "Scott is generally unpopular with the Company's employees, with a number of whom he has had quarrels. When asked whether he knew anyone who hated him sufficiently to kill him, he named without hesitation five men as coming in that category" (Post Wheeler, American minister, Asunción, Paraguay, to Stimson, September 9, 1931; State Department File 334.1121).

10. Robert Eaton recalled, "[McDonald] was hired in Buenos Aires by [John] Tippett [IPC president] and I traveled with [McDonald] to Asunción (Eaton to authors, April 9, 1998).

11. Craig wrote in "The Ambush" that he sold the revolver, with a 4 3/4-inch barrel, for eight hundred pesos. In reality, that was the price he had paid for the pistol (Burton, letter to authors, December 3, 1997). Craig identified the revolver as .45-caliber. However, .45 single actions were virtually unknown in the Chaco. "We could get 44:40 Remington, 44 S.W., and 38 revolver cartridges but never .45 caliber" (Eaton to authors, April 9, 1998).

12. Thurlow Craig, *Black Jack's Spurs*, p. 155.

13. Dr. Gerónimo Zubizarreta, Paraguay minister of foreign affairs, Asunción, to John B. Faust, United States chargé d'affaires, Asunción, February 18, 1931, State Department File 334.1121.

14. *El Ordan*, December 13, 1929; Eaton, to authors, April 9, 1998. Craig named the driver Rico Barrientos in "The Ambush," p. 213. No account states the actual name of the driver.

15. Eaton, to authors, April 9, 1998. Craig identified the site as kilometer nine (*Black Jack's Spurs*, p. 153). Zubizarreta located it at kilometer eight (Zubizarreta to Faust, February 18, 1931, State Department File 334.1121). *El Ordan* split the difference, placing the site between kilometer eight and nine (*El Ordan*, December 13, 1929).

16. Eaton, letter to authors, April 9, 1998.

17. Craig, *Black Jack's Spurs*, p. 156. The revolver then came into the hands of Silveira and finally to George Musgrave who paid Silveira two thousand pesos (Burton, to authors, December 3, 1997).

18. Gavilan, "The Ambush": 218; *El Ordan*, December 13, 1929; Faust to Stimson, December 29, 1930, State Department File 334.1121. There is no reference to the inconsistency between Wright's apparent payment of four thousand pesos and Dos Santos's claim of five thousand.

19. *El Ordan*, December 13, 1929; Zubizarreta to Faust, February 18, 1931, State Department File 334.1121.

20. Gavilan, "The Ambush": 219. Musgrave was apparently then living on a ranch in the *pantanal* in the northwest of Mato Grosso del Sul, Brazil (Craig, *River of Diamonds*, p. 111).

21. Craig, *Black Jack's Spurs*, p. 157.

22. Wright to Faust, June 10, 1931, State Department File 334.1121; *Buenos Aires Herald*, June 7, 1930.

23. Eaton, to authors, April 9, 1998; Wheeler to Stimson, September 9, 1931, State Department File 334.1121.

24. Faust to Stimson, December 29, 1930, State Department File 334.1121.

25. Ibid.

26. Faust, Denmark, S.C., to Orme Wilson, Department of State legal advisor, Washington, D.C., July 22, 1931, State Department File 334.1121.

27. Craig initially overstated the amount of the alleged bribe. After reviewing an account of the incident by Jeff Burton and Colin Rickards, he wrote, "I would like you to change 'a large sum of money—$9,000 U.S.— by the American consul' to 'a large sum of money—$5000 U.S.—through the American Consulate'" (Bill Craig to Jeff Burton and Colin Rickards, November 19, 1965, Burton, Miscellaneous Papers).

28. Eaton, to authors, September 20, 1998, April 9, 1998, and September 20, 1998; State Department File 334.1121.

29. Wheeler to Stimson, September 2, 1931, State Department File 334.1121.

30. Ibid.

31. Ibid.

32. *El Diario,* June 6, 1931; Gavilan, "The Ambush": 219.

33. Wright to Faust, June 10, 1931, State Department File 334.1121.

34. Craig, *Black Jack's Spurs,* p. 157; Eaton, to authors, April 9, 1998. For an account of Craig's later activities in Brazil, see: Craig, *A Rebel for a Horse* (London: Arthur Barker, Ltd, 1934).

35. Wheeler to Stimson, transcript of appellate hearing, no. 79, September 7, 1931, Supplement to Confidential Despatch #277, Despatch #280, September 19, 1931, State Department File 334.1121.

36. Tschiffely, *Bohemia Junction,* p. 143; Eaton, to authors, April 9, 1998.

37. Craig, *Paraguayan Interlude,* p. 23.

38. Eaton, to authors, June 12, 1999. Bill Craig's literary variation states that the captain "hankered for the glory of having laid a bad man low." He pulled a gun, exclaimed, "Now I'm going to shoot a bad man," and shot Musgrave in the face (Craig, *Black Jack's Spurs,* p. 64). Another variation relates that Musgrave was shooting at jaguars and, after having expended all of his bullets, the captain fired at him (Alejandro Langer, Costa Brava, Spain, to Colin Rickards, London November 5, 1965, Burton Papers).

39. Craig, *River of Diamonds,* p. 80.

40. Eaton, to authors, June 12, August 6, and May 11, 1999.

41. Cooney, to authors, October 2, 1999; *New York Times,* July 24, 1932.

42. Meredith Nicholson, American Legation to Paraguay, Asunción, to Cordell Hull, secretary of state, Washington D.C., June 15, 1934, File 324.115, Confidential Correspondence, 1930–1931, Records of the State Department, Central Files, Record Group 59; NACP, hereafter State Department File 324.115; Zook, *Conduct of the Chaco War,* pp. 91–102.

43. *Times* (London), May 11, 1933, October 30, 1935; Zook, *Conduct of the Chaco War,* pp. 142, 171–74; Beebe, "Yankee Found Paraguay—and

Success," *Miami Herald*, November 18, 1975; Justo Pastor Bení, minister of foreign affairs, Asunción, Paraguay, to United States chargé d'affaires, Asunción, May 9, 1933, State Department File 324.115; George Lohman, Pozo Colorado, Paraguay, to Findley Howard, American minister, Paraguay, March 10, 1938, State Department File 324.115.

44. Tschiffely, p. 150. In his fictional *River of Diamonds*, Thurlow Craig speaks of several Musgrave deals with a Paraguayan colonel who got so rich during the war that "they made him a brigadier-general and it looks like he's lined up for the next president [ca. 1938]" (pp. 101–2).

45. Danna Musgrave Crump, Redding, California, to authors, September 3, 1996.

46. Ibid., November 25, 1996; Eaton, to authors, August 7, 1997, November 6, 1999.

47. Craig, *Paraguayan Interlude*, p. 14. The Río Apa separates Bella Vista, Paraguay, from her twin city, Bela Vista, Brazil.

48. Eaton, to authors, July 6, 1997.

CHAPTER 18: END OF THE TRAIL

1. Eaton, to authors, May 21, 1997; William B. de Grace, American consul, Asunción, to Colin Rickards, London, July 1, 1965, Burton, Miscellaneous Papers. Edison Stewart was born in 1940 (Report of the Death of an American Citizen; File 334.113, Robert Steward; Confidential Correspondence, 1945–1949, State Department Central File, Record Group 59; NACP (hereafter Report of Death).

2. Eaton, to authors, May 28, 1998

3. Eaton, to authors, January 2, 2000, August 7, 1997, February 21, 1998, and February 21, 1998. There was no suggestion that the train robbery took place in South America. As for any involvement in the widespread smuggling of Chinese which was taking place following the Chinese Exclusion Act, the tale is believable but not documented; Musgrave had dealings with individuals who were involved. Lewis, of Uvalde, Texas, and a former Rough Rider in Captain Frank Frantz's Troop A, had drifted to Brazil working for the Anglo Packing Plant's cattle ranches. Flush with money, he later turned up in Concepción. Drinking and chasing women depleted most of his funds, and he went to work for Lohman. Lohman had convinced him to put the rest of his money into cattle. Lewis took his pay in additional cows. Eventually, he had a nice herd in partnership with Stanley Mobsby (Mrs. Eaton's uncle) and a common-law Lengua Indian wife. He sold out his cattle to George Lohman and returned to Texas where he died a few years later (Eaton, to authors, January 2, and March 26, 2000).

NOTES TO PAGES 255–58

4. Report of Death ("The wife possesses an apparently legitimate marriage certificate, birth certificates for her three children"); Shirley, "Buck Jones": 56.

5. Eaton, to authors, May 21.

6. Eaton, April 1, 1988, Eaton Letters; Robert W. Moore, American vice consul, Asunción, Paraguay, to Ola F. Skelton, Coolidge, Ariz., November 17, 1947, File 800.330 (Steward), Foreign Service Post Files, Asunción (Paraguay) Legation and Embassy, 1947, General Records of the Department of State, Record Group 84, NACP, hereafter File 800.330; Kenedon P. Steins, American vice consul, Asunción, to Herbert Mallamo, attorney, Phoenix, Ariz., December 29, 1947, File 800.330. Ora F. Skelton was the daughter of Musgrave's sister Julia and her first husband, Boyd Doak.

7. Petition of Joseph Walker, no. 355, May 19, 1873, Robb Commission, Memorial, volume 44, pp. 241–333, United States Board of Commissioners, United States and Mexico, Records of Boundary and Claims Commissions and Arbitrations, Record Group 76, NACP; *Amanda Walker v. The United States and Kickapoo Indians*, no. 10296, Indian Depredations Cases, Records of the United States Court of Claims, Record Group 123, NAB; Certificate of Death, Amanda Walker, Texas State Board of Health, Bureau of Vital Statistics, Reg. Dist no. 426, Reg no. 56658; Joseph Walker or Estate, Settlement of Records, Docket No. 2532, Agency #3355, General Records, United States General Claims Commission, United States and Mexico, Records of Boundary and Claims Commissions and Arbitrations, Record Group 76, NACP. Following payment of attorneys' fees and court costs, the distribution of the proceeds amounted to $660 to each of the children of Joseph Walker, with the share of each nonsurviving child to be divided among his or her heirs.

8. Report of Death; Eaton, February 22, 1988, Eaton Letters; Eaton, to authors, February 21, 1998.

9. Report of Death; *New York Times*, August 1, 1947.

10. Edward G. Trueblood, chargé d'affaires, Asunción, to General George C. Marshall, secretary of state, Washington, D.C., August 6, 1947, *Foreign Relations of the United States, 1947*, vol. 8, *The American Republics*, p. 991; *New York Times*, August 5, 6, and 7, 1947.

11. *New York Times*, August 11, 1947.

12. *Times* (London), August 16, 1947; Eaton to authors, May 21, 1997

13. Report of Death. The Eatons were convinced that he had throat cancer (Eaton, to authors, May 21, 1997, February 21, 1998).

14. *La Trubuna*, August 18, 1947 (author's translation); Report of Death.

15. De Grace to Rickards, July 1, 1965, Burton, Miscellaneous Papers; Eaton, February 2, 1988, Eaton Letters; Eaton, to authors, February 21, 1998. Musgrave was buried in Lot no. 1 of the Old Cemetery (*Cementerio de la Recoleta*) on Second Street. Government forces prevailed by August 19; the army announced the war's conclusion on August 21, 1947 (*Times* (London), August 20, 1947; *New York Times*, September 1, 1947).

BIBLIOGRAPHY

MANUSCRIPTS

Aguayo, Harry H. "The Murder of George Parker by George Musgraves [sic] in Sept, 1897 [sic]" (1957). Typed MS, photocopy provided by Howard T. Bryan, Albuquerque, New Mexico.

Alverson, Leonard. "Reminiscences of Leonard Alverson (1938), As Told to Mrs. George F. Kitt." MS 14. Arizona Historical Society, Tucson.

Atchison, Topeka and Santa Fe Railway Archives. Letter to Edward Payson Ripley, November 22, 1897. Kansas State Historical Society, Topeka.

Ballard, Charles L. "The Autobiography of Charles L. Ballard (n.d.)." Typed MS, photocopy provided by Mrs. Allene Ballard Mann (niece), Roswell, New Mexico.

Blachly, Louis Bradley. Transcripts of Oral Interviews. MSS 123 BC, Pioneers Foundation Oral History Collection. The Center for Southwest Research, University of New Mexico, Albuquerque.

Bursum, Holm O. Bursum Papers, 1873–1936. MSS 92 BC, Box 1. The Center for Southwestern Research, University of New Mexico, Albuquerque.

Burton, Jeffrey. Miscellaneous Papers. Photocopies and transcriptions provided by Jeffrey Burton, Gosport, Hampshire, England.

Crabe, Edmund. "Interview by Ludwig Stanley Landmichl. ca. 1939." WPA File #1806. Wyoming State Archives, Cheyenne.

Haley, J. Evetts. Transcripts of Interviews. The Nita Stewart Haley Memorial Library and J. Evetts Haley History Center, Midland, Texas.

Hayhurst, Sam J. "Reminiscences of Sam J. Hayhurst (September 27, 1937)." MS 419. Arizona Historical Society, Tucson.

Kelly, Charles. Charles Kelly Papers. Marriot Library, University of Utah, Salt Lake City.

McDaniel, Porter, Tombstone, Arizona Territory. Letter to Sheriff, White Oaks, New Mexico, April 25, 1906. New Mexico State Records Center and Archives, Santa Fe, New Mexico.

Moorman, Donald R. "A Political Biography of Holm Bursum: 1899–1924." Ph.D. diss, University of New Mexico, 1962. The Center for Southwestern Research, University of New Mexico, Albuquerque.

Musgrave, Bennett. Musgrave Family Bible. Owned by Danna Musgrave Crump, Redding, California. Photocopy in possession of the authors.

Otero, Miguel A. Papers of Governor Miguel A. Otero. New Mexico State Records Center and Archives, Sante Fe.

Peck, Arthur M. "In the Memory of Man." MS 652. Arizona Historical Society, Tucson.

Pinkerton Detective Agency. Dalton Gang Files. Pinkerton Detective Agency Archives, Encino, California.

Pointer, Larry. Larry Pointer Papers. Collection #10345, Box 5. American Heritage Center, University of Wyoming, Laramie.

Treat, Amanda, to Mr. Payton. "Eye witness to murder" [the reminiscences of Harry H. Aguayo] (newspaper clipping, Lincoln County News). Powell Collection, Lincoln County Historical Society, Lincoln, New Mexico.

Vandewart, Ralph. "Autobiography." Typed MS, transcribed by Joanna White, 1983. Photocopy provided by Mrs. Blanche Vandewart White (daughter), El Paso, Texas.

Walker, Joseph. Day Book of Joseph Walker, Dogtown, Texas, 1869. Owned by Ann Gibb Henry, McMullen County, Texas. Certified photocopy in possession of the authors.

———. Joseph Walker Family Bible. Owned by Ann Gibb Henry, McMullen County, Texas. Certified photocopy in possession of the authors.

Wells, Fargo & Co.'s Express. Attempted Robbery Report for October 2, 1896, and Robbery Report for November 6, 1897. Wells Fargo Bank History Room, San Francisco, California.

GOVERNMENT DOCUMENTS

Arizona, State of. Certificate of Death, Bennett Musgrave, Maricopa County. Certificate of Death, Dan Johnson, Santa Cruz County. Arizona State Library, Archives and Public Records, Phoenix.

Arizona, Territory of. Enlistment Papers, Boyd M. Doak, Arizona Rangers. Record Group 42. Arizona State Library, Archives and Public Records, Phoenix.

———. Records, Secretary of the Territory. Parole of J. J. Smith. Record Group 6. Arizona State Library, Archives and Public Records, Phoenix.

———. Records, Territorial Prison at Yuma, Arizona. No. 621, James Madison Shaw; no. 2853, Volney Campbell Musgrave. Record Group 85. Arizona State Library, Archives and Public Records, Phoenix.

Atascosa County, Texas. Deed Books B-1 through M-1.

———. District Court, Criminal Docket Book B.

———. District Court, Minute Books B and 3.

———. Index of Mortgages, Book 1.

———. Marks and Brands, Book 1.

———. Marriage Books 1 and 3.

———. Stock Record Book 6. Texas Pioneer, Trail Driver and Texas Ranger's Museum, San Antonio, Texas.

Brewster County, Texas. District Court, Minute Book 2 and Case File no. 396, *Fanny M. Mathis, et. ux. v. Galveston, Harrisburg & San Antonio Railroad.*

———. Deed Book 1.

———. Record of Marks and Brands, volume 1.

Caldwell County, Texas. Deed Books A, C, and D.

Carbon, County, Wyoming. District Court Records, District Number Three. No. 1996, *Jeanette Murray v. George W. Murray.* Wyoming State Archives, Laramie.

———. District Court Records, District Number Three. Estate Record no. 233, Eliza J. Magor. Wyoming State Archives, Laramie.

———. District Court Records, District Number Three. Criminal Record nos. 645, 664, 726, and 735, *State of Wyoming v. Jack Dempsey.* Wyoming State Archives, Laramie.

———. District Court Records, District Number Three. Guardianship Record no. 240, Jeanette Magor. Wyoming State Archives, Laramie.

———. Deed Books 28, 33, 38, 41.

Chaves County, Territory of New Mexico. Civil Records, Fifth Judicial District. *Prudence Musgrave v. Estate of George T. Parker,* case no. 147; *Dan Johnson v. Estate of George T. Parker,* case no. 152.

———. Criminal Records, Fifth Judicial District. *Territory of New Mexico v. George Musgrave,* case nos. 127–28, 143, 153, 1216; *Territory of New Mexico v. Dan Johnson,* case nos. 143, 219–24; *Territory of New Mexico v. Volney Campbell Musgrave,* case nos. 198, 1147, 1167–70, 1177, 1237; *Territory of New Mexico v. Charles Ware,* case nos. 225–30.

———. Deed Record Book 35.

———. Marriage Book A.

———. Record of Mortgage Deeds, Book 31.

Chester County, South Carolina. Philip Walker, Probate Record, Package no. 1148. South Carolina Department of Archives and History, Columbia

Cochise County, Arizona. Superior Court, Criminal Records. *State of Arizona v. V. C. Musgrave,* case no. 840; *Territory of Arizona v. B. H. Behrends,* case no. 1653.

———. Deed Books 25 and 38.

———. *Great Register of the County of Cochise, Territory of Arizona, for the Year 1884.* Reprint, Tombstone, Ariz.: Tombstone Commemorative Enterprises, n.d.

———. "Great Register of the County of Cochise, Territory of Arizona, For the Year 1890." Typed ms (photocopy), copyright 1978, Betty A. Boyer.

———. Marriage Book 1.

Colorado, State of. Denver District Court, Second Judicial District. *State of Colorado v. John Bradley,* case no. 18620.

Denver County, Colorado. Deed Book 2347 (microfilm roll #835).

———. Marriage License No. 44651.

———. Warranty Deed Book 2279 (microfilm roll #814).

Eddy County, Territory of New Mexico. Fifth Judicial District, Criminal Records. *Territory of New Mexico v. Charles Ware,* case nos. 224–28, 241; *Territory of New Mexico v. Samuel Morrow,* case nos. 229–33, 242; *Territory of New Mexico v. Dan Johnson,* case nos. 234–38, 243.

El Paso County, Texas. Deed Books C and D.

Frio County, Texas. District Court, Criminal Docket Book B.

———. District Court, Civil Docket. *State of Texas v. Bennett Musgrave,* et. al., case nos. 267–69, Texas State Archives, Austin.

Grant County, New Mexico. Deed Books 24 and 28.

———. Docket Book G.

———. Misc. Deed Record Book 32.

Kimble County, Texas. District Minutes, vol. 2.

La Salle County, Texas. District Court. *State of Texas v. Van Musgrave,* case file nos. 844, 859, 871; *State of Texas v. Volney Musgrave,* case file no. 858.

Lincoln County, New Mexico. Deed Book S.

———. Mining Records, Book S.

Live Oak County, Texas. District Court. *James Lowe v. Joseph Walker,* case file no. 180.

———. Marriage Book 1.

McMullen County, Texas. Marks and Brands and Bills of Sale, vol. 1.

———. Probate no. 152, Joseph Walker.

Maricopa County, Arizona. Marriage Book 15.

New Mexico, Territory of. New Mexico Territorial Penitentiary, Admission
    Records (Record of Convicts). New Mexico State Records Center and
    Archives, Santa Fe.
————. Records, New Mexico Territorial Penitentiary, File no. 2872, Volney
    Campbell Musgrave. New Mexico State Records Center and Archives,
    Santa Fe.
Santa Cruz County, Arizona. Marriage Book 1
Socorro County, New Mexico. Criminal Docket Book A. New Mexico State
    Records Center and Archives, Santa Fe.
Texas, Republic of. Joseph Walker, Conditional Certificate, Mgl. 10412,
    August 13, 1838; Headright Certificate #485, 2nd Class, Mgl. 10413, July
    12, 1847, File 347. Texas State Archives, Austin.
————. Department of State. Executive Clemency, no. 542, Van Musgrave,
    et. al., filed January 18, 1887. Texas State Archives, Austin.
————. Muster Roll, Captain Levi English's Company of Mounted Men,
    organized Aug. 1855, Bexar County, Texas, Nov. 13, 1855. Texas State
    Archives, Austin.
————. Muster Roll, Capt. Peter Tumlinson's Company of Mounted Vol-
    unteers on the 12th of November, 1859 thru Feb. 10, 1860. Texas State
    Archives, Austin.
United States Board of Commissioners, United States and Mexico. Petition
    of Joseph Walker, no. 355, May 19, 1873. Robb Commission, Memorial,
    vol. 44, pp. 241–333. Record Group 76, Records of Boundary and Claims
    Commissions and Arbitrations. National Archives at College Park, Md.
United States Bureau of the Census. Census enumerations for: Atascosa
    County, Texas (1850, 1860, 1870, 1880); Bexar County, Texas (1900);
    Caldwell County, Texas (1840); Carbon County, Wyoming (1880, 1900,
    1910); Chaves County, New Mexico (1910); Chickasaw Nation, Indian
    Territory (1900); Cochise County, Arizona (1900, 1910, 1920); Eddy
    County, New Mexico (1900); Gonzales County, Texas (1880); Hancock
    County, Iowa, (1880); Lawrence County, Tennessee (1820); Pecos
    County, Texas (1900); Santa Cruz County, Arizona (1900, 1910, 1920);
    Socorro County, New Mexico (1900); Throckmorton County, Texas
    (1880); Tom Green County, Texas (1880).
United States Bureau of Reclamation. See Ferguson, Bobbie H., below.
United States Court of Claims. *Amanda Walker v. The United States and Kick-
    apoo Indians,* case no. 10296; Indian Depredations Cases; Record Group
    123. National Archives Building, Washington, D.C.
United States Department of Justice. *Annual Report of the Attorney-General,
    1895.* Washington, D.C.: U.S. Government Printing Office, 1897.

———. *Annual Report of the Attorney-General, 1900.* Washington, D.C.: U.S. Government Printing Office, 1900.

———. File 13.065, The Black Jack Gang. Confidential Correspondence, 1896–1898, Central Files, Record Group 60. National Archives at College Park, Md.

United States Department of State. Despatches from the U.S. Consul in Nogales, Mexico, March 15, 1893–April 12, 1897 (National Archives Microfilm Publication M283, roll 2). State Department Central File, Record Group 59. National Archives at College Park, Md.

———. Despatches from the U.S. Ministers to Mexico 1823–1906. Files 239 and 356, November 1, 1897–May 14, 1898 (National Archives Microfilm Publication M–97, rolls 126–28). State Department Central File, Record Group 59. National Archives at College Park, Md.

———. File 130 ST 4211. Robert Steward. Administration Correspondence, 1920–1929. State Department Central File, Record Group 59. National Archives Building, Washington, D.C.

———. File 324.115, George Lohman; File 334.113, Robert Steward; File 334.1121, John Francis Wright. Confidential Correspondence, State Department Central File, Record Group 59. National Archives at College Park; Md.

———. File 334.330, Robert Steward. General Records, 1947, Asunción (Paraguay) Legation and Embasssy, Record Group 84. National Archives at College Park, Md.

———. File 834.00, Internal Affairs, Paraguay, 1910–1939 (National Archives Microfilm Publication M-1470, rolls 1–10). Record Group 84. National Archives at College Park, Md.

United States District Court. Arizona, Territory of. First Judicial District, County of Pima. Minute Book Volume N. Records of the District Courts of the United States, Record Group 21. National Archives and Administration—Pacific Southwest Region (Laguna Niguel).

———. Arkansas, Western District of, Fort Smith Division. Defendant Jacket File no. 9, *United States v. William Christain* [sic]; Defendant Jacket File no. 39, case nos. 1139 and 1563, *United States v. William Christian*; Defendant Jacket File #241, case no. 7018, *United States v. Ben Christian*; Defendant Jacket File #241, case no. 2059, *United States v. Mark Christian and one Christian*; Defendant Jacket File no. 287, case no. 2916, *United States v. Bob Christian, West Love, John Champion and Two Others*; Defendant Jacket File no. 287, *United States v. Bob Christian, Will Christian, John Fessington* [sic] *John Reeves, and Foster Holbrook*; Defendant Jacket File no. 287, case no. 349, *United States v. Bob Christian and One [Will] Christian*; Defendant Jacket File no. 287, case no. 1358, *United States v. Jim*

Castleberry, Bill Christian and Isaac Trett; Defendant Jacket File no. 352, case no. 47, *United States v. Joe Criner and Bob Christian.* Records of the District Courts of the United States, Record Group 21. National Archives and Records Administration—Southwest Region (Fort Worth).

————. New Mexico, Territory of. Third Judicial District. Case no.1174, *United States v. Jesse Miller, alias Jesse Williams, alias Jeff Davis, Cole Young, alias Cole Estis [sic], Robert Hoy, alias Robert Hayes, Thomas Anderson, and "Black Jack.* United States Department of Justice, File 13.065, The Black Jack Gang. Confidential Correspondence, 1896–1898, Central Files, Record Group 60. National Archives at College Park, Md.

————. New Mexico, Territory of. Third Judicial District. Case no. 1183, *United States v. George Musgrave, alias Jeff Davis, alias Jesse Williams.* Records of the District Courts of the United States, Record Group 21. United States National Archives and Record Administration—Rocky Mountain Region (Denver).

————. Texas, Eastern District of, Paris Division. Defendant Jacket File no. 287, case no. 1358, *United States v. Jim Castleberry, William M. Christian and Isaac Trett.* Records of the District Courts of the United States, Record Group 21. United States National Archives and Records Administration—Southwest Region (Fort Worth).

United States General Claims Commission, United States and Mexico. Joseph Walker or Estate, Settlement of Records, Agency no. 3355, General Records, Docket no. 2532. Records of Boundary and Claims Commissions and Arbitrations, Record Group 76. National Archives at College Park, Md.

United States Marshals Service. General Correspondence of the United States Marshals, Arizona, MS 820, William Kidder Meade, United States Marshal, July 1, 1896–March 2, 1897. Arizona Historical Society, Tucson.

————. General Correspondence of the United States Marshals, New Mexico, MS 322 BC, Creighton Foraker, United States Marshal (August 1, 1897–January 17, 1911). The Center for Southwest Research, University of New Mexico, Albuquerque.

United States Office of the Adjutant General. Document Files nos. 38212 and 29451, Office of the Adjutant General, Record Group 94. National Archives Building, Washington, D.C.

United States Post Office Department. *Annual Report of the Postmaster General, 1897 [3639-4].* Washington, D.C.: U.S. Government Printing Office, 1897.

————. *Annual Report of the Postmaster General, 1898.* Washington, D.C.: U.S. Government Printing Office, 1898.

———. Records of the Division of Postmasters, Post Office Appointments, Texas (National Archives Microfilm Publication M841); Record Group 28. National Archives Building, Washington, D.C.

———. Special Reports 1894–1897. Records of the Inspection Office, Denver, Colorado, 1879–1907, Record Group 28. National Archives Building, Washington, D.C.

United States War Department. Consolidated Index to Compiled Service Records of Confederate Soldiers (National Archives Microfilm Publication M253, roll 349). War Department Collection of Confederate Records, Record Group 109. National Archives at College Park, Md.

———. Muster Rolls, Co. D, Thirty-third Texas Cavalry Regiment (Bennett Musgrave). Records of the Adjutant and Inspector General's Department. War Department Collection of Confederate Records, Record Group 109. National Archives at College Park, Md.

———. Records of the Division of Postmasters, United States Post Office Appointments, Texas vol. 35 [ca. 1867–77], p. 562, also vol. 55, p. 20, and New Mexico, vol. 74, n.p. (National Archives Microfilm Publication M841), Record Group 28. U.S. National Archives—Pacific Southwest Region, Laguna Niguel, California.

Val Verde County, Texas. Deed Books 8 and 12.

———. District Court, C. V. Musgrave v. Ella Musgrave, case No. 426.

———. District Court, Index to Civil and Criminal District Court Minutes, 1885–1940.

———. Marriage Book 2.

Wyoming, State of. Wyoming State Penitentiary Records, Jack Dempsey, Convict no. 1311. Wyoming State Archives, Cheyenne.

Yavapai County, Arizona, Third Judicial District Court. Territory of Arizona v. John Halford, William D. Stiren, Daniel M. Harvick, and J. J. Smith, case file no. 36.

NEWSPAPERS

Argentina:
Buenos Aires Herald

Arizona:
Arizona Daily Citizen (Tucson)
Arizona Daily Star (Tucson)
Arizona Gazette (Phoenix)
Arizona Range News (Willcox)
Arizona Republican (Phoenix)
Arizona Silver Belt (Globe)

Douglas Daily Dispatch
Graham County Bulletin (Solomonville)
Oasis (Nogales)
St. Johns Herald
Sulpher Valley News (Willcox)
Tombstone Prospector
Yuma Daily Sun

Arkansas:
Elevator (Fort Smith)

California:
San Francisco Chronicle

Colorado:
Denver Rocky Mountain News
Grand Junction Daily Sentinel

England:
The Times (London)

Missouri:
Daily Globe-Democrat (St. Louis)

Nevada:
Elko Free Press
Goldfield News
Goldfield Sun

Nebraska:
The North Platte Semi-Weekly Tribune

New Mexico:
Albuquerque Daily Citizen
Albuquerque Morning Democrat
Albuquerque Morning Journal
The Carlsbad Argus
The Chieftain (Socorro)
The Chloride Black Range
The Eddy Current
Grant County Democrat (Silver City)
Independent Democrat (Las Cruces)
The Pecos Valley Argus (Carlsbad)
Rio Grande Republican (Las Cruces)
Roswell Daily Record

Roswell Record
Roswell Register
Roswell Register Tribune
Santa Fe Daily New Mexican
Sierra County Advocate (Hillsboro)
Silver City Enterprise
Silver City Independent
Weekly News (Albuquerque)
Western Liberal (Lordsburg)

New York:
New York Times
Variety

Oklahoma:
Indian Arrow (Tahlequah)
Indian Citizen (Atoka)
The Daily Oklahoman (Oklahoma City)
Daily Oklahoma State Capitol (Guthrie)
Daily Times-Journal (Oklahoma City)
The Democrat (Tecumseh)
Edmond Sun-Democrat
Guthrie Daily Leader
The Herald (Tecumseh)
Indian Chieftain (Vinita)
The Leader (Tecumseh)
The Weekly Oklahoman (Oklahoma City)

Paraguay:
La Critica (Asunción)
El Diaro (Asunción)
El Orden (Asunción)
La Tribuna (Asunción)

Texas:
The Daily Hesperian (Gainesville)
The Daily Light (San Antonio)
El Paso Daily Herald
El Paso International Daily Times

Wyoming:
Carbon County Journal
Rawlins Republican

BOOKS AND ARTICLES

Abente, Diego. "Foreign Capital, Economic Elites and the State in Paraguay during the Liberal Republic (1870–1936)." *Journal of Latin American Studies* 21:1 (February 1989): 61–88.

Atascosa History Committee. *Atascosa County History*. Jourdanton, Tex: Taylor Publishing Co., 1984.

Axford, Joseph Mack, *Around Western Campfires*. New York: Pageant Press, 1964.

Bailey, Lynn R. *"We'll All Wear Silk Hats": The Erie and Chiricahua Cattle Companies and the Rise of Corporate Ranching in the Sulphur Spring Valley of Arizona, 1883–1909*. Tucson: Westernlore Press, 1994.

Baker, Pearl. *The Wild Bunch at Robbers Roost*. Rev. ed. New York: Abelard-Schuman Limited, 1971.

Ball, Eve. "Charles Ballard: 'Lawman' of the Pecos." The English Westerners' *Brand Book* 7 (July 1965): 1–6.

———. "Lawman of the Pecos." *True West* 14 (May–June 1967): 20–21, 68–69.

———. *Ma'am Jones of the Pecos*. Tucson: University of Arizona Press, 1969.

Ball, Larry D. "Outlaws of the Southwest: 1895–1905." *Brand Book of the Denver Westerners* 20 (1964): 283–99.

———. *The United States Marshals of New Mexico and Arizona Territories, 1846–1912*. Albuquerque: University of New Mexico Press, 1978.

Ball, Larry, ed. "'No Cure, No Pay,' A Tom Horn Letter." *The Journal of Arizona History* 8 (Autumn 1967): 200–202.

Barnes, Frank C. *Cartridges of the World*. 5th ed. Northbrook, Ill.: DBI Books, 1985.

Bartholomew, Ed. *Black Jack Ketchum: Last of the Hold-up Kings*. Houston, Tex.: Frontier Press of Texas, 1955.

———. *Kill or Be Killed*. Houston, Tex.: Frontier Book Company of Texas, 1953.

Beebe, Ruth. *Reminiscing along the Sweetwater*. Boulder, Colo.: Johnson Publishing Co., 1973.

Bell, Peter Tumlinson. *Memories of Peter Tumlinson Bell*. Saint Jo, Tex.: S. J. T. Printing Company, 1980.

Biographical Directory of the Railway Officials of America, Edition of 1896. Edited by T. Addison Busbey. Chicago: Railway Age and Northwestern Railroader, 1896.

Bonney, Cecil. *Looking Over My Shoulder: Seventy-five Years in the Pecos Valley*. Roswell, N. Mex.: Hall-Poorbaugh Press, Inc., 1971.

Boyer, Glenn G. "Johnny Behan of Tombstone." *Frontier Times* 50 (June–July 1976): 6–9, 55–57.

Breakenridge, William M. *Helldorado: Bringing the Law to the Mesquite.* Boston: Houghton Mifflin, 1928. Reprint, Lincoln: University of Nebraska Press, 1992.

Bryan, Howard. *True Tales of the American Southwest: Pioneer Recollections of Frontier Adventures.* Santa Fe, N. Mex.: Clear Light Publishers, 1998.

Bryce, James. *South America: Observations and Impressions.* New York: MacMillan Company, 1912.

Buck, Daniel. "New Revelations about Harvey Logan Following the Parachute Train Robbery." Western Outlaw–Lawman History Association *Journal* 6 (Spring 1997): 6–13, 39–40.

Buck, Daniel, and Anne Meadows. "Did Butch Cassidy Return? His Family Can't Decide." Western Outlaw and Lawman Association *Journal* 6 (Spring 1998): 24–34, 48.

Buck's Directory of El Paso, Tex., for 1902. El Paso: El Paso Directory Company, 1902.

Burchett, Dennis. "They Called Her Jano." *True West* 45 (March 1998): 42–46.

Burroughs, John Rolfe. *Where the Old West Stayed Young.* New York: Bonanza Books, 1962.

Burton, Jeffrey. *Black Jack Christian: Outlaw.* Santa Fe, N. Mex.: Press of the Territories, 1967.

———. *Bureaucracy, Blood Money and Black Jack's Gang.* Vol. 22, *The Brand Book.* London: English Westerners' Society, 1984.

———. *Dynamite and Six-shooter.* Santa Fe, N. Mex.: Press of the Territories, 1970.

———. *Indian Territory and the United States, 1866–1906: Courts, Government, and the Movement for Oklahoma Statehood.* Norman: University of Oklahoma Press, 1995.

———. "Jail-Break," pts 1–3. The English Westerners' *Brand Book* 10, no. 2 (January 1968): 1–4; no. 3 (April 1968): 1–11; no. 4 (July 1968): 10–12.

———. "Jottings in the Margin; Bob Hall, Politics, and the Law." The English Westerners' *Tally Sheet* 20, no. 2 (January 1974): 9–11.

———. "Jottings in the Margin; Frank and Flavius Carver: A Pretty Pair of Scoundrels" The English Westerners' *Tally Sheet* 20, no. 3 (April 1974): 3–18.

———. "Jottings in the Margin; The Mysterious Kid." The English Westerners' *Tally Sheet* 20, no. 4 (July 1974): 4–10.

———. "'Suddenly in a Secluded and Rugged Place . . .' The Territory of New Mexico versus William H. McGinnis: Cause No. 2419—Murder." The English Westerners' Society *Brand Book.* London: English Westerners' Society, 1971–72.

Butler, Ken. *Oklahoma Renegades: Their Deeds and Misdeeds*. Gretna, La.: Pelican Publishing Company, 1997.

Carpenter, Frank. *Along the Paraná and the Amazon*. New York: Doubleday, Page and Company, 1926.

Carter, W. A. *McCurtain County and Southwest Oklahoma*. Idabel, Okla.: Tribune, 1923.

Charter, Anne Goddard. *Cowboys Don't Walk, A Tale of Two*. Billings, Mont.: Western Organization of Resource Councils, 1999.

Chesley, Hervey E. *Adventuring with the Old Timers Trails Travelled—Tales Told*. Midland, Tex.: Nita Haley Stewart Library, 1979.

Chrisman, Harry E. *Fifty Years on the Owl Hoot Trail: Jim Herron, The First Sheriff of No Man's Land Oklahoma Territory*. Chicago: Sage Books, 1969.

Clark, Ben R. "William Christian, Alias Black Jack." *Progressive Arizona and the Southwest* (December 1929): 24–25; (January 1930): 20–22.

Clarke, Mary Whatley. *The Slaughter Ranches and Their Makers*. Austin: Jenkins Publishing Company, 1979.

Craig, C. W. Thurlow. *Black Jack's Spurs*. London: Hutchinson, 1954.

———. *Paraguayan Interlude*. New York: Frederick A. Stokes Company, 1935.

———. *A Rebel for a Horse*. London: Arthur Barker, Ltd., 1934.

———. *The River of Diamonds*. London: Hutchinson & Co., ca. 1944.

Culley, Jack. *Cattle, Horses and Men*. Tucson: Univesity of Arizona Press, 1967.

Curry, George. *George Curry, 1861–1947: An Autobiography*. Edited by H. B. Henning. Albuquerque: University of New Mexico Press, 1958.

Dahl, Victor C. "A Montana Pioneer Abroad: Granville Stuart in South America." *Journal of the West* 4 (July 1965): 345–66.

DeArment, Robert K. *George Scarborough: The Life and Death of a Lawman on the Closing Frontier*. Norman: University of Oklahoma Press, 1992.

Debo, Angie. *The Rise and Fall of the Choctaw Republic*. Norman: University of Oklahoma Press, 1961.

Decoud, Héctor Francisco. *Geographia de la Republica del Paraguay*. Asunción, Paraguay: Escuela tip. Salesiana, 1901.

Deister, Bill, as told to Jane Pattie. "Outlaws I Have Known." *Old West* 9 (Spring 1973): 6–15, 52–55.

Dexter [N. Mex.] Old Timers. *As We Remembered It*. Roswell, N. Mex.: Hall-Poorbaugh Press, n.d.

Dobie, J. Frank. *A Vaquero of the Brush Country*. Boston: Little, Brown and Company, 1943.

Doshier, Inez Christian. "Lone Prairie Graves." *Frontier Times* 39 (December–January 1965): 38–40.

Dullenty, Jim. "The Farm Boy Who Became A Member of Butch Cassidy's Wild Bunch." National Association and Center for Outlaw and Lawman History *Quarterly* 10 (Winter 1986): 4–8.

———. "The Family Photo Album of 'Gentleman Outlaw' Elzy Lay." Western Outlaw and Lawman Association *Journal* 4 (Winter/Spring 1995): 24–25, 28–29, 51.

Dykstra, Robert R. *The Cattle Towns: A Social History of the Kansas Cattle Trading Centers.* New York: Alfred A. Knopf, 1968.

Egloff, Fred R. "Circle Z Ranch and the Sonoita Valley." The Chicago Westerners' *Brand Book* 34 (January–February 1978): 65–72.

Every, E[dward] F[rancis], D.D. *South American Memories of Thirty Years.* London: Society for Promoting Christian Knowledge, 1933.

———. *Twenty-five Years in South America.* London: Society for Promoting Christian Knowledge, 1929.

Farris, Frances Bramlette. *From Rattlesnakes to Road Agents: Rough Times on the Frio.* Edited by C. L. Sonnichsen. Fort Worth: Texas Christian University, 1985.

Ferguson, Bobbie H. ". . . and they laid them to rest in the little plot beside the Pecos": Final Report of the Relocation of Old Seven Rivers Cemetery, Eddy County, New Mexico.* Vol. 1. Denver: United States Bureau of Reclamation, 1993.

Fleming, Elvis, and Minor S. Huffman. *Roundup on the Pecos.* Roswell, N. Mex.: Chaves County Historical Society, 1978.

Ford, John Salmon. *Rip Ford's Texas.* Edited by Stephen B. Oates. Austin: University of Texas Press, 1987.

Foreign Relations of the United States, 1947. Vol. 7, *The American Republics.* Washington, D.C.: U.S. Government Printing Office, 1972.

French, Captain William. *Some Recollections of a Western Ranchman: New Mexico, 1883–1899, and Further Recollections of a Western Ranchman: New Mexico, 1883–1899.* New York: Argosy-Antiquarian Lts., 1965.

Gard, Wayne. *The Chisholm Trail.* Norman: University of Oklahoma Press, 1954.

Gauld, Charles A. *The Last Titan: Percival Farquhar, American Entrepreneur in Latin America.* Palo Alto: Institute of Hispanic American and Luso-Brazilian Studies, Stanford University, 1964.

Gavilan [C. W. Thurlow Craig]. "The Ambush." *The Wide World Magazine* (ca. February 1951): 210–19.

Gillett, James B. *A List of Fugitives from Justice: The Notebooks of Texas Ranger Sergeant James B. Gillet.* Introduction by Michael D. Morrison. Austin: State House Press, 1997.

Gonzales, J. Natalicio, and Pablo M. Ynsfran. *El Paraguay Contemporaneo.* Paris/Asunción: Editorial de Indias, 1929.

Haley, J. Evetts. *Jeff Milton: A Good Man with a Gun*. Norman: University of Oklahoma Press, 1948.

Hanratty, Dennis M., and Sandra W. Meditz, eds. *Paraguay: A Country Study*. Federal Research Division, Library of Congress. Washington, D.C.: Government Printing Office, 1990.

Hansen, Carl. *Harrowing Adventures of an old-time Cowboy and Sheriff*. Edited by Clarence S. and Joan N. Adams. Roswell, N. Mex.: Old-Time Publications, 1989.

Hanson, Simon G. "The Farquhar Syndicate in South America." *Hispanic American Historical Review* 17 (August 1937): 314–26.

Harkey, Dee. *Mean as Hell*. Albuquerque: University of New Mexico Press, 1948.

Hart, Robert L. "'She'll Be Comin' Round the Mountain': The Ozanne Stage to White Oaks and Lincoln, 1886–1895." *Southern New Mexico Historical Review* 3 (January 1996): 29–41.

Harvick, Dan, as told to William Sparks. "Canyon Diablo Train Robbery." *Frontier Times* 45 (January 1971): 8–11, 40, 48–51.

Hayes, Alden. *A Portal to Paradise*. Tucson: University of Arizona Press, 1999.

Hayhurst, Sam J. "Hayhurst Was with Arizona Rangers. . . ." *Douglas Daily Dispatch* (May 4, 1941), sec. 5, 1–2.

Herken, Juan Carlos. *Ferrocarriles, Concpiraciónes, y Negocios en el Paraguay, 1910–1914*. Asunción: Arte Nuevo Editores, 1984.

Hilliard, George. *A Hundred Years of Horse Tracks: The Story of the Gray Ranch*. Silver City, N. Mex.: High-Lonesome Books, 1996.

Hinkle, James F. *Early Days of a Cowboy on the Pecos*. Roswell, N. Mex.: N.p., 1938.

Hoover, H. A. "The Gentle Train Robber." *New Mexico* (January 1956): 21, 44–45.

———. *Tales from the Bloated Goat: Early Days in Mogollon*. El Paso: Texas Western Press, 1958.

Horton, Thomas F. *History of Jack County*. Jacksboro, Texas: Jacksboro Gazette-News, 1933. Reprinted 1975.

Hovey, Walter C. "Black Jack Ketchum Tried to Give Me a Break!" *True West* 19 (March–April 1972), 6–11, 48–52.

Huff, J. Wesley. "Malpais Mystery." *New Mexico* (April 1947): 17, 35–39.

Hughes, Dan de Lara. *South from Tombstone: A Life Story*. London: Methuen & Co., 1938.

Hunter, J. Marvin. *The Trail Drivers of Texas*. Austin: University of Texas, 1985.

Hutchinson, W. H. *The Life and Personal Writings of Eugene Manlove Rhodes: A Bar Cross Man*. Norman: University of Oklahoma Press, 1956.

Jinks, Roy G. *History of Smith & Wesson*. North Hollywood, Calif.: Beinfeld Publishing, 1977.

Katz, Frederick. *The Life and Times of Pancho Villa*. Stanford, Calif.: Stanford University Press, 1998.

Kelly, Charles. *The Outlaw Trail: The Story of Butch Cassidy and the "Wild Bunch"*. New York: Bonanza Books, 1959.

Kent, Constance. *Life in Paraguay*. Ilfracombe, Devon, England: Arthur H. Stockwell, 1958.

King, Frank M. *Mavericks: The Salty Comments of an Old-time Cowpuncher*. Pasadena, Calif.: Trail's End Publishing Co., 1947.

———. "Mavericks" (column). *Western Livestock Journal*, May 6, 1933, April 25, 1935, August 19, 1938.

———. *Pioneer Western Empire Builders*. Pasadena, Calif.: Trail's End Publishing Co., Inc., 1946.

———. *Wranglin' the Past: The Reminiscences of Frank M. King*. Pasadena, Calif.: Trail's End Publishing Co., Inc.,1946.

Kleinpenning, Jan M. G. *Rural Paraguay, 1870–1932*. Amsterdam: Centre for Latin American Research and Documentation, 1992.

Lauderdale, R. J., and John M. Doak. *Life on the Range and on the Trail*. San Antonio, Tex.: Naylor Company, 1936.

Lemmon, Ed. *Boss Cowman: The Recollections of Ed Lemmon, 1857–1946*. Edited by Nellie Snyder Yost. Lincoln: University of Nebraska Press, 1969.

Livingston, Carl. "Musgraves Own Law and Slew a Defender." Newspaper clipping (likely the *Roswell Daily Record*), ca. 1927. Files, Historical Center for Southeast New Mexico, Roswell, New Mexico.

———. "Rounding-up the 'Black Jack' Gang." *The Wide World Magazine* 65, no. 3 (March 1955): 339–50; no. 4 (April 1955): 471–82; no. 5 (May 1955): 45–55.

McCauley, J. E. *A Stove-up Cowboy's Story*. Dallas: Southern Methodist University Press, 1965.

MacDonald, Alesander K. *Picturesque Paraguay: A Land of Promise*. London: Charles H. Kelly, 1911.

McKinney, Grange B. *Art Acord and the Movies*. Raleigh, N.C.: Wyatt Classics, Inc., 2000.

McMullen County History. Tex.: McMullen County Book Committee, n.d.

Marquis, Albert Nelson. *The Book of Chicagoans* (1911). Chicago: A. N. Marquis & Co., 1911.

Mayer, Charles D. "Pioneer Story: 1938." *Old Lincoln County Pioneer Stories: Interviews from the WPA Writer's Project*. Lincoln County Historical Publications 3 (1994): 17–21.

Meed, Douglas V. *They Never Surrendered: Bronco Apaches of the Sierra Madres, 1890–1935.* Tucson, Ariz.: Westernlore Press, 1993.

Newsome, J. A. *The Life and Practice of the Wild and Modern Indian.* Oklahoma City: Harlow Publishing Co., 1923.

Otero, Miguel Antonio. *My Life on the Frontier: 1882–1897.* Vol 2. Albuquerque: University of New Mexico Press, 1939.

———. *My Nine Years as Governor: 1897–1906.* Albuquerque: University of New Mexico Press, 1940.

Parker, Morris B. *White Oaks: Life in a New Mexico Gold Camp, 1880–1900.* Edited by C. L. Sonnichsen. Tucson: University of Arizona Press, 1971.

Parker, William Belmont. *Casual Letters from South America.* London, New York: Hispanic Society of America, 1921.

Pinkerton, William A. *Train Robberies and Train Robbers.* 1907. Reprint, Fort Davis, Tex.: Frontier Book Company, 1968.

Pointer, Larry. *In Search of Butch Cassidy.* Norman: University of Oklahoma Press, 1977.

Richards, George L. *The Rest of the Diary and Scrapbook of Alonzo Van Oden.* Wimberley, Tex.: Privately printed, 1995.

Rickard, Mrs. "Tex," with Arch Oboler. *Everything Happened to Him: The Story of Tex Rickard.* New York: Frederick A. Stokes Company, 1936.

Rickards, Colin. *Charles Littlepage Ballard, Southwesterner.* Southwestern Studies, Monograph no. 16. El Paso: Texas Western Press, 1966.

———. "There Were All Kinds of Gunfighters." *Old West* 6 (Fall 1969): 22–23, 60–62.

Ringgold, Jennie Parks. *Frontier Days in the Southwest.* San Antonio, Tex.: Naylor Press, 1952.

Roosevelt, Theodore. *Through the Brazilian Wilderness.* New York: Charles Scribner's Sons, 1926.

Rose, Victor. *The Texas Vendetta: The Sutton-Taylor Feud.* New York: J. J. Little Co., 1880. Reprint, Houston: Frontier Press of Texas, 1956.

Samuels, Charles. *The Magnificent Rube: The Life and Gaudy Times of Tex Rickard.* New York: McGraw–Hill, 1957.

Samuelson, Nancy B. *The Dalton Gang Story: Lawmen to Outlaws.* Eastland, Conn.: Shooting Star Press, 1992.

———. "Who Really Robbed the Longview Bank?" *Quarterly* of the National Association for Outlaw and Lawman History 19 (April–June 1995): 26–33.

Second Decennial Edition of the American Digest: A Complete Digest of All Reported Cases from 1906 to 1916. St. Paul, Minn.: West Publishing Co., 1917–23.

Shinkle, James D. *Fifty Years of Roswell History, 1867–1917.* Roswell, N. Mex.: Hall-Poorbaugh Press, 1964.

————. *Reminiscences of Roswell Pioneers*. Roswell, N. Mex.: Hall-Poorbaugh Press, 1966.

Shirley, Glenn. "Buck Jones." *True West* 32 (Special Issue, 1985): 54–61.

————. *Law West of Fort Smith: A History of Frontier Justice in the Indian Territory, 1834–1896*. New York: Henry Holt and Company, 1957.

————. *Six-gun and Silver Star*. Albuquerque: University of New Mexico Press, 1955.

————. *West of Hell's Fringe: Crime, Criminals, and the Federal Peace Officer in Oklahoma Territory, 1889–1907*. Norman: University of Oklahoma Press, 1976.

Sonnichsen, C. L. *Colonel Greene and the Copper Skyrocket*. Tucson: University of Arizona Press, 1974.

Sowell, A. J. *Early Settlers and Indian Fighters in Southwest Texas*. Austin: Ben C. Jones, 1900. Reprint, Austin: State House Press, 1986.

————. *Rangers and Pioneers of Texas*. 1884. Reprint, Austin: State House Press, 1991.

Stanley, F. *No Tears for Black Jack Ketchum*. Denver: World Press, 1958.

Stephens, Henry. *Journey and Explorations in Argentina, Paraguay, and Chile*. New York: Knickerbocker Press, 1920.

Sterrett, Charles P. "Sam Butler—Cowboy Lawman." *True West* 22 (September–October 1974): 8–12, 53–54.

Tanner, Karen Holliday, and John D. Tanner, Jr. "Bank Heist at Nogales." *Western Outlaw-Lawman History Association Journal* 8 (Winter 1999): 22–30.

————. "Elzy Lay: New Mexico Prisoner #1348." *Western Outlaw-Lawman History Association Journal* 10 (Spring 2001): 14–20.

————. "The Great Grant's Robbery." *True West* 45 (August 1998): 12–17.

————. "Lon Oden: The Rhymin' Ranger." *Old West* 34 (Summer 1998): 10–14.

————. "Murder and Intrigue in the Chaco." *True West* 47 (January 2000): 39–44.

————. "The San Antonio–White Oaks Stagecoach Robberies of 1896." *Southern New Mexico Historical Review* 8 (January 2001): 20–23.

————. "Shoot-out at Parker's Well." *True West* 46 (September 1999): 20–25.

Theobald, John and Lillian. *Arizona Territory Post Offices and Postmasters*. Phoenix: Arizona Historical Foundation, 1961.

————. *Wells Fargo in Arizona Territory*. Tempe: Arizona Historical Foundation, 1978.

Thompson, Albert W. *They Were Open Range Days: Annals of a Western Frontier*. Denver: World Press, 1946.

Tschiffely, A. F. *Bohemia Junction*. London: Hodder and Stoughton, 1950.

Tucson City Directory: 1922. Tucson: Western Directory Co., 1922.

Van Pelt, Lori. *Dreamers and Schemers: Profiles from Carbon County, Wyoming's Past.* Glendo, Wyo.: High Plains Press, 1999.

Wagoner, Jay J. *Arizona Territory 1863–1912: A Political History.* Tucson: University of Arizona Press, 1970.

——. *History of the Cattle Industry in Southern Arizona, 1540–1940.* University of Arizona Social Science Bulletin no. 20. Tucson: University of Arizona, 1952.

Walters, Lorenzo D. *Tombstone's Yesterday.* Glorieta, N. Mex.: The Rio Grande Press, Inc., 1968.

Warner, Matt, as told to Murray E. King. *The Last of the Bandit Riders.* New York: Bonanza, 1940.

Webb, Walter Prescott. *The Texas Rangers: A Century of Frontier Defense.* Austin: University of Texas Press, 1965.

Weller, George. "American Cowboy in a Wild New Land." *Saturday Evening Post* (September 1, 1956): 31, 59–61.

Williams, Ernestine Chesser. "Diamond A. Ranch." In *Treasures of History II: Chaves County Vignettes.* Roswell, N. Mex.: Chaves County Historical Society, 1991.

Wilson, Edward. *An Unwritten History: A Record from the Exciting Days of Early Arizona.* Phoenix: H. H. McNeil Co., 1915. Reprint, Santa Fe, N. Mex.: Stagecoach Press, 1966.

Wright, Katheryn. "Dad Rode with the Wild Bunch." *True West* 26 (February 1979): 21–23; 42–43.

Zook, David H., Jr., *The Conduct of the Chaco War.* New Haven, Conn.: Bookman Associates, 1960.

INDEX

Gray Ranch, 51–52. *See also* Diamond A Ranch, Grant County, N.Mex.
Green, George H., 6, 173
Greene, Ella Roberts Moson (Mrs. William Cornell Greene), 269–70n.29, 314n.39
Greene, William Cornell, 48, 101–102, 106, 168, 171–72, 269–70n.29, 314n.39, 325n.23
Greene Cattle Company, 168
Griffith, William M., 7, 132, 139, 144–45, 305n.5
Griggs, John W., 144, 150, 309n.2
Grimes County, Tex., 106
Guadelupe Mountains, 48
Guild, Nolt E., 88
Guthrie, Okla., 28

Hachita, N.Mex., 22, 42–43, 92–93, 100
Hagan, W. F., 120
Halford, John, 299n.20
Hall, Edward L., 7, 52–53, 62–64, 68, 80, 92–93, 98, 108–109, 112, 115–16, 123, 127–29, 302n; reward announcements, 67, 102; U.S. justice department authorizations for funds, 79, 81–82, 121; U.S. marshal appointment, 132, 284n.40
Hall, Robert H., 29–31, 36, 273n.17
Hallenbeck, Albert, 79
Halprin, Maxine Texas Rickard, 206, 213
Hambleton, Ben E., 46
Hamilton, Tex., 188
Hammond, John S., 204
Hampson, Joe, 107, 111, 115–16
Hands, Alfred, 23
Hanna, Robert, 128
Hanson, Emmet, 41
Hardin (deputy sheriff), 43–44
Harkey, Dee R., 7, 39, 122, 153, 155–57, 159, 186
Harless, Thomas "Tom," 38
Harmon, Judson, 92
Harmon, Les, 70, 85, 191
Harper, Albert A., 176
Harper, Ira, 123–24, 136
Harper, James R., 137
Harrington, Loosely, 135
Harris, Bob. *See* Young, Code
Hart, William, 121

Harvick, Dan, 299n.20
Hassells, Sam, 269n.26
Hatchet Ranch, 22
Hawke, Nathaniel E., 294n.37
Hawks, G. V., 196
Hayes, Robert "Bob," 5, 54, 55–56, 90, 92, 105, 150, 269n.26; aliases, 22, 69; appearance and personality, 22–23; Central, N.Mex., robbery (alleged), 85; Deer Creek, N. Mex., killed at, 95–99, 104, 126, 128; Hassells, Sam, link to, 296n.9; High Five Gang forms, 24, 42; International Bank of Nogales robbery, 44–49, 57; Parker, George, killing, 69–74, 191, 194; Rio Puerco, N. Mex., train robbery, 59–62; San Simon, Ariz., robbery, 84–85; Separ, N.Mex., robberies, 42, 80–82, 109; Skeleton Canyon, Ariz., shootout, 50–53; White Oaks-San Antonio stage robberies, 64–66, 77–79
Haynes, Charles W., 73
Head, Edward, 135
Head and Hearst Ranch, 22
Heady, Sam, 59–61
Heather, William, 114–16, 134
Heitman, W. M., 194
Hereford, Ariz., 48, 180
Hermosa, N.Mex., 79
Herrera, Fred, 44–46
Herron, Frank, 109–10, 298–99n.15
Herron, James, 109–10, 151–53, 162, 270n.1
Hervey, James Madison, 186, 192, 194
Heywood, Billy. *See* Walker, Jerome McCowen
Hicks, Frank M., 220
Higgins, Dan, 109
Higgins, Frederick, 7, 76–77, 79–81, 93–95, 99–101, 106, 116, 121–127, 163, 291n.3
High Five Gang. *See* Christian, Robert "Bob"; Christian, Will "Black Jack"; Hayes, Robert "Bob"; Moore, Sid; Musgrave, Calvin Van; Musgrave, George West; and Young, Code
Hildebrand, Jake W., 176
Hildreth, Bill, 49–51, 128
Hill, Robert, 54, 285n.45
Hill, W. T., 174
Hillman, Ef. *See* Moore, Sid

"Jano," 177, 179–80, 199–200, 202–203, 206, 208–209, 212–13, 217–19, 224–26, 228; Nations, Joseph H., deal with, 199; Paraguay, move to, 202–203, 321–22n.4; Parker, George, cattle rustling with, 20–21; Parker, George, murder of, 69–74, 75, 104; Parker murder, arrest and trial for 181–83, 184–96, 198–99, 319n.15, 320n.32; personality traits, 3, 4, 5, 103, 210–11, 221, 224, 233, 235, 237, 259; physical characteristics, 3, 4, 220–21, 223, 228, 235–37, 248, 259, 266n.18; Rickard, George Lewis "Tex," association with, 172–73, 204, 209–10, 213–16; Rio Puerco, N.Mex., train robbery, 59–63; Roberts, Ed, employee of, 44, 162, 165; rodeo participant, 223–24; San Salvador packing plant, sells to, 218; San Simon, Ariz., robbery, 84–85; Separ, N.Mex., robberies, 42–43, 81–82, 109; Steins Pass, N.Mex., robbery, 90–91; Villa, Francisco "Pancho," association with, 199, 212, 321n.46; White Oaks-San Antonio stage robberies, 64–66, 77–79
Musgrave, Jeanette Magor "Jano" (Mrs. George West Musgrave), 181, 187–88, 203, 230, 324–25n.21, 330nn.31,32; childhood and family, 177–78, 202; death, 228; description and characteristics, 178–79, 325n.22; divorces Musgrave, 224–26; inheritance, 200, 206–207, 317n.22, 324n.17, 326n.30; Lay, Mary Calvert, friendship, 177–78, 226–27, 325n.27; marriages, 179–80, 227, 317n.22; Mexio trips, 199, 212–13; Paraguay, life in, 206–10, 217–19
Musgrave, Julia Elizabeth (sister). See Doak, Julia Elizabeth Musgrave (Mrs. Boyd M. Doak)
Musgrave, LeRoy Polk (brother), 14, 264n.16
Musgrave, Mariah (Mrs. Calvin S. Musgrave 1), 13, 263n.11
Musgrave, Mary Anderson (Mrs. Calvin S. Musgrave 2), 263n.12
Musgrave, Mary E. Remick (Mrs. Calvin Van Musgrave 2), 161–62, 312n.27

Musgrave, Samuel Houston (brother), 13, 263n.13
Musgrave, Sarah Prudence Walker (mother, Mrs. Bennett Musgrave), 11, 13–14, 18–19, 21, 161–62, 167, 171, 193, 219, 230, 257, 262n.6, 263n.11, 264n.16, 267n.20, 312n.27, 328n.7
Musgrave, Thomas James Harry (uncle), 13
Musgrave, Van. See Musgrave, Calvin Van
Musgrave, Volney Campbell "Vollie" (brother), 6, 111, 116, 153, 157–63, 165, 167, 172, 174, 196–98, 219, 264n.20, 321n.42, 328n.7
Mynett, Jeff D., 29, 273n.15

Naco, Ariz., 41, 174
Naco, Mexico, 151–53
Nacozari, Mexico, 107
Nation, Harry, 202
Nations, Joseph H., 199
Nelson, Oscar "Battling," 173
Newberry, William, 146, 307–308n.44. See also Shaw, James Madison
Newcomb, George D. "Bitter Creek," 27, 272n.8
Newman, Bill, 198
New Mexico and Arizona Railroad, 86
New Mexico Territorial Penitentiary, 135, 159, 163, 198, 298n.7, 305n.11
Newsom, J. A., 26–27, 275n.25
New York and Paraguay Company. See Paraguay Land and Cattle Company
Nite, James. See Knight, James
Nogales, Ariz., 44–47, 49, 55, 57, 117
Nogales, Sonora, Mexico, 47, 151
Noland, George, 36
Noland, Lee, 36
Northern Pacific Railroad, 146, 307–308n.44
North Platte, Nebr., 181
Norton and Stewart Cattle Company, 138
Nuckells, Claude, 36–37, 277n.43

O Bar O Ranch, 19, 22, 56, 58, 80, 106
O'Brien (rustler), 107–108, 111, 299n.19
Oden, Alonzo Van "Lon," 263n.13
OH Ranch, 23, 40, 100, 162, 168